Wilfred Sayers

ENGLAND

WITHOUT AND WITHIN.

BY

RICHARD GRANT WHITE.

"For me, with sorrow I embrace my fortune.
I have some rights of memory in this kingdom,
Which now to claim my vantage doth invite me."
HAMLET.

BOSTON:
HOUGHTON, MIFFLIN AND COMPANY.
The Riverside Press, Cambridge.
1882.

The Riverside Press, Cambridge:
Stereotyped and Printed by H. O. Houghton & Co.

To

CHARLES T. GOSTENHOFER,

OF BIRKENHEAD, LANCASHIRE, ESQUIRE.

———◆———

MY DEAR GOSTENHOFER:

I give myself the pleasure of inscribing this book to you, not only in recognition of the friendship between us, which began in early youth, and which you have constantly strengthened, but because your long residence in the United States, your candor, and your wide and generous sympathies make you, notwithstanding your love for England, which I share with you, the most competent person that I know to pronounce both upon the merits that it may have and the faults which I can hardly hope that it should be without.

Ever most truly yours,

R. G. W.

ADVERTISEMENT.

---·---

MOST of the chapters of this book have appeared in "The Atlantic Monthly." It is not, however, the writer wishes to say, a gathering of magazine articles to which he was tempted by the favor with which they have been received. Those articles were rather parts of a book which it was convenient for him to publish first serially, and which was from the first intended as a presentation of the subject indicated by its title.

CONTENTS

—◆—

CHAPTER I.

INTRODUCTORY.

CHAPTER II.

ENGLISH SKIES.

CHAPTER III.

ENGLAND ON THE RAILS.

CHAPTER IV.

LONDON STREETS.

CHAPTER XV.

PARKS AND PALACES.

CHAPTER XVI.

ENGLISH IN ENGLAND.

CHAPTER XVII.

A CANTERBURY PILGRIMAGE.

CHAPTER XVIII.

JOHN BULL.

CHAPTER XIX.

OXFORD AND CAMBRIDGE.

CHAPTER XX.

A NATIONAL VICE.

CHAPTER XXI.

THE HEART OF ENGLAND.

CHAPTER XXII.

A VISIT TO STRATFORD-ON-AVON.

CHAPTER XXIII.

IN LONDON AGAIN.

CHAPTER XXIV.

RANDOM RECOLLECTIONS.

CHAPTER XXV.

PHILISTIA.

ENGLAND, WITHOUT AND WITHIN.

CHAPTER I.

INTRODUCTORY.

IN the summer of 1876, long rest from work and a greater change of air than can be obtained by usual summer jaunting were needful for me; and as I had little interest in the Rocky Mountains, which were two thousand miles away from any place where my kindred had ever been, and a great interest in a land beyond the sea, but within ten days' steaming, where my forefathers had lived for about eleven hundred years, I went to England; to visit which had been one of the great unsatisfied longings of my life. I found there even more to interest me than I had looked for, although I saw less of the country and of my many friends within it than I had hoped to see. It was almost inevitable that a man who had written about matters much less near to him than this was to me should tell the tale of such a journey; and hence this book, which, although an honest one, I believe, and written in a candid spirit, is truly a labor of love.

The consideration of the manifold subject thus brought before me was not, however, merely a result of my visit to England. Of this subject I found myself thinking almost involuntarily, years ago, when-

1

ever it was accidentally presented. Indeed, English life and character have long been of such warm and close interest to me that my tour in England is rather the occasion than the cause of much that I have written about them. To say this is due to myself, if not to my readers.

Mr. Ruskin, in his "Fors Clavigera" (No. 42, June, 1874), says to his countrymen, "And yet that you do not care for dying Venice is the sign of your own ruin; and that the Americans do not care for dying England is only the sign of their inferiority to her." How ruinous England may be, and how sure a sign of her ruin may be found in her apathy towards Venice, I shall not venture the attempt to decide; but as to the latter clause of this condemnation, I offer this book as my protest. What the Oxford Graduate who became the Oxford Professor may mean by the vague, non-describing term "Americans" I do not exactly know; nor do I believe that, with all his skill in word-craft, he could define it in a way that would be quite satisfactory even to himself, upon a little consideration. This, however, I can presume to say, that among Yankees who think about anything but the business and the pleasure of their daily life there is no such indifference as that which he makes the occasion of his reproach. To them England is still the motherland, the "Old Home" of their fathers. To her they look with a feeling, strong and deep, of interest, of affection, almost of reverence, such as they have towards no other country in the world; and it is for them as well as to them that I have ventured to speak. This feeling in them may be a weak fondness; but it is natural, and a natural weakness of which they need not be ashamed. It is this very filial bond between them and the land of their fathers that has made the tone of most Englishmen towards them in time past so hard to bear. We all know the bitterness of a man's heart when he finds that his foes are they of his own household. Injustice, misapprehension, and misrepresentation on the part of Frenchmen and Germans touched us lightly. In them ignorance and prejudice might be excused, and indeed expected. Them we might flout or even pity; but to be reviled by our kindred in our own tongue was a sore trial to our patience. The truth was, however, that of all peoples with whom we had intercourse the English people of Great Britain were the most ignorant of us; and so as a whole they still remain. And strange to say, the very fact that the two peoples were essentially the same was the chief cause of their mutual misapprehension. Their likeness was so great that differences between them which could be made the subject of remark were to be found only in those trifling points of manners and customs, an unlikeness in which, among those of the same family, has ever been one of the most irritating causes of aversion. This ignorance and this dislike have been fostered and kept alive by writers whose interest and whose inclination joined in leading them to pander to the feeling of a day, rather than to use their pens and their opportunities in the interests of truth and of kindly feeling.

With a full knowledge and an often-recurring consciousness of all this, I went to England. I had got beyond — if I may not say above — being affected by it in my relations with Englishmen; and it was swept entirely from my mind by the experience of my visit.

My readers need hardly be told that my recollections of that pleasant sojourn include much with which I should not think of wearying them. It is no diary, no expanded note-book, that I have set before them. Indeed, I made hardly any notes when I was in England; all my memorandums being contained in two tiny books which would go into my waistcoat pocket, and having been hastily scrawled as I was walking or riding. My purpose has been to put England and English folk and English life before my readers just as I saw them. To do this, it was not necessary to write either an itinerary or an account of all my personal experiences, including the valuable information that I daily rose and breakfasted and walked, or rode and dined and slept, well or ill as the case might be. But of that experience I have here recorded only such incidents and facts as I thought characteristic. I have described such persons and such conditions of life as seemed, not, be it remarked, strange, striking, or amusing, but fairly representative of the country and the people. Because of a contrary practice, consequent upon a desire to satisfy a craving for novelty, books of travels are too often either caricatures of the people whom they profess to describe, or correct descriptions of persons as strange and incidents almost as unusual to the native inhabitant as to the foreigner. This is notably the case with books of travel in the United States, and also, but in a less degree, in those which have described England to "Americans." The people of the two countries are, or were until a few years ago, so nearly the same people, developing themselves under different forms of government and physical surroundings, that writing travelers, especially those from the motherland, have felt, it would seem, as if they must be sharply on the lookout for something strikingly characteristic. Tourists have gone about in both countries seizing eagerly upon the peculiar, the strange, the startling; and this they have set forth as portraiture. Thus, also, illustrators with the pencil have done; and not only in each other's country, but each in his own. The result of all this wonder-seeking is distortion, confusion, misapprehension, — ignorance instead of knowledge, aversion instead of liking.

I remember that on a drive, one pleasant afternoon, with a lady, through a gently rolling country near the eastern shore of England, where she was at home, and where there were fewer hedges and old timber houses than I saw in other shires, I was struck by the likeness of the land to that of the more level parts of New England, and spoke of it to my companion; and I remember the little tone of disappointment in her reply: "Then there was no use of your coming." It was in simple kindness that she was disappointed. She hoped to show me something new. She had it on her mind that I had gone forth, like Lord Bateman, "strange countries for to see;" and therefore she felt a little sense of short-coming in herself, and even in her country, that she could not show me something quite novel. But there was use in my coming; and there would have been had I found even more likeness than I did find between what I saw and what I had left behind me. I went to England not to see shows, nor to hunt up things new and strange, but to see it and its people as they are, to look upon them single-eyed as nearly as a man may look without a tinge of warm-hued feeling

upon the home of his fathers and upon his own kindred. I wished to know England as it is, so far as I
could learn that in the time that I had for the study
and with my opportunities. If I saw *that* there could
be no disappointment: like this or unlike the other,
what matter? I did not go to England as most Englishmen come to "America," where their object seems
to be to see a Niagara, or to shoot on the prairies the
bisons or the catamounts that they fail to find on Boston Common or in Central Park.

Nevertheless, the truth is that I passed my whole
time there, with the exception of that which was
darkened and dampened by two or three fogs, in a
succession of varying pleasures, the greatest of which
in degree and in extent was my intercourse — in the
old and better sense of the word, my conversation —
with the people into whose company I was thrown.
These were of all ranks and conditions in life; and
they were most of them average representatives of
the classes to which they severally belonged. I found
them, with some exceptions, very interesting, even
when they were not such persons as I would have
chosen for daily companionship. Moreover, notwithstanding the effect of railways, cheap newspapers,
and cheap postage, England is not yet without character in its society, nor without peculiar characters
who give zest and diversity to the intercourse of
every-day life. There are queer people yet in England. He who will go about the country in an easy,
familiar way, and keep his eyes open, may hope to
find them, — as odd, some of them, "as Dick's hat-
band;" and even if the people that he sees are themselves not very much out of the common, he will yet
be likely to meet with incidents, and even to become

a part of incidents, that will be both amusing and instructive, if he be but ready to enter into the spirit of what is going on around him.

Not unmindful of all the sources of confusion and misapprehension upon which I have just remarked, and yet doing only what seemed to me natural and right, I have been content to concern myself with that which is truly characteristic. Now the characteristic is always the commonplace. True generally, this is particularly true of peoples and countries. In my descriptions of England, therefore, I have told only what almost any man might see there on almost any day, — only what I believe no Englishman would regard as strange. For it is these every-day occurrences, these stable, homely facts, these commonplaces of life, that show what a people, what a country is, — what all the influences, political, moral, and telluric, that have been at work there for centuries have produced. And if, because I have not sought out the strange, the striking, and the grotesque, my recollections should lack interest, I pray my readers to remember that I have been dull in the interests of truth.

It may be well, also, that I should say that I saw and have written from a Yankee's point of view, applying the term Yankee necessarily to the descendants of those to whom it was originally and peculiarly applied, in whatever part of the country they may now dwell. When I speak of my countrymen I mean only those whose families were here at the time of the Revolution, who alone can be the true examples and representatives of the results of the social, political, and physical forces which have been in operation here for two centuries and a half. With others, whc are spoken of and who speak of themselves as "Americans," and who are the product of emigration during the last thirty or forty years, I do not here concern myself, however respectable, wealthy, or politically influential they may have become (and some of them are very respectable, very wealthy, and politically very influential), or however tenacious they may be (and they are apt to be very tenacious) of their "American" status. But to me, from my present point of view, they are no more than if they had remained at home, and had become respectable, wealthy, and politically influential there. Indeed, they are rather less. How could it be otherwise?

In regard to England, I have spoken freely as to myself, but with reserve as to others, of the pleasure of my life there during my first visit, — my only one. I have been sufficiently cautious, I hope, in my references to my personal experience, not to trespass upon privacy, nor to abuse hospitality. What I mean by this phrase no Yankee who is likely to read this book needs to be told; but if the language of a very widely-known war correspondent of a very superior London newspaper may be taken as evidence, an explanation may be necessary to some of his countrymen. Having been accused of violating hospitality in regard to 'the States," he says that the charge is untrue, because he "gave as many dinners as he received." It was with some surprise that I read this expression of the writer's apprehension of the duties and relations of hospitality. Apart from the business-like, debt-and-credit view taken of the matter, it was amazing that the writer did not see that the occasion of the reproach to which he referred was an alleged violation of that privacy and confidence which are implicit in the social intercourse of gentlemen, and that a man may abuse hospitality by giving improper and annoying publicity to matters spoken of at his own table, as well as if they were spoken of at another at which he was a guest. It is, however, unreasonable to expect that such implicit and purely sentimental obligations should be felt and acted upon by all men, even when they are able correspondents of superior newspapers. At any rate, this is the way in which I have felt the obligations of hospitality imperative on me, in relation to my friends in England no less than to those at home. It has of course been necessary for me to refer to individuals; and in writing of a country in which individuals are of different ranks it would have been an inept and confusing affectation to ignore them; but I believe that I have told my story in a way to which my friends, although they may recognize themselves in my pages, will make no objection, and which I am sure will conceal their identity from strangers.

Some expectation was expressed, during the serial publication of these chapters, that parts of them would be occupied by descriptions of distinguished literary people in England. That they are wholly lacking in this element of popular interest is not accidental, nor indeed unintentional. Having never made any special effort to meet literary people at home, I did not do so while I was in England. It would be difficult to prove, either by demonstration or by experience, that the fact that a man has the faculty of thinking well and writing agreeably makes him necessarily a pleasant companion. He may be so; and then he is likely to be the more so for his faculty of thinking; but the chances that he may be ill-natured or ill-bred, or at least uncompanionable, are quite as great as if his vocation were law, or farming, or fiddle-making. Indeed, I know one fiddle-maker, an uneducated artisan, who is found by some of the best bred and most intelligent men that I know much more companionable than most of those whom they meet in their own society. It seems to me an altogether erroneous notion, this assumption that similarity in occupation, or admiration on one side, must produce liking in personal intercourse. It was by no means certain, because of my delight in "Sartor Resartus" and in "In Memoriam," that I should personally like the writers of those books ; and it was very much more than uncertain whether they would like me. Therefore, as I did not happen to meet them at the houses of any of my friends, I did not visit them, nor others of their order, whom I need not name. For as to going to see them as shows, that I should not have presumed to do, even if I had had such an inclination.[1]

I thought myself very fortunate in the way in which I saw England and the life there ; for it was such an informal, matter-of-course, untourist-like way. Of the kindness that was shown me there, I shall say no more than I have said from time to

[1] Since the writing of this passage the author of *Sartor Resartus* has passed away, and his *Reminiscences* have been published. The latter confirm me in the opinion expressed above. Their writer, although not the wise and profound thinker that he deemed himself, was the greatest artist in words that this century has seen; and he gave to thousands, of whom I was one, more pleasure than they received from any other book-maker of his day. But he has revealed himself as one of those eminent persons whom I should prefer to know only through the protecting medium of some convenient Boswell: — albeit the invention of Boswellism and the elevation of it into a vocation is one of the literary nuisances and social afflictions of the last hundred years.

time, as occasion suggested. I can never cease to cherish its remembrance; and of this kindness no small part was that which made me at home in English houses. Indeed, I was hardly a stranger in any one in which I had the pleasure of being received; for, with three exceptions, I visited no one whom I had not had the like pleasure of receiving under my own roof; nor was I able to enter half the houses where I knew that for years welcome had awaited me. Moreover, I had the advantage of seeing England from two points of view, — that of a visiting stranger and that of one who is at home. Accustomed to be mistaken by my British kinsmen in the United States and Canada for an Englishman of British birth, I found the mistake still more common in Old England itself. There, by all who did not know me, it was quietly assumed as a matter of course that I was born on the soil; and as all who did know me knew to the contrary, I did not travel by rail or afoot with the announcement that I was a Yankee pasted on my hat; nor in my casual intercourse with strangers did I make the needless declaration. Therefore, as I went about a great deal alone from choice, and as, if I went by a highway, I often came back through a by-way, I saw Englishmen both as they appear to each other and as they appear to strangers. Under both aspects they commanded my respect and won my liking. Indeed, I must say of my sojourn in England, having both the people and the country in mind, that never that I can remember in my existence since I was a patch of protoplasm did I find it so easy to harmonize with the environment. Never was I, a Yankee of eight generations on both sides, so much at ease in mind and body, never, in one English word, so much at home, as I was in England.

My reader now knows my mood and my purpose in the writing of this book. It is not properly a book of travel, but the story of a semi-sentimental, semi-critical journey through various parts of England, in which what the writer thought and felt is told quite as much as what he saw. Whoever does not care to read such a book will do well to close this one here, and go no further.

CHAPTER II.

ENGLISH SKIES.

WHEN Horace wrote that they who cross the sea change their skies, but not their natures, he uttered a truth the full meaning and force of which is too little regarded by those who are ready to find men of the same race differing essentially because they live apart in different countries. True, the sea that Horace had in mind was but the Adriatic, or at the most the Mediterranean. For it should always be remembered that to the ancients lakes were seas, and that " the sea " was the Mediterranean ; a voyage upon which to Greece, mostly within sight of land, was probably the poet's only knowledge of those terrors of navigation which, with denunciations of its inventor, he uttered in his ode on the departure of Virgil for Athens. The exclamation of the Psalmist — " The floods have lifted up their voice ; the floods lift up their waves. The Lord on high is mightier than the noise of many waters ; yea, than the mighty waves of the sea " — had probably its inspiration in a squall upon the shores of the Levant, or in a tempest in the shallows of Gennesareth. So little can we measure the occasion by the expression which it receives from a poet. He tells us, not what the thing was, but what it seemed to him, what feeling it awoke in him ; and what is really measured is his capacity of emotion and of its utterance ; and even that is gauged by our capacity of apprehension and of sympathy.

The change of sky — I refer now to the visible heavens — made by passing from New England to Old England was very great. Upon its degree of physiological effect I shall remark hereafter. I am here concerned merely with its physical aspects. As, on my outward voyage, we neared land, and were on the lookout for the first sight of it, my attention was immediately attracted by the sky. Without the evidence of the ship's log, it seemed to me that I should have had no doubt that near by us there was another land than that from which I had come : certainly, above us there was another heaven.

It was in the afternoon of a fine summer day, and the outlook over the calm water was beautiful, with a radiance softly bright ; but those were not the clouds of the summer skies that I had left behind me. There were three layers of them, and well there might have been ; for the lowest were so low that it seemed as if our masts must tear them asunder if we should pass beneath them, and the highest were soaring in the empyrean. The former, however, were not heavy ; on the contrary, they seemed to be of the lightest texture ; and they stretched far away in long, low lines that could not yet be called bars, — not only were they so large, but their outlines were so soft and undefined. Clouds so formed — clouds which a meteorologist would probably pronounce to be of the same kind — I had seen above the bay of New York, and over the shores of Long Island and New England ; but they were high, so high that distance made them small ; their forms were sharply defined ; and when the sun was above the horizon, as it was now, or sinking gradually below it, they blazed in crimson and gold, whereas these were softly illumined with a mellow, grayish light. They seemed too unsubstantial to reflect the rays that fell upon them, and to need, and to absorb and retain as for their own use, all the brightness that the sun bestowed.

Far above these soared others, brighter, silvery, and fleecy; and yet again above the latter, but not apparently so far, were others, shaped in radiating curves. These layers, indeed, I had seen in western skies, generally moving in contrary motion; but the effect was not at all like that which now attracted my admiring attention. The difference appeared to be caused first by the lowness of the first layer, then by the great distance between this layer and the one next above it, and finally by the very perceptible and almost palpable nature of that vast intervening space. It was not mere space, mere distance. My sight seemed to pass through something that enabled me to measure this vast interval by gradation. And indeed so it was; for even at that great height the atmosphere was filled with a continuous vapor, which, although so thin as to be imperceptible, was yet of consistence enough to modify the light from the setting sun as the rays passed through its immensity. The skyey intervals were not so impalpable, so colorless, and therefore so immeasurable as they are in "America."

As we neared the land great headlands came to meet us, stepping out into the sea, and bearing sometimes these long, low clouds upon their fronts. The day was smiling; and this seemed a gigantic sort of welcome that under lowering skies might have been a more gigantic defiance. And then at once I felt as I never before had felt the significance of the first lines of that splendid stanza in the most splendid of modern lyric poems, —

> "Britannia needs no bulwarks,
> No towers along the steep."

With my glass, I saw upon the Irish side one or two little buildings, which proved to be lookouts and places for beacons, built at the time of the expected Spanish invasion, and one of those round towers which are of such remote antiquity and mysterious purpose that the most learned and sagacious antiquaries have failed to evolve an accepted theory as to their origin. Thus, even long before I touched the shore, was I made to feel the difference which the powers of nature and the hand of man had made between the land which I had left and the land to which I had come.

As we steamed on, and came within easy eye-sight of the land, the rocky height of the Irish coast impressed me, and the bright rich green of the surface of the country, as it stretched off into the distance. The island looked like a great stone set in the ocean jewel-wise, the top of which had been covered with a thin coating of green enamel. Soon we were near enough to see the waves dashing against the sides of these cliffs, which were so high that the ocean swell seemed but to plash playfully about their feet. And then I felt as I had never felt before the meaning of the lines, and saw as I had never seen before, in my flat-shored home, the scene of the lines, —

> "Break, break, break,
> On thy cold gray stones, O sea."

The position of the speaker I had imagined, — upon

a height looking down upon the sea ; but here it was before me : — those, or such, were the heights and crags, and there below was the bay.

When, after leaving Queenstown, we were well up the Channel, we were at times near enough to the eastern shore to see the surpassing beauty of the country : green field and darker wood, villages, farm-steads, country-seats, churches, castles, so uninten-tionally disposed by the hands of man and of nature working together that what was designed for conven-ience or made for use blended into a landscape of enchanting variety. And here I saw constantly something, a little thing, that delighted my eye, and I may almost say gladdened my heart, — windmills. There was a gentle breeze blowing, and these faith-ful servants of man for ages past were working away with that cheerful diligence which always marks their labors, and has always made me respect and like and almost love them, and feel a kind of sym-pathy with the poor dumb, willing things when a calm reduced them to idleness, which yet after all was well-earned rest. In my boyhood, there were two in sight from the Battery, on the Brooklyn side of the bay, and they were not far from my father's house ; but the places where they stood are now cov-ered by a howling wilderness of bricks and mortar, and the windmill seems to have disappeared from the land. At least, I have not seen one anywhere for twenty years and more ; and with them the tide-mill seems to have gone also. In England, although it is the country of coal and iron and the steam-engine, I found them more or less wherever I went, giving life to the landscape, and standing, like a link of develop-ment, between man and unmitigated nature.

2

Off Anglesea I made my first acquaintance with
that limited knowledge of manifest things on the
part of the British Philistine which I afterwards
found to be one of his distinctive traits of character.
My fellow-passengers were almost wholly Britons,
and they had assumed as a matter of course that
I was one of them. But there was one difference
between us : they had all been travelers, and had
crossed the ocean more than once, some of them
many times, while this was my first approach to the
shores to which they had often returned. As a knot
of us stood looking over the starboard quarter, our attention was attracted by a somewhat imposing structure set far out into the water. I waited to hear
what would be said about it. Presently one of my
companions observed it, and asked what it was.
Then there was a little discussion ; and to my surprise, I may say to my amazement, no one knew, or
seemed able to conjecture, at what we were looking.
After a little reserve, I said that I thought it was
Holyhead, — a suggestion which was received with
favor, and then with general acquiescence. Now my
knowledge was due to no sagacity or study ; but to
the fact that, before the days of the electric telegraph
and of fleets of commercial steamers, my father's
counting-house was in South Street, where the steep-
roofed old building still stands, and that on Saturdays
I was a frequent and not unwelcome visitor on board
the ships that lay at the wharves before his windows. Over the companion-ways into the cabins I
saw painted rows of little flags, with the legend
" Holyhead signals ; " and with a boy's inquisitiveness I asked a captain what that meant. His answer I need hardly give. Those were the signals

which each ship hoisted when she came in sight of
Holyhead light-house and lookout station, whence the
vessel was announced, by semaphore telegraph, in
Liverpool. Therefore, knowing where we were in the
Channel, it seemed plain enough that that was Holyhead. But there was a little crowd of my British
cousins, travelers and commercial persons, who had
passed the place again and again, and who did not
know what it was! I held my tongue; but, like a
wiser animal than I am, I kept up a great thinking.

When I landed, one of the very few differences
that I observed between the people whom I had left
and those among whom I had come was a calmer
and more placid expression of countenance. This in
the descending scale of intelligence became a stolid
look, the outward sign of mental sluggishness. But,
higher or lower, in degree or in kind there it was, —
placidity instead of a look of intentness and anxiety.
Now, to suppose that this difference is caused by less
thoughtfulness, less real anxiety, less laboriousness,
on the part of the Englishman is to draw a conclusion directly in face of the facts. The toil and struggle of life is harder in England than it is here: poor
men are more driven by necessity; rich men think
more; among all classes, except the frivolous part of
the aristocracy (not a large class), there is more mental strain, more real anxiety, than we know here,
where all the material conditions of life are easier,
and where there is less care for political and social
matters. Why, then, this difference of look? I am
inclined to think that it is due, in some measure, to
difference of climate, — not to such effect of climate
upon organization as makes a difference in the physical man, but to a result of climate which is almost

mechanical, and which operates directly upon each individual. Briefly, I think that an expression of anxiety is given to the " American " face by an effort to resist the irritating effect of our sun and wind. Watch the people as they pass you on a bright, windy day, and you will see that their brows are contracted, their eyes half closed, and their faces set to resist the glare of the sun and the flare of the wind ; and besides, in winter they are stung with cold, in summer scorched with heat. For some three hundred days of the three hundred and sixty-five they undergo this irritation, and brace themselves to meet it. Now, a scowling brow, half-closed eyes, and a set face unite to make an anxious, disturbed, struggling expression of countenance, although the wearer may be not really anxious, disturbed, and struggling. By the experience of years this look becomes more or less fixed in the majority of " American " faces.

In England, on the contrary, there is comparatively no glare of the sun, and comparatively little wind. The former assertion will be received without question by those who have been in both countries ; but the latter may be doubted, and may be regarded as strange, coming from a man who has to confess that, before he had been on English land forty-eight hours, he was almost blown bodily off Chester walls, and came near being wrecked in the Mersey. In fact, there are not unfrequently in England wind storms of a severity which, if not unknown, is very rare in the United States or in Canada. We have records of such storms in England in the past ; we read announcements of them at the present day. I had experience of one there more severe than any that I remember here, and heard little or nothing said about it. But in England, when a storm is over, the wind goes down. Here, on the contrary, our " clearing up " after a storm is effected by the setting in of a northwest wind, against which it is at first toilsome to walk, and which sometimes continues to blow out of a cloudless sky for days, with a virulence quite fiendish. Because it does not rain or snow, people call the weather fine, and delude themselves with the notion that the wind is " bracing; " but nevertheless they go about with scowling brows, watery eyes, and set faces, as they brace *themselves* up to endure it. On my return, this wind met me nearly two hundred miles at sea. It was something the like of which I had not felt once on the eastern side of the Atlantic. The air was as clear as a diamond; the sky was as blue as sapphire and as hard as steel; the moon, about fifty thousand miles higher than it was in England, blazed with a cold, cheerless light; life seemed made up of bright points; and the wind blew from the northwest, not tempestuously or in gusts, but with a steady, overbearing persistence for which nothing in nature affords any simile: it is itself alone. I knew that I was near home. There is nothing of this kind in England. Not only did I not find it in my brief experience, but I never heard of it, nor of it is there any record. The absence of it there and the presence of it here may, I think, be reasonably regarded as a very important influence in the fashioning the facial habit of the people of the two countries. All the more does this seem probable because I have observed that " Americans " who reside in England for a few years generally lose, in a great measure, if not entirely, the look in question, and on their return to their own shores soon acquire it again. It need hardly be said that there are numerous exceptions to these remarks in both countries.

To speak of the difference between the climate of England and the climate of the United States is as reasonable as it would be to speak of any difference between England, on the one hand, and Europe, Asia, or Africa, on the other. England is an isolated territory, — the southern half of an island, — and is about as large as the State of Virginia, or as the States of New York and New Jersey together; while the United States cover the greater third of a continent, stretching from ocean to ocean, and almost from the arctic regions to the tropics. England may be properly compared only with such several parts of the United States as are homogeneous in soil and climate. The difference between the climates, or rather the atmospheric conditions, of Old England and of New England, for example, or of the Middle States, is of course due, very largely, to the greater dampness of the former. Careful records of observations, extending through twenty-three years, show that rain falls in the valley of the Thames, on an average, one hundred and seventy-eight days in the year; that is, on nearly one half of the three hundred and sixty-five. Contrary to general supposition, the wettest month is July; and the wettest season is autumn, and not winter, as is generally believed. Spring is the least wet, winter comes next in rainfall and fog, summer next, and autumn stands highest. In this respect, autumn is to winter as 7.4 to 5.8. But I found rain in England to be a very different thing from rain in New England or in New York. With us it rarely rains but it pours; and excepting a few light show-

ers in May, all our rainfalls are more or less floods
from the sky, and are accompanied by storms, —
storms of thunder and wind in summer, violent winds
from the northeast in autumn and winter. This is
so much the case that loose speakers among us say that
it is storming, when they mean merely that it is raining; applying storm to a May shower as to a November gale. Now in England rain is generally a much
milder dispensation of moisture. It will rain there
steadily for hours together, a fine, softly-dropping
rain, without wind enough to shake a rose-bush.
Such rain is almost unknown in "America." Having
often observed our rains for purposes of comparison,
I find that about five minutes is the longest duration
of such fine, light rain as I have seen continue in
England for five hours, without either much increase
or much diminution, and without any appreciable
wind. This is why Portia says that mercy "drop-
peth as the *gentle* rain from heaven." We in America rarely see such rain as Shakespeare had in mind
when he wrote those lines.

Although the rain falls thus gently, the heavens
are very black. The earth is darkened by a murky
canopy. It is gloomier than it is with us even when
we have one of our three days' northeasters, or one
of our blackest thunder-storms. The clouds are of a
dirty, grimy hue and substance, and seem not to be
mere condensing vapor, but sloughs in mid-air. Looking at them, you would suppose that they would foul
the houses, the streets, and the fields, instead of washing them. The sight of them gives new force to Mi-
randa's description : —

"The sky, it seems, would pour down stinking pitch."

Fully to understand what that means, one must wake

up, as Shakespeare often had waked, to an autumn rain in London.

The reason of this seemed to me that the clouds lie so low. With us, even in a copious rain, the clouds are so high that the drops strike smartly as they come down, and we can look up to the lofty vapor level from which they fall. But in England the rain comes only from a little distance above the tops of the trees and the houses. (I am speaking not only of showers, but of steady rains.) Even when it does not rain and is not foggy the tops of the not lofty pinnacles of Westminster Abbey are sometimes hidden in mist; and once from the Thames I saw a gold-lined cloud descend upon the Parliament houses, as if to cast a royal robe around the Victoria Tower.

The changes of the sky, too, are sudden, although without violence. You will wake to find a steadily falling rain. The heavens will be of an impenetrable dun color; or rather, there will be no heavens, the very earth seeming to be wrapped around with a cloud of thick darkness, distilling water. You will naturally think that such a thick and settled mass can be dispersed and changed only by some great commotion of the elements. As you look out — no pleasant occupation — at long intervals, your judgment is confirmed. There is the same steady distillation of water out of the same darkness. Something, a book, or a newspaper, or a thought of faces far away, absorbs your attention, and suddenly there is a gleam of light. You look up; the clouds are breaking away, and before you can change your dress and get out the day is a beauty smiling through tears, and all the earth seems glad again. But you cannot count upon the continuance of this even for an hour. With us, if the wind changes and the clouds break, they are scattered, driven out of sight for days. Not so in England. Your bright sky there may be obscured in five minutes, and in less than five minutes more, if you are sensitive to damp, you will need an umbrella. This is what is meant in English literature by the changeability of the climate; not such sudden jumps from hot to cold and from cold to hot as those which we have to undergo. And again, in this variability of the heavens, I found an illustration of a passage in Shakespeare, that in King Henry VIII., where the doomed Buckingham says, —

> "My life is spann'd already:
> I am the shadow of poor Buckingham,
> Whose figure even this instant cloud puts on,
> By darkening my clear sun."

The passage at best is marred with the effects of the manifestly hasty composition of this play ; but the instant cloud darkening the clear sun is a simile — yet not a simile, for it is the glory of Shakespeare's style that he rarely wrote in set similes — that has an illustrative power in England which is given to it by no corresponding phenomenon in " America."

These passages are no after-thoughts with me, curiously sought out for the purpose of giving interest to my descriptions. The fitness of thing to thought was so exact and incisive that the latter came to me instantly as I was observing the phenomenon.

Rain is not looked upon in England, as it is with us, as a barrier to the open air, unless, as an Irishman might say, the open air is taken in a close carriage. Indeed, were it so regarded, the English people more than any other would live an indoor life, instead of being the most open-air loving of all Northern nations.

For the extravagant joke about the English weather, that on a fine day it is like looking up a chimney, and on a foul day like looking down, is more than set off by the truth of Charles II.'s sober saying, that the climate of England tempts a man more into the open air than any other. It is very rarely, I should think, that the weather in England is for many hours together so forbidding that a healthy man, not too dainty as to his dress, would be kept indoors, and lose by it invigorating exercise. It is not too warm in summer, nor too cold in winter; it is never too hot and dry, and, notwithstanding the frequent rains, it is rarely too wet. The mean temperature of the year is about fifty degrees; the mean temperature of the hottest month, July, only sixty-three degrees; and it is only on very exceptional days, in very exceptional years, that the mercury rises above eighty degrees, or falls below twenty degrees, the mean temperature of the coldest month, January, being thirty-five degrees. A comparison of these temperatures with those which we are called upon to bear in our long summers and in our longer winters shows the advantage which the people of England have over us in respect to out-door exercise. We cannot walk or ride as they do. During no small part of our year physical exertion in the open air is painful rather than pleasureful, injurious rather than beneficial. It is only in autumn that we can find health and enjoyment out of doors. Between the middle of September and the middle of December we may enjoy a mellow air and what is left of the verdure in our parched landscape; but at that season we strangely leave the country, whither we go in the blinding, blazing summer, when walking or driving, except in

the evening, is a fitting diversion only for salaman-
ders.

It is not, however, only men in England who are
not kept within doors by rain from their business, or
their pleasure, or their mere daily exercise. English
ladies, as is generally known, take open-air exercise
much more freely and regularly than women in the
same condition of life in most other countries. But
it is not so well known, I believe, how ready they are
to brave the rain, or rather to take it quietly, without braving, as a little inconvenience not to be
thought of within certain bounds. At first, I was
surprised to see, both in London and in the country,
ladies walking about in rain, coming out into rain,
which would have caused an " American " woman of
like condition to house herself, or if caught in it, and
not kept out by sheer necessity, to make for shelter
and for home. And not unfrequently I saw them doing thus umbrellaless. In England umbrellas would
seem to be a necessity of daily life ; but, according to
my observation, they are much more generally carried
by men than by women. In walking through the
Crescent in Regent Street on a wet morning, I have
met half a dozen women, lady-like in appearance, exposing themselves, and what is more their bonnets,
without protection to the fine, drizzling rain with an
air of the utmost unconcern.

I walked, one morning, from Canterbury to the
neighboring village of Harbledown, some three miles,
in a rain that, notwithstanding my umbrella, wet me
pretty well from the hips down. On my way I met,
or overtook, men, women, and children, but only one
of them had an umbrella, and that one was — of all
creatures — a butcher's boy! Just at the edge of

Canterbury — I cannot say the outskirts, for the towns in England do not have such ragged, draggled things as outskirts — I stopped at a little house to get a glass of milk (and good, rich milk it was, price one penny), led thereto by a sense of emptiness (for I was yet breakfastless), and by a small placard in the window announcing the sale of that fluid. It was served out to me by a middle-aged woman, lean, "slabsided," sharp-nosed, with a nasal, whining voice, who, looking through the window past her business card, said, by way of making herself agreeable, as I quaffed her liquid ware, "Seems suthin like rain, sir!" It was pouring so steadily, although not violently, that I had thought of turning back, and giving up Harbledown for that day ; but this determined me, and put me on my mettle. If a poor wisp of womanhood like that could see in such a down-pour only something like rain, flinching would be a shame to my beard and my inches. I was struck, too, by the thorough Yankeeness of her phrase : it might have been uttered on the outskirts of Boston. This likeness, however, struck me among the country folk in Kent on other occasions, to which I shall refer hereafter. In Kent I rarely heard an *h* dropped, and never one superfluously added.

At a country house where I was visiting in Essex, it was agreed at luncheon that we should have a walk in the park that afternoon, because it was fine, and we had had a drive the day before, and were to have lawn-tennis the day after. Now the phrase "it's fine" in England means merely that it is not actually raining at the time of speaking ; but when the hour of our walk came the rain came also with it. As our party was composed of two ladies and three gentlemen, I expected that it would be broken up. Not at all. With the most matter-of-course air, the ladies, neither of them notably robust in figure or apparently in health, donned light water-proof cloaks, and, taking each of us an umbrella, we soberly waded forth to our watery English walk. I hope the ladies enjoyed it, for they caused me to do so ; and we saw some noble trees and pretty views in the park and from it. We met a small flock of geese who did not hiss, but looking with goose-like sobriety seemed to recognize us, and to be ready to hold out to us the web-foot of fellowship. I observed that even the ladies did not put on overshoes, but trusted merely to stout, serviceable walking-shoes ; and although we walked over grass I found that my feet were not wet. I had made a similar observation on my walk to Harbledown. Then my feet became damp, of course ; but although there was neither a plank nor an asphaltum path by the roadside (one of which is commonly found in the more thickly inhabited rural districts in England), my strong walking-shoes were not soiled above the sole. This I found to be the case again and again, so firm are the tightly graveled roads in England. The harmlessness of wet grass was a puzzle to me. I walked all over the lawns at Hampton Court one morning after a rain, led to do so by a companion who knew how things should be done (you always walk on grass in England, if you like to do so), and I neither felt nor saw upon my shoes any evidence of water. Under similar circumstances in the United States, they would have been wet through in five minutes. It need hardly be said, however, that even when there is not a storm or an unusual rain the usual fall on alternate days is often too heavy to admit of parties of pleasure. Our lawn-tennis had to be given up as an out-of-doors perform-ance, although the lawn had been specially mowed for the occasion. But our hostess was not to be balked. We went into one of the drawing-rooms, and ourselves rolling the furniture out into the great hall, we stretched a rope across the room, hung cop-ies of the *Times* over it to make a barrier, and had our game out; in which, by the way, the most points were scored by my lady herself and by a Fellow of St. John's College, Oxford. Unlike the *America* in the famous yacht race, the " American " was " no-where."

In the gardens of such houses, or sometimes upon their walls, it is common to find sun-dials, relics of the past. Those upon the walls are very large, some of them being ten or twelve feet in diameter. They seem to have been as common as clocks, and to have been set up as a matter of course long after clocks were no rarities. But if, according to the pretty le-gend upon one of them, *Horas non numero nisi sere-nas*, they were useless unless the sun shone, they must have been mere ornaments for much more than half the days in the year. For even when it does not rain in England the days are comparatively few in which the sun casts a shadow strong enough to mark the hour upon a dial. The noon-mark on the kitchen window-sill of old New England farm-houses was almost always, once a day, a serviceable sign of the time; but a sun-dial in England must often have been little more useful than a chair to a cherub.

The low temperature of the country enables the people to bear the dampness, and even to find it con-ducive to health and enjoyment of life. " Let it be

cold," said an Englishman to me, as we walked from
his villa to the train through a chilling drizzle, " and
I care little if it is damp." And I found the combination, on the whole, wholesome and not unpleasant.
But if England, with its damp atmosphere, were subject to our extremes of heat and cold, it would be al-
almost uninhabitable : it would be as unhealthy in
winter as Labrador, in summer as India. I was surprised to see the freedom with which doors were left
open for the entrance of the air, and by the uncon-
sciousness of possible harm with which women of the
lower classes in the country went about in cold mist,
or even in rain, without bonnets or shawls. For as
to myself, at times I found this chilly fog pierce to
the very marrow of my bones, and make me long for
the fire which was not always attainable. And when
I did have it, the comfort that it gave me was not so
great as I expected it would be. Fire does not seem
to be very warm in England. I never saw a really
hot one.

It is this combination of cold and damp that makes
the Englishman so capable of food and drink. Nothing is more impressive about him than his diligence
in this respect. He never neglects an opportunity.
Hearty breakfast at nine o'clock ; luncheon at half
past one or two, at which there is a hot joint and
cold bird pies, with wine and beer ; at five o'clock
tea, generally delicious souchong, with thin bread and
butter ; dinner at eight, serious business ; sherry and
biscuit or sandwiches at eleven, as you take your bedroom candle. At home it would have killed me in
a month ; there I throve upon it mightily, and laid
pounds avoirdupois upon my ribs, which I lost within
a year after my return to the air of " America,"

which so often makes one feel like desiccated codfish. There is no shirking whatever of this matter of eating and drinking. It is not regarded as in the least indelicate, or, in the old-fashioned phrase,. " ungenteel," even for a lady to eat and drink anywhere at any time. I remarked this at a morning concert of the great triennial Birmingham musical festival. The concert began at eleven o'clock, and as the price of tickets was a pound (five dollars) it is to be supposed that every person of the thousands present in that great hall had breakfasted well about eight or nine o'clock ; but yet when the first part was over, around me and everywhere within sight, even in the seats roped off for the nobility, luncheon bags were produced, and flasks ; and men and women began to eat sandwiches and other wiches, and to drink sherry and water, or something else and water (but never the water without the something else), as if they feared that they would be famished before they could get home again.[1] And very careful in this respect are they of the stranger within their gates. The last words that I heard from a very elegant woman, as I parted from her to take a railway journey of three or four hours, were a charge to the butler to see that I had some sandwiches. Needless caution ! They had been prepared, and were produced to me in a faultless package, and put into my bag with gravity and unction. In due time I ate them, and with appetite, saying grace to my fair providence.

One effect of the climate of England (it must, I

[1] So the Scotsman Baillie, writing home about the trial of the Earl of Strafford, at which he was present, says that even then and there among the lords there was "much publict eating not only of confections, bot of flesh and bread, bottles of beer and wine going thick from mouth to mouth, and all this in the King's eye." (Bannatyne Club Ed., i. 314.)

think, be the climate) is the mellowing of all sights, and particularly of all sounds. Life there seems softer, richer, sweeter, than it is with us. Bells do not clang so sharp and harsh upon the ear. True, they are not rung so much as they are with us. Even in London on Sunday their sound is not obtrusive. Indeed, the only bell sound in the great city of which I have a distinct memory is Big Ben's delicious, mellow boom. In country walks on Sunday the distant chimes from the little antique spires or towers float to you like silver-tongued voices through the still air. Your own voice is hushed by them if you are with a companion, and you walk on in sweet and silent sadness. I shall never forget the soothing charm of the Bolney chime in Sussex, which, as the sun was leaving the weald to that long, slow-deepening twilight through which the day in England lapses gently into darkness, with no splendor of sunset obsequies, I heard in company with one whose sagacious lips, then hushed for a moment, are silent now forever. These English country chimes are very different from those that stun our ears from Broadway steeples. They are simple, and yet are not formless jangle; but the performers do not undertake to play opera airs *affetuoso* and *con expressione* with ropes and iron hammers upon hollow tons of metal.

At the Birmingham musical festival, I first remarked the effect of the climate upon sound. There was a large instrumental band, and a good one; and that it was well conducted need hardly be said, for the conductor was Sir Michael Costa. But in precision of attack, in perfection of *crescendo* and *diminuendo*, in the finish and the phrasing of the various salient passages as they were successively taken up

3

by the different instruments, and in sonority, I found the performance not quite equal to that of Mr. Thomas's band, the drill of which was very superior. A dozen bars, however, had not been played before I was conscious of a sweet, rich quality of tone, particularly in the string band, which contrasted with the clear, hard brilliancy of the Thomas orchestra. This impressed me more and more as the performance went on, although the enjoyment of it was marred by the organ being not perfectly in tune with the band. Another superiority in Costa's band attracted my attention : they accompanied much better than Thomas's ; with more feeling, sympathy, and intelligence. The singers could trust them and lean upon them. This was doubtless due in great part to Costa's long experience as an operatic conductor, while, on the other hand, Thomas has always worked in instrumental music pure and simple ; but I cannot doubt that it was due in part also to the feeling of the individual performers. As to the difference in the quality of the tone, I can find no other cause for that than the climate. Possibly, however, the English orchestras tune to the normal pitch (although it did not seem to me to be so), in which case some superiority in quality of tone would be accounted for ; the high, so-called and absurdly called, Philharmonic pitch being destructive of quality, which is sacrificed to a sharp sonority.[1]

[1] Some months after the first publication of this chapter Dr. Arthur Sullivan, who was then in New York, was reported in the *New York Herald* as having remarked upon this difference in tone between the string bands of the two countries, and as having accounted for it to himself by the supposition that the musicians in "America" were not careful in the selection of their instruments. His surmise was natural, but erroneous. He would find good instruments enough here; but the mellowing air of England cannot be bought and brought across the ocean. There is no more

One little performance of Costa's on this occasion was very interesting. My seat, although not too near, happened to be in such a position that I could see all his motions, and even his face. In a piece from Beethoven's Mass in C there was a little fugue, the rhythm and the intonation of which were both somewhat difficult. As the tenors entered with the subject they were unsteady, and speedily went into confusion. Ruin was imminent. But turning to Costa I saw him, little disturbed, merely increase the emphasis of his beat, while he himself took up the subject, and, looking eagerly at the tenors, sang it right out at them. They were soon whipped in, and the performance was not only saved, but was so good that its repetition was demanded by the president, the Marquis of Hertford (no applause being allowed) ; and on the repeat the tenors behaved handsomely in the presence of the enemy.

Whether I was favored by the English climate I do not know, but in addition to this soft, sweet charm which the air seemed to give to everything that was to be seen or heard, I found even late autumn there as verdant and as variously beautiful as early summer is with us, and without the heat from which we suffer. In Sussex the gardens were all abloom, wild flowers lit up the woods, blackberries were ripening in the hedges, birds singing, and everything was fresh and fragrant. Among the birds, I observed the thrush and the robin-redbreast ; the latter not that tawny-breasted variety of the singing thrush which

sensitive barometer than a stringed instrument. Dampness affects them all so much and so quickly that I have known the first and second strings of a 'cello to rise half a tone in an hour or so with a change of wind from dry to damp. This rise accompanies a slight increase of the thickness of the string, which gives its tone a little more body.

is here called a robin, but a little bird about half as
large, with a thin, pointed bill, a breast of crimson,
and a note like a loud and prolonged chirrup.   It
would be charming if we could have this man-trust-
ing little feathered fellow with us ; but I fear that
he could not bear our winters.   In Warwickshire I
found roses blooming, blooming in great masses half-
way up the sides of a two-story cottage on the road
from Stratford-on-Avon to Kenilworth ; and this was
in the very last days of October.   True, I had only
a few days before shivered through a rainy morning
drive in Essex, when the chill dampness seemed to
strike into my very heart ; but on the whole I found
myself under English skies healthy, happy, and the
enjoyer of a succession of new delights, which yet
seemed to me mine by birthright.

CHAPTER III.

ENGLAND ON THE RAILS.

JOUY, the author of "L'Hermite de la Chaussée d'Antin," which is the French "Spectator," has a remark which those who are ready to generalize upon national peculiarities would do well to consider. " Plus on réfléchit," he says, " et plus on observe, plus on se convainct de la fausseté de la plupart de ces jugements portés sur un nation entière par quelques écrivains et adoptés sans examen par les autres." [1] He illustrates and confirms this conclusion by asking, Who is the Frenchman that does not believe himself to be one of a people the most fickle and the most inconstant in the world ? Nevertheless, he adds, if we observe and study the character of our people elsewhere than in the capital, where it denaturalizes itself so easily, we shall discover that, so far from being inclined to change, the French is, of the peoples of Europe, the most enslaved by its prejudices, and the most bound down to routine.

The French Addison was right; and there could be no more impressive illustration of the truth of his judgment than the opinions formed of each other, and tenaciously held for more than half a century, by the people of England and those of " America,"

[1] The more we reflect, and the more we observe, the more we are convinced of the falsity of the greater part of those judgments passed upon a whole people by some writers and adopted without question by others. 'L'Hermite, etc. No. v., 21st September, 1811.)

or, as the latter is generally called in the former, "the States," both phrases being brief make-shifts for the long, complex, and purely political designation, "the United States of America." One of these notions is counterchanged, as the heralds say ; counterchanging being a quaint contrivance, by which a figure, a lion for example, is shown partly of one color and partly of another, in opposition to a party-colored background of the same tints. This correspondent perversion and antagonism has a grotesque resemblance to the opinions sometimes entertained of each other on one subject by two individuals or two peoples. Thus British writers, and generally the British people, adopting, as Jouy says, without question the opinions of their writers, speak of us as a nation of travelers ; while many of us, on the other hand, think of Englishmen as staid, immobile folk, slow in action, mental and physical, and, compared with ourselves, sluggish, stolid, and with a dislike of movement which is composed in equal parts of *vis inertiæ* and local attachment.

There was never a notion more incorrect, or set up more directly in the face of commonly known facts. Englishmen are, and always have been, the greatest travelers in the world. Englishmen, of all people, have been the readiest to leave an old home for a new one. They are the explorers, they are the colonizers, of the earth. It is because Englishmen are travelers and colonizers that two English-speaking nations monopolize the larger and the fairer part of this great continent ; that the vast continent-like island of Australia is rapidly becoming another New England ; that Victoria counts among her titles that of Empress of India ; and that the aborigines of the southern wilds of Africa are beginning to yield place to the Anglo-Saxon. Even on this continent more men from the Old England than from the New have traveled to the Western plains for curiosity or for the pleasures of the chase ; and in South America, — in the Brazils, in Peru, and in Chili, — of the English-speaking denizens and mercantile houses ten to one are British. Upon the latter point I speak not with personal knowledge, but by inference from what I do know and from testimony.

The notion that "the Americans" are a nation of travelers has sprung chiefly from the largeness of our hotels, and the freedom with which we use them. In former years the greater number of English travelers in England went, except when they were actually *en route*, to lodgings. It is only of late years that large hotels like ours have been established in the principal English cities ; but there, notwithstanding all that has been said of the Englishman's dislike of hotel life, they are profitable, and seem to be not unsuited to the habits of the people. Our large hotels were at first the result of a certain social condition. We had not a class of people who liked to let a part of their own houses to transient lodgers of a condition in life above their own. Keeping a hotel or a boarding-house as a business was quite another matter. It was undertaken like any other business. Hence our hotels and boarding-houses, and our free use of them merely as places where we could buy food and rest for a few hours, just as we could buy anything else at any shop, without concerning ourselves about the landlord in one case or the shopkeeper in the other. And this notion of our being so much more given to travel than Englishmen are had its origin many years ago, before railways were, and when we used steamboats even much more than we do now, which Englishmen can never use largely as a means of locomotion. A British traveler of that time, finding himself in one of our large river-boats, with one, two, or perhaps three or four hundred people, inferred, in his ignorance, that our whole population was constantly moving about in those to him wonderful vessels. He had never seen more than a stage-coach full of fellow-passengers at one time, and the great throng astonished him. But for one traveler in a stage-coach here there were a hundred in England, besides those who traveled post.

However all this may have been, nowadays half England seems to be every day upon the rails. High and low, rich and poor, they spend no small part of their time in railway carriages. Ladies who would not venture themselves in a London cab alone (although that they do now pretty freely) travel by rail unattended, or at most with a maid, who is generally in a second-class carriage, while they are in a first. Not only married and middle-aged women do this, but young ladies, even of the higher and the upper-middle classes.[1] The number of trains that enter and leave London, Liverpool, Birmingham, and other large cities daily is enormous. The great stations in London, of which there are six or seven, like the Victoria, the Charing Cross, and the Euston Street, swarm with crowds at all hours. The entire population of the island seems to be always " on the go." And all this is done without bustle or confusion. The Englishman and the Englishwoman of to-day are so

---

[1] *Teste :* the adventure of Colonel Valentine Baker, now, as Baker Pasha, restored to grace and good society in England.

accustomed to travel that they go about upon the rails with no more fuss than in going from the drawing-room to the dining-room, and from the dining-room back into the drawing-room ; and this freedom in locomotion is much aided by the perfect system of the railway management, and the comfort with which the whole proceeding is invested.

There has been much dispute as to the comparative convenience of the English and "American" systems of railway traveling. I give my voice, without hesitation or qualification, in favor of the English. In England a man in his traveling, as in all other affairs of life, does not lose his individuality. He does not become merely one of the traveling public. He is not transmuted, even by that great social change-worker, the railway, into a mere item in a congeries of so many things that are to be transported from one place to another *with the least trouble and the greatest gain to the common carrier*. His personal comfort is looked after ; his individual wishes are consulted so far as is possible. He arrives at the station with his luggage. One of the company's porters immediately appears, asks where he is going, and takes his trunks and bags. He buys his tickets, and directed, if he needs direction, by other servants of the company, all of whom are in uniform, he takes his seat in a first-class or second-class carriage, as he has chosen. He is assisted to find a comfortable place, and, if he appears at all at a loss, is prevented by the attendants from getting into a wrong train or a wrong carriage. For here, as in all similar places in England, there is always some authorized person at hand to answer questions ; and the answer is civil and pleasant and sufficient. His luggage, properly labeled, is placed in a van or compartment in the very carriage in which he takes his seat. For, contrary to the general supposition, first, second, and third class carriages are not distinct vehicles or, as we might say, cars, coupled together in a train. The body of the vehicle on each "truck" is divided into first, second, and third class carriages or compartments ; and each one of these composite vehicles has a luggage van. A minute or two before the train is to start a servant of the company, whose business it is, goes to the door of every carriage, and, examining the tickets of the passengers, sees that each one is properly placed. In more than one instance I saw the error of an ignorant passenger who had neglected to make the proper inquiries rectified by this precaution, which prevents mistakes that would prove very annoying. When this has been done the doors are closed but not locked, the word is given "all right," and the train starts, and with a motion so gentle that it is hardly perceptible. There is no clanging of bells or shrieking of whistles. The quiet of the whole proceeding is as impressive as its order.

And I will here remark that that most hideous of all sounds, the mingled shriek and howl of the steam-whistle, from the annoyance of which we are hardly free anywhere, in town or out, is rarely heard in England. At Morley's Hotel in London, which fronts on Trafalgar Square, within a stone's-throw of the great Charing Cross station, and where I stopped for some days, I did not once hear, even in the stillness of night, this hideous sound. On the rails it is rarely heard ; and there the noise is not very unpleasant. It is a short, sharp sound, — a real whistle, not a demoniac shriek, or a hollow, metallic roar.

The care that is taken of the safety of passengers is shown by an incident of which I was a witness when going to Canterbury. The way-stations are on both sides of the road. Passengers who are going up take the train on one side ; those going down, on the other. The communication between the two sides of the station is either by a bridge above the rails, or by a tunnel under-ground ; and no one who is not a servant of the company is allowed to walk on the tracks, or to cross them, under any circumstances whatever. On the occasion to which I refer, a man stepped down from the platform on one side, and was instantly met by a person in uniform who ordered him back. He submitted at once, and then said, good-humoredly, to the station-master, " I suppose you adopted that regulation because of the accidents that happened." " No," replied the other, with a smile ; " we adopted it before the accidents happened." In " America " we wait for the accident.

The carriages are the perfection of comfort. The first-class are in every way luxurious. You are as much at your ease as if you were in a large stuffed arm-chair with a back high enough to support your head as well as your shoulders. The second-class carriages on some of the lines are hardly inferior in real comfort, although they are not so handsomely fitted up ; the most important difference being a diminution of room. But even in the first-class carriages there is no glare of color or of tinsel, nor shining ornament of wood or metal. All is rich and sober ; and there are no sharp corners or hard surfaces. The holder of a first-class ticket may ride in a second or a third class carriage if he desires to do so and there is room for him ; and I have again and again, on the stopping of the train at a way station, gone from one to the other to observe the passengers in each and to talk with them, — for English people are much more talkative and communicative than we are, particularly when they are traveling. In this way I had the pleasure of many long conversations, even with ladies whom I never saw before and whom I shall probably never see again. When a train stops the doors are all immediately thrown open, and if it is at a way-station the passengers give up their tickets as they pass out through the station. If you choose to go beyond the point for which you have bought your ticket, you merely pay the additional fare, for which a receipt is given; doing which causes no appreciable delay.

When the train reaches its destination it is stopped a short distance from the station, and an officer of the company comes to the door of the carriage and asks for your ticket. Sometimes this is done at the last way-station, if that is very near the end of the line. The train then moves on and quietly enters the station, slowing its gentle movement so gradually that motion insensibly becomes rest. There is no clanging, bumping, or shaking. If you have only your hand-bag and your rug, you step out, and if you do not choose to walk, you take the first of the line of cabs in order as they stand, and are off in a minute. If you are in London, and are observant, you will see as you pass the gate that your cabman gives your address to a policeman, who writes it down with the number of the cab, taking a look at you as this is done; but the cab does not perceptibly stop for it, and then is off on a trot. If you have luggage and more than a single trunk, you hold up your

finger, and one of the company's porters is instantly
at the carriage window. You tell him to get you a
four-wheeler, and give him a bag, a rug, a book, or a
newspaper, which he puts into some four-wheeled
cab, which is thereby engaged for you. You get out,
go with the porter to the luggage van, which is not
one of two or three huge cars, full of trunks and
boxes, away at the end of the train, but a small compartment just at your side ; and the contents are not
numerous, of course, as each van has only the luggage of the passengers on one vehicle. You point
out your own trunks and boxes, the porter whisks
them up to the cab, and in five minutes or less from
the time when the train stopped you are trotting off
to your house, your lodgings, or your hotel, and *all
your baggage is with you* for immediate use, without
the bother of checks and expressmen and a delivery
of your bags and boxes at some time within half a
day afterwards. If by chance any mistake has been
made as to the disposition of your baggage, which
happens with extremest rarity, according to my observation, it is discovered at once, and there is the
whole force of the company's porters and higher officers to rectify it, and to search for and produce your
property under your own observation; and the thing
is done in a few minutes. Police officers are there,
too, not lounging or indifferent, but ready, quick,
and active to give you protection and help. The result is expedition and the keeping of your property
under your own eye, and the having it immediately
at your residence. It is customary to give the porter
who gets your cab and takes your luggage to it sixpence or fourpence for his trouble.

Nothing is more remarkable on an English railway

than the civility of the company's servants ; and this is the more impressive because it does not at all diminish their firmness and precision in obedience to orders.   I happened on two occasions to remark this particularly.   But before telling my own experience in England I will relate that of another person under similar circumstances in "America."

A young gentleman, whom I know very well, started from Philadelphia to New York, buying a through ticket.   He stopped on the way and remained a night, and the next morning resumed his journey.   When he presented his "coupon" ticket to the conductor, he was told that it was worthless, as it was dated the day before, and was good only for the day on which it was issued.   He insisted that as he had paid to be taken from Philadelphia to New York he had the right to be taken the whole distance, whether he stopped on the way six hours or twenty-four, and he refused to pay the double fare demanded. At the next station the conductor ordered him out of the car.   He refused to go, and thereupon the other undertook to remove him; but this, even with the assistance of a brakeman, was not found highly practicable, and was given up as a bad job.   When the train reached Trenton the conductor and his assistants entered the car with a man in plain clothes who said that he was an officer, and who arrested the passenger.   This officer said that he was commissioned by the governor and by the mayor of Trenton, but that he was also in the employ of the company.   The passenger demanded the intervention of the mayor, was able to enforce his demand, and the result was his immediate release.   The matter was then placed in the hands of a lawyer, and I believe has not yet been settled.

Now it so happened that at that very time I was in a precisely similar position in England. The affair being in all its circumstances very illustrative of the difference between the two countries in railway regulations, and in the manners of those who administered them, I shall relate it in detail. While at the Great Western Hotel at Liverpool, which belongs to the Great Western Company and is the Liverpool terminus of the line, I had spoken to a porter of the house, who did me some little services, of my intention to go to London in a day or two, stopping at Birmingham for the great triennial musical festival. On the afternoon when I was to start, I came in belated and in great haste. I had but twenty minutes in which to pack, pay my bill, buy my ticket, and get off. I sent this porter to get me a second-class ticket. He went, and my luggage was taken in charge by another porter. I reached the train just in time, and the first porter, whom I found standing at a carriage door, handed me my ticket with some silver change, all of which I thrust into my waistcoat pocket without looking at it, and got into the carriage which he had selected for me. The other porter, who had taken my luggage, came to the door, said, "All right, sir," and we were off. I was so close upon the time of starting that the inquiry as to my destination was made just as the train began to move. To my surprise the ticket examiner said, as I showed him my ticket, which of course I had not yet had time to look at, "This ticket is for London, sir, and you said Birmingham." As it proved, the first porter, having heard me speak of going to London, had in his haste forgotten what I said about Birmingham, and had bought me a London ticket.

I was immediately in a state of unpleasant doubt as to what my experience would be and what would become of my luggage, for I had been in the country hardly a week. At the first stopping-place I made inquiry of the guard, and was told that the stops were so short that nothing could be done until we reached Stafford, where the train would stop ten minutes. The train had hardly come to a stand-still at Stafford when he made his appearance and took me immediately to a superior official, who, when I had stated my case, said that I must see the station-master; and in less than half a minute that personage appeared before me. He was an intelligent, middle-aged man, very respectable in his appearance, and very respectful in his bearing. The guard told him the case briefly. He ordered the luggage in the van of my carriage to be taken out. It was all turned out, and mine was not found. I was asked to describe it particularly. I did so, and the order was given to take out all the luggage from all the Birmingham and London carriages. It was now quite dark, and the search was made with lanterns; but in two or three minutes (so many hands were engaged, so quickly did they work, and so little luggage, comparatively, was there in each van) my trunks were found, duly labeled "Birmingham." The second porter had made no mistake. I then told the station-master that I had intended, as he saw by the labeling of my luggage, to stop at Birmingham, and asked him if with a London ticket I might break my journey for a day or two. He said that he thought that I might, bade me good-evening, and the train started without the delay of a minute.

I stopped at Birmingham, stayed two days, and

then resumed my journey to London. At a short distance from the Euston Street Station the train halted, and we were asked for our tickets. I gave mine, and the ticket taker, glancing at it as he was moving on, stopped short, and said, " This is a ——— day's ticket, sir. I cannot take this." " You 'll have to take it," I said, " for I have no other." " Then I must ask you, sir, to pay me your fare from Birmingham." " I 've paid it once, and I certainly shall not pay it twice on this line until I have been taken to London." " I beg pardon, sir, but I must positively refuse to take this ticket. It 's against my orders ; and I must ask you for your fare from Birmingham." I was struck by the man's respectfulness, civility, and quiet good humor, but none the less by his unflinching firmness ; and I answered him with, I believe, equal respect and firmness, " I am sorry, but I shall not pay double fare. I refuse positively." " Then, sir," was his reply, " I must ask you for your name and address." I took out my card, wrote upon it the name of the hotel in London to which I was going, and handed it to him. He touched his cap, saying, " Thank you, sir. Good evening." I replied, " Good evening," and he passed on. The affair had, of course, attracted the attention of my carriage inmates, one of whom said to me, as the train started again, " I think you 'll find you 're wrong. This is a matter the companies are very particular about ; I don't know why ; and I believe the question has been decided in their favor ; I can't see why. You 'd better write to the general superintendent of the company when you get to London," and he gave me that officer's name. The next morning I did write, stated my case, received a courteous

4

reply, and the matter was settled quietly, good-naturedly, decently, sensibly, with respect on both sides, and with the least possible trouble. I think so much could not be said of the proceedings in the case of my young friend between Philadelphia and New York, even although he was a resident of New York and was able to give a name and references very well known, and I was a stranger in England and had never been in London.

At the great railway stations such is the throng of travelers ceaselessly passing back and forth, or waiting for trains, accompanied sometimes, in the case of ladies who are going alone, by friends, that these places afford very favorable opportunities for the observation of all sorts of people from all parts of the country, whose superficial traits may be thus conveniently studied and compared. The variety of classes and conditions is great; the difference unmistakable. Here we see nothing like it. True, we can tell Northerners from Southerners, Eastern from Western men, and can distinguish by the outside between a denizen of one of the great cities and one from the rural districts. An observant eye can even detect slight variations between the urban and the suburban man or woman, none the less easily when the latter has had her garments carefully made according to the patterns in " Harper's Bazaar." But beyond this a close observation of our travelers tells us little. In England, notwithstanding the leveling and assimilating tendencies of the last half century, due largely to the railway itself, the gradation of classes is readily perceptible, even to a stranger's eye; nor is the condition, or in many cases the occupation, less distinguishable than the class. Agri cultural laborers are very rarely seen upon the railway, except when they move in gangs for special work ; and then they are quite likely to be Irishmen. The farmers travel much more than I supposed they did, — very much more than they do with us. I met with them and talked with them in second-class cars on every line on which I traveled ; for as I have said it was my habit, when alone, to change my place at station and station. I found that my apprehension of their class and condition from their appearance was rarely, if ever, wrong; and so it proved (within certain limits, of course) in regard to other classes. Not only are the upper classes, that is, we may say, those who are educated at Eton and Harrow and the two great universities, unmistakable by their bearing and expression of countenance, but among the professional classes a barrister would hardly be taken for a physician, or either of these for a clergyman, or a clergyman for either of those. The London city man, " commercial person," is also unmistakable, unless he is one of those highly educated great bankers or merchants which are found in England, but are very rare in " America." Such a person might be taken for a peer, unless you were to see him and the peer together, when, with a few " tiptop " exceptions on the city side, the difference would manifest itself, if in no other way, by the countenance, if not in the behavior, of the city man himself.

The intermediate classes — commercial travelers, small attorneys, tradesmen, and so forth — have also their distinctive outside and expression, difficult to define in words when dress has come to be so identical in form and color among all classes, but still, as I found it, quite unmistakable. I remember that on one Sunday, when I went to morning service at a little village church with the "lady of the manor," I observed in the choir, near which her pew was, a man so very earnest in his singing that he attracted my attention. As we walked back through the shrubbery, just beyond which the church stood, shut off by a wall through which was a little gate, I spoke to my hostess of this man's singing, and asked if he was not a carpenter. "Yes," she answered, with a look of surprise; "but how did you know that?" (I had come to —— only the day before.) "Oh," I said, "I knew that he must be an artisan, for he was plainly neither a farmer nor a laborer; and as he did not look like the village blacksmith or wheelwright, I therefore concluded that he must be a carpenter. And besides, he sawed away so at his singing." The man's dress was like that of my host in fashion and material, a black cloth frock and trousers, and they were perfectly fresh and good, and his linen was clean; but the difference of rank and breeding between the two men was as manifest as if the one had worn his coronet, and the other his paper cap and apron.

All these various classes are nowhere seen together as they are at the railway stations; for, except the agricultural laborer and the lowest classes in the city, all travel. I therefore never was near a station without entering it and walking about for a while among the people there. A trifling incident at one, which was connected with a hotel at which I was, interested me. I had gone down to breakfast in my slippers; and when I rose from the table I walked out into the station, from which two or three trains were about starting. As I was quietly eying the motley multitude, I heard a small voice: "Black your shoes, sir? — only a penny;" and as I did not immediately reply, my attention being fixed upon a group at a little distance from me, the words were repeated, and I turned my head. The speaker was looking up earnestly into my face. I, smiling, pointed down to my slippered feet; and the boy, a good-looking little fellow, smiled too, but shyly, and, seeing his mistake, blushed to the edges of his hair. Wonder of wonders! thought I. Here is a country in which boys can blush; where boys who speak English without a brogue, and yet black boots, have some shamefacedness in the presence of their elders. The little fellow gained somewhat by my not having a job for him to do; but what he took so joyfully should have been more, by a hundred-fold, to acknowledge fitly the pleasure that I had from his shy, glowing face.

This was on the 31st of August, and I saw in the station and elsewhere signs of the time unknown to me before. These were keepers, with leashes of dogs, going hither and thither to the preserves; for shooting was to begin on the morrow. There was such a fuss and talk about it that one would have thought that it was a matter of life and death to some thousands of gentlemen that they should burn powder and propel lead into birds on that day, and that some other thousands of men, and three or four times as many thousands of dogs, should be promptly on the spot to help them. The dogs were mostly handsome, intelligent animals; the keepers were smallish, tight-built fellows in long gaiters, with a strange mixture of shrewdness and brutality in their faces.

On my journey to London I had the good fortune

to witness an incident very characteristic of the society in which I was. I took the train at Birmingham at about four o'clock in the afternoon. Although I had a second-class ticket, as I have said, I was put by mistake into a first-class carriage. The grades of the carriages are indicated on the glass of the upper half of the doors; but as the doors were opened and thrown back, I did not see "First Class" on the door of the one I entered. When the train started I was alone. At the next station, or the next but one, a party of three, a young gentleman and two ladies, approached the carriage, and one of the ladies entered it and took the seat next me on my left hand, between me and the door, I having one of the middle seats. Her companions appeared to be her brother and sister, or her sister-in-law; and from their talk, which I could not avoid hearing, I learned that she was going a short distance, and was to be met by her husband at the station where she was to stop.

When the train began its gentle, almost imperceptible motion, both of them kissed her, — the lady with feminine effusion, but the young gentleman in a perfunctory manner; and when I saw his cool salute, and heard his "Take care of yourself, old girl," I was sure he was her brother. No other man having his privilege could have availed himself of it with such indifference. For my carriage companion was a beautiful woman; and her beauty impressed me the more because of its delicate character, and because she was the first really beautiful woman of her class that I had yet seen in England. She was just tall enough to be noticeably so, and the noble elegance of her figure could not be concealed by her traveling dress. This was a long garment, of a soft texture and light color between buff and cream, buttoned from the throat to the lower hem with buttons of the same tint as that of the dress. Her hat, or bonnet, was also of the same material, and was without ornament of any kind. As a bonnet has strings, I believe, and a hat has not, it was probably a hat; for no woman not inhumanly disposed could conceal by a ribbon the inner outline of such a cheek as hers; and she was not inhuman. In her dainty ears were small earrings of dull gold set with turquoises, which were matched by the brooch which confined a lace frill around her lovely throat. Her eyes were blue, her brow fair; her mouth had the child-like sweetness which Murillo gave to the lips of his Virgins; in expression her face was cherubic. Why I describe her with so much care my reader will soon see. She apparently had no other luggage than a small Russia-leather bag, which she put into the rack above our heads.

We sat in silence; for there was no occasion for my speaking to her, and she looked mostly out of the window. After we had passed one or two stations she took down the little hand-bag, opened it, took out a bottle and a small silver cup, and turning herself somewhat more to the window poured something into the cup and drank it off at a draught. I did not see what she drank; but in an instant I knew. The perfume filled the whole carriage. It was brandy; and the penetrating odor with which I was surrounded told me of the strength of her draught as well as if I had mixed her grog myself, or had joined her in a sociable cup. At this I was not so much astonished as I should have been two or

three days before ; for at the Birmingham festival I
had seen, during the interval between the two parts
of a morning performance, potation of the same kind
by ladies of whose respectability there could be no
question. We went on in silence. After passing
one or two more stations we stopped at one — Rugby,
I believe — for a little longer time than usual. Soon
I was conscious that some persons whom I did not
see were about entering the open door, when my angelic beauty sprang from her seat, and placing herself before the door cried out, " No, you shan't come
in ! I won't have third-class people in the carriage ! "
There was remonstrance which I did not clearly hear,
and the people attempted to enter. She then threw
her arm across the door-way like a bar, clasping
firmly one side of the carriage with a beautiful white
dimpled hand. Catherine Douglas, when she thrust
her arm through the staples of the door, to keep out
the pursuers of her king, could not have been more
terribly in earnest. She (*my* Catherine Douglas)
almost screamed out, " Go back! go back ! You
shan't come in ! This is a first-class carriage, and I
won't have third-class people put into it ! " Then
came counter-cries, and there was a hubbub which
certainly was of the very first class. She turned her
beautiful head to me with an appealing look ; but I
sat still and made no sign. A guard, or other official
person, who accompanied the inferior intruders ex-
postulated with her; and I heard him explain that
the train was so full that all the third and even the
second class carriages were occupied, and that as
these people had their tickets and said they must get
on he was obliged to put them into our carriage. It
would be for but a little while, only till we reached a

certain station. My fair companion was obdurate, and perhaps was a little set up by the contents of the silver cup. But two first-class passengers came in, and as they pleaded for the admission of the luckless third-class people, and the assurances that there was no alternative and that the period of contamination would be brief were repeated, she at last subsided into her seat, although still grumbling, and the objectionable persons were admitted.

They certainly were not people with whom it would have been pleasant to sit down to dinner. One, a woman, took the seat on my right, and the other, a coarse, ill-looking fellow, sat himself opposite to her. The face and hands of the woman, sallow and leathery, although she was young, might have been cleaner, and contrasted very unfavorably with the lovely, fair, and fresh complexion of the angry beauty. Her nails were like claws, with long black tips. She had a red woolen tippet around her neck, and her bonnet was a hopeless mass of crumpled ribbons and dingy, flaring flowers. Her companion was the male proper to such a female, — a little less noisome, however; for when a woman sets out to be dirty or disagreeable she succeeds better than a man. Immediately a war of words began between the two "ladies," and it was fought across me. The beauty repeated her objection to third-class people, and protested that as she had paid for a first-class place it was a shame that she should be made to travel third class whether she would or no. She with the red tippet wished to know what harm she would do anybody by riding in the same carriage with them, and added, " Some peepull that *coll* themselves first-clawss peepull because they paid for a first-clawss ticket

might be no better than other peepull that paid for a
third-clawss ticket." A sniff and a toss of the beautiful head. Then she of the tippet: " As for me,
I 'm not going to stop in Rugby all night with race-
peepull." (It appeared that there had been races
somewhere in the neighborhood of Rugby that day.)
" If peepull *were* honly third-clawss peepull, they
could n't be expected to stop hall night in a place
wen the 'ole town was filled with honly race-peepull."
This proposition seemed to meet with general bland
assent from all the company in the carriage ; and I
was delighted to find that below the deep of common third-class people there was admitted to be still
a lower deep, into which certain third-class people
could not be expected to descend. Opposite my fair
neighbor now sat a rubicund, well-rounded clergyman, to the establishing of whose local color many
gallons of richly-flavored port must have gone. He
had not an apron nor even a dean's hat, but either
would have become him well. He soothed the fair
first-class being with a mild mixture of sympathy and
expostulation. There was a general discussion of the
situation, in which every one of my fellow-passengers
had something to say ; and the impropriety of third-
class people being put into contact with first-class
people was generally admitted, without the least regard for the presence of her of the red tippet and of
her companion. At last I was appealed to ; for all
the while I had sat silent. I replied, " Really, I
ought n't to say anything about the matter ; for I myself am only a second-class passenger out of place."
The beauty turned upon me a stare of surprise, and
with a bewildered look " wilted down " into her
corner. She of the dingy claws and flowers tittered
and the subject was dropped.

After a while the silence was broken by the third-class person's saying that she wanted to get to a certain place that night, and asking vaguely, of no one in particular, if she could do so. There was no reply at first; but after a moment or two I was surprised by hearing the first-class dame say " Yes," softly, with a mild surliness, and looking straight before her. Her former foe then asked, " How ? " A shorter pause; then, " Take the train that meets this one at Blisworth Junction," came from the beautiful lips between the turquoises,— the head turned slightly toward the questioner, and the words dropped sidelong. This seemingly announced a treaty of peace; and again to my surprise, and much more to my pleasure, a conversation went on across me, but now in perfect amity, and information as to the minutest particulars was freely asked for with respectful deference, and given with gracious affability.

The fact that my fair neighbor was accompanied to the station by her brother and sister showed that she was what is called " a respectable woman ; " and the manner and speech of the three were those of cultivated people. Moreover, upon reflection I became convinced that she was neither a termagant nor a particularly ill-natured person. She had merely done, in a manner rather unusual, I believe, even in England, and somewhat too aggressive to suit all tastes, what it is the habit of the whole people of England to do : she had insisted upon her rights, and resisted an imposition. She meant to have what she had paid for. This the custom and the manner there. English people are, according to my observation, kind and considerate, notably so, and ready to do a service to any one in need of it; but they resist, *vi et armis*, tooth and nail, the slightest attempt to impose upon them; and they do it instantly, upon the spot, and follow the matter up vigorously. The habit is productive of unpleasantness sometimes, and it may cause some disenchantments, but it has its advantages, and they are not small.[1]

Another characteristic of the country is shown in its railway vocabulary. There are, for example, a "guard" or guards on the train, and a "booking office" at the station. The guard guards nothing, and has nothing to guard. The steam-horse was not only "vara bad for the coo," but for the highwayman, who long ago ceased to labor in his vocation. At the "booking office" no booking is done. You merely say, to an unseen if not invisible person, through a small hole, "First (or second) class, single (or return)," put down your money, receive your ticket, and depart. But as there were booking offices for the stage-coaches which used to run between all the towns and through nearly all of the villages of England, the term had become fixed in the minds and upon the lips of this nation of travelers. So it was with the guard and his name; and when the railway carriage supplanted, or rather drove out, the stage-coach, the old names were given to the new things, and the continuity of life was not completely broken. The railway carriages are even now often

1 This incident, which I have told without embellishment, will remind the reader of Fielding of the indignation of Miss Graveairs at the entrance of Joseph Andrews into the stage-coach with her, and her declaration that "she would pay for two places, but would suffer no such fellow to come in." And it may also bring to mind that when the coach was stopped by highwaymen the lady gave up a little silver bottle, "which the rogue applied to his lips and declared that it contained some of the best Nantes he had ever tasted." There continues to be a great deal of human nature in men, and some in women.

called coaches. We, however, had traveled so little comparatively, owing in a great measure to the long distances between our principal towns and even between our villages, and stage-coaches were so comparatively rare and so little used, that when the railway engine came, not only they, but all connected with them, words as well as men and things, disappeared silently into the past, and left no trace behind. In such continuity on the one hand, and such lack of it on the other, is one of the characteristic differences between the Old England the New; and its cause, as it will be seen, is not in the unlikeness of the people, but in that of their circumstances.

CHAPTER IV.

LONDON STREETS.

I LIVED in London. I did not merely pass through it on my way elsewhere, stopping for two or three days at a hotel while I drove about the vast den of lions; nor was I content with passing a longer time in the same way. After a week or so of hotel life and sight-seeing, I sought diligently, and found not easily, lodgings in which I established myself as if I had been a bachelor born within the sound of Big Ben. Hence I made excursions on foot or by rail, but usually by both ways of travel, into the neighboring country, and chiefly into that which lies around the beautiful banks of the Thames. Into the great city itself, however, I made daily excursions; for so the walks by which I explored the various parts, far and near, of that thickly peopled region of bricks and stones might well be called. I set out sometimes with an end to my journey clearly in mind, but oftenest without one, wandering on over the vast distances, watching the people that I met, and scanning the houses and them that looked from the windows. But I never got to the end of London unless I took a steam-engine into service. Cabs and omnibuses were of no avail. I used them, but generally I walked, following no guide but my curiosity.

I never felt so lonely as I did in these solitary rambles in London, — never so much cut off from my family and my home, I may almost say from human-kind. In mid-ocean I did not feel so far removed from living contact with the world. Within these boundless stretches of streets, and of houses so same, and yet each with a physiognomy of its own, just like so many men and women, — and I came to look at them as if they were human, and in the poor parts, which are of astonishing extent, where they stand crowded together as far every way as the eye can reach, to pity them for the gloomy life they led there, with the sweat and dirt oozing from their sad faces, — within these precincts, made oppressive, if not melancholy, by the apparently endless repetition of units, it seemed to me farther than I could con-ceive, not only to the land that I had come from, but to any other place out of my range of vision. I could not take in even London; and what was out of Lon-don was beyond beyond.

After I had walked about it enough to have in my mind a loose, exaggerated apprehension of distance, such as we have in childhood, and was yet not so much at home in the place as to become familiar with it and to lose its impression of strangeness, the thought of its vastness became vague and unmeaning, like that of astronomical distances, which are so far beyond apprehension that a change in them by the addition or subtraction of a million of miles or so is of no significance. And the feeling that the rest of the world was very far removed from me transferred itself afterward to England, with some variation. England began to seem to me the one place that I knew upon all the earth : out of England was out of the world. What we call "America," although I had come from there in ten days, and although my eyes

hungered for the sight of faces and my ears thirsted
for the sound of voices there, took on a nebulous
shape and substance, not much more cognizable than
any other inchoate body within or without the solar
system ; and I began to understand the long indifference, and the ignorance, indifference-born, of Englishmen to the country which lay beyond the horizon edge
of the ocean.

There is little architectural beauty in London, besides that of the wondrous nave of the great Abbey
church.   Externally, even that venerable and most
interesting structure is so marred by Wren's towers
that the feeling which it excites is one of constant
regret.   Within, a very considerable part of it is defaced with ugly monuments, chiefly to titled nobodies;
and generally the more insignificant the body and the
grander the title, the more pretentious and ugly the
monument.   It is offensive to see the statues of great
men jostled by such a mob of vulgar marbles.

St. Paul's, outside and inside, is the ugliest building of any pretension that I ever saw.   A large inclosed space is always impressive ; and the effect thus
produced is all of which St. Paul's can boast.   Its
forms are without beauty, its lines without meaning ;
its round windows are ridiculous.   Its outside is not
only ugly in form, a huge piece of frivolity, but its
discoloration by the black deposit from the London
atmosphere, and the after-peeling-off of this in patches,
give it a most unpleasant look.   It seems to be suffering from a disease that covers it with blains and
blotches.

The public buildings in the City, the Bank and the
Mansion House and the Post-Office, and so forth,
have the beauty of fitness ; for they look just like

what they are, — the creations, the abode, and the stronghold of British Philistinism ; rich, substantial, tasteless, and oppressively respectable. The new Houses of Parliament present a succession of faint perpendicular lines in stone ; even distance cannot make them imposing. Only the bell-tower, whence Big Ben utters, four times hourly, his grand, sweet voice, has beauty for the eye as well as for the ear. The parish churches are mostly by Wren, or in his style, and are ugly with all the the ugliness possible to a perversion of the forms of classic architecture.

In looking for lodgings, in which I had not even the help of advice, I went over no small part of London, and into many London houses of the middling order. My search extended from Covent Garden to South Kensington, and from Euston Square to the Thames, and even across it ; for I was led off into Surrey by advertisements, of the locality of which I knew nothing. As to the lodgings that I saw, they had for the most part a tendency towards the suicide of the lodgers ; so gloomy were they, so dingy, so stuffy, and so comfórtless. On inquiry as to what rooms there were to let, I was generally told that there was "the dron-room floor ; " and when I replied that I did n't want a whole floor, but a bedroom and a sitting-room, I was also generally told that there was a room to let " at the top o' the aouse." I found that these rooms were literally at the top of the house. In those which I looked at I found an iron bedstead with a bulgy bed, the stuffiness of which I smelt as soon as the door was open, and upon which was a dingy brown coverlet drawn over the pillow. A small wash-stand with small ewer and basin, a chest of drawers, a looking-glass, and one or two not

very robust chairs completed the furniture of the
apartment, which always looked out upon the windows of like apartments, and the roofs above and the
chimneys around them. For these rooms the price
demanded was almost invariably "a paound a week."
In Surrey and some other places it was somewhat
less,—from fifteen to eighteen shillings. Bath-rooms
were unknown, but " the servant would bring me a
can of 'ot water in the morning."

I spent the greater part of four days in this search,
not altogether unwillingly, because of the places into
which it took me and the people with whom it brought
me into contact. With some of these places I seemed
to myself not unacquainted, so familiar was I with their
names and their localities. This was particularly the
case with the smaller streets around the lower end of
St. James's Park. The houses in these, — old-fashioned, and yet not old enough to be venerable or even
antiquated, — with their plain, sombre brick fronts,
the look of character and respectability which lingered about them, although they had long been deserted as the dwelling-places of people of condition,
and the elaborate iron-work on the steps and before
the areas of many of them, in which I observed large
conical iron cups, set at an angle, which, strangely
never mentioned by any writer that I remember,
were plainly huge extinguishers into which the link-
boys thrust their links, — all these seemed to me
like respectable, decorous old friends of my family
who had been waiting to see me, and who now looked
at me with serious and yet not unkindly eyes.

The newer part of London, near South Kensington,
and by Hyde Park Gate and Prince's Gate, did not
interest me so much externally ; although some of

the houses were made delightful to me by friends who had really been waiting to give me welcome. The houses here are very handsome. The pretentious talk that I have heard about Fifth Avenue houses leads me to say that there are hundreds of houses in the best parts of London — around Hyde Park, on Carlton Terrace, and in other like places — which are far finer, much more noble, as Pepys would have said, than any that are to be found in New York, in Boston, or in Philadelphia. I except some of the old houses in Philadelphia, — those built in the beginning of this century, in which, although there is little show of gilding, color, and French polish, there is that far higher beauty in domestic architecture which is given by ample and well-ordered space. I was in many of the houses in May Fair; in not a few into which I was not invited. For if I passed a house which I saw was undergoing repairs, and the family was absent, I entered, and inquiring for the person in charge, I was generally able to go through it at the cost of a shilling or half a crown to my attendant. Sometimes houses were thrown open to workmen, and these I always went through unquestioned. The difference between houses of this class and those which may be regarded as of a corresponding class in New York is that the former, while less showy than the latter, are more spacious, and have more of the dignity which accompanies large and well-proportioned size. The entrances, the passage-ways, and the staircases are very much wider; the halls in some are large enough to admit of support with pillars. The drawing-rooms are notably spacious, and are not directly accessible from the front door. Both a drawing-room and a parlor are common in these houses, and two drawing-rooms and a parlor are not rare. But what is known in New York as an English basement house (that is, one in which the staircase comes up into a dark hybrid sort of room between the front and the back parlor) must be so called because there are none such in England. I did not see one in London, or in any other English town that I visited. The houses are generally like the basement houses built in New York more than thirty years ago. The notion also that rows of houses all alike are not found in England is altogether wrong. In the new part of London such rows, and of very handsome houses, are common ; while in the new parts of smaller towns the houses built for people of moderate means stand in rows of from a dozen to two dozen, as like each other as one brick is like another. The pretense, and the consequent misrepresentation, of some British travelers on this score is like much more of their pretension, unfounded. There is, however, a heavy, monotonous effect given to a long row of houses in New York by the hideous device known as a " high stoop," which is much more oppressive than that which could be produced by the indefinite repetition of any house that I saw in London, and which makes a row of " brown stone fronts" in New York the most unsightly and unhome-like-looking structures that the mind of man ever conceived.

Two simple contrivances are found in almost all London houses of the better class which might be adopted with great advantage elsewhere. The first is a handsome square lantern, which is set in the wall over the street-door, and which lights from the inside the vestibule and from the outer the porch and steps.

The comfort of this lighting is very great, as every one accustomed to our dark steps and porches sees immediately. The other is two bells, the pulls of which are marked severally " visitors " and " servants ; " the convenience of which in the daily working of a household need not be told to any housekeeper. And much more numerous as servants are in London (and as much better as they are more numerous) than here, more pains are taken there than here to save their labor and their steps. Over the street-door bellpulls, or over the letter-boxes, of the best houses, it is common to see on bronze plates, " Please do not ring unless an answer is required." These little precautions tend much to the common comfort of master and mistress, and of servants.

There is a remarkable absence of show and pretension in the shops of London. Even in Regent Street and New Bond Street and St. James's Street there is little display, and hardly anything is done merely to catch the eye. And even in these quarters the shops are comparatively small. You may find the most splendid jewels, the richest fabrics, and treasures of art and of literature in little places that would provoke the scorn of the smallest dealer in Broadway. The publishers make no show at all. The greatest of them are to be found in unpretending quarters, with little display of their literary goods, which are stored elsewhere. The principals are in their counting rooms or their parlors up-stairs, and quite inaccessible, except when they choose to see those who send up their names. The book-sellers are hardly more expansive. I found that, with one or two exceptions, the men from whom I had received, when I was a book-buyer, catalogues of books of great rarity and price were in small, unpretending shops which in New York would attract no attention. But a glance at their shelves was provocative of a woful sense of impecuniosity; and I found them intelligent, and with a notable knowledge of their business and of the literary world, and also of the why and the wherefore of the value of their books. They were not all William Pickerings; still they were generally men of whom Pickering was in some degree the type and the model.

One day, as I turned the corner of a little street nor far from Covent Garden, my eye and my admiration were attracted by a pair of little old yellow and blue vases which stood in a window among some other articles of the same sort, and I wished to inquire the price. The entrance to the shop or salesroom was in the cross-street, and proved to be merely the somewhat imposing door of a large, old-fashioned dwelling-house. I rang the bell; which seemed to be rather an odd way of getting into a place where articles were exposed to public sale. The door was opened. I ventured to say that I wished to know the price of a pair of vases in the window, speaking, I am sure, with some shyness and hesitation; for I felt rather as if I were intruding upon household privacy. This feeling was not diminished by the sequel. First, a stout, middle-aged man appeared, descending the stairs. He was in a dressing-gown and slippers, with a smoking-cap on his head. He was closely followed by a middle-aged woman, plainly his wife, also stout, and clad in dingy garments of heterogeneous fashion. I was received with great distinction, almost with ceremony; and while I was repeating my simple wish to know the price of those vases, a young woman, doubtless the daughter of the respectable persons before me, descended the stairs, and, taking up a position in the rear, joined her parents in looking at me. After her came a blowsy little Scotch terrier, who trotted to the front of the group, and stood, with nervous nostrils, looking up into my face through the chinks in his soft shock of hair. The servant who had opened the door withdrew slowly and by stages, facing about like the rearguard of a retreating army ; and thus she, for a while, was added to the group. And all this merely because I wished to know the price of a pair of vases, — vases put in the window to catch the eye of the passer-by.

I was marshaled into the show-room. I walked across it at the head of the party, keeping my countenance and pretending, impostor that I was, to take the whole performance as a matter of course, when in fact I felt as if I were making believe that I was a Highland chief with his tail on. I pointed out the pottery, whereupon my host — for such I felt he was — bowed, and blandly smiling said, " Hah ! yessur, yessur ; most helegant vawses ; quite rococo, indeed ; hin the Rennysawnce style ; *hand* only sixty guineas." The stout wife repeated, "Quite hin the Rennysawnce style." The daughter did not speak, but I saw that she longed to do so ; and if the terrier could have barked Rennysawnce I am sure he would have done so in fine style, for he seemed by far the most intelligent of the party. I thanked my host, and said I would think about it ; — another base imposture on my part, for I could not afford to give sixty guineas for a pair of little blue and yellow pots. But what was I to do when a man turned out the guard as if I were officer of the day making grand rounds, and all just because I wished to know the price of a pair of vases? I was about to withdraw promptly, feeling very much ashamed of myself; but I was not allowed to do so. I was asked to look at the rest of the stock, and with such heartiness of manner that I saw plainly that, altogether apart from the question of present purchase, they would all like to have me examine what they had for sale. I made the round of two rooms, escorted by the family; and after seeing many beautiful things, I bade good-morning to my entertainers, who courteously attended me to the door in a body, and stood there until I turned the corner; and all because I wished to inquire the price of a pair of vases.

I did not have quite such a formidable reception at any other of the many little shops which I entered to buy, or to make inquiries; but this instance is indicative of the style which I found in vogue. On the first occasion or two when I did not buy, I felt quite ashamed of myself for putting such very polite people to so much trouble; but I soon got used to the fashion, and liked it. For indeed it is pleasanter than that carriage of the salesman or the saleswoman (who advertises herself as a "saleslady") which seems to say, "I would die on the spot, or ruin my employer, rather than show you the least deference, or take any trouble to please you."

I was struck by the readiness to sell to me, a perfect stranger and chance passer-by, and to send home my purchases without even asking payment. These good people could not have been readier to supply my wants if I had been an old customer. I remember buying an umbrella in Burlington Arcade, and ordering my name to be engraved upon the handle

It was on my second day in London. I had given my
address, but I expected to stop at the shop on my return, look at the engraving, and pay for the whole,
and have it sent home. This I did not do, wandering
back by another way. On reaching my hotel, there
I found my umbrella, with the engraving nicely done,
but not even a bill. The next morning I went and
paid for it, and thanked the shop-keeper for sending
it to me, a perfect stranger, and jestingly added,
" How did you know I should come back again ? "
The answer, with a smiling shake of the head, was,
" Oh, sir, we don't lose much money in that way."
There was always a readiness to " book " anything I
liked, but seemed reluctant to buy. Once, when the
keeper of an old curiosity shop, a woman, earnestly
suggested that she should send me home a magnificent pair of fire-dogs, which I lingered over in admiration, the dog part being reduced copies in bronze
of Michael Angelo's Day and Night on the Tomb of
the Medici, and, the price being eighty guineas, I had
replied rather curtly, " Thanks, but I can't afford it ;
I 've no money," the answer was, immediately, " Oh,
sir, we 'd book it for you with pleasure." This readiness was but one mode of the manifestation of a general confidence which seemed to me remarkable, and
the existence of which was a most pleasing social
trait. If I had been a resident of London, and these
good people had known but my name, the matter
would have had a different aspect ; but in every case
it was my first visit to the shop and I was quite alone.[1]

---

[1] A singular exception to this confidence is worthy of remark. I wished
to hire a violoncello, that in odd moments I might keep my fingers from
rusting.   I was required to give a reference ; and there was so much
fuss that I simply deposited the value of the instrument.   Not being satisfied with the one I got, I went elsewhere for another, to have the same ex-

And when bills do come in with goods, or afterwards, they are sent " with the compliments " of Messrs. So-and-So, and with a request for further orders and the honor of your recommendation. If you express a wish to examine anything, it is sent to you for approval " with compliments." If it is desirable that you should inspect anything which is in making for you, you have a respectful note asking you to do Messrs. So-and-So the favor of calling at your convenience ; and this although your order may be only a matter of a pound or two, and Messrs. So-and-So may be able to " buy you " a thousand times over, and know it. If this is a result or a necessary accompaniment of aristocratic institutions, they certainly in one respect have a wholesome and elevating influence.

London shop-streets are in a great measure free from the abominable defacement not only of telegraph poles, but of what we now call signs. Even in the Strand, in Oxford Street, and in Edgeware Road, where the shops are second-rate, there are few such great, glaring, gilded boards as affront the eye in every trading quarter of New York. There are signs, but they are comparatively few and small and inoffensive ; and of flag-staffs and transparencies and other rag-fair appurtenances there are none. This is one characteristic of London streets that makes walking through them a pleasant and a soothing process. And this unmarring modesty of outward

perience. This argues rather ill for the good behavior of my fellow-fiddlers. But having this time given a reference, I found that I might have had all the fiddles in the shop on my bare word. And besides, having hired one for a month, on giving it up in a few days less than a month, I offered, of course, the price for the time for which I had engaged it, and was surprised to receive back a shilling or two, deducted for those days.

show involves no inconvenience. I never had the least difficulty in finding any shop to which I wished to go, but once; and in that case the fault was my own. But there is one peculiarity of London streets which is somewhat embarrassing to a stranger: they are not, the long ones at least, numbered regularly from end to end, with the odd numbers on one side and the even on the other, but very irregularly and in sections; the sections being those parts of the street which run through certain quarters; and the same street has different names in different quarters. The quarter in which a house or shop stands is generally named, as well as the street itself. This produces those double designations which are found in most London addresses; for example, " Bedford Street, Covent Garden;" " Wellington Street, Strand;" or "Bond Street, Regent Street;" and I have one, "11 Vigo Street, Regent Street, W. Poultry." The complication makes no difficulty when once you are used to it; and it has a picturesqueness and individuality which seemed to me far preferable to the right-angled and numerical street arrangement which rules off a city in square blocks, and numbers the houses in the first 100, 101, and so on, those in the second 200, 201, and so on. It is difficult to attach any idea of personal possession or peculiarity to such an address as No. 1347 Chestnut Street, or No. 100 West Fifty-First Street. How much more character there is in the Black Swan without Temple Bar, the Queen's Head against St. Dunstan's Church, the Golden Ball in St. Paul's Churchyard, or the Kings Arms in Little Britain!

What we call signs, nowadays, are really not signs, but quite the contrary. A sign is a symbol, — a thing of one kind which represents or indicates something of another kind, or which is adopted as a designation for a particular place or person. Indeed, a sign is not a description in words, but as Bardolph might say, a sign is — something — which — whereby — we make a sign of something. Thus we read in old books of such addresses as those mentioned above, and of the sign of the Bible, or of the Crown, or of the Rising Sun, or of the Cock, or of the Eagle, or of the Red Lion, or what not. These were really signs, and they came into use to designate shops or inns in times when few people could read. A board on which is written the name of the person over whose door it is, with a description of his business and the number of the house, is not properly a sign; although when these descriptions took the place of the old signs the name of the latter was transferred to the former.

A few of the old sort of signs remain in London, and in some instances the name of an old sign remains as the designation of the house. One of these is the famous hostelry, The Cock, in Fleet Street, hard by Temple Bar. But lately Temple Bar has been removed from Fleet Street, and I believe the Cock itself has come down from the old perch, and crows no more. I took my luncheon there one day in a low, dark room, with a sanded floor. There were boxes, with little dingy green curtains along the top; the seats were as hard and straight as those of a pew in an old New England meeting-house. It was probably in the same condition when Dr. Johnson, who lived not far off, took his dinner there. I observed that the score was still kept with chalk. The attendants were very sad and solemn. But for their black swallow-tailed coats and neckties that had once been white, you might have supposed them the very waiters that had just heard the news of the death of Queen Anne. The spirit of British Philistinism was concentrated there. The beef and the beer were indeed supremely good; but notwithstanding this and the interest attaching to the place, my luncheon was a rather doleful and depressing performance.

What is to be done without Temple Bar across Fleet Street who shall say? I had thought that this obstruction, architecturally not very admirable, had its title to respect in some close connection with the British constitution, which is of about the same age; and this notion was not unsettled when I saw the props and make-shifts by which it was kept from falling into disastrous ruin. Its removal shows how, at the last moment, the English mind can rise to the emergency of a great reform; and its preservation in one of the parks shows equally that respectful consideration for the memory of the past which is one of the estimable and lovable traits of the national character.

Nothing is more remarkable in London than the suddenness with which you may pass from a thronged street bustling with the business of the modern world into quiet and silence amid verdure and venerable memories. Out of Fleet Street you go through a small gate-way and a narrow, dim passage which promises nothing, into the Temple Gardens, where, hearing no sound but that of leaves rustling lazily and a fountain plashing drowsily, you may walk, on such a beautiful day as that on which I walked there, musing amid a sweet stillness that could not be more undisturbed if you were in the rural heart of England. If you know one of the resident benchers or barristers, and choose to visit him, you will find his name painted in small black letters on the lintel of a door; and you will go up a rude staircase with a heavy beam hand-rail that will remind you of the stairs at Harvard and Yale in the halls that are the most old-fashioned and the rudest. You will see your friend's card upon the outside of a plain, dingy deal door; but that passed, you are likely to find yourself in chambers that are the perfection of unpretending luxury and comfort; and your friend's talk and the wine that he will offer you are likely to be such that you would gladly sit the whole day enjoying both, quite oblivious of London, the hum of which steals so lightly to your ears in the pauses that it seems less a thing of time present than a dim memory.

Stretching down to the Thames for half a mile below Charing Cross are little streets with narrow entrances which suddenly widen, and on either side of which are old houses now mostly let out in lodgings. They lead to gardens by the river-side; and there, too, you may walk or sit in silence, while just behind you roars the Strand. These streets bear the names of great families whose city residences were built there when the Strand was a suburban road by the river-side. The great houses have disappeared, most of them long ago; but the last of them, Northumberland House, was taken down quite lately. Three years ago its dilapidated basement and foundations still stood just beyond Trafalgar Square, the last ragged remnant of feudal magnificence in London.

From the upper end of Trafalgar Square, out of

which issues Pall Mall, the street of the great clubs, and hard by which are the public offices of Downing Street, it is not five minutes' walk to St. James's Park, with its long stretches of green turf, its great trees and its water, where wild fowl dive and flit into hiding. Here Dorimants and Bellairs might make appointments, and keep them unobserved, just as they did in the days of Charles II. and of Etherege; although, indeed, prying eyes might look down from the gardens of the noble houses on Carlton Terrace, built in the reign of a king who had all of Charles's vices without any of his manly good nature or his wit. Beyond St. James's, Green Park stretches along the unbuilt side of Piccadilly to Hyde Park, which is a wilderness of arboral beauty, and where, if you prefer silence and solitude to the throng and display of Rotten Row, you may sit under the branches of great trees, and fancy yourself in the Forest of Arden, although cabs and omnibuses are dashing along within half a mile of you. There I saw clumps of oaks casting shadows that covered nearly an acre, with acres of sunlit greensward lying beyond them; and after a ramble of a mile or more I struck diagonally across the park, and came to a straight avenue about half a mile long between lofty elms, which were the edges of a noble wood, so free from undergrowth that the eye could pass from trunk to trunk until distance brought obscurity.

The London omnibus, or 'bus as it is universally called, is a much less pretentious vehicle than that which plies up and down Broadway and Madison Avenue; and in some respects it is much less comfortable. It is small, sober in color, and in form a mere ugly square box on wheels. It is in constant use as an advertising van. Its windows are immovable. At the upper end there is no window or aperture at all, nor is there any in the roof; the only means of ventilation being the window through which you see the conductor standing upon the step, where, like the head-waiter at the Cock, he keeps his score (on some lines, at least) in chalk. On a muggy day one of these air-tight London 'busses, filled with the Queen's liege subjects, not of the upper classes (who rarely or never enter one), is not pervaded with the odors of Ceylon, or with the freshness of the breezes on the top of Mount Washington. If you use an omnibus, ride upon the outside; and this is something to do; for you have not seen London streets unless you have looked down upon them from the top of an omnibus.

There is one comfort in the London 'bus which distinguishes it and all other public vehicles in England from those in the United States. They are not overcrowded. No one is permitted to enter a full 'bus or tramway car and stand up in it to the annoyance of other persons. Neither in London nor in any other part of England did I see this offense against good manners committed even once. If an omnibus were full, the conductor took up no more passengers. And yet the street travel in London is of course much greater than it is in New York, where omnibus proprietors and the managers of street railways, practicing for their profit upon the supineness of one part of the public and the dull perceptions and rude manners of another part, are permitted to carry people packed so closely together that they are pressed into a somewhat lasting semblance of sameness, like the wax cells in a bee-hive. Entering a car once on a tramway in Birkenhead, near Liverpool, I found every seat occupied. I purposely stood up to see what would come of it. I had found all sorts of public servants, guards on railways, beadles in churches and vergers in cathedrals, very considerate and accommodating; but I had not stood a moment when the conductor of this car came to me, and said, with that mixture of deference and firmness which I have mentioned before, "Beg pardon, sir, but you can't stand here." I yielded, of course, immediately, and went out; but stopped, again purposely, upon the platform. "Beg pardon, sir," immediately said my conductor, "but you know no one is allowed to stand upon the platform. Please go on top; plenty of room there." And thither I went, where I had intended to go from the first.

Everything in the England of to-day is bound by visible links to the England of the past. This is manifest even on the railways, as I have before remarked; and the very omnibuses in London preserve these signs of the continuity of English national, municipal, and social life. London, from the time when it was a little walled town, has always had suburbs lying a mile or two away, and these suburbs it has gradually absorbed; being in this respect like, but only in a certain degree, other great cities in other countries. No other great city has had so many suburban villages around it. But though London has taken them to itself, it has not destroyed them; they preserve their names, and still to a certain degree their individual existence. Thus Charing Cross, Kensington, Paddington, Putney, Hackney, Bayswater, Brompton, etc., which are quarters more or less new of metropolitan London (not the city

6

proper), were once villages and parishes, separated
from the city by green fields. Of this fact the London omnibus is a daily witness and record. It is not
quite a mere public vehicle running through streets
to take up chance passengers, but is still a sort of
stage-coach plying between stage and stage, stopping
regularly at each to take up passengers who assemble
there. The fares are determined by this custom.
They are not so much for the whole distance run by
the 'bus, or for any part of it, but twopence from one
stage to another, or threepence for a longer trip.
Chance passengers are of course taken up and set
down at any point; but much the greater number
are taken up at these distinct stages, and leave the
'bus at some one of them. The various stages are
set forth, with their proper fares, on a board at the
upper end of the vehicle.

The practice in the United States has been just
the reverse of this, and deliberately so. For example, omnibuses began to run in New York just as they
did in London, between the centre of trade and suburbs which had become attached to the city. Greenwich and Chelsea were suburban villages, to the first
of which people fled *from* New York, when the city
was visited by yellow fever, only some fifty and odd
years ago. Fifteen or twenty years afterwards the
first line of omnibuses was set up to ply between
Wall Street and Greenwich, and " Greenwich " was
painted on the 'bus, as " Charing Cross," or " Ham-
mersmith," or " The Elephant and Castle," is upon
a 'bus in London. But what trace of Greenwich is
there now in New York? The name is never seen nor
heard; and few inhabitants of New York know that
there ever was such a village at a place on the west

side, not quite half-way from the Battery to Central Park. So Williamsburgh, a considerable town, has been united to Brooklyn within the last twenty-five years; but its old name is rapidly fading away before the glories of its new appellation, " Brooklyn East District," for which its real name has been changed, with conspicuous loss of convenience, individuality, and dignity. Names of streets are changed in the most ruthless manner. We have in New York not only the destruction of history long ago in the change of Queen Street into Pearl Street, and the late snobbish and silly change of Laurens Street to South Fifth Avenue, but within a year or two Amity Street has been made into Third Street; and there has been an attempt to wipe away the name of Lord Chatham from the thoroughfare to which it was given in honor of his protest against the oppression of the American colonies.

This foolish and vulgar fashion cannot rightly be called " American." It belongs chiefly to New York, the most characterless place in every respect that is known to me; but I am unacquainted with any of its Western imitations. In Boston they do not thus blot out all memories of the past, nor at the South. I have a friend in Annapolis who lives in Duke of Gloucester Street; and there is comfort in the date of her letters. But the New York numerical system will probably prevail until States and counties and cities are subjected to it, — why not? — and we shall have letters addressed to No. 243½ West 1279th Street, City Seven, County Twenty-Three, State Five. A lovely arrangement this will be, when it takes place. But it is merely a consistent carrying out of the plan already adopted. What associations of home or of happiness can there be with a number? With what face can a man speak of the time when he lived in dear old One Hundred and Seventy-Fifth Street? For my part, I would rather than this go back to the obsolete addresses of London, and live over against the sign of the Black-Boy and Stomach-Ache in Little Britain. London does not retain these old names and things in their old form and force, but she does not wipe them out as with a wet sponge, and begin the world anew for every generation. As to finding one's way about in London, there is no difficulty in it whatever; at least I had none, although I was a perfect stranger, and generally — because I preferred to be so — without guide or companion.

I saw no beggars in London streets. Even in the poorest quarters, where, but for the half-drunken look of half the people, it seemed to me that the very tap-rooms must have shut up for want of custom, and where I felt as if I were five miles from decency, so long had I walked without seeing a clean shirt on a man or a clean face on a woman, I was not asked for alms. This was not peculiar to London. In all England, town and country, I was begged of but once, and that was in effect for food, not money. Having at home every day, and many times a day, proof that there is nothing about me to forbid the asking of alms, I was soon struck by this absolute absence of beggars, and I threw myself in the way of solicitation, but with no success. I thought once that I should succeed with a poor woman who had a few faded little nosegays for sale, and who importuned me to buy. I said no, that I could do nothing with her flowers, but spoke kindly. She entreated me to buy, and followed me out of Bond Street as I turned into another street, holding out her sickly little bouquets, which I thought might be like the wan, feeble children that she had left at home. I still shook my head, but did not tell her to go away, and I am sure must have looked the compassion that I felt. I meant to buy a nosegay, but I thought, Surely this woman will ask me to give her something. But no ; she even followed me to the very door of the house where I was going, thrusting the flowers almost into my face, and saying, "Only sixpence, sir ; please buy one : " but she did not beg. I remained obdurate in vain, until the door opened, and then I took her nosegay, and put something into her hand which, little as it was, brought joy into her face, and the door closed upon her looking on her palm and making a half-dazed courtesy.

It was in the Strand, about nine o'clock in the evening, that I met my only beggar. As I walked leisurely through that thronged thoroughfare, suddenly I was conscious of a woman's presence, and a woman's voice asking, "Please, sir, would you give me tuppence to buy one of those pork-pies in that shop ? I 'm so hungry." I paused. The face that was looking up into mine with entreaty in the eyes was that of a young woman about twenty years old, not pretty, but with that coarse comeliness which is not uncommon among lowly born Englishwomen. Her dress was neat and comfortable, but not at all smart. As I looked at her doubtingly, she said, "You think I want it for drink ; but indeed, indeed, I don't, sir. You need n't give me the tuppence ; you may come and buy the pie yourself, sir, and see me eat it, if you will." She pointed across the street to a little shop where pastry and other viands were in the window. I had no doubt that her object in walking the Strand at that hour in the evening was not to beg for pork pies, but I decided to do as she suggested. We crossed the street and entered the shop. It was a very small place, humble and rude; much more so than I expected to find it from the look of the window. However, it seemed perfectly quiet and respectable, — merely a tiny eating-house that lived by the chance custom of the poorest wayfarers along the Strand. Behind the little counter stood a woman so fat that she looked like a huge pork-pie in petticoats. I said to the girl, "Never mind the pie; call for what you like." "May I?" she cried, her eyes brightening wide with pleasure; and then, turning to the little counter, she said, with a largeness of manner and an intensity of satisfaction the sight of which was worth a Cincinnati of pork-pies, "Stewed tripe and potatoes!"

We sat down in a little pen upon deal seats and at a deal board that had once been painted, but, I think, never washed. Stewed tripe was manifestly a standing dish; for we had hardly taken our seats when a plate, a soup plate, of it came up through a sort of trap-door just outside our pen, with two large unpeeled potatoes on a smaller plate. My companion made a hasty plunge outside, and set them smilingly upon the table. The principal dish looked like a bucket of bill-sticker's paste, into which a piece of a bill had fallen, as sometimes happens, and become thoroughly soaked. It was steaming hot, and gave out a faint, sickening smell, in which I detected an element that reminded me of an occasion when, upon the recommendation of a professed good liver, I had vainly tried to eat a little tripe broiled after some wonderful fashion. The girl seized upon the potatoes; and although they were so hot that she plainly could not touch them without pain, she squeezed them out of their skins into the pasty fluid in which the tripe was wallowing. At once she began to eat the grumous mess, and ate so hastily, almost voraciously, that she burnt her mouth. I told her not to eat so fast, but to take her time, and let the stuff cool. "But I'm so hungry," was her reply. She abated but little of her eagerness, and soon finished her portion to the last morsel and the last drop. Upon my invitation she ate some trifle more; but when I asked her if she would have some beer, to my surprise she said no, adding, "They've no tap here." This is the case in many eating-houses in London, of the better as well as of the lower order. At one where, early in my London experience, I was eating a chop, I was asked if I would like anything to drink, and ordering a pint of half-and-half, I was surprised at the waiter's saying, "Please to give me the money." To my look of inquiry he replied, "We've no license, sir, and we send out." This just reverses the practice in New York, where the keeper of a bar will add a skeleton restaurant and two beds to his establishment for the purpose of making sure his license to sell beer and spirits. I suppose that there are not half a dozen restaurants in New York where ale and beer may not be had for the asking.

When the girl had stayed her hunger, I led her to talk, to which she seemed not at all unwilling. She proved to be one of those simple, good-natured, common-sensible, but not quick or clever, women who abound in England. She told me a story, — with a

man in it, of course.   When was a woman's story
without one ?   A man's story sometimes, although
rarely, may have no woman in it; but a woman's
without a man, — never.   This one had no incident,
no peculiarity, which gave it the slightest interest.
It was the baldest possible narration of fact.   She
had been at service, and her child was born about
four months ago; that was all.   But there was also
an entire absence of the pretensions and the com-
plaints common in such cases; universal in the
United States, but more rarely heard in England, I
believe, where there is less sham upon all subjects.
In this case, at least, there was not a word of reproach, and no talk of betrayal or of ruin.   On the
contrary, she said frankly, " I 've no call to find any
fault with him."   I respected the girl for this candor.   " But," she added, " I did think he need n't
have run away just before my baby was going to be
born.   The poor little kid would n't have done him
any harm."   I more than heartily agreed with her
here, when I found that she had neither seen the father of her child nor heard from him for nearly six
months.   But I could not but respect her simplicity,
her uncomplaining endurance, and her cheerfulness;
for she spoke hopefully, and with such slight but loving reference to her baby that I was sure that when
it left her breast she would hunger before it did.
To be sure, she had health and strength and youth
and courage, and some humble friends who did not
cast her off; but for all that that selfish and cowardly
fellow knew, she might have been dead, or worse,
lying ill and starving with his child on straw in a
garret.   Her feeling toward him seemed to be that
of mild contempt, because he had lacked the manli-

ness to face the consequences of his own conduct.
She made no claim upon him whatever. From what
I saw and heard I came to the conclusion that among
the lower classes in England an unmarried mother
is not in general treated so cruelly by her friends as
in corresponding circumstances she is with us. As I
made a slight contribution to the comfort of her baby,
she begged me to go home with her and "see the
little kid," with regard to whose prettiness she gave
me very confident assurances. To this invitation I
did not seriously incline. We went out into the
glaring, gas-lit, bustling Strand. She shook hands
with me in a hearty way, and with no profusion of
thanks from her we parted. I turned after I had
walked a few steps, and saw her standing still amid
the hurrying throng, looking earnestly after me. I
nodded to her, went on my way, and saw her no
more.

I observed, as she was talking with me, that she
did not maltreat her *h*'s. I found other instances of
a like correctness of speech among people of her low
condition of life in England ; but they are very rare,
— rarest of all in London. The others that I met
with were, if I remember rightly, chiefly in Kent and
in Lancashire.

CHAPTER V.

My search for lodgings in London ended in my fixing myself in Maddox Street, which runs from Regent Street near its upper end across New Bond Street. Here I had a parlor, bedroom, and dressing-room on the second floor; and, although they were not handsome, perhaps hardly cheerful, I was very comfortable. I did not mind it that my little side-board, my sofa, and my chairs were old mahogany of the hideous fashion of George IV.'s day. They were respectable, and there was a keeping between them and the street into which I looked through chintz window-curtains that reminded me not unpleasantly of those that had hung over my mother's bed in my boyhood. They were much more grateful to my eye than those which formed the canopy of my bed, which were heavy moreen of such undisturbed antiquity that they made the room somewhat stuffy. But I liked the old bedstead, which was a four-poster so high that I ascended to it by steps; and those also brought back my boyhood to me in the recollection of a dreadful fall which I had from just such a pair, which I had mounted to blow a feather into the air, in defiance of parental injunction. The low French bedstead long ago drove the four-poster out of " American " bedrooms, in the Northern cities at least; but in England the stately and, to uneasy sleepers, somewhat dangerous old night pavilions still hold their own, not only in London lodgings of the higher class, but in great country houses, where they have stood, many of them, for more than a century, some of them for more than two.

English beds are, in the day-time, among the few things in England which I did not find pleasant to look upon. This is because of the fashion in which they are made up, which seems to be invariable. The coverlet is drawn up over the pillows; and the curtains, hanging from the canopy or pushed up to the head-posts, are then drawn across the upper part of the bed, one curtain being folded over the other. To an eye accustomed to the sight of white pillow-cases and of the upper sheet turned down over the coverlet, the effect of the English arrangement is gloomy, stuffy, and forbidding. But at night, when the maid has released and half drawn the curtains and turned down the coverlet, and has prepared everything for your night toilet, an English bed-chamber, even in lodgings, has a very attractive and sleep-inviting aspect. The bed, too, keeps the promise to the eye. English beds are delightful to sleep upon, and are something in feeling between a hair mattress and a well-stuffed feather bed, soft upon the surface, yet firm beneath. I found all English beds so, even in the inns of small provincial towns.

The neighborhood in which my rooms were had some little interest for me, and would have had more if I had been a woman, from the fact that they were within a few yards of St. George's Church, Hanover Square, where the marriages of which accounts are published in the London newspapers almost always take place. My fair readers I believe have won-

dered, some of them I know have wondered, why the
Lady Arabella must always be married at St. George's.
The reason is simply this: that St. George's was until
lately the westernmost parish of London, the "West
End" parish, that which is nearest the quarter known
as Belgravia.[1] Now an Englishwoman, whatever her
position, is married, as a rule, at her parish church;
if from her father's country-seat, at the little old
stone building which has stood just outside the park
perhaps for centuries; if in London, at St. George's,
Hanover Square. The church is, however, not upon
Hanover Square; not nearer it, indeed, than Grace
Church is to Union Square, or than the "Old South"
is to Boston Common. It has its designation, after
the London fashion which I have mentioned before,
because it is in the neighborhood of Hanover Square.
The church itself is ugly enough, like most of the
London churches built in the last century; but it is
somewhat imposing from its large portico, over which
is a handsome pediment supported by six Corinthian
pillars. Inside, however, it is mean and frivolous,
almost vulgar. It is remarkable that this portico
stands out over the pavement or sidewalk, the steps
rising abruptly from the edge of the road, so that pe-
destrians walking upon that side of the street must
go into the road, or mount the steps and pass within
the pillars as if they were going to church. The effect is somewhat that of a huge ecclesiastical trap set
to catch wayfaring sinners.

When I took these lodgings, I was struck with another manifestation of that confidence which I have

---

[1] Of late such marriages have been "celebrated" at All Saints' Church,
Knightsbridge, and at Christ Church, May Fair, as well as at St. George's.
The first two are very much farther west than the third.

already mentioned. One day, as I passed through the street, I stopped and looked at the rooms, attracted by a neat little card in the lower window, announcing that there were "apartments to be let." [1] Three days afterwards I came unannounced in a cab with my luggage, and, finding that the rooms were still unlet, said that I would take them for an indefinite time between a fortnight and six weeks. I was made welcome, and my luggage was taken up-stairs. I had not yet given even my name; but now I presented my card, the name on which I am sure my landlady had never seen before, and asked if I should pay a week in advance. The answer was, " Oh, no, we don't want that, sir." Inquiries were then made as to how I would like to be taken care of, at what hour I should breakfast, and so forth. For the rooms I paid a guinea and a half a week, exclusive of fire and candles. For breakfast, and for luncheon when I chose to take it there, I was to pay just the cost of what was furnished to me. I found the bills for these " extras " very moderate; and from the time when this arrangement was made I never saw my landlady, heard the sound of her voice, or was reminded of her existence, except by her bill, which appeared, with every item carefully priced, weekly upon my breakfast table. I was expected to pay for every article that I asked for, no matter how trifling. An extra candle appeared in the bill; and I remarked, when the arrangement as to my occupation of the rooms was making, that Mrs. —— said, " As you won't dine at 'ome, you say, there 'll be no

---

[1] I have heard this phrase, " to *be* let," called an Americanism, — what, indeed, have I not? But I found it, to my surprise, very much more common in England than in the United States, where, so far as my observation extends, it is comparatively rare.

charge for kitchen fire." It seems that the cost of heat expended in making breakfast is counted in the room rent of London lodgings, but that for every dinner that may be served there is an extra charge for kitchen fire.

I paid also for the washing of my bed-linen, towels, and napkins. My own clothes were sent out for me to the laundress, of whom I knew nothing but the wonderfully written bills on minute scraps of paper which came with the returned garments. The price of their lavation looked very small to me, as indeed it should have been if price bore any porportion to purification. For it seemed to me sometimes, when they came back, as if the smoke and dirt of London, which was upon them in streaks and patches when they were sent out, had been merely dissolved and diffused through them, and fixed in them by heat and starch. For once I sympathized heartily with that selfish snob, George Brummell, — the sufferance of whose impudent vulgarity by English gentlemen and gentlewomen was always a marvel to me, — in his insistence upon country washing. Was his charm a singularity in being clean in his person and neat in his dress? Charles James Fox was a dirty sloven. Country washing in England is as fine as can be; the clothes come to you as white as snow, and seeming to bring with them a suggestion of daisies and lavender. But London washing seems to be done in a dilution of grime; and how, indeed, could it be otherwise?

This homely subject leads me to remark upon the relief of the English housekeeper of middling rank from one great trial of her "American" sister in a corresponding condition of life. In no English household of a station above that in which washing is done

as a means of livelihood is any washing done at all,
except in great houses in the country where there is
a laundry service. The weekly wash which is the
ever-recurring torment of most "American" housekeepers is unknown in England. Everything is sent
out to a laundress. I think that the effect of this is
one element of the greater serenity and repose of
English life. Nor would English kitchens — and I
saw not a few, in full operation, in houses of all
grades — admit of the laundry work that is carried
on in so many "American" kitchens where there is
no separate laundry. The English kitchen in the
houses of men of moderate means — for example,
professional men and merchants not wealthy — is
not half so large as that in corresponding houses
with us. A set of standing-tubs would more than
half fill it. And that Moloch of the "American"
kitchen, the great mass of heated iron known as a
range, is almost unknown in England. The fire-
places are comparatively small; the fire is open, and
although there is the hob and the hot closet and the
boiler, the whole affair is much less formidable than
our range, which looks like an iron-clad gun-boat
stranded upon the hearth-stone.

I dined, when not at the house of a friend, at restaurants of various grades. Eating and drinking is
such serious business in England, and is taken so
much to heart by everybody, that one expects to find
ample and worthy provision for it in the great capital. But although a stranger need not go hungry in
London if he has money in his pocket, he is not sure
of being able to breakfast, lunch, dine, or sup to his
satisfaction, at short notice, if he is at all fastidious
as to viands, cookery, or table service. There are

eating-houses in great numbers and variety, at some of which you may fare sumptuously, and at many of which excellent cold beef and hot, tender chops may be had, with good beer, and even good wine ; but of restaurants at which you may order from a copious bill of fare to your liking, there are very few. I did not find one that would compare favorably with half a dozen that I could name in New York, or with Parker's in Boston.

At most of the London eating-houses of the first class there is a set dinner at set hours, or rather two or three set dinners of different grades, which are served at corresponding prices. The courses, few or many, are placed before you in due order, and the cooking is tolerably good ; but you cannot travel out of the record ; and as to coming in at your own hour and making up your own *menu*, the preparation of which begins while you are dallying with oysters and soup, that is almost out of the question.

Of course, there is good reason for this ; for it need hardly be said that London can and will have anything that it wants ; and I find the reason in the habits of the people, who are prone to regularity of life, and as a rule have a liking for the simple and the solid, and are not inclined to be fanciful. Notwithstanding the introduction of French cookery and dinners *à la Russe* among the luxurious classes, the " average " Englishman, even if he can afford to be fanciful and luxurious, has a liking for his joint, and is satisfied with that if it is well cooked, juicy, and large enough. Lord Palmerston used to tell his butler, when people were coming to dinner, to get what he pleased for the rest, but to be sure to have a good joint of roast mutton and an apple-pie for him, —

and " Pam " was a typical Englishman. Moreover, the Englishman generally likes to eat his dinner at home, even if he is living at lodgings; if not at home, at his club; if neither at home nor at his club, then at some eating-house, where he goes regularly and takes the regular course of things, content if his dinner is plentiful, his wine sound and strong, and his cheese mild, but reserving the right to grumble, with good occasion or without. He is not inclined, like the Frenchman, to take his wife and children to a restaurant and make his dinner a work of art, more or less varied and rich in design and costliness, according to the condition of his purse or the festivousness of the occasion. Such, too, if I mistake not, were the habits and tastes of Yankees, until the Delmonicos introduced into New York, some thirty or forty years ago, I believe, the French restaurant system, which has gradually exercised a modifying influence upon habits of life in this respect throughout the country. It may be questioned whether, all circumstances and consequences being considered, this influence has been in every respect benign, even upon cookery.

The joint is still dominant upon the average English table. Its rule is visible, tangible, almost oppressive. It appears in various forms, even at breakfast. That greasy Juggernaut of many American breakfast tables, a hot beefsteak, or a beefsteak which is not hot, is almost unknown as a morning dish in England; at least, I had the pleasure of never seeing it, even at an inn; but mighty cold sirloins, and legs of mutton, and hams, and birds in pies, and mysterious potted creatures weigh down the buffet at all the great hotels. Your eggs and bacon, your sole or your whiting, with your muffin kept hot by a bowl of hot water beneath the plate, are set before you upon your special table; but to yonder mountainous holocaust of cold heterogeneous flesh you may take your plate at pleasure, and carve for yourself, and cut and come again. In private houses the same arrangement obtains, but modified and gently tempered to eyes more fastidious and appetites more delicate than are generally found in a public coffee-room.

In the windows of the middling restaurants, soon after noon, placards begin to appear, announcing in large letters, "A Hot Joint at 2 o'clock," and a like promulgation is made at intervals of an hour or thereabout. It seemed to me as if there was a degree of solemnity about this; and I am sure that the word joint in reference to the table is uttered with a notable unctuousness and emphasis by the average Englishman.

At the Garrick club a member may have a friend not a member to dine with him, and the stranger may have any kind of soup, fish, made dish, or pastry; but he may not have a slice of the joint. Of that sacred thing only the initiated may partake. To maintain the *cultus* of the joint in its purity, and at the same time to meet the requirements of English hospitality, a peculiar kind of steak has been invented at this club where it is served to visitors instead of roast meat.

At a restaurant of high class just out of Regent Street, at which I dined twice, the worship of the joint was impressively brought home to me. The room was a handsome one, and the service rich, almost elegant; the diners seemed to be all of such a condition in life as one would expect to find in such a place. In due time I was asked whether I would have roast beef or roast mutton. I chose mutton, of course. Whereupon my waiter disappeared, and presently returned, slowly followed by a man clothed in a white garment and with a white cap upon his head. In one hand he bore a huge naked blade that looked like a sabre, in the other what seemed to be some pronged instrument of torture. Behind him came an assistant who pushed forward on rollers a small staging of dark wood, which was solemnly set before me. I looked in amazement, but with little apprehension of peril; for was I not in the land of Magna Charta, and trial by jury, and the Bill of Rights? It was in truth not a block, and the man in the white cap was not a headsman who had come to take my head, although upon the seeming block was a charger large enough to have held that of John the Baptist if he had been as big as Goliath of Gath. But it was already occupied by a huge roast saddle of mutton, and the man in white was only the carver. The blade gleamed in the air and descended upon the joint, and the only result of this solemnity was that there lay upon my plate a large slice of mutton so delicious that the eating of it marks an era in my gastronomic life. I shall date my dinners back and forth from the day when I ate that mutton.

In no other eating-house that I remember was there so formal and elaborate a *cultus* of the joint as this, which I believe is peculiar to the house where I saw it. But in all others, and particularly in those of a somewhat lower grade, I observed that the joint was spoken of with a certain deference and unction, much as, for example, when it was said that Mr. Blank was particularly engaged; "Lord So-and-so was with him." The manager of the place where the joint was solemnly sacrificed to the god of Philistia had but finely apprehended and boldly conformed to the spirit of the public, one of whose priests he was. His carving performance was a little above and yet closely akin to that of the grill-rooms, the attraction of which is that your chop, or your kidney, or your steak, is broiled before your eyes. You may pick out your chop, if you like to do so, see it put upon the gridiron, and stand by while it steams and smokes and hisses and sputters before you, and, hastening to your table, send it steaming, smoking, hissing, and sputtering down your throat. The smell of cooking is one of the sensuous miseries of life ; and the sight of a gashed and dismembered joint, with its severed tendons and fibres, its gory gravy, and the sickening smell of its greasy vapor, is, it would seem, what any man not a Fijian of the old school would gladly avoid. But in England, eating, with us a necessity, with the French an art, is a religion, and the joint is, like some other fetiches, at once god and sacrifice. The devouring of hot, red, half-roasted flesh is high among the duties and the beatitudes.

I said that when asked to choose between beef and mutton of course I chose mutton, and that I was richly rewarded for my preference. Much as English mutton has been praised, not half enough, so far as I know, has been said of its excellence. As to the roast beef of Old England, it is good enough, but although I suppose that I had opportunities of eating the best that could be had, I found it no better in flavor or in fibre than that to which I had been accustomed. On the whole, I think that, although we have nothing better, one is rather surer of getting very good beef here than there. I found the beef·

steaks decidedly inferior to ours. But with English mutton, eaten in England, there is none to be compared. Canada mutton, and even English eaten here, is inferior in every respect. Although I had such a distaste for mutton, particularly when roasted, that I had often said, to the discomfiture of the domestic powers, that I should be glad never to see it again upon the table, in England I ate it always when it was to be had. There it was mutton which was mutton, and yet was not muttony. For tenderness, juiciness, and flavor, it was beyond praise. It was merely to be eaten with thankfulness.

To return to my lodgings : for my comfort in them I was chiefly, and indeed it seemed almost entirely, dependent upon a maid-servant who took care of them and of me, and who was always ready when I touched my bell. Emma — for that was her name — was a typical specimen of her class. The prettiest women I saw in England were, with few exceptions, among the chamber-maids and the bar-maids; and Emma's fine figure, bright eyes, and ever pleasant and respectful manner of course enhanced the agreeable effect of her careful and thoughtful service. They even caused me to be somewhat disturbed by the consciousness of the fact that she cleaned the shoes which she brought up with my can of hot water in the morning. I did not quite like to feel that a woman, and a pretty young woman, performed that service for me.[1]

The freedom, innocent and unconscious, of the English chamber-maid was also a surprise to me. At

[1] I let this passage stand as it was first written : yet how much more reluctant I ought to have been were the woman old! But a man cannot help being a man.

the house of a friend, in one of the suburbs of London, soon after my arrival, I was awakened by a slight tap at the door, and a rosy, blue-eyed, fair-haired young woman, of that type of English beauty which is not too often seen in England, walked into my bedroom with a can of hot water. I was startled, although I did not find the shock at all unpleasant. She set out my " tub " and my rough towels, and disappeared with a pleasant " Good-morning, sir." One reason for this agreeable ceremony is that bath-rooms are rare in English houses; and in households in which men-servants are not kept, the maid-servants perform all such offices. For that a " gentleman " should do anything for himself, even in the preparation for his own toilet, is not to be thought of, except in some great emergency.

The care with which one is looked after by these good creatures — and they seemed to me to be the perfection of good nature and of thoughtful kindliness, and made me wish that I had sovereigns to give them instead of shillings — was illustrated to me on my return to my lodgings from my first dining out. It was after midnight when I came in. In the passage below stood a lighted candle, and against it leaned something, I forget now what, which showed that it was meant for me. I found the door of my sitting-room wide open, with a chair set against it to keep it so; for, like all the other doors in my rooms, it was hung upon beveled hinges, which caused it to shut gently of itself. Upon the table directly in front of the door stood two candles unlighted; between them were the letters and cards that had been left for me during the evening. The door between my sitting-room and bedroom was also wide open, and was stayed back, as also was that of my dressing-room. In both bedroom and dressing-room everything was prepared for my night toilet, even to the laying out of my night-shirt "in a wow" upon the bed, like Dundreary's dozen. This careful setting open of all the doors did indeed suggest to me a suspicion on Emma's part of the condition in which I might possibly return from dinner ; but that I readily forgave her for the forethought. Briefly, there was nothing that I could wish or reasonably expect to have done for my comfort that this good girl did not do for me, generally without my asking it. After I had been in my rooms a day or two, she seemed to understand me, and to know what I should like, and to set herself to making my stay as pleasant as possible. And, like most of her class that I saw, she added to her ministrations the grace of cheerfulness, while at the same time, although she was not without the capacity of enjoying a little complimentary chaff, her manner was perfectly modest and proper, mingling respect for herself and for me with an ease of manner very uncommon in the Hibernian maid-servant of "America."

She illustrated to me one day a superstition which had quite faded out of my memory. I had asked for a fire, which she laid and lit, but which, owing to some ill condition of the air, smouldered in blackness. I went into my bedroom for a minute, and, returning, found the open tongs laid over the top of the coals, and Emma standing over the grate watching it intently. "What is that for?" I asked, pointing to the tongs. "To draw up the fire, thir," replied the girl, who added a little lisp to the charm of her soft English voice ; and then I remembered that I had read of this superstition, but I did not suppose that it still held its own in England, and that I should ever see it acted upon in simple good faith. The blaze at last came up, and the girl lifted off the tongs with a little look of triumph at my face, which I suppose showed some of the amusement and the doubt I meant to conceal.

With all their respectfulness and deference, English servants and people in humble life indulge in a freedom of speech of which democracy has unfortunately deprived us. I made purchases from day to day; they were greater in number and in bulk than in value; and one day, being a little annoyed by the clutter which they made upon my table and sofa, when Emma brought in an addition to it which had just come home, I cried out against them. "And yet they keepth a-comin', thir," said the girl, as she turned to go out. Another time, sitting in solitude, and being very much vexed at a mistake that I had made, I exclaimed, "I do sometimes think that I act like a born fool!" "I thuppoth tho, thir," demurely said Emma, who had entered from my bedroom just as I spoke. I looked at her a moment, and we both laughed, — I heartily, she shyly and blushing. And yet in all this there was not the slightest lack of respect; she never forgot her place, and I could not but think in regard to her, as I thought in regard to others in like condition, how much better this freedom of intercourse was, how much more human, than an absolute interdiction of all communion between the server and the served, and how much it might do to smooth and sweeten life for both.

I was witness to a scene of freedom between the server and the served in which the conditions and the sexes were reversed. One morning I went to take an early walk in Hyde Park. It was not later than nine o'clock, which for London, and particularly for that end of London, is very early. And indeed, as I walked at my will through path, or over lawn, and beneath great trees, with that perfect freedom the consciousness, or rather the unconscious possession, of which adds so much to the charms of an English park, the rays of the sun slanting through a golden mist, the cool freshness of the turf, and a moisture yet upon the leaves made the landscape seem like one seen soon after dawn in an American summer. I had crossed the Serpentine, and was walking slowly along the foot-path by the side of the road, when I saw coming towards me a young lady on horseback. She was riding alone; but at the usual distance behind her I saw her groom. Till then I had found the park as deserted as if it were midnight; and now I and the two distant riders were the only living things in sight; and sound there was none except a gentle murmur faintly coming from the town, as it slowly wakened into life. The riders walked their horses, and as we gradually approached each other I saw that my horsewoman was a large, fair girl, some twenty years of age. She rode a handsome bright bay, remarkably tall and powerful, as indeed the horse that carried her had need to be; for she herself was notably tall, and her figure was full to the utmost amplitude of outline consistent with beauty. Plainly, neither she nor the groom saw me, and as I wished to have a good look at her without seeming rude I withdrew myself into a position which enabled me to do so, as she passed within a few yards of me. She was not beautiful, and pretty

would have been too small a word to apply to her in
any case, but she certainly was a fine, handsome girl;
her face breathed health and sweetness and good nature ; she was very fair, with glowing cheeks, and
teeth that made me thank her for smiling as she
passed. She wore a blue riding-habit that fitted
very close, and of course a chimney-pot hat. As
she drew near to me, I saw that the groom gradually
shortened the distance between them, and spoke to
her, he speaking first. She answered, and they began to talk, he bringing his horse step by step nearer
hers. Looking at him attentively, I found him one
of the handsomest men I had ever seen. He was tall,
and strongly although sparely built, with fair skin,
dark hair and whiskers, steel-gray eyes, and a firm
yet persuasive-looking mouth. He was in complete
groom's costume, top-boots, livery-buttons, and striped
waistcoat, but these did not seem able to subdue a
certain distinction in his bearing. Perhaps, however, he was only a fine, handsome animal, and would
have been vulgarized by being put into a dress-coat
and a white neck-tie, — that crucial test of a man's
ability to look like a gentleman. Nearer and nearer
he came to his young mistress, closer and closer his
horse sidled up to hers, till when they had just passed
me he was hardly a head behind her, — just enough
to say behind. He spoke earnestly now, leaning over
toward her from his saddle ; and she did not lean the
other way, but turned her head slightly to him, and
looked down with a sidelong glance upon the ground.
I could hear her voice as well as his, and although I
was not able to distinguish the words of either, and
the sounds became fainter with the slow stepping of
their horses, I felt somewhat ashamed of my position.

And yet the place was public, and I had expected only to see a young lady ride past me. Gradually I lost the sound of their voices, but I still saw the groom leaning toward her and her head not turned away from him. At length it seemed as if their saddle-girths must touch, and as if he must be tempted to put his arm around her, as she sat there, except for the blue woolen surface, Lady Godiva from the saddle up. But he was discreet, and merely held his place : — the blue outlines of her noble figure became indistinct, the great gleaming knot of her golden hair waned and faded in the distance, and they rode out of my sight, leaving me to wonder what might come of all this.

Another of my early walks was to Covent Garden market, where I went soon after sunrise to see the early traffic. Covent Garden, with an adherence to the signification of its name, is a market for flowers and vegetables only. It is not much frequented by private purchasers, but is the place where dealers, green-grocers and coster-mongers supply themselves. Half London gets its supply of garden stuff from Covent Garden. I found little peculiar in the place, except its size and the filling of this vast expanse with vegetable produce. I arrived in the height of the early business. All around the place were the little carts of the little dealers, waiting to be filled, or just filled and hurrying off at that break-neck pace with which such people think it necessary to drive as well in London as in New York. Even the donkey-carts went off with rapidity. The number of these was amazing and amusing. I never saw so many donkeys on four legs before, nor shall I ever see so many again. There were ears enough there to have stretched in a straight line through London. The hurry and the bustle were bewildering. Every dealer seemed to think that his fortune for the day depended upon his making his purchases and getting off with his load five minutes before his neighbor. But in the midst of all, here and there auctions went on, — Dutch auctions as they are called. For it has long been the strange custom to sell vegetables and flowers every morning by auction at Covent Garden ; but the sale is called an auction because the offered price does *not* increase, but diminish. The things are put up at a certain price, which is gradually lowered by the crier, until they are taken at the rate last named. When this so-called Dutch form of auction came in I did not learn. The vegetables were much what may be found in our own markets, but seemed fresher, perhaps because I saw them earlier in the morning than it is my wont to see anything. I took note of no novelty except the vegetable marrow, that fruit of the soil which Mrs. Nickleby's admirer cast at her feet. On eating this vegetable, I thought it most ill adapted to the expression of an ardent passion, in which it might yield to the pretensions of a pumpkin. It looks like a long, smooth squash ; and even when it passes through the hands of a skillful cook, it tastes like squash and water.

The fruit at Covent Garden, some of it, was fine and fair to the eye ; but in this respect I found in England much to be desired. I shall not say with Hawthorne that I never tasted anything there that had half the flavor of a New England turnip ; but, excepting grapes, I found the flavor even of wall fruit and hot-house fruit comparatively tame. Apples were small and tough ; pears, mostly from France

were better, but still inferior; peaches were often
fair to the eye, yet at best rather greenish in tint,
and within always almost tasteless, little more than
a pleasantly acid watery pulp. Indeed, the climate
of England is not well adapted to the growth either
of fruit or of grain. For both there seems to be
required a drier and longer continued heat than her
skies afford. The hot-house supplies this in part for
fruit, but only in part, except, I am told, as to the
strawberry; but that I did not eat; it was not in season. The melons, even those which came from Spain,
were poor, flashy things, far past the help even of
pepper and salt. Yet it is poor melon the flavor of
which is not spoiled by condiments. As to grain, it
remains to be proved, and will probably erelong be
tested, whether England might not better abandon
its culture, and depend, for wheat at least, upon other
countries. To this end come the corn laws.

It is not very far from Covent Garden to Seven
Dials. This place is so called from the fact that by
the meeting of seven streets seven corners are formed,
at each of which there was once, it is said, a dial.
This place has a reputation like that of Five Points
in New York; and it is remarkable that the meeting
of many streets should in both cities have been followed by a degradation of the neighborhood. But
Seven Dials, although I found that it richly deserved
the ill odor in which it stands, is not, as Five Points
is, or was, the lowest and most wretched part of the
town. There are neighborhoods in London which
are to Seven Dials as Seven Dials is to May Fair.
These are regions which stretch away to the east and
north from the city proper. They are a town in themselves. The formation of a nest of slums one can

understand ; but it was inconceivable to me how this vast area of wretchedness and vice, and of moral and physical filth and gloom, could have come into existence in a civilized country. I went into the innermost recesses of it, — into quarters which I found few London men knew of, and where I was warned by those who did know them that there was danger. But although remarked and gazed at, I was not molested ; and although I had nothing with me for self-protection but an umbrella, I came out unharmed. Indeed, I have found that a man may go almost anywhere and among almost any people, if he will only behave to them as if he neither fears nor hates them ; and the only way of doing that is neither to fear nor to hate.

I found here nothing to provoke hate, nothing ludicrous, nothing amusing. The sadness of it weighed heavily upon my spirit. The houses were high and without any character whatever ; plain brick walls, lead-colored for the most part, and pierced with modern windows. Indeed, all this part of London is quite modern. In one little court, however, that I penetrated running out of Whitecross Street (a street named twice by Defoe in his "History of the Plague in London : " once as the street in which a shop-keeper lived who was summoned to the closed door of his deserted shop to pay money, and who, with death in his face, told the messenger to stop at Cripplegate church and bid them ring the passing bell for him, and died that day ; next as the scene of the burning to death of a plague-stricken citizen in his bed, and, as it was supposed, by his own hand), I found a remnant of the old city, a relic of the great fire which so closely followed the great plague, more than two hun dred years ago. It was the rounded corner of an old peak-roofed stone or plaster house, only two stories high, which had escaped the burning; and although not more than about twenty feet square of it seemed to have been left, this had characteristically been preserved, and was built into the modern building. From the quaint windows of this ancient habitation two girls, not more than twelve or thirteen years old, but with pallid faces and a hideous leer, began to chaff me as I stood in the little court. I felt that to be the most dangerous place that I had ever been in, although I had walked under the walls in Havana more than twenty years ago; and I turned away and got out of it as soon as possible, but went leisurely, nodding good-by to the girls.

And in these streets there were shops, although of what forlornness of aspect who can tell! But they told that even these people buy and sell and get gain, and live upon each other. It would seem that they must live altogether by thieving and burglary. One business was strange to me. Cooked food was sold at stands, at not very remote distances from each other. A board or two was stretched across two trestles or two barrels, and on this were a few potatoes, bits of bacon, and other viands. I saw no one eating; at which I did not wonder. There might have been much of interest to be learned from the people in these houses, but upon that I could hardly venture; externally, they only oppressed me by the endless sameness of the dull and formless misery which seemed to dwell within them and about them.

The mention of the great fire reminds me that one day I passed the place where it was stayed. This is Pye Corner; and the fact is recorded in a little in-

scription on one of the houses. It had an interest to
me beyond that of the event thus announced; for
Pye Corner is the place where Mrs. Quickly tells us
that Falstaff came continuantly to buy a saddle. Most
unexpectedly I came upon this memorial of the old
London of Elizabeth's and Henry V.'s days; and I
confess that by the help of Mrs. Quickly I felt myself nearer to Shakespeare there than when I stood
in his father's cottage in Stratford, or looked upon
his signature in the British Museum.

The scene of Falstaff's continuant shopping for a
saddle is also celebrated by Defoe, who tells us, in
his "History of the Devil," that the fact that Satan
had a cloven foot is certified by "that learned famil-
iarist Mother Hazel, whose writings are to be found
at the famous library at Pye Corner." Did the circulating library spring up at Pye Corner to flower
into Mudie and the Grosvenor?

What proportion of intelligent Londoners know
that there is such a place as Pye Corner, and such a
street as Whitecross Street, I shall not undertake to
say; but my experience leads me to think that the
number must be very, very small. And apart from
the general ignorance about places of interest, but not
of celebrity, which is not peculiar to Londoners, I
was much impressed by the Englishman's ignorance
of everything that did not concern him, if it were a
little out of his daily beat, even if it were daily before his eyes. I was walking, one day, with an elderly London friend through precincts where he told
me he had passed his boyhood and his youth. Going
from one charmingly secret and mysterious court to
another, as much in private, it would seem, as if we
were going through a succession of back yards, I saw

on one hand a great gate-way with square posts
surmounted with balls: it must have been twelve
feet high. I asked my friend what it was. He hesitated a moment, and then said, smiling, "Indeed, I
don't know. Strange to say, although I've seen it
all my life, I never did know." Just then another
elderly gentleman crept out of some hidden by-way
to worm himself into another, and my friend exclaimed, "Oh, here's A——! He'll tell us; he's
lived near here all his life." But A—— knew no
more about the great gate-way than my friend did
himself; and they were not such Philistines but that
they laughed at each other for their common ignorance.

Not only did I find this sort of ignorance, but actual ignorance of their own neighborhoods, of the
principal streets, great thoroughfares, and public
places. The very cabmen were not to be trusted;
and I had to set one right by most impudent guess-
work when I had been in London only a week or two.
I found that it was much better to trust to my own
general knowledge, and to my feeling for form and
distance, than to ask direction from any one but a
policeman.[1] They were always right, always attentive, always civil. Before I left London I came to
look upon every policeman that I met as a personal
friend.

I was lost but once, and that was after midnight,
and because, instead of trusting to the providence
that watches over wayfarers, I was misled and misdi-
rected. I was on my way home from dinner at a

[1] I find this memorandum in my pocket-book: "London, September
20th. A commissionaire, in full uniform, asked me the way to Hyde Park
Gate."

suburban house (it was the occasion when the maid
set all the doors open for me), and found myself set
down, or turned out, at the Victoria Station about
twelve o'clock. I had been there only once before,
but I wanted the walk home; and, confident in my
ability to go back over any road by which I had
passed one way, I called no cab, and set out to walk
to my lodgings by way of St. James's Park, St.
James's Street, and Regent Street. To my surprise,
as I was turning into the street leading, as I thought,
to Buckingham Palace Road, I saw the cabs going my way turn off at another street. I waited a
few moments, and, seeing that they all went that
way, I inferred that I had gone wrong, and I followed the lead of the cabs. I had not walked a hundred yards before I thought that I must be astray.
That was not the street I had come through before;
everything was strange to me. But I reflected that
the night was very dark, and I kept on for a while,
the impression of strangeness and of lengthening distance still increasing on me. The cabs were out of
sight and out of hearing long ago.

Just as I was about stopping to reconsider my
ways, I saw a young man come out of a house a little
ahead of me. When we met I asked him if that
was the way to St. James's Park. "Oh, yes," he
cheerily replied, "quite so, quite so. You'll keep
on for about off a mile, and then go straight through
it." The distance, half a mile in addition to what I
had walked, struck me as too great, and I asked if
he was sure, and mentioned again that it was St.
James's Park I wanted. "Oh, yes," he replied,
"quite sure, quite so, quite so." I thanked him, and
walked on. But at every step I was more and more

impressed by the feeling that I had not been driven through that street on my way to the station, and after walking full " off a mile " I saw no sign of the park, nor of any of its surroundings. I did, however, see a policeman, and glad I was of the sight. To my inquiry how far it was to St. James's Park, he replied, " Wy, bless your art, sir, I dun know ow far it may be the way you 're a-goin'. You 're a-walkin' halmost right away from it. You must turn back for near a mile," etc., etc. In a word, I was to go back to where I had first turned off. I started, but before I got there along came a belated cab, which, thinking I had had walk enough for that night, I hailed and took. It was well that I did so. My cabman astonished me by the route *he* took; so much so that I turned and called to him, " Maddox Street, Maddox Street ! " " All right, sir," he answered, and on he drove, up and down, through ways unknown to me. At last I recognized my street through the darkness, and was set down at my own door. " Why did n't you come by Buckingham Palace Road ? " I asked. " It 's much shorter." " I knows it, sir. *Hof* course. But the pok was shut up this afternoon, sir ; mendin' the road, sir." And this was the reason that the cabs had turned off into another street, to my misleading.

Another little experience of this kind amused me and made me wonder. A gentleman had asked me to his house on Sunday morning. He lived in Knightsbridge, and was an author of high repute. I had never been to Knightsbridge ; did not even know where it was ; but I found out that it was to be reached through Piccadilly, and I set out to walk there. I had come, I was sure, pretty near to the

place, and I thought that I would ask to be directed
to this gentleman's house; less that I felt in need of
direction, than for the sake of trying an experiment;
for the ignorance of London people about London
had become a matter of observation to me, and of
amusement. I looked about and saw a gentleman
descending the steps of a very handsome house near
Albert Gate, Hyde Park. I went to him and asked
if he could tell me where my friend lived, mentioning the celebrated name, of course, and adding that
I was sure it was very near there. The gentleman
was not only polite, but kind, as I always found people in England; but he hemmed and hawed, and said
he ought to know, yet at last was obliged to confess
that he did n't. "But come," he said, "we 'll find
somebody to tell you. Here 's a crossing-sweeper;
he 'll be sure to know, if it 's near by." But the
old sweeper was as ignorant as the gentleman, and
touched his hat and looked at us with a lack-lustre
eye. I had a delightful inward smile, said good-
morning, and in less than three minutes I was at
Charles Reade's door, which was not more than a
hundred yards off, and in five minutes more I was
sitting with him in a pleasant parlor (not a drawing-
room) before a sea-coal fire, talking fiddle, — a subject which he understands better and warms up about
more than any other except one; and what that is no
woman need be told who has read his novels, from
"Peg Woffington" down to "The Cloister and the
Hearth," and onward through the brilliant list. I
wish to write of things, not persons, but I may say
that I found Charles Reade far more attractive than
authors generally are to me. He is tall, distinguished
in person and in manner, yet easy and simple in

speech and bearing, with no more vanity than he has the right to have (and this I mention only because he is credited with more) ; and as to his companionableness, I only wished for greater opportunity of testing it. I did not tell him that his near neighbors did not know where he lived; but I wish that I had done so, for the sake of the hearty laugh that we should have had together.

CHAPTER VI.

A SUNDAY ON THE THAMES.

I DID not spend a whole Sunday on the Thames; but as I was going to morning service at the Abbey, and to evening service at St. Paul's, I chose to make the river my way from one to the other; and doing this it seemed to me good to go leisurely over the whole of it within what is called the metropolitan district. This one is enabled to do easily and pleasantly by the little steamers that ply back and forth constantly within those limits. The day was as beautiful as a summer sky, with its bright blue tempered by lazy clouds smiling with light and sailing upon a soft, gentle breeze, could make it; the sense of Sunday seemed to pervade the air; and even the great city sat in sweet solemnity at rest. When science has taken entire possession of mankind, and we find no more anything to worship, will the Sunday-less man possess, in virtue of his rule of pure reason, any element of happiness that will quite compensate him for that calm, sweet, elevating sense — so delicate as to be indefinable, and yet so strong and penetrating as to pervade his whole being and seem to him to pervade all nature — of divine serenity in the first day of the Christian week? It is passing from us, fading gradually away, not into the forgotten, — for it can never be forgotten by those who have once felt it, — but into the unknown.

There are men now living who have never known it; their numbers will increase; and at last, in the long by and by, there will be a generation of civilized men who will say, that there should ever have been a difference between one day and another passes human understanding. This sense of Sunday is much stronger in the country than in the town; — strangely, for the current of life is there much less visibly interrupted; and it is always deepened by a sky at once bright and placid. And such a sky has its effect even in town. I felt it on this day, as I glided, through sunny hours and over gentle waters, past the solid stateliness and homely grandeur that are presented on the Thames side of London.

I walked across the lower end of St. James's Park, passing over much the same ground that King Charles trod on the 30th of January when, in the midst of a regiment of Cromwell's Ironsides, but attended personally by his own private guard and his gentlemen of the bed-chamber, and with the Parliamentary colonel in command walking uncovered by his side, he went to lay down his handsome, weak, treacherous head upon the block before the outraged Commonwealth of England: — an event which, notwithstanding the Restoration and the subsequent two centuries of monarchy in England, is the greatest and most significant of modern times, and is also of all grand retributive public actions the most thoroughly and characteristically English. Tyrants have been put to death or driven from their thrones at other times and by other peoples; but then for the first time, and first by men of English blood and speech, was a tyrant solemnly and formally tried like an accused criminal, condemned as a criminal, and put to death in execution of a warrant issuing from a court constituted by the highest power in the land. Compared with this high-handed justice the assassination of a Cæsar is like a brawl among " high-toned " politicians, and the expulsion of the Bourbons the chance consequence of a great popular tumult. And in this was its endless worth and its significance ; and hence it was that from that time there was a new tenure of kingship. Then for the first time the great law of government was written, — that it should be for the best interests of the governed ; and it was written in the blood of a king. This was the one boon of that great act to England, to the English race, to all civilized Christendom; for politically the beheading of Charles was a blunder ; and the Commonwealth, after living an artificial life for a few years, died an inevitable death, because it was born out of due time.

None the less because it was Sunday did I find the cows at the place towards the lower end of the park, whither I strolled, and where they and their predecessors have stood day after day for centuries, professing to give new milk to visitors thirsting for this rustic beverage, either for its own sake, or that it might by its associations enhance the rural effect of the meadows and the trees. I did not drink of the product of their maternal founts ; but my experience leads me to the unhesitating conclusion that if those cows give milk instead of milk-and-water they must be of a breed which, or the product of which, cannot be found in Middlesex without St. James's Park. The milk of London is a little thicker, a little more opaque, and a little whiter than its fog. Whether or no it is more nourishing I shall not venture to say.

Probably these cows do give milk-and-water, and produce instinctively, as becomes metropolitan British
kine, their article of trade ready adulterated. For,
many times as I passed the place where they stand, I
never saw man, woman, or child drinking; and I am
sure that if they gave real milk there would at least
be a procession to them of mothers and nurses with
their weanlings. They seemed to be of the homely
variety known as the red cow, to which belonged she
of the crumpled horn and she that jumped over the
moon. And if this were so it is yet another witness
to the perpetuity of things in England; for the fa-
cetious Tom Brown, who lived and wrote in the days
of James II., tells of the intrusion of the milk-folks
upon the strollers through the Green Walk with the
cry, "A can of milk, ladies! A can of red cow's
milk, sir!"

I could not but think that if kine could communi-
cate their thoughts there would be in that little knot
of horned creatures a tradition of the looks of Charles
I. and of Cromwell, and of Charles II. and of the
Duchess of Cleveland, and of Nell Gwynne, and of
dear, vain, clever, self-candid, close-fisted, kind-hearted Pepys, and of the beautiful Gunnings, and of
the captivating, high-tempered Sarah Jennings, who
could cut off her own auburn hair to spite the Duke
of Marlborough, and fling it into his face, and of the
'Duchess of Devonshire, who kissed the butcher and
wore the hat, and of all those noted beauties, wits,
gallants, and heroes whose names and traits are the
gilded flies in the amber of English literature. For
there probably has been no time since the park ceased
to be a royal chase when there was not at least some
one of the herd, and probably more, that could have

learned all these things in direct line of tradition from predecessors. So, to be sure, the same is true of the men and the women of London ; but the directness of such a course of transmission was brought more home to me in considering these cattle, as they stood there, the representatives and perpetuators of a little custom, older than any commonwealth, in one of the richest, most populous, and most powerful countries of the earth.

Chewing the cud of my fancies, I passed out of the park, and soon was at the Abbey door ; but not soon was I much farther. I had not troubled myself upon the score of punctuality ; and being a few minutes late I found the Abbey — that part of it which is used for service — full, even to the crowding of the aisles down to the very doors. I managed to squeeze myself in, but was obliged to stand, and moreover to be leaned against like a post, through service and through sermon. In these I found no noteworthy unlikeness, even of a minor sort, to what I had been accustomed to hear from my boyhood. The changes in the language of the Book of Common Prayer to adapt it to the political constitution and the social condition of the United States of America are so few and so slight that they must be closely watched for to be detected. The preacher was Canon Duckworth, canon in residence, who reminded me in voice, in accent, and in manner very much, and somewhat in person, although he was less ruddy, of a distinguished clergyman of the same church in New York, and whose sermon was the same sensible, gentleman-like, moderately high-church talk which may be heard from half a dozen pulpits in that city every Sunday. Not every one, however, of those who preach them, or the like of them in England, has Canon Duckworth's rich, vibrating voice and fine, dignified presence. The long hood of colored silk that he wore (his was crimson), like all English clergymen that I saw within the chancel, was not, as I find many persons suppose it to be, an article of ecclesiastical costume. It was merely his master's hood, — that which belonged to him as Master of Arts. The different colors of the linings of these academic hoods indicate the degree of the wearer and the university by which it was bestowed. They are worn by university "clerks" on all formal occasions.

After the sermon there was an administration of the communion, and all persons who were not partakers were required to leave the church. The exodus was very slow. Even after the throng was thinned and movement was easy, many lingered, looking up into the mysterious beauty of that noble nave. These the vergers did not hesitate to hasten, addressing them in some cases very roughly, as I thought, and even putting their hands upon their shoulders; but on my telling one of them that although I did not mean to commune I should like to remain during the service, he with ready civility, and with no shilling-expectant expression of countenance, took me to a seat within a gate and very near the outer rails. In this service, too, I found nothing peculiar to the place or to the building, — indeed, how could there well be? — but I observed that certain of the communicants, as they passed through the railing on their way to the table (which they, I suppose, would call the altar), and as they returned, carried their hands upright before them, holding the palms closely together and bowing their heads over them, with an air which conveyed the impression that they thought they were behaving like the saints in an altar-piece or in a missal. Perhaps I might have observed the same practice at home if my church-going had been more frequent since the outbreak of "ritualism."

It was strange, as I came out from such a solemn service in that venerable and sacred pile, and strongly indicative of the political position of the church in England, to be met just outside the door by a man who carried under his arm a huge bundle of hand-bills, calling a meeting and making a protest about some municipal matter. These he distributed freely to the communicants, as they issued from the cele-bration of the mystery, who took them as a matter of course into the same hands which had been pressed together with such ascetic fervor only a few minutes before, and, glancing at them, put them for the most part carefully into their pockets. We know that the English Church is a part of the government of Eng-land; but its peculiar place is shown by practices which to us would seem highly indecorous. In the rural counties I saw posted on the doors of parish churches — beautiful with the beauty of a lost in-spiration, and venerable with the historic associations of centuries thick with acts of import — notices of those persons in the parish who had taken out licenses to keep dogs; the list being always led by the name of the lord of the manor. There this was no sacri-lege. A parish in England is a political and legal entity, with material boundaries within which cer-tain officers have power; and the parish church is its moral centre. Why, therefore, should not the licenses to keep dogs be announced upon its doors?

Soon after leaving the Abbey I was at the river

side ; and in a minute or two along came a small black steamer, in length about twice that of the little tug-boats that run puffing and bustling about New York harbor, and no wider. It seemed to me more than simple, indeed almost rude in its bare discomfort ; and certainly it was as far from anything gay or festive in appearance as such a boat could be. The absence of bright paint and gilding, and of all that glare of decoration which it is thought necessary to make "Americans" pay for, commended the little craft to my favor ; but I thought that without these it yet might have been made a little less coarse and much more comfortable. On the dingy deck were some benches or long settles of unmitigated wood ; and that was all. There was not even an awning ; but perhaps awnings would interfere with the vailing of the funnel as these boats pass under the bridges, and they might perhaps also be in danger of fire from the small cinders that then escape. The passengers, in number about a score, were all of what would be called in England the lower-middle class, with one exception, a fine-looking man, manifestly a "gentleman," and with an unmistakable military air.

As I sat upon my hard seat, worn shiny by the sitting of countless predecessors, and looked around upon my fellow-passengers, I was impressed by the stolidity of their faces. The beauty of the sky, the soft, fresh breeze, the motion, the fact that it was a holiday, a fine Sunday, seemed to awaken no glow of feeling in their bosoms. And yet they were, most of them, plainly pleasure-seekers. As we moved swiftly on (I had taken an up boat) we soon passed over toward the Surrey side of the river. Erelong an elderly woman by whom I sat turned to me, and, pointing out at some distance ahead on our left a square tower, the familiar outlines of which had attracted my attention some minutes before, asked, " Wot buildin 's that there ? " " Lambeth, madam ; the Archbishop of Canterbury's palace." " The Harchbishop o' Cantubbury ! Well, well ! deary me ! A many times as I 've bin on the river, I never see that afore." To be asked such a question by a Londoner in my first half hour upon the Thames astonished me, and the confession that followed it was amazing ; for Lambeth palace is almost opposite Westminster. This was within the first fortnight after my arrival in England, and although, as I have already mentioned, I met with an exhibition of this kind of ignorance even before I set foot on English ground, I was not yet prepared for quite such an example. Before another fortnight had passed I had learned better.

As I turned to look at the questioner, I saw that she was a neatly-dressed, obese female, and that she was accompanied by a neatly-dressed, obese man, who plainly was her husband. The couple had lived together a long while ; they had grown old together ; they had grown fat together ; together they had sunk, year after year, deeper into a slough of stupidity ; together they had, as they passed through the world and life, become more and more ignorant of the one, and more and more indifferent to all of the other, except eating and drinking and the little round of their daily duties that enabled them to eat and drink. Their faces had grown like each other, not only in expression but in form. The noses had become more shapeless ; the chinless jaws had swelled and rounded imperceptibly into the short, thick neck.

Those faces probably had once expressed some of the vivacity of youth; but this had passed away, and nothing, no trace of thought or feeling, had come into its place, — only fat; a greasy witness of content; and the result was two great sleepy moons of flabby flesh pierced here and there by orifices for animal uses. I made surreptitiously an outline sketch of their two faces, as they sat side by side staring stupidly before them; and it looked like two Bourbon heads on a medal. He was one of those long-bodied, short-legged Englishmen who are framed with facilities for a great development of paunch. Man and wife were about the same height; and at the next landing they got up and waddled off together. I laughed within myself, as I am laughing now; and yet why should I have sat there and scoffed at those good folk for being what nature and circumstance had made them?

Of a very different fabric in every way was the military-looking man whom I have already mentioned. He was tall and strong, although not stout; a well-made, good-looking man, with a certain consciousness of good looks not uncommon among handsome Englishmen, and not unpleasant. His dress showed that union of sobriety with scrupulous neatness and snugness which is characteristic of the Englishman of the upper classes.

He alone of all my male fellow-passengers kept me in countenance in my chimney-pot hat. The round-topped hat, called "wide awake," or what not, has become so common in London that a crowd looked down upon from window or from 'bus seems like a swarm of great black beetles. I walked toward this gentleman, thinking that I would speak to him if he appeared willing; but he dismissed my doubts by speaking first. Brief as my experience in England had been, this did not surprise me; for I had already learned that English folk — women as well as men — are free in their intercourse with strangers to a degree that made me wonder whence came their reputation for gruff reserve. I should say that the chances of a pleasant chat with a fellow-traveler in England compared with those in the United States were as seven to three. I have again and again traveled from New York to Boston, and from New York to Washington and back (both journeys being of about two hundred and thirty miles each way), without having one word spoken to me by a stranger, although my journeys have mostly been by daylight; but in England I never went a dozen miles in company with other people without pleasant talk with one or more of them. Nor is such intercourse limited to traveling; there is a freedom of intercourse there to which we are comparative strangers; this, notwithstanding the visible limitations and restraints of rank, — perhaps rather by reason of them.

We sat down and talked as the boat glided swiftly up the river, the banks of which became gradually more suburban in appearance. The Thames, wherever I saw it, whether below London Bridge, or above that landmark and within the metropolitan district, or beyond, where it passes Kew and Isleworth and Twickenham and Richmond and Hampton, is remarkable for its character. It is nowhere common-looking; and the variety of its traits within a few miles surprises the eye at every stage with new delight. From the wide-expanding shores, the vast gloomy docks, the huge black hulls, and the strange, clumsy lighter craft of the Pool and Limehouse

Beach, past the stately magnificence of the embankment and the Abbey, with the Houses of Parliament on one side, and Lambeth on the other, up to the enchanting rural scene at Richmond, is not farther than it is from one village to another one just like it, through miles of sameness upon the Hudson.

My talk with my temporary companion was the mere chat of fellow-travelers under a bright sky; but even he managed to illustrate that narrowness of knowledge of which I found so many examples. As we looked off toward the west end of the town, there were in sight three or four rows of new houses, all unfinished, and some not yet roofed. He spoke of "so much buildin' goin' on" and "sellin' houses," and wondered how it was, and why gentlemen built houses and sold them. Thereupon I told him of the associations of builders, masons, carpenters, and the like, who built houses by a sort of club arrangement, and had their pay in an interest in the houses, which they sold at a good profit. Now this I merely remembered having read some two or three years before in the London Building News. It was nothing in me to know it; the remarkable thing was that a Yankee, hardly a fortnight in England, should be called upon to tell it to an intelligent Englishman.

Our little boat soon reached her upper landing, and then turned back. I went down the river to London Bridge, and there, after visiting the Monument and looking at the plain and unpretending solidity of the warehouses, which had the look of holding untold wealth, and after loitering about the murky purlieus of Thames Street, I crossed the bridge and was in Southwark. But of course the bridge was like a short street across the river (it

9

used to be a street with houses on either side), and one end of it was much the same as the other. In the people that I met, who were generally of the lower classes, there was a pleasant appearance of homogeneousness. They were all English people ; and the speech that I heard, although it was not cultivated and was sometimes even rude, was English. I heard no brogue' nor other transformation of my mother tongue. Little else attracted my attention, except the general inferiority of the men in height and weight to those we see in New England, and the rarity of good looks, not to say of beauty, in the women. They were all plainly in their Sunday clothes, which did not much become them, and in which they were at once much set up and ill at ease.

Not far from here I encountered a flock of girls between eight and twelve years old, who proved to belong to the Bridgewater School. They were dressed in blue and white, with straw bonnets trimmed with blue. They were neat, and looked comfortable and happy ; and some of the elder girls with whom I talked said that they were so. The school contained forty-two girls and sixty-five boys. The best that I learned about it was that the girls made their own dresses, and were taught every afternoon to sew by hand. But I looked in vain among them for the rosy, golden-haired, blue-eyed cherubs which I had been led to suppose were as thick in England as in an antique altar-piece.

On my way to St. James's Park I had stopped at a little coster-monger's stand and bought an apple, merely for the sake of a few words with the man and his wife, who were both in attendance. I took up an apple carelessly as I was going away, when the man said, " No, sir, don't take that; it's no good. Let me get you a better ; " and he picked out one of the best he could find. He appeared pleased when I thanked him and said that was a good one. Ungratefully, I gave the fruit to the first urchin I met ; for although I might have been willing to walk down St. James's Street munching an apple on a Sunday morning, it was not for an English apple that I would have done so. But none the less I reflected that the like of that had never happened to me in my boyhood, when I did buy apples to eat them anywhere, in doors or out of doors ; and I thought that most persons in trade would not have regarded that transaction as " business " on the part of my coster-monger. If he could " work off " his poor stock first, at good prices, he should do so, and — *caveat emptor*. I do not mean to imply that all coster-mongers in England are like him ; but, notwithstanding all that we hear about the tricks of British traders, adulteration, and the like, I will say that his was the spirit which seemed to me to prevail among the retail dealers of whom I bought in England. The seller seemed to be willing to take some trouble to please me, and — without making any fuss about it — to be pleased when I was pleased.

Not far from the Southwark end of London Bridge I passed a little fruiter's stall. It was plainly a temporary affair set up for the Sunday trade ; but in it were hanging some bunches of very fine white grapes, and I bought some that I might take them down to the river-side and eat them. They were only eight pence a pound. Down to the river-side I went, and, finding an old deserted boat or scow, I seated myself upon it, and ate my grapes and flung the skins into the water, as it ebbed swiftly past me, but gently and almost without a ripple. As I lay there the beauty of the day began to sink into my soul. The air had a softness that was new to me, and which yet I felt that I was born to breathe. The light in the low, swelling, slowly moving clouds seemed to come from a heaven that I once believed was beyond the sky, and did not smite my eyes with blindness as I looked upward. The stillness in such a place impressed me, and took possession of me. There was not a sound, except the distant plash of the wheels of one of the little steamers, and a faint laugh borne lightly down from the parapet of the bridge. And there lay before me, stretching either way beyond my sight, the great, silent city, — London, the metropolis of my race; the typical city of my boyhood's dreams and my manhood's musings; the port from which my forefather had set sail two hundred and fifty years ago, to help to make a new England beyond the sea; the place whose name was upon all the books that I had loved to read; the scene of all the great historical events by which I had been most deeply moved. It was worth the Atlantic voyage to enjoy that vision in that silent hour. Within my range of sight, as I turned my head, were the square turrets of the Tower and the pinnacles of Westminster; and I must have been made of duller stuff than most of that which either came from or remained in England between 1620 and 1645 not to be stirred by the thoughts of what had passed, of mighty moment to my people, at those two places, or between them. Many of those events flitted through my mind; but that which settled in it and took possession of it was the return of Hampden and Pym and the other Five

Members who had fled from Westminster to London before King Charles and his halberdiers. From where I sat, had I sat there on the 11th of January, 1642, I might have seen that now calm and almost vacant stretch of water swarming with wherries and decorated barges outside two lines of armed vessels that began at London Bridge and ended at Wesminster, while up the river, between this guard of honor, sailed to Westminster a ship bearing the five men whose safety was the pledge of English liberty ; and along that opposite bank, now silent and almost deserted (not indeed the Embankment, but the Strand, then the river street, as its name indicates), marched the trained-bands of London, with the sheriffs and all the city magnates and the shouting citizens, amid the booming of guns, the roll of drums, and the blare of trumpets. It was London that received and sheltered the Five Members ; it was London that protected them against the king ; it was London that carried them back in triumph past Whitehall, then purged of its royal tyrant, to resume their seats at Westminster, at the command of the outraged but undaunted House of Commons. That was the brightest, greatest day in London's history ; that the most memorable pageant of the many memorable seen upon the bosom of old Thames. I should not have enjoyed this vision and these thoughts if I had not lusted for those grapes, and for the pleasure of eating them to the music of the rippling water.

Again I took a steamer and went up the river and returned, that I might mark well the bulwarks and the palaces of this royal city, and see it all from the outside by daylight ; and also that I might enjoy the day, which was beautiful with a rich, soft, cool beauty unknown to the land from which we are driving the Sitting Bulls and Squatting Bears, to whose coarse constitutions and rude perceptions the fierce glories of its skies are best adapted. On the return trip the few passengers thinned rapidly away, so that at Charing Cross (I believe it was) every one but myself went ashore; and as no one came on board I was left actually alone upon the deck. This did not suit me, for I wanted to see the people as well as the place; and I too, just in time, went hastily ashore to wait for another steamer.

The landings are made at long, floating piers or platforms; and upon one of these I walked up and down, after having bought another ticket. Erelong another steamer came, well loaded, and I watched the people as they came ashore. Thoughtlessly I turned and walked with the last of them toward the stairs by which they made their exit to the city. It was my first day on the Thames, and I had not observed how very brief the stoppages of the boats were: they touch and go. I was startled by the plash of the wheels, and, turning, I saw the boat in motion. Instinctively I made for her, and having the length of the platform as the start for a running jump, I easily cleared the widening distance and the taffrail, and landed lightly on the deck. But it was a wonder that I was not frightened out of my jump and into the water; for there was sensation and commotion on the boat, and cries; two of the deck hands sprang forward, and stretched out their arms to catch me as if I had been a flying cricket-ball; and when I was seen safely on the deck there were cheers, — decorous cheers, after the English fashion. Indeed, I was sitting comfortably down and opening a newspaper be-

fore the little stir that I had caused was over. I did
not read my paper; for I was in the condition in
which Montaigne supposed his cat might be when he
played with her. The action of the people interested
me quite as much as mine interested them. These
English folk, whom I had been taught were phleg-
matic and impassible, had been roused to visible and
audible manifestation of excitement by an act that
would not have caused an " American " to turn his
head. The passengers on our crowded ferry-boats
saw men jump on board them after they were under
way day after day without moving a muscle, until,
too many having jumped into the water, and too
many of these having been drowned, we put up gates
and chains, not long ago, to stop the performance.
I should not take that jump again, nor should I have
taken it then if I had stopped to think about it; but
I was glad that I did take it then, not for the saving
of the five or ten minutes that I did not know what
to do with, but for the revelation that it made to me
of English character.

I landed again at London Bridge, and went to
evening service at St. Paul's. I have said before that
this great cathedral church has no attractions for my
eye externally, except in its dome, that heaves itself
heavily up into the dim atmosphere; nor has its interior to me any grand or even religious aspect. The
service there, too, as we sat on settles under the
dome, seemed to me entirely lacking in the impressiveness of that at Westminster. The voices of the
clergymen were indistinct, almost inaudible; the
singing sounded comparatively feeble, like the wail-
ing of forlorn and doleful creatures in a great cave.
The introit, although the dean was there, with a

stronger array of assisting clergymen, and choir boys
in surplices, and vergers than I had seen before,
seemed a comparatively ragged, childish performance. I took a distaste to the whole thing, and managed to slip away between the service and the sermon, in which movement I found myself kept in
countenance by others.

I strolled for a little while about the silent city,
meeting not more people than I should have met in
Wall Street or the lower part of Broadway on a Sunday afternoon. Moreover, during service the bright
skies had darkened, and it had begun to rain; but
it soon stopped, and the black clouds were white
again. Feeling hungry, I began to look about for
a place where I could get luncheon. I soon found
one, but the door was closed; and this was the case
with another, and yet another. The reason of this,
as I learned, was that during the hours of divine
service all public-houses are required to be closed in
England: another witness to the political position
of the Established Church. I had been startled in
the morning, while at breakfast, by hearing street
cries, and looking from my window had seen peri-
patetic coster-mongers uttering the inarticulate and
incomprehensible noises by which they allure people
to buy their wares, which seemed to me very strange
on a Sunday morning in England; but I found that
everything of this kind is allowed, except during the
hours of morning and evening service. This brought
up to me the religious discipline of New York in
my boyhood, or rather my infancy; for I remember
that when I, not yet five years old, was taken to
St. George's Church, in Beekman Street, there were
chains stretched across the street above and below

the church, to prevent the passing of vehicles, and also to keep away the carriages of those who did not let their beasts and their servants rest on Sunday. And I remember in the summer time, when the church doors were open, the faint, distant stamp of the waiting horses mingling drowsily with the monotonous sing-song of the worthy clergyman, and lulling my wearied little brain to slumber that was broken only by the burst of the great organ. Think how the liberty-loving people of a city which has produced a Tweed for its chief manager and a Fernando Wood for its mayor and its representative would now endure chains across a street to prevent them from disturbing the devotions of others! The right to obstruct and mar our streets is now only to be had by great corporations who are rich enough to pay (but not us) handsomely for the privilege.

Erelong the prescribed hour had gone by, and the doors of the churches and of the eating-houses and the tap-rooms were opened, and more people appeared in the streets. I went to two or three of the latter, but did not go in. They repelled me; they were in such out-of-the-way places, they were so small, so unsightly, so rude and dirty; and, moreover, there was an "uncanny" air about them that took away my appetite. At last, however, I saw an entrance that attracted me, and I went in, expecting to find myself on the threshold or in the porch, at least, of an eating-house. But I was only at the street end of a long, narrow passage, which was like an alley. This I followed to a place where there were doors; and by the exercise of some ingenuity I discovered the public-house, which, like so many public places in English cities, seemed to shrink into the remotest recesses of privacy.

It was a queer-looking place. The room was very small. In the open space a table for six people could not have been set conveniently. On one side was a small, semicircular bar, — so small that the stout publican behind it seemed to be standing in a barrel out of which he produced his liquors. On another side, nearly at right angles, was a large window opening into a room, half tap-room, half kitchen, where two bar-maids waited. On the broad ledge of this window were two or three cold joints. Into the room, on another side, a singular structure projected itself. It had three sides, and was sashed, and in fact was an indoor bay-window. Its floor was about three feet above that of the principal room, and it was about eight feet across. It was entered by steps along-side the bar, and also from behind by a door on its own level. It was carpeted, and furnished with a table and two chairs. In one of the chairs sat a woman who was evidently the hostess. She was a large woman, red of face, rotund of figure; but indeed as to figure she had long ceased to be of any particular shape. As to the dress of her, she was very imposing. She wore a gown of pale lilac-purple *moiré antique;* and her every movement betrayed a consciousness that it was very moiré and, although quite fresh, very antique. She was right. I never before saw such an obtrusive garment. It invaded all the senses; for it was highly perfumed and so stiff that the *frou-frou* of it was like the crackling of stout wrapping-paper. She wore a lace cap (real, O female reader!), and a lace collar confined by an enormous and brilliant brooch. Around her neck was a thick, dull-gold chain, by which hung a locket that would have served a fop of George II.'s time for

a snuff-box ; in her shapeless ears were glaring, jingling pendants ; and her fat fingers flashed with
rings. She spoke familiarly with the man in the
bar, who came out of his pen once in a while and
stumped about the place ; but whether he was her
husband, or she intended him to be so at some future time, I could not quite make out. But I suspected, from a certain subdued air about him, that
his case was the former ; and besides, how otherwise such a gorgeous creature could look with favor
upon a little semi-bald-headed, paunchy fellow in his
shirt sleeves was quite incomprehensible.

I asked for some beef and a glass of Burton ale,
which were soon cheerily placed before me by one
of the bar-maids. Both were excellent ; but I was
obliged to stand as I ate and drank, and indeed half
a dozen persons on chairs would have so filled up
the place that it would have been impassable. I
soon drained my glass, and asked for another. When
it was brought me, at the first sip I set it down, and
said, " That's not the same ale ; and it's not Burton." It proved that the bar-maid who had first
served me did not fill my glass the second time, and
that the other had by mistake done so from the wrong
tap. But I was amused by the impression that I
had plainly made upon these Hebes by my quick detection of the error. The mistake was of course
corrected at once, with apologies ; but then I saw
them put their heads together and look at me with
the great respect due to a man who was not to be
imposed upon in the matter of ale, to my great enjoyment. But why laugh at these poor she-tapsters ?
Are there not men, gentlemen, who have " a reputation " as wine tasters, and who are " authorities " on

the subject, and who are mightily set up because
thereof? I remember that, once dining at the table
of a newly rich man, he told me, as he gave me some
Cos, that one of his friends, when in Europe, had
some wine set before him as to which there were serious doubts; and he, tasting it, said at once that it
was Cos, which proved to be true. "And that, you
know," said Lucullus, "was a great thing for him."
I cannot see how any one who has once drunk either
Cos or castor-oil can ever mistake its flavor; but why
a man should be respected because he knows the taste
of what he eats and drinks, and makes a talk about
it, it is not very easy to discover. In England, however, such accomplishment seems to be more highly
prized than it is with us; or I should rather say that
there are more people there who respect it, — both
in great dining-rooms and in little tap-rooms.

While I was still occupied with my beef and beer,
there entered to the hostess a visitor, another stout
middle-aged woman richly arrayed in black silk.
Indeed, when she had mounted the steps and got,
somewhat in the manner of a burglary, into the little bay-window, it was an engineer's problem to determine how two such women in two such silk dresses
could both be and move in that narrow space. The
sweep of their two trains was portentous. Each was
a threatening silken comet. But the hostess had
the happiness of far eclipsing the other. The sheen
and the shimmer of that lilac silk were not to be
dimmed by the approach of any black, however much
it might have "cost a yard." There was large performance in the way of ceremony and courtesying,
which, owing to the formation of the place, had the
air of private theatricals, and for which I, another

hungry man, and the bar-maids were the audience.
" *Ow* do you do, Mrs. ——? I *ope* you 're well."
" Quite well, Mrs. ——, an' I opes you 're the same."
" Thenk you; my 'ellth 's yery good. Could I hoffer
you anythink ? " " Ho, no, my dear Mrs. ——, not
on hany account." " Ho, now, indeed you must
obleege me by takin' a little somethink. Juss a drop
o' sherry, now, an' a biscuit." " Well, Mrs. ——,
since you 're so wery pressin', I think I will." This
performance went on amid contortions of civility.
Indeed, these large ladies threatened the very existence of the little structure by the transaction of their
tremendous courtesies ; and I expected to see certain
rearward portions of the moiré antique and of the
black silk appear through the riven glass on either
side. Was the contrast between the fine dresses of
these women and their affectation of fine manners on
the one side, and their reality and what would have
been truly becoming to them on the other, peculiar
to England ? I am inclined to think not. The peculiarity was that the play was played before me on
Sunday on a little stage in a little tap-room.

Leaving these *grandes dames* to the discussion of
their sherry and biscuit, I walked home, and after a
solitary dinner on English mutton slept soundly upon
my first Sunday in London.

CHAPTER VII.

A DAY AT WINDSOR.

It was on a bright October morning that I took an early train from London to Windsor. No autumnal tints had yet touched the trees, which stood full clad in vivid green, nor was the grass a blade thinner or a shade paler than it was in summer. The sky was almost cloudless, and of that pale gray-blue which is its brightest color between the narrow seas. I never saw the heaven quite void of clouds in England; and I am sure that if I had seen it so I should not have liked it better. The wind — but there did not seem to be any wind, not even a breeze, only a gentle motion of soft air which stirred just enough to make you conscious of its presence. There was not that glow above and that rich, deep-hued splendor below that make the autumn of New England appear so glorious ; but the absence of those bright colors which our year, like a dolphin, takes on as it is dying was more than made up for me by the fullness of life and the freshness of beauty which, when we had left the city behind us, I saw all around me. I admit that I am quite willing to do without any evidences of decay, however brilliant may be its phosphorescence, and that there is no flower which compensates me for the loss of June roses.

In the approach to Windsor there is nothing remarkable ; but rural England under a bright sky is

always beautiful; and it was after as pleasant an
hour as railway traveling will permit that I left the
train at the town which clusters around the base of
England's royal castle.

What a little place! It seemed hardly big enough
to hold so fat a man as Falstaff. And then it is so
small for its age. Think that it should have been
there these eight hundred years, and yet have grown
no larger! Moreover, there is the surprise of finding in such a very small town such a very big castle.
Indeed, it is absurd to say that the castle is at Windsor: it is Windsor that is at the castle. But the
smallness of the town, its age, and its apparent incapacity for becoming any larger were all charms in
my eyes. It was a new and delightful sensation in
England, — the coming upon places that were finished, that were neither great nor growing, and that
plainly had no enterprise. It gave rest to a certain
stunned and weary feeling which comes upon one in
the streets of New York, and in the streets of other
places which are daily, with more or less success,
doing all they can to be like New York, that dashing, dirty, demirep of cities.

Before going to the castle I walked about the town
a little, — not, however, with any Shakespearean purpose. Not in the town, nor in the park, nor in the
neighborhood did I make passionate pilgrimage to
the scenes of Shakespeare's only comedy of English
life. To what good end or pleasant thought should
I have done so? Among the places and objects at
Windsor that Shakespeare has mentioned there is
now not one which is what he saw or had in mind, or
which he himself would recognize were he brought
back to earth again. Herne's oak is gone; and if it

were not, in what would it differ from any other old oak? And why should I go to Frogmore simply because it is mentioned in "The Merry Wives"? If places have any beauty or any real charm of association, the sight of them is a source of a great and a pure pleasure. Could I have seen the house that Shakespeare had in mind as Ford's, or that might have been Ford's house; could I have seen Mistress Ford or sweet Anne Page, or portraits of the women that stood to Shakespeare as models for those personages, — if he had any models, — I would gladly have gone twenty miles afoot to enjoy the sight; but since I could not, since I could see nothing of the sort, not even the "bare ruined choirs where late the sweet birds sang," what need to follow the shadow of an empty name! Therefore I left the places mentioned in "The Merry Wives" unvisited.

In Windsor itself I found little of interest. The town is not new, but it is modern. Its Elizabethan features have all been improved away. It is chiefly filled with people who live upon the castle, and upon the railway that brings other people to the castle. The glorifying beams of royalty fall upon everything. On a little hut by the river-side I saw a sign, "All Kinds of Bait. Patronized by the Royal Family;" and I had some comfort in picturing to myself the Prince of Wales and the Dukes of Edinburgh and Connaught going there for worms and minnows when they went out fishing on half holidays, — although, poor fellows, I fear they never had the true boyish pleasure of carrying their worms, not exactly, like Mr. Punch's boy, in their mouths, but in boxes in their own pockets, and of putting them on the hooks themselves, and then of taking home a good catch of fish for the royal breakfast-table. Who would be a prince, to have his hook baited by an attendant, and his gun loaded by a game-keeper! Dignity in pleasure dulls the edge of enjoyment. But nevertheless a bait-house patronized by the royal family was a thing to see.

In a little public-house in a by-street I saw in the window a card: "Bean Feasts and Parties Supplied." This I hailed as evidence that pork and beans came into New England with the Mayflower, quite as trustworthy, to say the least, as that on which some noble families are said to have come into Old England with the Conqueror. And I was also glad to see in it evidence that the bean-eaters had their little merrymakings and picnickings, not unlike those festivals which produce here a dreadful variety of iced-cream and consequent stomachic derangements for Sunday-school children.

In the course of my stroll I came upon a house which had recently been burned, the ruins of which stood just as they had been left by the fire. The house had not been wholly destroyed, and the skeleton still held together. It seemed to have been built some forty or fifty years ago. I was surprised at the flimsiness of its construction. The bricks were poor and the mortar was bad; the beams were out of proportion, small, and badly joined; the tenon and mortise work was not only clumsy, but weak and insufficient. A house so built may be found anywhere; and I should not mention this but as the occasion of remarking that I found the same inferior builder's work wherever I went in England. According to my observation, modern English houses, unless they are built with special care and unusual expense, are

10

very slightly put together, with bad materials and poor workmanship.

It is the custom there to put up the shells of houses, usually three or four together, and to leave them to be finished according to the wishes of an intending tenant or purchaser. They are called " carcasses." I examined many of these without finding one even tolerably well built. The walls brought to mind the scoff of Tobiah the Ammonite against the newly rebuilt wall of Jerusalem, — " If a fox go up he shall break down their stone wall," and Panurge's declaration that a cow could destroy, in a not very quotable manner, six fathoms of the walls of old Paris. The mortar, although it had been set for years, would crumble under the touch of my stick, or even of my thumb nail. And walls of the modern-built villa houses that I visited were rarely more substantial, while the joiner's work was both slight and coarse. I also remarked that where recent additions had been made to the height of garden walls the mortar in the new part, although in general it was plainly ten or twenty, or even thirty, years old, was more like mud than like mortar. Indeed, I did not see in England, in a new private building of moderate pretensions, any mortar worthy of the name. This attracted my attention, I need hardly say, because of the notion generally prevailing, and sedulously encouraged by British writers, that all English work is distinguished from other work of its kind by excellence of material and thoroughness of workmanship; that although it might not have elegance it was sure to be substantial. I did not find it so. In this respect, in many ways, I was disappointed. That such was once the character of the

work of English artisans and manufacturers I believe is not to be disputed; but during the last fifty
years this glory of England seems to have departed.

Visitors to Windsor Castle are required to register
their names in a book before they receive the tickets
without which they cannot pass the gate. No fee is
expected or allowed to be taken for this preliminary
process, which is performed at a little shop in the
principal street of the town. I offered a half crown
to the respectable and cheerful dame who thus
equipped me; but she told me, with a smile, that
she could take nothing, but that she had guide-books
which she could sell me. Whereupon I whipped her
particular devil around her particular stump, to her
entire satisfaction. As to her books, they were naught,
as such books are most commonly.

While I was doing this it occurred to me that I
wanted some ginger-pop, a potation which I had not
yet tasted, and which I would by no means have left
England without enjoying. For in my boyhood I
had been made thirsty by reading of the revelings of
English boys in this exhilarating drink, just as I had
been made hungry by reading in Scott's novels of
knights and cavaliers devouring venison pasties. I
asked for ginger-pop. But the lady replied with some
dignity that she did not keep it, adding kindly and
with gentle condescension that I might get it at a
little shop down the street. Hereupon a cheery
young voice broke out, "I'll show you, sir, where
you can get some pop." I turned, and saw a lad
some twelve or fourteen years old, and, thanking
him, asked him if the pop would be good. He assured me that it would, adding by way of proof,
"All the fellows of our school go there." Moment-

arily forgetful, I asked, What school? "Why, Eton,
of course," he replied. We went off together, and
soon pledged each other in the fizzing fluid, which,
to my great disappointment, I found to be nothing
more than poor soda-water flavored with poor ginger
syrup. But I was well recompensed for this disillu-
sion. My companion's views upon the subject of
ginger-pop were different from mine, and he beamed
and expanded under its influence. I told him that I
had come to see the castle, and asked him some questions about it. Of course he knew Windsor through
and through ; and after we had chatted a while he
offered to go with me and be my guide.

We set off immediately, and at the castle we became part of a group or squad of visitors who were
about to make the round of the state apartments. I
shall not be so superfluous as to give any description
of these apartments, which did not impress me either
with their magnificence or their good taste. I expected both ; I should have been satisfied with one ;
I found neither. There was an absence of grandeur
and stateliness in proportion and in arrangement, a
lack both of splendor and of elegance in decoration,
which surprised me. Nor was there any impression
of antiquity in keeping with the age of this venerable
palace and fortress. Two of the apartments were of
great interest, — the Vandyke room and St. George's
Hall. The Vandyke room is filled with portraits by
that master-painter of gentlemen and gentlewomen.
Of the twenty-two canvases one half are portraits of
Charles I. or of his family. There are three of
Charles himself ; of Henrietta Maria four, besides
that in the family group. One wearies a little of
Charles's handsome, high-bred, melancholy face, with

its peaked beard dividing the singularly elegant, but certainly most unmanly, Vandyke collar. And after all, notwithstanding Charles's beauty and his air of refinement, he had not a kingly look. His face lacked strength. The Earl of Strafford, whose portrait is perhaps the greatest head that Vandyke ever painted, looked far more kingly; and, with all Strafford's faults, he was more kingly than his master. The most interesting of the other and not royal portraits are those of Tom Killigrew, of Carew, and of Vandyke himself.

St. George's Hall is interesting from the fact that it has upon its walls and its ceiling the arms and the names of all the knights of the Garter who have been installed since the foundation of the order. The general effect is that of a rich series of heraldic mosaics. As to the knights, there is, as Sir Pertinax Macsycophant might say, "sic an admeexture." Not that there was a " Jew and a beeshop," — at least there was no Jew's name yet visible when I was there in 1876; but the names of men of mark and distinction are mingled with those of men who were merely the commonplace sons of commonplace fathers, inheritors of high rank and great estates, who but for their inheritance would never have been heard of beyond the bounds of their own parishes, and who as simple gentlemen would have had no claim to admiration and little to respect. And yet the Garter is the great prize of life in England. To win it men will peril body and soul, although it is the emptiest of all distinctions. For a knight of the Most Noble Order, except by his star and his garter, does not differ in virtue of his knighthood from any other human mortal. A peerage brings station and power and privilege and ennobling duty and opportunity; but the Garter and the Golden Fleece and the Black Eagle, — what are they? Can any one tell what good they do the man who wears them, or of what merit they are the sign? They are not, like the Victoria Cross, or the Order of Merit, or even like that much-cheapened distinction the Legion of Honor, tokens of courage, or of ability, or of character. But a knight of the Garter is one of a body of not more than some fifty men (originally but twenty-five), who have the sovereign for their chief and foreign kings and princes among their number; and therefore it is the most coveted distinction in Europe, although it means nothing, and the order does nothing. This hall of the order of St. George is two hundred feet long, but as it is only thirty-four feet wide its effect is not one of grandeur; on the contrary, it seems like a decorated corridor to some really grand apartment.

The Waterloo Chamber, although not very spacious, considering that it is one of the principal state apartments in the principal palace of the British sovereign, is yet a noble room. It is hung with some thirty or forty portraits, nearly all at full length, of distinguished personages who were connected in some way with the great battle which ended Napoleon's career. Most of these portraits are by Sir Thomas Lawrence. As one looks around it, the old exclamation, "My stars and garters!" (which was still heard in New England till recently, if, indeed, it is yet obsolete), is brought forcibly to mind. Such an exhibition of starred coats and gartered legs, and of ermined robes and of human upholstery in general, with faces appended thereto in Lawrence's weak, pretty style, is not to be found elsewhere. It is

amusing to see that whatever the figures of the men
may be, which are hidden by the velvet and the fur,
their legs are all alike. Lawrence evidently had one
pair as models, and furnished them to all his sitters
with impartial pencil.

It was more amusing to see the awful admiration
with which these and other magnificences were regarded by the visitors, who were all, with the single
exception of myself, British sight-seers of the middle
and lower-middle classes, out on a holiday. Of the
Vandykes they took little notice; they were more
disposed to admire the vast inanities of Verrio and
Zuccarelli in the audience-chamber and the drawing-
room. But these robed and jeweled full-length portraits of kings and princes and dukes and earls, some
of whose names they had heard, were to them manifestly glimpses of glory. They were also much interested in furniture, gilded chairs and tables and
vases, and the like.

My Eton boy kept near me, but he had found two
or three young companions, and when he was not
playing good-natured cicerone to me (and he showed
intelligence and good taste in what he said) he chatted with them.

I saw that our official attendant fretted at this,
particularly when the lad spoke to me. He was a
consequential man, more like one of John Leech's
butlers than any real butler that I saw in England.
His squat figure was carefully dressed in black; his
shoes were polished to an obtrusive brightness, so
that they looked like large lumps of anthracite coal;
and he shone at both ends, for he must have had
half a teacupful of highly perfumed oil upon his
straight black hair, which was coaxed into the sem

blance of a curl above each ear. He delivered himself of his explanations with pompous dignity. At
last, on one occasion, when my young companion
had spoken somewhat eagerly to me, and had then
turned to his fellows, and their tongues disturbed the
almost awful hush with which the small crowd of
Philistines listened to his descriptions, the man
stopped short in the midst of an harangue, and,
wheeling about upon my Eton guide, broke out,
" Wot *har* you a-talkin' about ? Wot do *you* know
about hanythink in the castle ? *Will* you be quiet
wen hI'm a-talkin' ! 'Ow *can* the ladies and gentlemen hunderstand the castle if they can't 'ear me
speak ? " The boy held his peace, of course ; but
as soon as the man turned round again, looked up
at me with a most impenitent wink, and thrust his
tongue into his cheek with an expression that, if his
rebuker had seen it, would have made him choke
with suppressed wrath.

The weary round of the state apartments having
been finished, we descended a staircase at the head
of which our guide pointed out to us the " harmor of
the Hearl of Hessex," and I went to St. George's
Chapel, which, although worth seeing, seemed to me
less so than any church of note that I visited in England. The monument to the Princess Charlotte is
one of those elaborate exhibitions of bad taste which
were put up at great expense in England at the end
of the last century and the beginning of this. Indeed,
I did not see in any church in the country a modern
monument which was well designed or really beautiful. The modern monuments in Westminster Abbey are mostly monstrosities in marble.

The noble round tower of Windsor Castle is its

chief beauty. It dominates and harmonizes all the other architectural features of the pile. It is the round tower that makes Windsor Castle imposing. We all know Windsor by that tower, which sits like a great crown upon the castle-palace of the British sovereigns. Up the hundred stone steps of this tower I went with my young Eton friend; and if the steps had been a thousand I should have been well repaid for the ascent by the sight that greeted me on all sides, as I looked off from the battlements. The guide-books say that when the atmosphere is un clouded twelve counties, Middlesex, Hertford, Essex, Oxford, Wilts, Kent, Hants, Bedford, Sussex, Berks, Bucks, and Surrey, may be seen from this elevation. I must then have seen my full dozen; for although there were clouds, they were few and light, and themselves so beautiful that I would not have given the sight of them for the sight of six more counties; and the day was bright and clear with a soft, golden clearness. Except from Richmond Hill, off which I looked on such another day, I had no sight of English land that was to be compared with this in its beauty and in its peculiarly English character. It was picturesque, but it had no striking features. Its charm consisted in the blending of man's work with nature's; in the alternation of the noble and the simple; in the grand harmony of things which although beautiful in themselves, would not have been very striking if alone, — like the rich interweaving of simple themes in great orchestral music. It was a grand symphony in form and color. For it seemed, like a symphony, to have been constructed with design, yet with such art that the succession and relation of its beauties were perfectly natural. To have disturbed

their order, or to have regarded one without regard-
ing the others also, would have been destructive of
its highest charm, — that of the extension and continuity of varied, self-developed beauty. I wandered
around the great circle of the parapet, and leaning
into the topaz-tinted air drank in delight that filled
me with a gentle happiness.

But I was not allowed to muse in solitude. Soon
a warder came up to me, telescope in hand, and began his official function. He called my attention to
this great house and to the other, seeming to think
that the chief pleasure in looking from Windsor
walls consisted in seeing the seat of this or that
nobleman. I did not take his prying telescope, and
after a word or two walked away and changed my
point of view. Soon he followed me, and began
again his verbal catalogue and index, and again offered me his brazen tube. Annoyed by his persistence, and wishing at once to be left alone and not to
offend him in the performance of his office, as the
easiest way of accomplishing my double purpose I
listened to him a moment, took the telescope, and
sweeping the horizon slowly with it, handed it back
to him with thanks and the customary shilling. He
took the telescope, of course, but to my surprise he
refused the shilling.[1] His manner was very respectful, but equally decided. Fearing that he might
fasten himself upon me as a gratuitous guide, I
pressed the coin upon him on the ground that I had
used his telescope. "No, indeed, sir, you did n't,"
he replied, with civil and even deferential manner.
"I saw you did n't, and I 've done nothing for the
tip." I yielded, and was moving away again, when

[1] My only experience of this kind in England.

after looking at me a moment, he said, "I beg your pardon, but I think you must be an American gentleman. I should n't have thought it, if you had n't been so suspicious. American gentlemen are always so suspicious."

The man's outspoken but respectful manner pleased me. I was a little puzzled by his epithet, but apprehended him in a moment. He had no conception of the feeling which made me desire to be alone, and supposed that I regarded him as a sort of impostor, who for the sake of my shilling professed to show me what he did not know himself. For the rest, — 'ow was I to hunderstand the castle if I did n't 'ear him speak? Then I put myself into his hands, and let him show me his landscape and his country-seats; and in the course of our talk I learned from him that "Americans" were more apt than Englishmen to decline his offices. This he thought was because they were so sharp, "bein' so accustomed, you see, sir, to be taken in at 'ome." That was richly worth the shilling, which I offered him again, and which he now took thankfully.

My nativity had been detected by a stranger only once before; and that was by a tailor, who spoke of it casually as, soon after my arrival, I was trying on a water-proof overcoat at a shop in Regent Street. I asked him how he knew it. He smiled, and said, pointing to my coat, "I knew that coat, sir, was never made in England." He was right; and I should have known it myself if I had seen the coat upon another man, although it was cut after a London pattern, and was made of English cloth by an English tailor. This stamp of nationality in handiwork is universally borne. Why it is so seems almost

unaccountable. But a book, for example, bound in
New York or at Riverside by an English binder, with
English tools and English materials, after an English
pattern carefully copied, can be distinguished from a
London-bound book almost at a glance by an observant book lover. It may be as well-bound, or better,
but it will not be precisely the same. So a London-
made watch-case copied here line for line, and in tint
of metal to a shade, will be easily distinguishable from
the original, even although the pattern is "engine-
turned" and worked by a machine in both cases.
The critic would not perhaps find a ready reason for
his discrimination, and might find it impossible to
give one; but none the less he would be safe in
making it.

Just as I was turning from my warder, he said,
"If you like old churches, sir, yonder 's one that 's
one of the three or four oldest in the kingdom, they
say, — St. Andrew's of Clewer;" and he pointed off
to a little spire that shot up from among some trees
and hay-stacks two or three miles off. This was welcome news; and after a word or two with him on
the subject, I sought and found my Eton boy, and
asked him if he knew the way to that little church.
"To be sure," he said, mentioning the name. "I 've
been there many a time. Would you like to go?
We need n't go by the road; I know paths through
the fields." We set off without more words. He
took me down through by-streets, and then through
workshops and stables, and at last brought me out
upon a broad, low meadow; and then we followed
by-paths and lanes. And here, from this out-of-the-
way place, I got a view of the castle which surpassed
in grandeur and in noble picturesqueness all views of

it that I had seen before, either with my own eyes or in prints and pictures. The sky line was more richly varied, the whole pile had much more dignity, and the long, level foreground over which I looked stretched out directly to the base of the mound out of which that majestic growth of stone seems to spring.

As we walked, the lad, upon a little leading, told me about himself. He was a foundation scholar. His family had once been wealthy, but had decayed and become poor, — by means, I suspect, from what dropped casually with his story, of a scampish father and grandfather. His friends had interest enough to get him a foundation scholarship at Eton, where he had been two years. But the poor fellow had not prospered; for he confessed to me that he had been plucked twice. Moreover, he told me how hard a life he led among the sons of noblemen and rich gentlemen who filled the school; how they scorned him and scoffed him, and at best slighted him, and took no more notice of him " than if he had been a puppy dog." I did not tell him, but I saw that the reason of this treatment was not only his being on the foundation, as he said, but his being neither clever nor strong. He was intelligent enough, and not quite a weakling; but he had been plucked twice, and I saw that he would not have counted for much at football or at cricket. He lacked both nervous energy and strength of fibre; and this in a foundation boy who was nothing at his books of course made him a nonentity at such a school as Eton, where, most of all places in England, the traditionary creed is held that

> " They should take who have the power,
> And they should keep who can."

But he was a good-hearted fellow, and with some independence, as I found; for he would take no tip from me, and had declined, as we came through the town from the castle, to have luncheon, suspecting, as I saw plainly, that I proposed it on his account. Poor, weak, sensitive soul!—sure not to succeed in life; able neither to take nor to keep, and ashamed to receive, yet far more worthy of respect than many who get both gain and glory.

After a pleasant walk we came out close by the little church, which stood almost literally among the hay-stacks, and which might have been hidden entirely from view, except its spire, by any one of many hay-stacks that I have seen in Pennsylvania; for it was not much larger than a country school-house. But outside and inside it was a little jewel, of quaintest design, if design could be asserted of what bore the marks of different hands and different periods,—Saxon, Norman, and Early English. Part of it is said to have been built in the seventh century. It stood in its church-yard almost like a summer-house in a garden. It was composed of two parts, one much longer than the other. Its walls were of chalk and flint, and its roof was of flat, red tiles. It had a low, square tower, very heavily buttressed at the angles, from which rose, with a curved base, a small, sharp spire. The little porch at the side showed its rafters, as the whole church did; those of the porch were like an A. Although so small, it had a nave and side aisles, and little clere-story windows, the sills of which almost rested upon round arches supported by rude pillars. It had a pretty carved altarpiece; and there were the old high pews,—actually old, but comparatively very new; for at least one part of the church had been built centuries before

pews and Protestantism came in together.   It was by
far the prettiest country church that I saw in England, and much the most interesting, notwithstanding
the superior age claimed for St. Martin's at Canterbury and the associations of the Hospital church at
Harbledown.   Yet upon after-inquiry among those
of my friends who had been educated at Eton, I did
not find one who had seen St. Andrew's of Clewer, although he had been within one hour's easy walk of
it for three years.

As I entered the church, there appeared at the
porch, I know not how, as if she had come up out of
a vault, an old woman, who smiled and courtesied
and gave me good-day as I went in.   She wore a cap,
a folded kerchief, and an apron, all as neat as wax
and as white as snow.   I saw, of course, that the little place was her show ; but how she managed to be
there as I came in, the Queen's head upon a shilling
only knows ; for there cannot be a visitor a day to
this little place.   I expected to hear her soon whining beside me ; but no, she remained quietly at the
porch, while I sauntered about the church until I got
my fill of it ; nor did she offer to speak to me until I
called her up and asked a question.   She answered
in so sweet a voice and with so pleasant a manner
that she won my heart on the spot ; but it had been
half won, as I encountered her, by her smile, her cap,
her kerchief, and her apron.   She showed me the little that there was to be shown, and told me the little
that there was to be told, about the church, which
for its age was very bare of legend and of monument.
As I passed out I observed the font close by the
porch, -- a large, low, dark-colored bath of stone, half
filled with water.   Around the edge, which was a full

span deep, was arranged a garland of roses, the most beautiful, I think, that I ever saw. They were white and red and yellow, and their perfume filled the whole of the quaint old shrine; for the little church was hardly more. The old woman, seeing my admiration of them, told me that the rector's daughters had put them there "because to-day was St. Michael's and hall hangels." She dropped a little courtesy as she said it; and if St. Michael and all the other angels were not pleased with her simple obeisance they must be harder to propitiate than I believe they are.

We went out into the church-yard, which had as much beauty as such a place can have, — more than any other of its kind that I have seen. It was full of small dark evergreens (the Irish yew), which shot up, pointed like spires, from the emerald grass, the flowers, and the old head-stones. Although the place was so small and so rustic, there were others than "the rude forefathers of the hamlet" buried there. And as I went about among the stones, the old woman, whom I kept near me by constant questions, that I might enjoy the pleasure of her speech, stooped to some planks which I had thought were the temporary cover of a new and unfilled grave, and removing one of them, showed me a large and handsome vault. It was of white marble, finely finished, and had slabs for two coffins. She told me that a Colonel —— was building it for himself and for his wife; and she pointed out to me with evident pride its elegance and costliness. "See, sir," she said, "what a beautiful resting-place the Colonel is building for himself, and for his lady too, when it pleases God to call them. Could there be anything finer? See, sir, white marble and polished, that the porch of your own house could n't be finer. [No, indeed, good soul; there you are nearer right than you seem to think.] It must be such a consolation to them, sir." And she spoke quite as if she thought that the Colonel and his " lady " ought to be very thankful, when it pleased God to call them, to be laid away in so grand and elegant a place.

I left her smiling and courtesying, and walked back to Windsor with my young Eton friend. I have since heard that she herself lies now in the churchyard; and although there will be no marble around or above her humble coffin, I have no doubt that she sleeps as well as if she lay in the tomb that she regarded as so inviting. Peace be with her; for she had a gentle way, a sweet voice, and she did not speak unbidden.

We crossed the Thames, going thus over a tiny bridge, from Windsor to Eton, and from Berkshire into Bucks; and indeed it seemed to me as if, excepting the castle, both places could be covered with a large blanket. In this is one of the charms of England, and I believe of other European countries, — that in small towns which have always been small you may find buildings, like Windsor Castle and Eton College, which have always been large ; and the cultivated fields and the green meadows come close up to the walls or to the houses. Eton is a very small place, but is full of houses in which it must be a delight to live, so indicative are their outsides of comfort and refinement, and, not least, of reserve. And this expression of reserve, which pertains more or less to the houses in all small towns in England, is much helped in all by the winding, irregular streets. You cannot stand and look down a row of

11

houses a quarter of a mile long as if you were in-
specting a file of soldiers.

It was now long after noon, and I saw in a field an
Eton game of foot-ball. It was played with spirit,
but with less dash than I had been led to expect.
At another time, however, there may have been more.
Apart from their uniforms, the players could not
have been distinguished from the same number of
Yankee boys, of like condition in life, engaged in the
same sport. I also met a large party of "old boys,"
as they came up, in their uniforms, from a cricket
match. A lathier lot of young fellows I never saw.
Not that they were either weak looking or unhealthy;
but they were not at all what the writings of British
critics had led me to expect. Not one was robust;
only one had color; and there was not a curling
auburn head among them. I saw Eton boys by
scores, and found them neither ruddy nor plump,
but, like most other boys between twelve and twenty,
rather pale and slender.

The full-dress Eton costume is a ridiculous one.
It is a short jacket or roundabout, with a very broad
turn-over shirt collar, and a chimney-pot hat. The
combination is grotesque; and it is made more so
by the solemnity of most of the young chaps when
they have it on.

Hunger drove me and my young companion into
a restaurant, and I shall never forget the looks of a
little Eton prig who entered as we were sitting, and
took a place over against us. He kept on his preposterous hat, gave his order as if it were for his
own capital execution, and ate his cakes and drank
his chocolate as if that event were to take place at
the conclusion of his repast. My poor fellow was not

one tenth part so dignified, although he was, I am sure, a hundred times more agreeable. And when the time came for us to part, and I thanked him for his company, he stood up and made me a bow, and said, " I have had a very pleasant day, sir, and I hope you have." We went out and shook hands, and he turned toward the school, and I across the Thames toward Windsor. I should be glad to know that he was no longer snubbed, or worse, and that he was not plucked at his next examination.

I was soon in the train, and as we steamed away towards London, although it was only five o'clock in the afternoon, I saw the mist rising and lying in level bars across the trees some six or eight feet above the ground. It was so dense that it was plainly visible at a distance of not more than one hundred yards, — plain enough for me to make a memorandum sketch of it. But this seems to breed no malaria. The tertian ague of our forefathers has departed from England. Did it come over here with bacon and beans and some other English blessings in the Mayflower?

CHAPTER VIII.

WHILE I was in England I saw nothing of its factory life. I kept away from mills and mines and everything connected with them, — from all mills except grist-mills and saw-mills, finding very few of the latter. As to factories, I saw only " the black country " around Wolverhampton, as I passed through it ; and the sight tempted me to no closer acquaintance. It looked like the valley and shadow of death, " a wilderness, a land of deserts and pits, a land of drought, and of the shadow of death, a land that no man passeth through, and where no man dwelt." And like Christian in the midst of this valley, I perceived the mouth of hell to be there, and it stood hard by the wayside, and ever and anon the flame and smoke would come out in such abundance with sparks and hideous noises, and still the flames would be reaching toward me ; also I heard doleful voices and rushings to and fro ; and this frightful sight was seen and these dreadful noises were heard by me for several miles together. Poor Christian went through it on foot; I had the advantage of him in doing it by rail, which would have helped him much ; but then there would have been no story, and the world would have lost one of the most vivid and stirring descriptions of the terrible and of terror that exists in all literature.[1] Of the grievous blasphemies that the pilgrim, so hard bestead, had whispered into his ears, I heard nothing; but I fear that I supplied that deficiency myself, in my heart at least, at the sight of such dark desolation wrought upon earth and sky, in a country that else might have been bright with beauty and glad with meadows and trees and fields of corn.

It is impossible not to see that railways and mills and forges and towns are gradually, and not very slowly, destroying rural England. Railways, however, are not so barely hideous there as they are in the United States. All that can be done is done to soften and mitigate their harsh unloveliness. They are carried over the roads or under them; and this precaution against danger does much to preserve beauty and diminish unsightliness. The glimpses of country roads and village streets, undisturbed by the passing train, that are caught from the windows of railway carriages are charming in themselves, and are witnesses of the care that is taken there that those who wish " rapid transit " shall not have it at the cost of the property, the business, the safety, the comfort, or even the pleasure of the neighborhoods through which it suits their convenience or their interest to hasten. The maxim " Sic utere tuo ut alienum non lædas " (So use your own that you injure not that which is another's) seems to be a guiding one in the administration of British affairs — at home. Indeed, as compared with the United States, and with many other countries, England may be defined as the country in which every man has

---

[1] I need not tell the reader of *Pilgrim's Progress* that in the passage above I have borrowed Bunyan's phraseology.

rights which every other man is bound to respect.
The rights are not always the same rights, but they
may always be enforced even by the humblest and
poorest, and they are usually asserted and maintained. In England private independence and public spirit are constant forces, and both have at their
back the two great powers of the land, — the law
and public opinion. There are great lords and great
corporations in England; but neither lord nor corporation can do a wrong to the poorest laborer, much
less to a great body of people, with impunity, or
lawfully take a penny without restoring it. The
remedy lies at hand in the courts, which are incor-
ruptible; and it is always availed of. If any one
should by chance suppose that I have in mind the
elevated railways, existing and proposed in New
York, he is quite right in his supposition.

English railways are banked and sodded, and, if
need be, walled, so that as you travel over them it
does not seem as if the country had been rudely torn
in twain and left at ragged ends for your passage.
Even the stations are made sightly, and some of
them are very pleasant to the eye. Many of them
have little gardens on either side which are cultivated
by the station-master's family; and in not a few
places I observed that these gardens, containing vegetables and flowers and shrubs and even small trees,
extended many rods on both sides of the station-
house. Telegraph poles, such as those which traverse
our roads and stand thickly in our very streets, looking like posts and lines on which Brobdingnag wash-
erwomen might dry the petticoats of Glumdalclitch,
are unknown in England. All unsightly things are
kept out of sight as much as possible; all unpleasant

sounds are suppressed as much as possible. In the cities manufacturers are not allowed to fill the air four times a day with the shrieks of steam-whistles, simply because it is convenient for them to mark their hours of work by turning a steam-cock. They are not permitted to save themselves trouble and a little money by annoying all others who are within hearing. Indeed, as I have mentioned before, even the railway whistle is rarely heard, and when heard it is a very mild and inoffensive creature compared with that which shrieks and howls over the plains and through the towns of our favored land. For generations England has been a manufacturing country, and the manufacturing interest is now the most powerful influence in its affairs ; but there even manufacturers are obliged to respect the minor rights and little comforts of other people. It might be so with us if in our so-called " land of liberty " we had personal independence and public spirit. But we have neither ; and the peculiarity of our liberty seems to be that it is the liberty of every man, and especially the liberty of any combination of rich men, to get gain at the cost and by the annoyance of other people.

But no care or contrivance can make railways and steam-mills and forges other than an offense to all the senses, or cause them to harmonize with human surroundings. If we will have what they give us, we must yet accept them as necessary evils. Therefore it is that, there being so many of them in so small a country, they are destroying rural England. By means of the first, and chiefly because of the others, the great towns encroach upon the country. This is true of all the great towns, but it is especially true of London. London not only grows monstrously itself, but like some germs of corruption, it throws out prehensile feelers which draw other objects to it, to be changed into its own likeness, and made in fact part of itself. London town already in reality lies upon four counties, and spreads so rapidly, changing every place to London as it goes, that it seems as if in a not very remote future it must meet the off-shoots thrown out by other great towns, that it will absorb and assimilate them, and that England will become one great London, an island city of trade and manufacture and art, the political and commercial metropolis of a peerless empire, yet dependent for its food and its rural recreation upon other countries, which its imperial people will use as their grain fields and as their grazing and hunting grounds. "Moab is my wash-pot; over Edom will I cast out my shoe."

Enough of rural England, however, still remains to make it the most beautiful country in the world to those who love to see nature humanized, and her spontaneous beauties moulded by the hand of man and blended with his work. They who like rugged roads better than green meadows and cultivated slopes, or palms better than oaks and elms and beeches, or who like to live by rivers upon which fleets may sail, may seek their enjoyment of the beauties of nature in other climes. They to whom the blending of castle and cottage and spire with forest and field brings no enhancement of the beauty of unmitigated nature may find that beauty elsewhere, or have it " dry shod at home." But the lover of humanized nature may find it in England in a perfection which imagination can hardly surpass. If the climate of England tempts a man into the open air more than that of any other country, the beauty which rural England spreads before his eyes more than doubles the temptation. I expected much ; but although I am a man and did not come from Sheba, I was obliged to borrow the words of the woman who did, and say that the half had not been told me. When Wordsworth wrote —

> " One impulse from a vernal wood
> May teach you more of man,
> Of moral evil, and of good,
> Than all the sages can,"

it was an English landscape that he had in his mind's eye. No true brother of the angle, no contemplative man whom any pursuit or taste tempts into communion with nature, even in our raw, rude country, can fail to apprehend and feel, although he may not quite comprehend, what Wordsworth endeavored to express by his somewhat extravagant utterance ; but in England its truth comes home to him with tenfold strength.[1] Nature there is informed with humanity ; there the landscape, without being artificial, has been redeemed from savagery. And this has been done not with purpose, but simply by man's taking nature to himself, to love her and to cherish. It is remark-

[1] The mood of Wordsworth's mind which is expressed in the stanza quoted above is that which is most characteristic. It found its finest and subtlest as well as its sweetest utterance in *The Daffodils.* If I were asked to point out a passage in Wordsworth's writings which would in a few words illustrate the peculiar trait of his genius, although not its full strength and range, I should choose the last two lines but two of *The Daffodils ;* the beauty and significance of which, however, grow out of their immediate context : —

> " I gazed, and gazed, but little thought
> What wealth the show to me had brought :
> For oft, when on my couch I lie,
> In vacant or in pensive mood
> *They flash upon that inward eye*
> *Which is the bliss of solitude ;*
> And then my heart with pleasure fills,
> And dances with the daffodils."

able that a people so inferior in the arts of design should have been able so to treat nature that art may look to the result as a model, almost as a realized ideal. The beauty of English scenery is a set-off against many acres of painted canvas of which other peoples boast. Eye-full and soul-full with pleasure, I often thought it would be good if England could be preserved from further encroachment of towns and railways, and be kept beautiful for all the English peoples to go home to, and visit, and feel that they had the right of children in their father's house, although they had left it perforce for another.

In my country walks I was interested not only in the beauty of rural England, which in greater or less degree never failed to delight my eyes, but in the people; and indeed it was in my endeavors to observe them, and in my way to see places and buildings of note, that I found the beauty which I did not seek. I wished to know something by personal contact of the English country folk, the farmers and the peasants; and I was able to do so. I found them accessible, good-natured, and truly hospitable.

A fine afternoon tempted me to a long stroll in the country around Canterbury, and as the twilight came on I saw a little cottage in the midst of a great sprout-field. The approach to it from the road was by a narrow path. In this I found a poor man, a farm-laborer, standing by a plow which he was untackling, and by him stood his little child, ragged and barefooted. The man's face was sad, and his child was sad, too, and silent. He answered my greeting civilly, but so heavily and with such manifest reserve that I did not stop and speak with him, as was my custom. The incident was nothing, even to me, ex

cept that it seemed to show how little change had
been made in men of his condition by the lapse of
centuries. For it brought up at once to me that passage in "Piers Plowman's Creed," which even in my
boyhood, and before I had pondered the sorrowful
problem of life, had moved me to tears, in which the
writer tells of his meeting with the poor man who
hung upon the plow, whose hood was full of holes so
that his hair came out, and whose toes looked out of
his clouted shoes as he wallowed in the fen almost to
his ankle ; whose wife was with him using the goad,
barefooted on the bare ice that the blood followed ;
and their children were there : —

> " And al they songen o song
> That sorwe was to heren ;
> They crieden alle o cry,
> A careful note."

And this wretched man, when he sees Piers Plowman
weeping, stills his children, lets the plow stand, asks
him why he grieves, and says that if he lacks livelihood he shall share with him such good as God hath
sent : — " Go we, leeve brother."

Passing the poor man and his child, I went to the
cottage door, which proved not to be his. It was
half open, and at the sound of my step a woman appeared. She was homely of feature, but pleasant of
look, healthy seeming, and comfortably clad. She
bade me " Good-even," which I returned, and asked
if she could give me a glass of water, saying that I
had had a long walk, and that there was no ale-house
near. This I did because I had been told that the
peasants were very shy of the curious, and resented
sullenly the mere intrusion of their superiors. She
answered, cheerily, " 'Deed I can, sir, and I will.

But will ye walk in, sir, an' sit down. We 're just havin' supper." This was just what I wanted, and more than I had hoped for, and I said, Yes, if she would n't let me disturb them. " 'Deed an' ye won't, sir ; an' if ye 'd sit with us an' take a cup o' tea, ye 'd be kindly welcome." Then, turning to her husband, who sat munching his supper in stolid but not ill-natured silence, — the usual mood of the inferior man animal here when not under excitement, — she said, " Mate, the gentleman wants a glass of water ; step out and draw him some fresh." He obeyed in silence ; and while he was out she said, " We 've good water here, sir ; sweet an' soft, an' it comes cool from the well." The water when it came was worthy of her praise, and was one of but two draughts of sweet, soft water that I had in England. For there all over the country (as I found it) the water is hard ; it does not adapt itself to your thirsty throat ; and when you wash, the soap does not mix with it, but forms a patchy scum with eyes, that float about and look at you.

I accepted the invitation to sit with them at table, and was pleased, and, after what I had heard and read of the hard lot of the famished English farm-laborer, surprised at the comfort of their meal. The bread was good, better than that which is sold by most bakers in New York ; and they had butter (good also), and cheese, and tea which although not very good was still tea, and quite drinkable when concocted with milk and white sugar, both which they had of good quality. They had also a dish of cabbage and potatoes, of which I did not eat. As I took my cup of tea and ate my slice of bread and butter, I talked with them, and asked questions about their life. I say with them, but it was the woman who did all the talking, the man sitting silent, only uttering a few words or a simple "aye" when she appealed to him : "Mate, how is that?" or, "Mate, is n't that so?" I liked her use of "mate" instead of that unlovely word "husband."

The sum of my observation and information at this visit was as follows. The cottage was of three rooms, entered, after the first, in which we sat, one from the other. These rooms were about ten feet square, and the walls, which were of rough stone plastered, were about seven feet high. The rooms were ceiled, and the roof was thatched. For this cottage they paid half a crown (sixty-three cents) a week. The man earned twenty shillings a week, and the woman got washing and odd jobs to do. They were cheerful, and seemed to think themselves very comfortable. They complained of the odd sixpence in the rent (half a crown is two and sixpence), and thought that they ought to have the cottage for two shillings. If they could but do this and have a patch of ground for a vegetable garden, the woman said they "would be made ; " but of the latter there was no hope. To my surprise, I found wherever I went among the peasants this absolute lack of a square foot of ground on which to grow a radish. What is the cause of the universal, or at least the general, unwillingness to let these poor people have the use of a few yards of idle land beside their cottages I did not learn, and cannot conjecture. It cannot be the value of the land, for at least as much as they could use is thrown out of cultivation by the very presence of the cottage. I afterwards found that this cottage and the fare and fortune of its inmates were fairly representative of the housing and living of the peasants in such parts of England as I visited, but I was not in the western counties, where, I believe, the peasants fare most hardly. This couple had no children, as, in answer to me, the woman said, with a droop in her voice that showed that she had ceased to hope for one. Poor creature! if her natural longing had been satisfied, perhaps there would have been less comfort in her cottage and less cheerfulness in her face.

The landlord of the cottager is not, or is rarely, the squire or the lord of the manor. His landlord is the farmer; and my observation and inquiry led me to the opinion that the farmers as a class are disposed to be hard upon the farm-laborers. It is they who refuse them little garden allotments; it is they who exact for miserable hovels rents which are entirely out of proportion to their value, and to the rent of the ground on which they stand. It is the English farmer who is most strongly opposed to household suffrage in the rural districts. I do not mean to say that upon the latter point he is in error, or to express any opinion in regard to the subject; I merely remark upon it as a fact not unsignificant. In truth, the English farmer is an aristocrat. He is willing to take his place in a system of caste, and to look up, if he may also look down. He will touch his hat to the squire, and think it quite right that people should be respectful to their superiors; and he is confirmed in this opinion, or rather this feeling, when Hodge touches his hat to him. To give Hodge a vote would be to take away one of the marks of his inferior condition, and so to level him up, in every respect except money, to the position of his employer. With my limited opportunities for observation, it would not become me to pronounce upon the social and political feelings of whole classes in England; but I believe the farmers to be the most conservative body in the kingdom, the least disposed to change, and to be the main-stay of the tory party.

The English farmer must be a man of some money capital. It is not uncommon for him to have from one thousand to five thousand pounds (that is from five thousand to twenty-five thousand dollars), and some farmers are worth much more than that. As none of his money is invested in the land which he tills, he has it all for current expense, as an improvement fund, and as a reserve. This gives him the position and the importance of a capitalist, and brings him a certain consideration even from the great land-holders; but it does not make him independent, or, I should say, even aspiring, with extremely rare exceptions. If crops are good, if his wife and his sons and daughters are healthy and do his will, and if the squire is " haffable " when they meet, he is content; and who shall say that he does not wisely? So long as his rent is paid with fair punctuality and his family live decent lives, he may be sure of not being disturbed; and indeed he is not uncommonly living in the same house in which his father and his grandfather lived before him, and his plows are following theirs along the old furrows. And if he cannot pay his rent, his landlord, the son or the grandson of theirs, would be an exceptional English squire if he were not ready to do anything in reason to make it easy for him in the present, and to help him in the future. But however prosperous, he does not think of such a thing as setting up for a gentleman; nor does he seek to acquire the tastes or the habits of one, although he may be better able to afford them than many of those who have them by birth and breeding. The truth is, they would not suit him; to be obliged to live like a gentleman would be to him a daily affliction. He sometimes hunts a little ; but hunting is a rough, out-o'-doors amusement, which may be enjoyed to the full by the dullest and coarsest of human creatures, as well as by their superiors in intellect and refinement. But here the English farmer generally stops in his direct contact with the gentry and his imitation of them. He reads little, and thinks less. He has his place in the social scale, and with that he is content. His wife and daughters are often more ambitious.

English cottages and farm-houses are generally picturesque objects in a landscape, their forms and colors being almost always pleasing in themselves and harmonious with their surroundings. And within doors, the cottages, although they may be very rude and comfortless, have a character which is not to be found in houses of a corresponding or of a much higher class in the United States. These, square, sharp-edged, flat-roofed, built yesterday, directly on the road-side, of clapboards and shingles, and painted white or lead color, are very unsightly objects in themselves, and compared with English cottages of stone or brick, or beams and plaster, with their pitched roofs tiled or thatched, their softened outlines and rich color, are much inferior in beauty. But in real comfort and in healthiness I am inclined to think that our flimsy wooden houses are superior. For they are dry and warm. Their shingle roofs keep out the rain, which comes through thatch, or soaks and rots it, and their clapboard sides do not become reservoirs of cold dampness. Rheumatism is not so common among those who live in them as it is among the English rustic folk. In an English village, or along an English country road, you see more old men leaning upon sticks, or sunning themselves as they sit crooked over by their doors, than you do in the farming districts of New England and the Middle States.

Picturesque, too, as the English farm-house is at a distance, and picturesque as it often is within, — made so by old brown beams and red brick and mellow-tinted stone left in sight, and old tables and settles browned by the smoke and the use of generations, — when seen close by, it generally bears without, as it does within, the mark of the inferior condition and habits of its occupants. Sight and smell are offended by objects that are in unnecessary nearness; and there are no indications that the in habitants are anything more than tillers of the ground, and that when work is done they put it and its belongings out of sight and out of mind, and change their occupation with their clothes. The family live generally in the kitchen, although there is a parlor, or keeping room, which is used on high days and holidays, and sometimes on other days in the evening.

I have in mind one of the farm-houses in which I was, which might be taken as a type of its class. The occupant paid £150 a year for one hundred and eighty acres with a comfortable stone house. The kitchen, where I found the family, was paved with large red brick, which is the common flooring of farm-house kitchens. Damp as it must be, it is pre-

12

ferred. A landlord told me that he had offered to put down plank floors, but that the offer had been declined. It might be reasonably supposed that the women would gladly change the bricks for wood; but they have been accustomed to the bricks, and they cling to them. Certainly the advantage in appearance is largely on the side of the old flooring. I remember another farm-house kitchen in which I drank buttermilk, which with its unceiled beams, its old oaken window casings and settles, its gigantic chimney-piece of the same, its soft, sombre plaster, its red brick floor, and rows of red flower-pots standing behind the lattice in the deep window, presented one of the richest and most charming combinations of color that I ever saw. And it was a notably home-like-looking place, with individual traits and a physiognomy of its own, to which one might become attached; being in this respect far superior to the possibly more comfortable, but utterly blank and characterless rooms corresponding to it in our country.

In the other farm-house I was hospitably offered cider, for which the neighborhood had reputation, and was invited into the keeping room to drink it. Compared with Newark cider, or any of our cider of like grade, it was a dull, flavorless fluid; but the drinking it gave me an opportunity to chat and look about me. In the former way, however, I effected little. It was difficult to extract anything more than monosyllables from my entertainer. Indeed, I found the farmers the most taciturn class in England; and I may say that they were the only people that I met there who as a whole were silent and reserved. The peasantry I found very ready to talk, as I did also the higher classes; but the farmer sat mumchance. The cause of this of course I do not know; but it occurred to me that it might be his position. He knows little more than the peasant, and can talk but little better ; and yet he has a consciousness of superiority which makes him, in the presence of his betters, ashamed of his great mental inequality with them, and therefore he is silent. Certainly, the furnishing of this parlor showed the barest possible condition of mind in those for whom it was prepared. There was a heavy, clumsy old mahogany sideboard, evidently looked upon with great respect, upon which stood some old decanters and glasses, deeply cut and very ugly ; upon the walls were three or four colored prints of the cheapest kind, ugly also ; on the table was a large Bible and an almanac, or some book of the sort; and these, with the chairs, one of which was a rocker, completed the furnishing of the room, compared with which the kitchen was cheerful and attractive. The holder of such a farm as this in New England or the Middle States would have taken me into another sort of room, would have received me more on a footing of equality, and would have had more to say in reply to my inquiries. Whether he would have been so good a farmer I very much doubt ; whether he would have been a more respectable man, or even a happier, I shall not pretend to decide.

An English village is not at all like one in New England ; at least I saw none such, and I walked through scores of them, north, south, and east. Instead of the long, wide street, with its great elms and maples, on which are the churches and meeting-houses, the houses of the principal farmers, of the clergyman, the lawyer, and the physician, as well as

of the minor people, an English village shows a knot
of little brick, or stone, or antique beam and plaster
houses, very close together, and mostly without grass
or trees of any kind.   There is an ale-house, which
has for its sign and name the head or body of some
wild beast of impossible color, or the arms of the
nearest nobleman or gentleman, a shop or two, and
in the middle the town pump.   These villages generally belong bodily to the bearer of the arms aforesaid, and in some cases they are not more than half a
mile apart.   It impressed me strangely when a gentleman who was driving me through one of these said,
as we passed a group of houses, from one of which a
coat of arms hung out, " This is Lord —'s village."
" Then," I replied, " that one we drove through last
[it was about fifteen minutes before] was yours."
" Yes," he said, with a little smile at my question.
He had said nothing of it as we passed through.

One of the remarkable conditions of rural England is this nearness to each other of places regarded
as distinct.   I asked a little fellow in Essex if he
was born in the village in which we were.   " Oa
noa ! " he answered with surprise, almost with resentment.   " I were born in — " (I forget the name).
" And where is — ? "   " Yon," he said, pointing
to a nest of half a dozen little houses, about as far
off as the width of Boston Common.   Every place,
every clump of wood, every little knoll, every hollow, has a name by which it is known to the whole
neighborhood.   Even the shaws, which are hollows
filled with a growth of shrubs and dwarf trees, are
named, and have been named for centuries.

The smallest isolated village through which I
walked was Speke, in Lancashire.   Its utter insig-

nificance may be gathered from the fact that it contained no shop, and not even an ale-house. The absence of this customary place of refreshment (where you may be pretty sure of good beer and good bread and cheese, if not of a good chop) caused me, after I had walked out a few miles into the country around, to look about me for luncheon. Two pretty little cottages at the end of a short lane attracted my attention, and I resolved to try them. As I walked up the lane I passed three boys playing, whose names, oddly enough, were Tom, Dick, and Harry. After a few words, I proposed that each of them should accept a penny. The proposition was received in silence, but with a delight manifested by flushed cheeks and brightened eyes, and, when the pennies had been bestowed, by a mutual exhibition of them, accompanied by that twist of the head which means so much in a boy, and which is of no race or people; or if it be peculiar to Anglo-Saxons, then all boys of English blood may pity the French and German and other boys who have it not. The like sum, however, would have elicited no such signs of pleasure from "American" boys. But in England a penny is a possession to a child, of whatever rank. One day a little lady, some six or seven years old, who was sitting on my knee, while her younger sister sat with mamma, hard by, said to me with an amusing air of importance, "I had a penny yesterday," — the room in which she made this announcement was hung with antique tapestry that was given to one of her ancestors by a king, — "and I had it," she went on, "for reading." Whereupon her little ladyship opposite spoke up, saying, "And I had a penny, too; and ι had it for not reading," at which charming *non*

sequitur there was a merry peal of laughter from
mamma and me that greatly disconcerted the little
damsel. I thought at the time how much better this
restriction as to money was than that lavish use of it
to which "American" children are accustomed. A
young lady whom I knew well was at a famous school
on the continent of Europe, where she had not a few
titled school-mates. Certain exercises being required
which were mere manual drudgery, and a certain
orderly arrangement of the toilette table, *et cetera*,
my fair friend, being somewhat lazily disposed, was
able by her excess of pocket money over that of her
noble companions to have her exercise copied by a
princess, and her toilette table kept in order by a
countess. As to which I think that, looking forward, the discipline of the noble young ladies was
of better omen than that of the New-York merchant's daughter.

But I am long on my way to the cottages, where
indeed I found little of peculiar interest, not even the
thing of most interest to me just then, — luncheon.
The one which I entered seemed to have but two
rooms, but it may have had three. The room at the
door of which I found myself was, as usual, the
kitchen and living room. The walls were plastered;
the beams and the thatch showed; the floor was
paved with flat stones, which were much broken in
places, so as to show the ground beneath. This floor
must have "heaved," to use the word by which the
peasants express the striking up of the wet ground
and the dampness in these floors. Nearly opposite
the door was a large dresser, on which was a not
copious array of crockery. A fire-place, as large as
that in the kitchen of an old-fashioned New England
farm-house, stood out into the room.

Notwithstanding the condition which I have described, the aspect of the place was cheerful, much more cheerful than that of many " best parlors " in which I have been. Perhaps this cheerfulness was somewhat owing to the fact that it was a bright, genial day, and that a mellow light and a soft air entered the door with me: perhaps, also, to the fact that one of three women whom I found seated before the chimney (from habit, for there was no fire) was a handsome mother, who was suckling her child, which sweet sight, with charming freedom from shame, she did not hesitate to allow me to enjoy. But no small part of the attraction of the room was a flowering vine which climbed up the cottage wall and strayed in through the open lattice. And there, too, in this humble habitation, stood a row of pots with flowers, common flowers, the grandest of them a geranium ; but all were well cared for and nearly all were blooming.

Nothing struck me more forcibly as peculiar to the lower classes in England, or won me more in their favor, than their love of flowers. It is universal. Go where I would, in the abode of the poorest farm-laborer, through the back streets of little country towns, where the houses were hovels grimier and gloomier than any cottage I entered, I saw flowers. Sometimes it was a single flower that could have cost nothing, set in an old broken tea-pot or other shard of earthenware ; but it was there, and it was put in the window, and plainly was prized and tended. The beautiful feeling of which this is a manifestation seems to be almost lost to us. For it has absolutely nothing in common with that fashion of cutting flowers off by the head and making them up into huge artificial masses for decorative purposes at feasts and at funerals, which has prevailed among us for many years. That fashion, on the contrary, is actually at war with this feeling; for it destroys the very beauty which the flower-lover so much prizes; it does away with the character of the flower, which is only to be seen as it stands upon its stem and amid its leaves; and it deprives the flower nurse of her tender pleasure. This flower-loving and flower-tending, although of course it has no moral significance, no more than Robespierre's love of cats, seems to me a very charming trait in the character of English women.

After giving the woman with the child good-day, I asked her (for she plainly was at home) if she could give me some bread and milk, mentioning as my excuse that even if I walked back to the village it had no public-house. She replied pleasantly, " No offense, sir, but I 'm sorry I can't give you any milk; we 've no cow." Whereupon there was a consultation between her and the two old crones, who sat with their chins between their hands and their elbows on their knees. One cottage and another in the neighborhood was suggested, but in vain; not one had a cow. And this, by the way, I found very general. If the cottager has a pig he does well; the possession of a cow is a mark of somewhat high grade in agricultural society. At last the name of such an aristocrat was remembered, and I was told how to reach him or her. I had merely to go back through the lane, cross the road, and take the next by-road, and follow it about a mile.

On my way thither I passed a man doing work that we hear of sometimes, but never see, — breaking stones on the highway. He was an old man, and

he sat flat upon the road, with a heap of small square
stones between his legs, at which he pegged away
with a hammer having a small head and a long han
dle. I stopped and talked with him. He had on a
pair of wire goggles to protect his eyes from the
splinters of the stone. They stood well out from his
face, and as he lifted his head to answer my greeting
he had the look of a large, benevolent lobster set
upon end in the road-way. He was not stolid, but
talked intelligently, speaking very good English, and
seemed cheerful and contented. His wage was eighteen shillings a week ; and as he had now no one dependent upon him he was quite at his ease. That
at his age, he being certainly sixty-five years old, he
should sit all day upon a damp road-way and smite
small stones into smaller pieces he seemed to take as
the ordinary and inevitable course of things. I
learned from him that the wages paid in that neighborhood were, for plowing twenty shillings a week,
for harvesting twenty shillings, for digging and piece
work eighteen shillings. On my telling him that he
would get nineteen shillings that week, and proving
it to him, he was very grateful. I turned away and
resumed my walk and he his hammering.

I soon found the house to which I had been sent,
and the mistress was at home ; and a very comfortable body she was to have about a house, ample,
healthy, very cheerful, and, without being at all
pretty, not uncomely. I made a hungry man's request. Her reply was prompt and cheery. Indeed
I could have some bread and milk, and cheese too, if
I would walk in and sit. This I did at once, taking
a seat by a small table by the kitchen fire (for it was
the kitchen) ; and while she went off on her Eve's

business, just as if I had been an archangel, I looked
about me. All that I saw was very homely; but
comfort and plenty were manifest on every side,
with neatness and order. I got a glimpse of the living room through a half-open door, and it was much
more attractive than what I saw in the south of England. Indeed, the farm-houses and even the cottages
in Lancashire seemed to me better in every respect
than those in the southern and eastern shires.

My hostess soon returned, and set a pitcher of milk
(she would have called it a jug, and so would her
betters, but it was a pitcher), a loaf of bread, and a
big wedge of cheese before me, and bade me welcome. I fell to, and she turned to an ironing table
and began to sprinkle clothes that lay in a large
buck-basket. As I ate and she worked we chatted;
and I learned that her husband was a small farmer,
paying for twenty acres of land, this nice stone house,
with a stable and barn, twenty pounds a year, if I
remember aright. Her goodman was kind to her (I
saw plainly that she loved him); they were fore-
handed folk; and she was "as happy as the Queen,
God bless her majesty,"— with a little courtesy. I
slackened the working of my jaws, and stopped,
when she pressed me to my food, begging me to eat
the whole, for there was plenty more. But although
I had not eaten for six hours, and had walked many
miles, I was quite inadequate to what she proposed,
which gave me an astonishing notion of her goodman's performances at table. Hearty thanks and a
shilling at parting were pleasantly received as full
payment, and I went on my now aimless way.

I walked straight on into the country, by the rich
ness and the fine farming of which I was strongly

impressed. In the newly plowed fields the ground
turned up a dark, rich loam, and the furrows across
a twelve-acre field were drawn as straight as if they
had been ruled. I had observed this highly finished
plowing elsewhere in England. In some fields, for a
reason that I know not, there was an alternation of
four or five furrows with an unplowed green space
of about the same width all across the field. The
lines were drawn so accurately, and the sides of the
unplowed spaces were so exactly parallel, that the
effect was as if a gigantic piece of green music-paper
had been spread upon the earth. The farm-houses
and their out-buildings were substantial, comfortable,
and in good repair, and I passed some well-trimmed
hedges that were quite ten feet high. As I walked
I was conscious of a difference between this country
and that in the middle and southern shires from
which I had just come. At first I did not see to
what the different impression was owing; but all at
once it came upon me, — the land was level and there
were no trees. As far as I could see, all around me,
the land lay flat, or in very gentle undulation, and
there was scarcely a tree in sight. The only green
was that of the fields and the hedges; and the latter
were confined to the grounds just around the houses.
This absence of trees and scarcity of hedges deprived
the landscape of what we regard as its peculiarly
English traits. But the notion that the hedge is the
universal fence in England is erroneous. Even in
the south, where hedges are most common, post and
rail fences are even more common; for the hedge is
used chiefly on the road-line, and to mark the more
important divisions of property. Elsewhere, post
and rail fences and palings are frequently found.

The hedges that line the roads are generally not more than three feet and a half high, and are not thick, but grow so thin and hungrily that the light shines through them. In various parts of Essex I found miles of ugly board-fence, and palings along the sides of the roads, and houses built of clapboards. There were not so many trees nor such fine ones as I saw elsewhere; the sides of the roads were ragged, the hedges low and thin. Indeed, it would be difficult to find a difference between some parts of rural Essex and the neglected parts of the flat country in New England, New York, or New Jersey.

Near houses, especially in suburban places, brick walls are common; and I observed in these a fact which seemed significant. In most cases I saw that the walls in such places had been raised by an addition of some two or three feet. The upper courses of bricks were plainly discernible to be of a make different from that of the original wall, and the joint and the newer mortar could easily be detected. This seemed to show unmistakably an increase in the feeling of reserve, and perhaps in the necessity for it. The walls that would sufficiently exclude the public a hundred years and more ago were found insufficient, and some fifty years ago (for even the top courses were old and well set and mossy) the barriers were made higher, — high enough to be screens against all passing eyes.

Another change seemed to me to be witnessed by the fields all over the country. I observed not uncommonly trees standing in lines in fields or meadows, but chiefly in the latter. Seen from any point but one, their linear arrangement was hardly apparent, but with a little trouble they might be sighted

in line. Now such an arrangement of trees in an
open field is almost certain evidence that the line in
which they stand was once that of a fence of some
kind ; and these trees therefore bore witness to the
increase of the size of fields in England in late years,
— a natural accompaniment of an increase in the
size of farms and holdings generally. The Lancashire fields past which I now was walking were free
from these trees and from hedges. I cannot but believe that they had been removed for purposes of
agricultural thrift : for trees in fields and hedges between them are greedy devourers of the nourishment
that is needed for the crops. I found a plowman
sitting on a rail fence, but he could tell me nothing
about this, although he seemed to be a sensible fellow. "The land was as he had allus knowed it."
He gave me the same information as to wages that I
received from my old lobster friend, and like him
praised the soil without stint. I found all the Lancashire country folk proud of their land, and with
good reason.

My road soon became very lonely. I had not met
one human creature since I ate my luncheon; but
now not even a human habitation was in sight. The
road narrowed and wound about, following the course
of a sluggish little stream, which, with alders and
ragged bushes stooping over it was always at my
right hand, and began to be offensive to me. What
business had it there, stealing along in noiseless
shadow? It was neither beautiful nor useful, but a
mere ditch of running water. I began to hate it.
The sun was going down, darkened by heavy dun
clouds, casting a gloom upon the landscape. As I
walked on I thought, Why should not some of these
people that I have seen this afternoon, that plow-

man on the fence, for instance, murder me and throw
me into that hateful stream ? The few sovereigns
that I have with me and my watch would be ample
temptation; and if any one or two of them should do
it they would quite surely escape detection. For I
should not soon be missed. The friend whom I left
in Liverpool, even if I did not return within a day
or two, would merely suppose that I was off on some
traveler's expedition, and would await letters for a
week or perhaps a fortnight, may be, before making
any inquiry. And if inquiry were made, I might
possibly be traced to the farm-house where I took my
luncheon, but no farther ; for in all this distance of
some miles I had not seen man, woman, or child.
Such things are often done in England, and this is
just the time and place and occasion.

The ideas of time and place suddenly suggested to
me that to be back in Liverpool that evening I must
be at the railway station at a certain hour, and I was
miles away from it. I looked at my watch, and
found that at my best pace I had barely time to
make the distance. I turned, and set off at a swing
ing gait that I knew I could keep up for half a day.
As I walked, the gloom vanished from my soul ; my
quickened pace and my settled purpose almost
changed the face of nature to me, and made even
the sluggish stream not quite hateful. As I passed
the great field where I had left my murderous plowman on the fence, I saw him whistling behind his
plow, half a furrow's length off. At the farm-house,
my comely hostess looked out at the door and gave
me a smiling, cheery " Good-even, sir." Just as I
reached the station I heard the little chirp of the
steam-whistle on the coming train, and by nine
o'clock I was in Liverpool.

CHAPTER IX.

ENGLISH MEN.

ONE of the earliest records of modern history in regard to the race which peopled the Old England and the New refers to its beauty. Most of us have heard the story: how three young captives, brought from an almost unknown island on the verge of civilization, and indeed at the western limit of the then known world, were exposed for sale in Rome; and how Gregory the Great, not yet Pope, seeing them, was struck by their beauty, and asked what they were, and being told, *Angli* (English), replied, "*Non Angli, sed angeli*" (not Angles, but angels), — which was a tolerable pun for a future Pope and saint. This was twelve hundred years ago; and since that time the English race has enjoyed the reputation (subject to some carping criticism, due to the self-love of other peoples) of being the handsomest in the world. It is well deserved; indeed, if it were not, it would long ago have been jealously extinguished.

Not improbably, however, the impression made upon Gregory was greatly due to the fair complexion, blue eyes, and golden brown hair of the English captives, which, indeed, are mentioned in the story. For Southern Europe is peopled with dark-skinned, dark-haired races; and the superior beauty of the blonde type was recognized by the painters, who always, from the earliest days, represented angels as of that type. The Devil was painted black so much as a matter of course that his pictured appearance gave rise to a well-known proverb; ordinary mortals were represented as more or less dark; celestial people were white and golden-haired; whence the epithet "divinely fair." [1] When therefore the good Gregory saw the fair, blue-eyed English youths, his comparison was at once suggested, and his pun was almost made to his hand. And I am inclined to believe that it is of much later origin, although he ought to have made it; just as Sydney Smith ought to have said to Landseer, when he asked the Reverend wit to sit for his portrait, "Is thy servant a dog that he should do this thing?" and as the innkeeper ought to have said to Mr. Seward that not he was Governor of New York, but "Thurlow Weed, by thunder!" but did not. In each of these cases, however, and in all such, a significant fact is at the bottom of the story, which otherwise would have no reason for its being.

It is hardly true, however, that other races do not produce individuals approaching as nearly to an ideal standard of beauty as any that are seen among the English. These are found, as we all know, among the various Latin races, the Celts and the Sclaves, and even, as Mr. Julian Hawthorne himself would hardly venture to deny, among the Teutons, the very Saxons themselves. Who has not seen French women and French men, Italians, Spaniards, Russians, Poles, Irish, and even Germans of both sexes, dis-

---

[1] So Shakespeare in his 127th Sonnet: —

> " In the old time black was not counted fair,
> Or if it were, it bore not beauty's name;
> But now is black beauty's successive heir,
> And beauty slander'd with a bastard's shame "

tinguished by striking and captivating personal beauty both of face and figure? But the average beauty of the English race appears to be in a marked degree above that of all others. Among a thousand men and women of that race there will not only be found more "beauties" than among the same number of other races, but the majority will be handsomer, "finer," more symmetrically formed, better featured, with clearer skins, and a more dignified bearing and presence than the majority of any other European race with which they may be compared.

A notion prevailed for some time that this English distinction did not obtain in America, but that the race had degenerated here. It was a mere notion, having its origin in a prejudiced perversion of isolated facts; in the desire of book-writing travelers to find something strange, and also derogatory, with which to spice their pages; and in a craving, which amounts to a mild insanity, among European people, and particularly among all classes of the British nation, to lay hold of some distinctive "American" quality, whether physiological, literary, political, or other, and label it, and file it away, and pigeon-hole it for reference by way of differencing "Americans" from themselves.

The notion, I venture to say, was essentially absurd. That a race of men should materially change its physical traits in the course of two centuries, under whatever conditions of climate or other external influence, is inconsistent with all that we know upon this subject. The very temples of Egypt protest against it by their pictured records. According to the history of mankind, as it is thus far known to us, such a change could not take place within such a

13

period, unless to external influences of great modifying power there were added such an intermingling of races as has not yet taken place here more than in England itself, although plainly it is to come in future generations. Down to twenty or thirty years ago the intermarriage of Yankees — by which name, for lack of another, I designate people of English blood born in this country — with Irish and Germans was so rare as practically, in regard to this question, not to exist; and at that period there was not in England itself a more purely English people than that of New England.

What Horace found to be true of the effect of a migration across the Adriatic, or the Ægean, or the Mediterranean, is equally true of one across the vast, storm-vexed Atlantic. Englishmen remain English, Frenchmen French, Germans German, and Irishmen Irish, even unto the third and the fourth generation. It is not lightly that I say this; not without long and careful consideration of the subject; not without knowledge of opinions received, too readily, to the contrary. That emigrants to this country or to any other find, in many cases, that a change in climate and in habits of life produces such temporary and superficial changes in habit of body as may attract the attention, if not require the aid, of a physician may be true enough. This is not to the point in question. Let those of my Yankee readers who are really observant upon such subjects consider their acquaintances of French, of Highland Scotch, or of Dutch descent, or those of Irish and German descent, if they have any, and see whether to this day they do not show, both mentally and bodily, the distinctive traits of race, even if their blood has been under the influence of American skies for eight generations, — whether at this day there is in them any greater modification of race characteristics than might be reasonably expected if each one of these persons had been brought to this country in his early youth.

The notion of English degeneracy in "America" has, however, been rapidly dying out in Europe, and even in England during the last ten or fifteen years. The change has been brought about partly by the events of our civil war. For the blindest prejudice saw that that war was not fought by a physically degenerate people, and partly by the increase of knowledge obtained, not from carping travelers writing books to please a carping public, but from personal observation. This I know, not by inference, but from Englishmen and others who have been here, and who have not written books. The belief, formerly prevalent, that "American" women had in their youth pretty doll faces, but at no period of life womanly beauty of figure, is passing away before a knowledge of the truth; and I have heard it scouted here by Englishmen, who, pointing to the charming evidence to the contrary before their eyes, have expressed surprise that the traveling book-writers, who had given them their previous notions on the subject, could have so misrepresented the truth. A colonel in the British army, who had been all over the world, and with whom I was in New England during the war, at a time when a large number of our volunteers were home on furlough, expressed constantly his surprise at the "fine men" he saw going about in uniform, the equals of whom he said that he had never seen as a whole in any army; although he did not hesitate to express his dislike of their uniform, or his disgust at the slouching, slovenly way in which they carried themselves. I was ready to believe what he said ; for I had then just seen the Coldstreams in Montreal ; and I had before seen the Spanish regular troops in Cuba, who, even the regiment of the Queen, were so small that they looked to me like toy soldiers to be kept in a box.

After I had been in London a week or two, having previously visited other places, a London friend, who had twice visited "the States," said to me, " Well, I suppose you 've been looking at the people here and comparing them with those you 've left at home ? " " Yes, of course." " Do you find much difference in them really ? " " No; very little ; almost none." " You 're right, — quite right. There may be a little more fullness of figure and a little more ruddiness ; but it 's been greatly exaggerated, — greatly." One reason for this exaggeration I learned from the remarks of two English friends to me in this country. Some years ago I took one, a gentleman who had traveled a good deal, and who held an important position in the Queen's household, — and a very outspoken man he was, — to a " private view," at which, for a wonder, there was not a miscellaneous throng, but just enough people to fill the rooms pleasantly. As we sat together after a tour of the room, looking at the company, I asked him to tell me the difference between the people he saw there and those he would see on a like occasion at the Royal Academy. He sat looking around him in silence for so long a time that I thought he was going to pass my question unnoticed, when he said, " I can see no difference; none at all, except that there would not be quite so many pretty women there, and that there

would be more stout old men and women." The
other, a lady, of like social position and opportunities
of observation, who also did not hesitate in her criticisms, remarked that the chief difference in appearance between people of the same condition here and
in England was that here she " did n't see any fat old
men." *She* said nothing about fat old women ; not,
however, that she herself was either fat or old.

There is this difference among old people, although even this has been exaggerated ; and it is this
which gives a certain color of truth to the notion I
have referred to. English men and women do not
always grow stout and red-faced as they grow old ;
but after they have passed middle age more of them
do tend to rubicundity and to protuberant rotundity
of figure than people of the same age do in " America." The cause, I am quite sure, is simply — beer.
Both the color and the rotundity come to a large proportion of the " Americans " who live in England and
drink English beer, in English allowance ; which, it
need hardly be said, could not be the case if there
had been any essential change in the type of the race.
But among men under forty and women under thirty,
the difference either in complexion or figure is almost
inappreciable.

As to the women, there are at least as many in
England who are spare and angular of figure as here,
and of those who have not passed thirty I think
rather more. The London " Spectator " said some
years ago, in discussing the Banting diet, I believe,
that " scragginess was more common in England
among women than stoutness · " and it is remarkable
that the French caricatures of English women always
represent them as thin, bony, and sharp-featured.

In this of course there is a little malice; but it shows the impression left upon the French people by their near neighbors. I cannot do better here than to offer my readers, in the following passage, a share in one of my letters written home; it has at least the advantage of recording on the spot impressions received by me after careful examination under the most favorable circumstances. I was writing about the beauty of the parks: —

"It is amazing to see the great space of this little island that these English folk have reserved for air and health and beauty; and it is for all, — the poorest and meanest, as well as the richest and noblest; there are no privileged classes in this. As to the effect upon their health, I suppose it must be something, but it shows for very little. G—— [a gentleman who is very strong upon the subject of degeneracy, which I have always doubted] will laugh, and say that it was a foregone conclusion with me; but to set aside my inference he will be obliged to take the position that there is nothing so misleading as facts, except figures. I have now seen many hundreds of thousands of English men and English women of all classes. I have placed myself in positions to examine them closely. At the great Birmingham musical festival my seat gave me full view of the house, chorus and all. The vast hall was filled with people of the middle and upper-middle classes, and at one end with members of the highest aristocracy, who occupied seats roped off from the rest, and called 'the President's 'eats;' — the President being the Marquis of Hertford. At the end of the performance, both evening and morning, I hastened to a place where a great part of the audience would pass out close before me. At Westminster Abbey I stood again and again at the principal door and watched the congregation as they came out; I have done the same in swarming railway stations; I have walked through country villages and cathedral towns; I know the human physiognomy of all quarters of London pretty well; I have seen the Guards and the Heavy Dragoons; and I say without any hesitation that thus far I find that the men and the women are generally smaller and less robust than ours, and above all that the women are mostly sparer in figure and less blooming than ours. The men are ruddier, on the whole; that is, there are more very ruddy men here; but the number of men without color in their cheeks seems to be nearly the same as with us. The apparent inconsistency of what I have said is due to the fact that the ruddy men and women here are generally so very red that they produce a great impression of redness, an impression that lasts and remains salient in the memory. A delicately graduated and healthy bloom is not very common. But the little London 'gent,' with whom Leech has made us so familiar, you meet everywhere in the great city. Sunday before last, loitering in the cloisters of Westminster, I stopped to look at a tablet in the wall. There were three of these men before me, and the number soon increased to seven. I looked over *the hats* — round felt hats — of the whole seven without raising my chin. I remember that, like Rosalind, I am 'more than common tall,' but I never did anything like that at home. At the Horse Guards they put their finest men as mounted sentinels on each side of the gate. Well, they are fine fellows, and would be very uncomfortable chaps to meet, except in a friendly way. A detachment of them riding up St. James's Street, the other morning, with their cuirasses like mirrors, and the coats of their big black horses almost as bright, was a spectacle which it seemed to me could not be surpassed for its union of military splendor and the promise of bitter business in a fight; but Maine, or Vermont, or Connecticut, or Kentucky can turn out whole regiments of bigger and stronger men. Colonel M——, whom I met in Canada, said the same to me when he thought he was talking to an Englishman. I wonder that he ever forgave me the things he said to me during his brief self-deception; for they were true. But he was a good fellow, and bore no malice. Nevertheless, you sometimes meet here a very fine man, or a big, blooming beauty, and in either case the impression is stronger and more memorable than in a like case it is apt to be with us; chiefly, I think, because of their dress and ' set up,' which in such cases — as in that of the Guards and Dragoons — is apt to be very pronounced."

I will add here, in passing, that this English " set up," particularly in the case of almost all Englishmen of any pretensions, is distinctive, and is in a great measure the cause of the impression of superior good looks and strength on their side. It appears in a marked degree in all military persons, rank and file as well as officers, and in the police force, the men of which are on the whole inferior in stature and bulk to ours, — leaving the big Broadway squad (most of them Yankees) out of the question, — and yet it is far superior in appearance to ours, owing to the " set up " of the men, and the way in which they carry themselves. I observed that, although the upper classes contained a fair proportion, although no notable excess, of large and well-formed men and women, the burly men and the big-bodied, large-limbed women were generally of the lower and the lower-middle class.[1] The peasantry are mostly spare in figure and short in stature. This made me wonder where all the pretty house-maids and shop-girls came from; for, as I have said before, the prettiest faces,

[1] The photographic portraits of Sir Walter and Lady Trevelyan, in *Selections from the Literary and Artistic Remains* of the latter, show types of the Englishman and Englishwoman which are so common in the upper classes and in the lowest as to be almost characteristic. I may thus refer to these portraits without offense, I hope, as they were made public by one of the originals, of whom neither is now living.

the most delicately blooming complexions, and the finest figures that I saw in England were among them. In a letter written from the Rose Inn at Canterbury, a cosy, comfortable old hostelry, I find the following passage, which is to the purpose : —

"I ate my bacon and eggs this morning in the coffee-room, where, at another table, were three queer English-women, yet nice looking, — apparently a mother and two daughters. The elder daughter was, I will not say a lathy girl, but very slim, not only in the waist, but above and below it. The mother and the younger were plump and rosy, absurdly alike, and with that cocked-up nose which is one of the very few distinctive peculiarities of feature that you see here, — but even this is not common ; and their black hair was curled in tight curls all over their heads. I was struck by this, because curling hair is comparatively rare here, and I had expected to find it common. Theirs was cut just like a man's, and plainly so because, if it were allowed to grow long, it would have been impossible to dress it in woman fashion. They were very jolly and pleasant, chaffing each other in low, soft voices, and breaking out in rich, sweet laughter. They looked like boys masquerading in women's clothes ; for the eldest was quite young looking, and may have been an elder sister. The youngest, who was some seventeen or eighteen years old, looked very fair and blooming across the room ; but when I came close to her, which I had an opportunity of doing, I found that her color, both white and red, was coarse, which is very often the case here when there is color. In the mother, or eldest sister, this coarseness was apparent even at a distance. But see : — Lady —— and her daughters, although pretty and elegant, had no tinge of color in their cheeks, and they were all as thin as rails ; and the girls' hair, as well as their mother's, was as straight as fiddle-strings. I came here expecting to see golden curls in plentiful crops, or at least not uncommonly. But it seems to me that I have n't seen

a dozen curly-haired children since I have been in the country ; and I have seen them — the children — by tens of
thousands, and examined them closely, making memorandums of my observation. Nor have the ladies of this family (I am now at ——) any more bloom than this paper,
and they are both as thin as Lady —— and her daughters ; Mrs. —— painfully so. The men, belonging of
course to another family, are stout, well-built fellows
enough, but the other two guests are as lean as greyhounds.
I went to a little dinner party the other evening, and the
carriage sent to the station for me (for they think nothing
here of asking you fifteen or twenty miles to dinner, even
when you are not expected to stay over night) took also a
Major-General Sir —— ——. I was told that he would
join me, and I expected to see a portly, ruddy man of
inches, with sweeping whiskers and mustache. I found a
short, slender, meek-looking, pale-faced man ; but his bearing was very military ; he was a charming companion and
the pink of courtesy. We entered the drawing-room together, of course ; but, notwithstanding his rank, he waved
me in before him, and my plain Mistership was announced
before his titles. I have seen no men here at all equal in
face or figure to General Hooker, General Hancock, General Augur, or General Terry, to say nothing of General
Scott, who was something out of the common even with us.
And Burnside and McDowell and Grant and McClellan
are all stouter men than you are apt to find here. The
biggest men that I have seen were from the north, Yorkshire and Northumberland. Those of the south, particularly in Kent, are the shortest ; although, as a Kent man
said to me, they are generally ' stocky.' " [1]

[1] Mr. Jennings, formerly the resident New York correspondent of the
London *Times*, late editor of the New York *Times*, now London correspondent of the *World*, in a recent letter describing the opening of Parliament by the Queen in person, on which occasion the House of Lords
was filled with peers and peeresses, writes thus with regard to the beauty
of the women and the presence and figures of the men : —

" On this occasion the ladies overflowed the House. Early as it still

A New England man now living in England, who
made his house very delightful to me, first by the
presence of himself and his family, and next by the
kindest and most considerate hospitality, is an ever-
present rebuke of the stoutest sort to the British
notion of the physical degeneracy of the English race
in "America." He, a Yankee of the old Puritan
emigration, is five feet ten and a half inches high, is
forty-eight inches, four good feet, in girth around the
chest, weighs two hundred pounds, and yet has not
the least appearance even of stoutness, — rather the
contrary. He is the only man I ever met whose
friendly grip was rather more than I liked to bear.
I spoke to his wife about his strength and his figure,
and she told me that when he went to get his life in-
sured here the surgeons said that they very rarely saw

was, the floor was covered with them; large blocks of the benches were
occupied, and the galleries were crowded. All these ladies were in evening toilets, the peeresses wearing coronets of diamonds, — most of them
being fairly ablaze with diamonds on head and neck. If the daylight was
not very favorable to the shoulders or complexions of some of these noble
dames, the gorgeousness of their costumes and the glitter of their precious
stones served to divert attention from the defects of nature or the ravages
of time. . . . . Not many of these ladies in the House were very pretty,
although here and there was a face such as makes one stop short and
hold one's breath, and wonder at the divine perfection of nature's handiwork when she is at her best. . . . . As for the old bald-headed gentlemen,
some of them very short and stumpy, they looked painfully like a collection of 'senators' in some opera bouffe. One of them in particular,
with four ermine bars on his cloak, denoting his high rank, was exactly
like the funny-looking dummy Englishman which the French delight to
exhibit in their farces. He had very little hair left to boast of, and that
little was very red; and his face was round and red also; and he was altogether so comic a little man that one could not look at him without a
smile. I could not find out who he was till the royal procession entered,
when he suddenly reappeared in great pomp and state. . . . . So much for
appearances."

Mr. Jennings, it should be remembered, is an Englishman, but he lived
eight or ten years in New York; and I may be pardoned for saying that
he carried away a constant reminder of "American" beauty, and a standard of comparison which would be likely to make him fastidious.

such a powerful, finely formed, and perfectly healthy man as he is, and never any finer or healthier. That would be impossible. And as he is so was his father. Were they exceptions? Only of a sort that constantly occur among real Yankees, — "Americans" whose families have been in the country for generations, and who are the only proper examples of the influence of the climate and the social conditions of the country.

I have, perhaps, said too much upon this subject of the comparative physical condition of the race in the two countries ; but I have been led to do so because of the very great inconsistency I found between the facts and the common notion as to stout English men and lean "Americans," blooming, buxom English women and pale, slender "American" women, — a notion which one writer has repeated, parrot-like, after the other, until even we ourselves have accepted it without question. Like many other notions which no one disputes, it is false. But the world has gone on accepting it and assuming it to be true, until it has so taken possession of the general mind that if in a room full of English people only one man were found ruddy and burly, and only one woman blooming and well rounded (and this, or something very like it, I have seen more than once), they would be picked out and spoken of as English-looking, to the disregard of all the others. The exceptions would be taken as examples of the rule ; and this by the English themselves ; so swayed are we all by tradition and authority, even in such an every-day matter. Nay, even I myself, skeptical and carping, was thus misled.

The steamer in which I went over was filled chiefly

with English people. Two of my fellow-passengers
I selected in my mind as notably and typically English, not only in person, but in bearing. They
proved to be, one a Massachusetts Yankee and the
other a Western man ; but both had from association
contracted English habits of dress and of manner.
Two Englishwomen, however, attracted my particular attention. One was, I think, the very largest
human female I ever saw outside of a " show." She
was a fearful manifestation of the enormous development of solid flesh which the British fair sometimes
attain. As she stood by her husband she was the
taller from the ear upward. She must have weighed
about twenty stone. I think that a plumb line
dropped from the front of her corsage would have
reached the deck without touching her ample skirts.
Her tread was hippopotamic. And yet she showed
traces of beauty, and not improbably had been a fine,
fair girl ; and even at the present time she managed
to effect a very palpable waist. I mused wonder-
ingly upon the process by which she did this ; but
still more upon that sad gradual enormification by
which she passed from a tall blooming beauty into
her present tremendous proportions. The other was
exactly the reverse. She could hardly be called ill-
looking in the face ; but her pale, blank, unfeatured
countenance reminded one instantly of a sheep. She
was a washed-out and, although young, a faded creature, with no more shape than my forefinger. And
yet she was a perfect English type, and so like some
of John Leech's women that I could not look at her
without internal laughter.[1] Her husband — for even

[1] Mr. Du Maurier, characterist rather than caricaturist, gives this sheep
face to his typical Duchess of Stilton, and to her two daughters. See
Punch for February 26, 1881.

such women by some mysterious process known to themselves will get husbands — was like unto her in face, in feature, and in expression; and yet he was so strikingly, so aggressively British in look and in manner that I heard some Yankees on board say that they would like to kick him. At first I somewhat shared their prejudice, of which, before we landed I learned to be ashamed; for I found him a very intelligent, well-informed, pleasant man, reserved in his manners, and although firm in his opinions, which were strongly British, very respectful of other men's, and very careful of giving offense. His union of firmness and courtesy seemed to me worthy of admiration; and if he did wish to kick any of the Yankees on board, for which in one or two cases I could have forgiven him, I am sure that he never let the desire manifest itself in their presence.

Another prevalent notion, which is reciprocal between the people of the two countries, is mistaken, according to my observation. It is generally believed, or at least very often said, in "America" that the men in England are very much handsomer than the women; and, conversely, it is commonly believed in England, or said, that the women in "America" are handsomer than the men. An absurd and truly preposterous notion, as will be seen upon a moment's reflection. For the women in both countries are the mothers of both the men and the women; and the men are the fathers of both the men and the women; and as some of the women are of their fathers' types and some of the men of their mothers', the imputed difference of the two in personal beauty could not be brought about. It is physiologically impossible that the women of a race should be handsomer than the men, and *vice versa*.

It is nevertheless true that the men in England are on the whole more attractive to the eye than the women, and that the women in " America " are generally much more attractive than the men. The cause of this is a fact very distinctive of the social surface of the two countries. I have spoken of the " set up " and the bearing of the men in England. It is very remarkable, and is far superior to anything of the kind that is found even among the most cultivated people in this country, except in comparatively rare individual cases. But in England it is common ; it is the rule. There, from the middle classes up, a slovenly man is a rare exception. There men are almost universally neat and tidy, and they carry themselves with a conscious self-respect. They do not slouch. They do not go about, even in the morning, with coats unbuttoned, skirts flying, and their hands in their overcoat pockets. They dress soberly, quietly, with manly simplicity, but almost always in good taste, and with notable neatness. They are manly-looking men, with an air of conscious manhood. Moreover, in England the man is still recognized as the superior. England has been called the purgatory of horses and the paradise of women. But that saying came from the continent of Europe, where women, except in the very highest and most cultivated classes, are not treated with that tenderness and consideration for their weakness and their womanly functions which I am inclined to think is somewhat peculiar to the English race.

I should call England the paradise of men, for there the world is made for them ; and women are happy in making it so. An Englishman who is the head of a family is not only master of his house, but of the whole household. His will is recognized as the law of that household. No one thinks of disputing it. It is not deemed unreasonable that in the house which he provides and keeps up, his comfort and his convenience should be first considered, or that, as he is responsible for his household both to the law and to society, authority should go with responsibility. And yet — perhaps for this very reason — wives there have the household affairs more absolutely in their hands than they have here. A man whose absolute authority is acknowledged, practically as well as theoretically, is very ready to make concessions and to lay aside what at any time he may assume. Real monarchs, like the Czars or like the Tudors, are careless of the protection of royal etiquette. The consciousness of this acknowledged, or rather unquestioned, superiority shows itself in the men's faces, and in their bearing, simple and unpretending as their manner is.

Besides all this, men in England (I am leaving out of consideration the lower classes) show the effect of cultivation, of breeding, of discipline. Even in the middle classes they are well informed, and, what is of more importance to the present question, they have been taught to behave themselves respectfully to others. They do so behave; they feel that they ought to do so, and that they must. There are two gods worshiped in England, and one is propriety; and a very good god he is, when he is not made a Juggernaut. The result of all this is, a man not much unlike in reality, but very different in appearance from him who generally pervades "America."

The latter may be, and generally is, as handsome physically as the former; he may be, and generally is, as good morally: but the one generally shows for all that he is, and perhaps for more, while the other does not, and frequently does for less. And yet again: — among such men in England as those whom I have described another sort, who, for example, say "had n't oughter" and "have came," and who spit upon the floor, are not generally found mingling. They are kept in social pens by themselves. And thus in judging of English society they are left out.

14

CHAPTER X.

ENGLISH WOMEN.

A LADY whom I had the honor and the pleasure of taking in to dinner at a country house near London, and whom I had soon found to be one of those simple-minded, good-natured, truth-telling women who are notably common in England, spoke to me about some ladies who on a previous day had attracted her attention, adding, " I knew they were Americans." " How?" I asked. " Oh, we always know American women!" " But how, pray?" She thought a moment, and answered, " By their beauty, — they are almost always pretty, if not more, — by their fine complexions, and by their exquisite dress." I did not tell her that I thought her discrimination just; but that it was so I had by that time become convinced. And yet I should say that the most beautiful women I have ever seen were Englishwomen, were it not for the memory of an Irishwoman, a Frenchwoman, a German, and a Czech. But the latter were exceptional. Beauty is very much commoner among women of the English race than among those of any other with which I am acquainted; and among that race it is commoner in " America " than in England. I saw more beauty of face and figure at the first two receptions which I attended after my return than I had found among the hundreds of thousands of women whom I had seen in England.

The types are the same in both countries; but they seem to come near to perfection oftener here than there. Beauty of feature, however, although rarer, is sometimes found more clearly defined in England. The mouth in particular, when it is beautiful, is more statuesque. The curves are more decided, and at the junction of the red of the lips with the white there is a delicately raised outline which marks the form of the feature in a very noble way. This may also be said of the nostril. It gives a chiseled effect to those features which is not so often found in "America;" but the nose itself, the brow, and the set and carriage of the head are generally finer among "Americans." In both countries, however, the head is apt to be too large for perfect proportion. This is a characteristic defect of the English type of beauty. Its effect is seen in Stothard's figures, in Etty's, and in those of other English painters. Another defect is in the heaviness of the articulations. Plump arms are not uncommon, but really fine arms are rare; and fine wrists are still rarer. Such wrists as the Viennoise women have — of which I saw a wonderful example in the Viennoise wife of a Sussex gentleman — are almost unknown among women of English race in either country. It is often said, even in England, that the feet of "American" women are more beautiful than those of Englishwomen. This I am inclined to doubt. The feet may be smaller here; and they generally look smaller because Englishwomen wear larger and heavier shoes. They are obliged to do so because they walk more, and because of their moister climate. But mere smallness is not beauty either in the feet or in any other part of the body. Beauty is the result of shape, proportion, and color; and feet are often cramped out of shape and out of proportion in other countries than China. To be beautiful the foot should seem the fit support for the body, in rest or in motion. It is said by some persons, who by saying it profess to know, that nature, prodigal of charms to Englishwomen in bust, shoulders, and arms, is chary of them elsewhere, and that their beauty of figure is apt to stop at the waist. Upon this point I do not venture to give an opinion; but I am inclined to doubt the judgment in question upon general physiological principles. The human figure is the development of a germ; and it is not natural that, whatever may be the case with individuals, the type of a whole race in one country should present this inconsistency. Possibly those who started this notion were unfortunate in their occasions of observation and comparison.

There is more beauty in the south of England than in the north. When I left Birmingham on my way southward, although in addition to my observation northward I had there the opportunity of seeing the great throngs, chiefly of women, called together by the triennial musical festival, my eyes had begun to long for the sight of beauty. The women were not all homely; but they were mostly hard-featured, without bloom, and whether thick or thin, ungainly. I found a great improvement in this respect in the lower counties; and in London of course more than elsewhere. For it is remarkable that, according to some law which has never yet been formulated, or from some cause quite undiscovered, perhaps undiscoverable, beautiful women are always found in the greatest numbers where there are the most men and the most money.

Much has been said about the complexion of the women of England, which has been greatly praised. I did not find it exceptionally beautiful. It is often fresh, oftener ruddy, but still oftener coarse. A delicate, finely-graduated bloom is not common; and the white is still oftener not like that of a lily, or, better, of a white rose, but of some much coarser object in nature. Pale, sallow women are quite as common as they are in any of the United States with which I am acquainted. It is true that in making these odious comparisons I cannot forget certain women, too common in "America," who seem to be composed in equal parts of mind and leather, the elements of body and soul being left out so far as is consistent with existence in human form. But such women are also to be found in England, although perhaps in fewer numbers than here.[1]

As to dress, that, as a man, I must regard as a purely adventitious and an essentially unimportant matter. If a woman be beautiful, or charming without positive beauty, a man cares very little in what she is dressed, if she but seems at ease in her apparel, and its color is becoming and harmonious. Moreover, there is no greater mistake than the assumption that being dressed in good taste is indicative of good breeding, of education, or of social ad

[1] I find, in the not very justifiable description given in a New York newspaper of a distinguished English family resident in an "American" town, the following paragraph, from which I omit the name: —

"The young daughters of the —— family are described as tall and slender, with sweet but rather plain faces, and complexions of that sallow paleness supposed to be unknown to consumers of the roast beef and plum pudding of England. They dress with the greatest plainness, their abundant light hair braided and tied with ribbons, their dresses rather short and free from unnatural expansion, and their shoes, which are not at all diminutive, have soles thicker than any American shoemaker would care to make."

vantage of any kind. Nor is it even a sign of good taste in any other particular. You shall see a woman who has come out of the slums, and whose life is worthy of her origin and her breeding, and she shall dress herself daily, morning, noon, and night, with such an exquisite sense of fitness in all things, with such an instinctive appreciation of harmony of outline and color, that your eye will be soothed with the sight of her garments ; and she shall nevertheless be vulgar in mind and manners, sordid in soul, in her life equally gross and frivolous. And the converse is no less true. Women most happy in the circumstances of their birth and breeding, intelligent, cultivated, charming, of whose sympathy in regard to anything good or beautiful you may be sure, will dress themselves in such an incongruous, heterogeneous fashion that the beauty which they often possess triumphs with difficulty over their effort to adorn it.

I feel, therefore, that I am saying very little in dispraise of Englishwomen when I say that in general they are the worst dressed human creatures that I ever saw, except, perhaps, the female half of a certain class of Germans. The reputation that they have in this respect among Frenchwomen and " Americans " is richly deserved. Good taste is simply absent. The notion of fitness, congruity, and " concatenation accordingly " does not exist. In form the Englishwoman's dress is too often dowdy, in color frightful. If not color-blind, she seems generally to be blind to the effect of color, either singly or in combination. At a morning concert I saw a lady in a rich red-purple (plum color) silk, — high around the neck, of course, — and over this swept a necklace of enormous coral beads ! It made one's eyes ache to look at her. This was not an uncommon, but a characteristic instance. Such combinations may be justly regarded as the rule in Englishwomen's dress. For purple they have strong liking. They not only wear it in gowns, but they use it for trimming, in bands and flounces, in ribbons, in feathers. They combine it with all other colors. An Englishwoman seems to think herself " made " if she can deck herself in some way with purple silk or velvet, or ribbons or feathers. Of course I am excepting from these remarks a few who have intuitive good taste, and other few who employ French *modistes*, and who submit without question to their authority. The latter condition is essential ; for even when the main body of an Englishwoman's dress is in good taste, she is very apt to destroy its effect by some incongruous addition from her stores of heterogeneous jewels, or by some other ornament, — a collar, a cape, a *fichu*, or a ribbon. They have a sad way of putting forlorn things about their necks and on their heads which is very depressing, unless it is astonishing, which sometimes happens. An Englishwoman will be tolerably well dressed, and then will make a bundle of herself by tying up her neck and shoulders in a huge piece of lace ; or she will wear specimens of two or three sets of jewels ; or she will put a colored feather in her hair, or a bonnet on her head, that would tempt a tyrant to bring it to the block. I remember seeing a peeress whose family was noble in the Middle Ages riding with an " American." lady who had not as much to spend in a year as the other had in a week ; but the former was so obtrusively ill dressed and the latter with such good taste and simplicity that, both being unusually intelligent, both perfectly well bred and self-possessed, and both fine healthy women, a person ignorant of their rank would have been likely to mistake the latter for the noblewoman.

It has been said that Englishwomen dress better in full evening dress than in what is known as *demi-toilette*. I cannot think so. It is not the English dress that then looks better, but the English woman; that is, if she has fine shoulders, breasts, and arms. It is the beauty that is revealed, the woman pure and simple, that pleases the eye, just as is the case elsewhere. For the things that an Englishwoman will put on, or put half off herself, in the evening, are amazing to behold. An Englishwoman in full dress who has not a fine figure is even more dowdy than she is in the morning. For then she is likely to be at least neat and tidy, and she may wear a gown that is comparatively unobtrusive in form and color. Indeed, the best dress that the average Englishwoman wears is that in which she walks, which is apt to be of some sober color, — black, gray, light or dark, or a dark soft blue, — and to be entirely without ornament, — not a flounce or a bow, or even a button except for use, — with a bonnet, or oftener a hat, equally sober in tint and in form. And this is best for her; in this she is safe. If she would not risk offense, let her enfold herself thus. Let her by no means wander forth into the wilderness of mingled colors: "that way madness lies." This outward show is in no way the consequence of carelessness. No one in England seems to be careless about anything, least of all a woman about her dress. It is helpless, hopeless, elaborated dowdyism.

And yet as I write there rise up against me, with sweet, reproachful faces, figures draped worthily of their beauty; and more could not be said even for the work of Worth himself. One of many I particularly remember, with whom I took five o'clock tea at the house of a clergyman of distinction, and who bore a name that may be found in the " Peveril of the Peak." Her bright intelligence and her rich beauty (her oval cheek was olive) would have made me indifferent to her dress had it been a homespun bed-gown. But shall I ever forget the beautiful curves and tint of that soft-gray broad-leafed felt hat and feather, the elegance of the dark carriage dress that harmonized so well with it, or the perfect glove upon the hand that was held out so frankly to bid me good-by? No, fair British friends, it is not you that I mean; it is those other women whom I saw, but did not know.

It is because of the average Englishwoman's sad failure in dressing herself that the notion has got abroad that Englishmen are finer looking than Englishwomen. For the dress of the men is notably in good taste. It is simple, manly, neat; and although sober in tint and snug in cut, it is likely to have its general sobriety lightened up with a little touch of bright, warm color. On the other hand, the dress of " American " men is generally far, very, very far, inferior to that of the women in the corresponding conditions of life. This helps to produce the corresponding mistaken notion that the women in " America " are handsomer than the men; upon the incorrectness and essential absurdity of which I have already commented.

As to another attributed superiority of the Yankee woman I must express my surprised dissent. It is not uncommon to hear their intelligence and their social qualities rated much higher than those of their sisters in England. Fair countrywomen, heed not this flattery. It is not true. The typical Englishwoman of the upper and upper-middle class has in strength of mind and in information no type counterpart in "America." She may not know Latin, or she may and get little good by it; she may not be brilliant, or quick, or self-adaptive, and she generally is not; but she is well informed both as to the past and the present; she shows the effect rather of true education than of school cramming, of culture inherited and slowly acquired, and of intercourse with able, highly educated, and cultivated men. She generally has some accomplishment, which she has acquired in no mere showy boarding-school fashion, but with a respectable thoroughness. England is full of ladies who draw well in water-colors, or who are musicians, not mere piano players, or who are botanists, or who write well, and who add one or more of such acquirements to a solid general education, a considerable knowledge of affairs, and the ability to manage a large household.

The conversation of the society in which such women are found is far more interesting, far worthier of respect, than that which is heard in fashionable society (and these women are fashionable) in "America." And this without any reproach to the latter. For how could it be otherwise than that women who are the daughters, sisters, and wives of men who are themselves highly educated, and who have the affairs of a great empire, if not in their hands, at least upon their minds, should in all that can be acquired by intercourse with such men be superior to others, most of whom bear the same relations to men who are necessarily inferior in all these respects, who are absorbed in business, and who know little beyond their business, except what can be learned from the hurried reading of newspapers not of the highest type of journalism?

In England there is not only accumulated wealth, but accumulated culture; and of this the result appears hardly more in the men than in the women. It could not be otherwise. Englishwomen are companions and friends and helps to their fathers, their husbands, to all the men of their household. They are not absorbed in the mere external affairs of society; and society is not entirely in their hands. Men, men of mature years, form the substance of English society; they give it its tone; women, its grace and its ornament. Even in the Englishwoman's drawing-room the Englishman is looked up to and treated with deference. The talk and the tone must be such as he approves. She finds her pleasure as well as her duty in making it such as pleases him. She is even there his companion, his friend, his help. No matter how clever or brilliant she may be, she does not seek *tenir salon*, like the French female *bel esprit*. No matter how beautiful or how fashionable she may be, she does not leave him out of her society arrangements; unless, indeed, in either case, she chooses to set propriety at naught, and brave an accusation of "bad form." And should she attempt this, she would in most cases soon be checked by a very decided interposition of marital authority. One result of all this is a soberer tone in mixed society than we are accustomed to, and the discussion of graver topics in general conversation.

And yet in the English household the woman is quite supreme, — much more so, I think, than she is in "America." She really manages all household affairs, troubling her husband with no details, but being careful to manage in such a way as to meet his wishes. For, as I have said before, the wish of the master of an English household is the law of that household. Notwithstanding which, I have been led to the firm belief that henpecking is far more common in England than it is with us, and that curtain lectures are much oftener delivered there than here. "Mrs. Caudle's Curtain Lectures" would hardly have suggested themselves to an "American" humorist, although the thing itself — if not in its perfection, in its germ — is sufficiently known here to make the humor and the satire of that series not quite inappreciable. And, strange to say, the average English husband seems to be a less independent creature than the "American." English wives more generally insist upon their prerogative of sitting solemnly up for their husbands at night; and latch-keys are regarded as a personal grievance. What "American" wife would think of making a fuss about a man's having a latch-key? Not a few of them, indeed, have one themselves. And yet I have seen an Englishwoman of the lower-middle class flush and choke and whimper when the subject of the inalienable right of a man to a latch-key to his own house was broached, and begin to talk about the worm turning when it is trampled upon.

The devotion of Englishwomen to their families, and particularly to their children, cannot be surpassed. I believe that they are the best, the most self-sacrificing daughters, wives, and mothers in the world, ex-

cept the good daughters and wives and mothers in
" America ; " and even them I believe they generally
surpass in submissiveness and thoughtful consideration. But this is the result of the general subordination which in all things pervades English society.
They have little coquetry, and are not remarkable
for social tact. They are chiefly the sensible companions and helpers, subordinate but trusted, of their
fathers, brothers, husbands, and lovers, over whose
interests they watch with fond assiduity ; but in a
very simple, direct way. Mrs. Grote, with her " I 'll
thank you for a sovereign," when she lent a book,
was a characteristic manifestation, grotesquely exaggerated indeed, of a large and very valuable, if not
very charming, sort of Englishwoman, who does not
disdain to show and to put in practice, particularly
for her family, a certain hard common-sense selfishness, which is felt more directly as an active social
force in England than in " America."

It is generally believed in England, I cannot tell
why, that women in " America " take part in public
affairs, and are much more in the eye of the world
than Englishwomen are. Of this belief I met with
an amusing instance. One day at dinner in a country house, I had on one side of me a gentleman who
had come in alone for lack of ladies enough to "go
round ; " it was a small family party. He was the
brother of my hostess, a fine, intelligent fellow about
twenty-three years old, who had just taken his bachelor's degree at Oxford. As I turned from his sister
to him, in a pause of conversation, he asked me with
great earnestness, almost with solemnity, " Is — it —
true — that — in — America — the — women — sit —
on — juries ? " I instantly answered, in the most

matter-of-course way, " Yes ; all of them who are
not on duty as sergeants of dragoons." For one perceptible delightful moment doubt and bewilderment
flashed through his bright, handsome eyes, and then
he, as well as others within ear-shot, appreciated the
situation, and there was a hearty laugh and an in-
genuous blush mantled his cheeks, — for young men
can blush in England. When I explained that in no
part of that strange country, " America," with which
I was acquainted did women sit on juries, or take
any part in public affairs, or even vote or go to public meetings, and that nine in ten of the women that
I knew would be puzzled to tell who represented in
Congress the districts in which they lived, who were
the senators from their States, and possibly who
were their governors, I was listened to with profound attention ; and the surprise of my hearers was
very manifest, and was strongly expressed. It could
hardly have been otherwise ; for nothing that I could
have said would have brought into clearer light the
fact that women in " America " are very much less
informed upon public affairs and take very much less
interest in them than is the case with almost all Englishwomen of the cultivated classes.[1]

In England almost all intelligent women of the
upper and upper-middle classes take a very lively interest in politics, and are tolerably well informed
upon the public questions of the day, upon which in
many cases they have no inconsiderable influence.

---

[1] Mr. Edward Everett Hale, of Boston, recently said that he has " within
s.x months talked with a highly cultivated American woman who did not
know the difference between a senator and a representative in Congress."
And he " went into a public school one day, and asked a question about
the battle of Brandywine, to find that the class had never heard of it, and
was only amused by the drollness of the name."

The reason of this is that political life and the social life of the upper classes there are so thoroughly intermingled. Politics form the chief concern of the members of those classes; apart, of course, from their own private affairs. Hardly a woman of that class is without a husband, brother, kinsman, or friend who is, or who has been, or who hopes to be, a member of Parliament, or who is in diplomacy or connected in some way with colonial affairs. Politics there are intimately connected with the great object of woman's life in modern days, — social success. It is difficult for women in England, and even for men, to understand the entire severance of politics and society which obtains in " America," and to believe that a man may be a member of Congress, or even a senator, and yet be entirely without social position. Politics there are the most interesting topic of conversation among intelligent and cultivated people in general society; and such an acquaintance with political questions and party manœuvres as is here confined to a very small class of women whose relations to public men are peculiar, and who " go to Washington," is there very common among all women of superior position.

Of this I met with a striking illustration on my way from Warwick to Coventry. As I was about entering the railway carriage, a friend, an Englishman, who was kindly traveling with me for a day or two, and " coaching " me, told the porter who had my portmanteau to put it into the carriage. This, by the way, is permitted there. If there is room, and no one objects, you may take a huge trunk into a first-class railway carriage. One could hardly be taken into a second-class carriage for lack of room; and a third-class carriage is hardly larger than that marvelous institution known to American women — but to no others — as a Saratoga trunk. I objected to my friend's proposal, because there was a lady in the carriage. She was standing with her back to me as I spoke, but she immediately turned, and said, in a clear, sweet voice, " Oh, yes; bring it in; never mind me; there's quite room enough." I never saw a more elegant woman. She was about forty years old, still very handsome, tall, with a fine, lithe figure, and a gentle loftiness of manner which I might have called aristocratic, had she not reminded me strongly in every way of an " American " woman whom I had known from my boyhood. Nothing could have been more simple, frank, and good-natured than the way in which she made me and my luggage welcome. Her maid, who was standing by her, and who was herself quite a lady-like person, soon left us to take her place in a second-class carriage, and we three were left in possession.

The train started with that gentle, unobtrusive motion which is usual on English railways, and we fell into the chat of fellow-travelers. I was charmed with her. Her voice and her manner of speech would have made the recitation of the multiplication table agreeable. She had a son at Oxford, which I had left a few days before, and it proved that we had common acquaintances there. She showed, with all her superiority of manner, social and personal, — for she was what would have been called in the last generation a superior woman, — that deference to manhood which I have mentioned before as a trait of Englishwomen. Erelong my companion mentioned that we had been at Kenilworth that day. She replied, "Oh, I must go there. I have never been. Why! it is just like Americans to go to Kenilworth. All the Americans go to Kenilworth, and to Warwick Castle, and to Stratford." My companion replied that we had been at all those places. She laughed merrily, and said, "You ought to have been Americans to do that." My friend then told her that I was an "American." She turned upon me almost with a stare, and after a moment of silence spoke to me again, but with a perceptible and very remarkable change of manner. It was very slight, — of a delicate fineness. Her courtesy was not in the least diminished, nor her frankness; but the perfectly unconscious and careless expression of her face was impaired, and her attention to me was a little more pronounced than it had been before. She inquired if I had been pleased with my visit to Kenilworth, and told me that a novel had been written about it by Sir Walter Scott. "But," she added, "perhaps you have read it. Have you met with it?" I answered, "I have heard of it;" and my inward satisfaction was great when I saw that I had done so with a face so unmoved that she replied with a gracious instructiveness of manner, "Oh, you should have read it before you went to Kenilworth; it would so have increased your pleasure. But the next best thing for you is to read it now." I thanked her, and said that I should like to do so. I think that she would have gone on to recommend a perusal of the works of William Shakespeare to me in connection with my visit to Stratford-on-Avon, although she looked at me in a puzzled way once or twice. But my companion, although I saw he was amused at something in her talk, marred whatever hopes I had of further

15

instruction by breaking in with some remark upon
the politics of Warwickshire. She rose to his fly
like a trout on a hazy day, and in a minute or two
she had forgotten my existence in her discussion with
him of a topic which plainly was to her of far more
interest than all the Scotts that could have dwelt in
Kenilworth, and all the Shakespeares that could have
stood in Stratford. He was a Birmingham notable,
and knew everything that was going on in the county ;
but she was his equal in information, and it seemed
to me his superior in political craft. To every suggestion of his she made some reply that showed that the
question was not new to her. She knew all the ins
and outs of the politics of the county: who could be
expected to support this measure, who was sure to
oppose that. She knew all about the manufacturing
interests of Birmingham : who had retired from active management; who was coming in; what money
had been taken out of this establishment, what
changes had taken place in the other, — and had an
opinion as to what effect this was going to have upon
Parliament. I never heard the beginning of such
political talk from a woman in " America," even
from one whose husband was in politics. The train
stopped ; her maid appeared, and she bade us courteously good-by, with the puzzled look in her eye as
it rested upon the fellow-passenger to whom she had
recommended the perusal of " Kenilworth ; " and
then my companion told me, what indeed I had been
sure of all along, that she was a member of the governing class.

A few days before, I had observed in Oxford,
where a local election was impending, small posters
addressed to " The Burgesses," and these invariably

began, "*Ladies* and Gentlemen," a form of "campaign document" as foreign to us as it would be to peoples subject to the Salique law, — than which worse laws have long prevailed in many countries.

Not only in politics but in business women appear much more prominently than they do in "America." If they do not keep hotels, which they sometimes do, they manage them, whether they are great or small. The place which in "America" is filled by that exquisite, awful, and imperturbable being, the hotel clerk, is filled invariably in England by a woman, — so at least I always found it, and the change seemed to me a very happy one. To be met by the cheery, pleasant faces of these bright, well-mannered women, to be spoken to as if you were a human being whom, in consideration of what you are to pay, it was a pleasure to make as comfortable as possible, instead of being treated with lofty condescension, or at best with serene indifference, was a pleasant sensation. And these women did their work so quietly and cheerfully, and yet in such a business-like way, that it was a constant pleasure to come into contact with them. Dressed in black serge or alpaca, they affected no flirting airs, and directed or obeyed promptly and quietly. And yet their womanhood constantly appeared in their manner and in their thoughtfulness for the comfort of those who were in their care. They always had a pleasant word or a smile in answer to a passing remark, were always ready to answer any question or give any information, and were pleased at any acknowledgment of satisfaction. Naturally it was so; for they were women ; and they were chosen, it seemed to me, for their pleasant ways as well as for their efficiency. From not one of them,

from one end of England to the other, in great cities
or in quiet country towns and villages, did I receive
one surly word or look, or anything but the kindest
and promptest attention. I can say the same of the
shop-women, who waited upon customers not as if
they were consciously condescending in the performing of such duties, but cheerfully and pleasantly, and
with a show of interest that a purchaser should be
satisfied. Their dress was almost invariably the same,
— black, unornamented serge or alpaca, which, by the
way, is the commonest street dress of all women of
their condition. In the telegraph offices the clerks are
generally women; and, indeed, women seem to do
everything except plow, drive omnibuses and railway engines, and be soldiers and policemen. They
keep turnpikes, where turnpikes still exist; and in
Sussex I saw a woman's name with her husband's
upon the pike-house. Indeed, it seemed to me that
in all public affairs, from politics down to turnpike
keeping, women were very much more engaged and
before the world in England than in "America," although I saw no jury-women or she-sergeants.

As to the manners of Englishwomen, they are, like
the manners of other women, good, bad, and indifferent. And chiefly they are indifferent, being in this
particular also like the manners common to the Teutonic races; which races, some of my readers may
like to be reminded, are the Deutsch (which we call
German), the Hollanders, the Anglo-Saxon (or, better, the English), and the Scandinavians (Swedes,
Norsemen, Danes, and Icelanders). The average
manners of these people, even of the women among
them, are on the whole truly indifferent. They are
not coarse, but as surely they are not polished. Man-

ner, however, is a very different thing from manners ; and in manner Englishwomen, from the highest class to the lowest, are all more or less charming, — strong-minded women and lodging-house keepers being of course excepted. This charm, like all traits and effects of manner, is not easy to describe ; but it left upon me at all times and among all classes an impression of its being the outcoming of a consciousness of womanhood combined with a feeling of modest but very firm self-respect. The most intelligent Englishwoman, even in her most exalted moments, never seems to resolve herself into a bare intelligence. Her mind is always clad in woman's flesh ; and her body thinks. Thus conscious of her own womanhood, she keeps you conscious of it by a subtle influence of sex, — the only subtlety of which she is usually capable, — and not merely by the facts that her hair is long, her face beardless, and her body covered with voluminous and marvelous apparel, — in a word, not merely by outer show.

All this is but the outward sign ; and it might exist — as it so often does, I shall not say where — in females, who are wholly without that grace, not of movement or of speech, or even of thought, but of moral condition, which is to man the chiefest charm in woman. How often have I sat by one of those women talking — no, talked at (for it reduces me to silence) — in such a splendid and overwhelming manner, and with such a superior consciousness of intellectuality, that I could not but think that, except for the silk and the lace, and the lack of mustaches, and the evident expectation of a compliment, I might as well have been talking with a man, and that I longed for the companionship of some pretty, well bred igno ramus, whose head was full only of common sense, and whose soul as well as whose body was of the female sex.

England is not without women of the former kind, I suppose, but they are so rare that I met with none; while all the women that I did meet had the soft, sweet charm given by the contented consciousness of their womanhood. Womanhood looks out from an Englishwoman's eyes; it speaks in every inflection of her voice. No matter how clever she may be, how well informed, she never utters mind pure and simple; she never lays a bare statement of thought or of fact before you. She is too modest. A piece of her mind she does, indeed, sometimes give you. But then, be sure, she is, of all times, the most thoroughly woman-like and absolved from intellectuality; being thus, however, in her excitement not peculiar among her sex. At all other times she leaves an impression of gentleness and a lack of intellectual robustness; and, at least if you are a man, she, without any seeming intention of so doing, keeps you constantly in mind that she is trusting to you — to your strength, your ability, your position — to insure that she shall be treated with respect and tenderness, and cared for; and that therefore she owes you deference, and that it becomes her to be not only as charming, but as serviceable as possible. Even in the hardest women there is at least a remnant of this. An Englishwoman shall be a sort of she-bagman, a traveler for manufacturers, and in the habit of riding second or even third class alone, from one end of England to the other (and I talked with such women), and she shall yet show you this gentle, womanly consciousness. A woman's eye there never looks straight and steady into yours, saying, "I am quite able to take care of my own person and interests and reputation. Don't trouble yourself about me in those respects. Meantime, sir, I am taking your measure." There is always a mute appeal from her womanhood to your manhood. This charm belongs to the Englishwoman of all ranks, and beautifies everything that she does, even if she does it awkwardly, which is not always. She shows it if she is a great lady and welcomes you, or if she is a house-maid and serves you. Not absolutely every Englishwoman is thus, of course; for there are hard and proud and cruel and debased women in England, as there are elsewhere. But, apart from these exceptions, this is the manner of Englishwomen; and in so far as a man may judge, this manner, or the counterpart of it, does not forsake them when they are among themselves.

This gentle charm of the Englishwoman's manner is greatly helped and heightened by her voice and her way of speaking. In these she is not only without an equal, but beyond comparison with the women of any other people, except the few of her own blood and tongue in this country, who have like voices and the same utterance. The voices and the speech of Englishwomen of all classes are, with few exceptions, pleasant to the ear, — soft and clear; their words are well articulated, but not precisely pronounced. They speak without much emphasis, yet not monotonously, but with gentle modulation. Their speech is therefore very easily understood, — much more so than that of persons who speak louder and with stronger emphasis. You rarely or never are obliged to ask an Englishwoman to repeat what she has said because you have failed to catch her words. This soft, yet crisp and clear and easily flowing speech is, as I have said, common to the whole sex there.

I remember that in one of my prowlings about London I found myself in a little, dingy court that opened off Thames Street, — a low water-side street that runs under London Bridge. It was Sunday morning, and I had come down from Charing Cross to attend service at St. Paul's, and had half an hour to spare. The street was almost deserted, and so quiet that my footsteps echoed from the walls of the dull and smoke-browned houses. In this court I found two women talking. One was Sairey Gamp. I am sure it was Sairey. The leer upon her heavy face could not be mistaken, and she had grown even a little stouter than when I was so happy as to make her acquaintance years ago. The other was probably Betsey Prig; she was a mere wisp of a woman; or, indeed, she may have been Mrs. Harris herself, — her shadow-like figure being the next thing in woman form to nonentity. As I passed these two humble people, I was struck by the tone and manner of their speech as they talked earnestly together. Their words and their pronunciation were vulgar enough; but, as a whole, the speech of both was rich and musical. The whole of that otherwise silent court was filled with the soft murmur of their voices. I had no business there, but I pretended to have, and went from dingy door to dingy door, lingering and loitering all round the court, that I might listen. They did not stare at me any more than I did at them, — plainly, they would not have thought of such rudeness, — but they went on with their talk, speaking their language and mine with tones and inflections that I never heard from two women of like position in "America."

I was reminded of this afterwards when one morning, at a country house, I lingered chatting with my hostess at the breakfast table after all the rest of the family had risen. She touched a bell, and a maid, an upper servant, answered the summons. No servants, by the way, wait at breakfast there, even in great houses. After you are once started, and the tea is made, you are left alone, to wait upon yourselves, — a fashion full of comfort, making breakfast the most sociable meal of the day. When the maid appeared her mistress spoke at once, and she stopped at the door and replied; and there was a little dialogue about some household matter. The young woman's answers were little more than, "Yes, my lady," and, "No, my lady," but I was charmed by them, — more so than I have ever been by a lecture or a recitation from the lips of one of the sex. She spoke in a subdued tone; but every syllable was distinct, although she was at the further end of a large dining-room. Her mistress' voice was no less clear and sweet and charming, and as they talked, in their low, even tones, with perfect ease and understanding at this distance, the whole of the great room resounded sweetly with this spoken music. When English is spoken in this way by a woman of superior breeding and intelligence there is of course an added charm, and it is then the most delightful speech that I ever heard, or can imagine. Compared with it, German becomes harsh and ridiculous, French mean and snappish, Spanish too weak and open-mouthed, and even Italian, noble and sweet as it is, seems to lack a certain firmness and crispness, and to be without a homely charm which it may not lack to those whose mother tongue is bastard Latin.

One reason of this beauty of the speech of English-women is doubtless in the voice itself. An English-woman's voice is soft, but it is not weak. It is nota-bly firm, clear, and vibrating. It is neither guttural nor nasal. While it soothes the ear, it compels atten-tion. Like the tone of a fine old Cremona violin, its softest vibrations make themselves heard and under-stood, when mere noise makes only confusion. Such voices are not entirely lacking among women in "Amer-ica;" but, alas, how few of the fortunate possessors of such voices here use them worthily! For the other element of the beauty of the Englishwoman's speech is in her utterance. We all remember poor Lear's words about a voice soft, gentle, and low, being an excellent thing in woman. Shakespeare knew the truth in this, as in so many other things. One of the very few points on which we may be sure of his personal preferences is that he disliked high voices and sharp speech in women. Singular man! The Englishwoman's voice is strong as well as sweet, but her speech is low. She rarely raises her voice. I do not remember having ever heard an Englishwoman try to compel attention in that way; but I have heard French and Spanish and Italian women, ladies of unquestionable position and breeding, almost scream, and that, too, in "society." Nor does the English-woman use much emphasis. Her manner of speech is calm, although without any suggestion of dignity, and her inflections, which rise often, although they are full of meaning, are gentle. I remarked this difference in her speech of itself, but much more when I heard again the speech of some "American' ladies whom I accidentally met in England. I had not been in their company five minutes when I was pierced through from ear to ear. They seemed to me to be talking in italics, to be emphasizing every word, as if they would thrust it into my ears, whether I would or not. I am sure that to their too emphatic utterance is due, in a very great measure, the inferior charm of the speech of most American women, when compared with that of their kinswomen who have remained in the "old home." If they would be a little more gentle, a little less self-asserting, a little less determined, and a little more persuasive in their utterance as well as in their manner, who could doubt that, with all their other advantages, they need fear no rivalry in womanly charm, even with the truly feminine, sensible, gentle-mannered, sweet-voiced women of England!

To make an end of this embarrassing discussion, it may be said, but not confidently, that on the whole women are more beautiful in "America," but more lovable in England; that in "America" they are better dressed, but in England better housekeepers and companions. There are as lovable women here as there, and as beautiful women there as here; but the preponderance of numbers is probably as it is above set forth. Perhaps erelong time will bless the men of both countries by making the balance perfect.

CHAPTER XI.

When I took passage for Liverpool I naturally inquired what kind of man he was in whose charge and under whose command I was to be for some ten days upon the ocean. I was told that he was an excellent seaman and a good ship-master, but that he was unsociable and surly; in fact positively disagreeable; had English manners, and was in brief "a perfect John Bull." I took all this with some grains of allowance, and was content to be in the hands of a good seaman and commander. For as to reserve of manner on the part of a man who has upon his mind the responsibility for a great steamship and her cargo, and a thousand or twelve hundred souls, upon the storm-vexed, fog-shrouded Atlantic, I could not only make allowance for it, but respect it; having some knowledge, although at second hand, of the way in which "the captain" is often pestered by the he and she gadflies among his passengers. And therefore on the voyage, although the sea was calm and the skies were bright, and we went smoothly and swiftly on under steam and sails, I did not for several days speak to any officer of the vessel, except the purser and the surgeon. When I passed the captain I merely bowed silently in acknowledgment of his position, and of mine as his subordinate and dependent. I should have been better pleased if he had made some acknowledgment, however slight, of my salute, of which he took not the least notice. But even this neglect, although I had never met with it before even in the commander of a man-of-war, I should have passed by without setting it down against him, had it not been that I observed that he made himself deferentially agreeable to a passenger who was connected in some way with the British embassy, and who seemed to have no higher claim to exceptional attention. Other passengers complained outright of the surly indifference of his manner even to ladies; and one of the latter, a very gracious and agreeable woman, of such social position that she could have safely snubbed the whole British embassy, and of such spirit that upon good occasion she would have done so, told me that he had replied to a civil and simple question of hers so rudely that she did not mean to pass over the offense unnoticed.

One day, as we were just passing out of the Gulf Stream, I saw him standing near me, and stepping up to him and raising my hat I said, " I beg pardon for interrupting you, captain [he was doing nothing], but will you be kind enough to tell me how wide the Gulf Stream is where we cross it?" He replied very curtly and gruffly, " Indeed, I don't know. It's a matter I 've never thought about, — don't know anything at all about it." The manner was more than the words. It was not insulting; I could not complain of it; but it was insolent, and insolent in a way which showed that the speaker was an ill-conditioned person who did not know how to behave himself. And if the reply was true, it was amazing. For the Gulf Stream is a very important fact in navigation; and here was an accomplished seaman who for years had been crossing it twenty times and more in a year, and yet he had, as he said, not even thought how many miles of it he had to pass over. If what he said was true, it was an astonishing exposition of Philistinism, or something worse. For as to the information for which I asked, I soon got at that easily by an examination of a chart and a brief and simple calculation. The reply was, however, probably a simple exposition of personal character. But the feeling aroused among the passengers by our commander's behavior (although most of them were his countrymen) was such that there was some talk of sending to the owners a formal complaint against it ; and although this project was abandoned, the lady whom I have mentioned did not forget her feminine mischief.

She got up one of those little entertainments by which the tedium of a voyage is not unfrequently relieved, making herself hostess, and providing a little supper. To this she invited every passenger with whom she or any one of her party had exchanged a word, and by special note every officer of the ship, except the captain, who was pointedly omitted. The slight was extreme, and I am not prepared to say that it was quite defensible ; for, whatever his manners, he was the commanding officer of the vessel · but it was generally regarded as fully justified by his conduct, and as permissible on the part of a woman. His captainship, surly sea-dog as he was, felt the cut very deeply, and was furious; and in the midst of our little festival, at which all the officers not on duty were present, he sent in orders for them to appear on deck. Of course they were obliged to go ; but none the less the lady had accomplished **her** purpose.

Some years before my voyage to England, I had an experience of this sort of English manners, and as it was in every way very characteristic, the story of it is not here inappropriate, and may be instructive. I knew and was on the pleasantest terms with an English gentleman of a very different sort from Captain ——, a man whom I had respected, liked, and even admired. He was a man of intelligence, of wide information, and of remarkably good-breeding, — a man distinguished in person and in manner. When he applied to me to perform a certain responsible duty for him during his absence, I was pleased at such a mark of his confidence, and I accepted his proposal. While he was away a gentleman connected with him in business thought that he had reason to be dissatisfied with some of my arrangements, and on my declining to admit any interference with my discharge of the duties which I had undertaken, he took the responsibility of breaking the agreement, to which, for peace' sake, I assented, on the understanding that my rights in the matter were to be held in abeyance until the return of my friend from England. When he did return we met in the pleasantest way; and after waiting until he was well settled again, I brought the matter to his attention briefly by letter, and asked his decision. To my surprise, and I may almost say to my grief, I received a very curt reply, in which he said that he did not propose to trouble himself at all about the past. The purpose of his response was so plain, and its utter lack of consideration was so manifest and so insufferable, that in sorrow, and without a disrespectful word, I wrote to him that our acquaintance must cease immediately.

I determined, of course, that the matter should not

drop there; but on looking for the letters in which his proposals were made and the terms of our agreement settled, I could not find them. They were carefully preserved, but had been mislaid, and many months passed before they were discovered. During this time his partner became convinced that, however correct his judgment might have been, I was right in the position which I had taken; and in a courteous note he inclosed me a check for his half of what was due to me under the agreement. This check I returned to him, telling him, with thanks, that the question on my part was not one of money.

When I found the letters, I wrote to my former friend, bringing the matter again to his attention, and asking his consideration of it. He took no notice of my letter. I then brought a suit against him, which he defended. I was very sorry for the whole affair, and just before the trial was coming on I went to a common acquaintance, and, showing him the whole matter, said, " This case ought not to be tried. I don't want —— to pay me a dollar. Go to him from me and say so, and see if you can't induce him to behave differently." He agreed with me, and did what I asked. But his intercession was in vain; Sir John Bull refused to hear a word about the matter. The trial came on; and after the evidence was all in my counsel offered to submit the case to the jury without argument, but the other side refused. The judge charged briefly, and the jury, after a minute's consultation without leaving their seats, gave a verdict in my favor for the full amount claimed, to which the judge added the largest permissible " allowance." And thus ended the only suit in which I, although bred to the bar, and the loser of not a little much-needed money, was ever plaintiff. If my former friend had treated me with the consideration which one man — I shall not say one gentleman — owes to another; if he had merely said to me, even at the last moment, "My position in this matter is such that I cannot without great inconvenience interfere in anything that passed during my absence; I am sorry that it is so," that would have been an end of the affair. His arrogance and his ignorance of me except as a man of letters led him to take a position which proved untenable and costly. By many persons, perhaps by most persons who were not born and bred in England, his conduct will be regarded as thoroughly English, and as a typical example of English manners.[1]

[1] A gentleman whose opinion on such a subject would be valued by all who knew him — I do not know why I should not mention the name of my friend the late Maunsell Field, a man who could learn nothing in courtesy from the courts with which he was familiar — told me of an experience of British high-class manners which he pronounced characteristic. He was at a small town in the south of France or north of Spain, — Pau, perhaps, — in company with a friend, and they had a bedroom and a sitting-room together. The latter was the only apartment of the kind in the little inn, except the general parlor, which was made unpleasant by some rude army officers. The dowager Duchess of —— (a well-known English title) arrived with her family, including girls and the young duke. They needed a sitting-room for their comfort; and under the circumstances the two Yankees sent their compliments to her Grace, with the offer to give up their sitting-room to her; regretting only that they should be obliged to pass through it once in the evening on the way to their bedroom. It was accepted. When the gentlemen passed through their room, the lady who by their favor was occupying it looked up at them; they bowed, and expressed themselves sorry to disturb her. She in return only stared at them in silence, as the young ladies and the boy duke also did; and that was all. This was repeated three evenings; and then, finding it intolerable, the self-sacrificing gentlemen shortened their visit, and left the inn without a word of thanks from her Grace. I never met with such conduct on the part of decent English folk, however high their rank, and never but once anything like it, and that not in England. Another friend, not inferior in social tact or knowledge of the world, told me that when he was at Gibraltar the Duchess of —— (another very noted title) used to

16

To a certain extent it was typical of English manners, but only of one narrow strongly marked phase of them; and although I had had other opportunities of observing similar conduct on the part of Englishmen, in some of which I was directly interested, but in others of which I was not, I had refused to accept these as evidence against a whole people, and a people in whom, apart from all considerations of kindred, which to me were great and abiding, I felt an interest which I had felt in no other. It will be seen, however, that when I stepped from the deck of my steamer I did so with sufficient reason for some prejudice against the manners of my British kinsmen.

I found, however, good reason to be glad that my experience of a few individuals had not led me into a foregone conclusion against a people. Those who have gone with me thus far will not be surprised at my saying that I found the manners of English folk in most respects pleasing and admirable. And by manners I mean not merely the attitude and the action and the speech which appear upon the surface of social intercourse, but the motive feeling which underlies this surface, and which influences the actual conduct, as well as the bearing of man toward man. Moreover, the distinction between manners and manner must be constantly kept in mind.

It is a trite remark that the English manner lacks both warmth and grace. Indeed, as a people, the English have no manner. I would not say, as Malvolio says of Viola in her page's dress, that their manner is "a very ill manner." There is simply the

come out in the gallery that surrounded the court of the old inn, and rate her servants there like a termagant; and that unless she was in full dress she was slatternly and — I refrain from using a word which would assert that an English duchess could be other than irreproachable in person.

absence of pleasing outward demonstration, a reserve so absolute and yet so unconscious (unconscious, perhaps, through long habit and continued practice) that it is very like indifference. But even to this judgment there must be made many exceptions, — exceptions so numerous that sometimes it seems as if, like the exceptions to the conjugation of French verbs, they almost invalidate the rule. Certainly, I have never seen, nor could I desire to see, more show of heartiness and warmth than I have met in Englishmen. And even as to polish of manner I could hardly deny that the finest examples of it that I have met with were afforded by Englishmen, although these were few in number. It would seem as if the hard, tough material had, like some agates, under its natural rough coating the possibility of a smoothness and transparency of surface which shows all the beauty of the structure beneath, and which yet will turn an edge of hardest steel. Soft-natured things take no such polish. On the other hand, it is not often that you find that union of simplicity and courtesy, that lack of self-assertion and that thoughtfulness of others' feelings, which was not uncommon among New England folk of the best breeding in the last generation (for, alas, we have lost it, rubbed rudely down as it has been by the rush of railway trains, and war, and the flood of wealth and emigration), and which seemed to be the outward manifestation of a gentle, kindly, fine-fibred nature.[1] But of good

[1] To most of my readers I need hardly say that in my parenthetical censure I am not one of Horace's praisers of the manners of the days of their youth. But all they whose social experience began like mine in railway times, and who yet had youthful glimpses of the fading charm of old New England manners among those whose sons have since gone West or South, will agree with me in my admiring and reverential memories.

manners and kindly intentions, accompanied by a manifest consciousness of superior position and of its duties, it is hard to imagine finer examples than may be found among the higher classes in England.

English people impress you first of all by a sense of the genuineness of their actions and of their speech.   Warm or cold they may be, gracious or ungracious, arrogant or considerate, but you see that they are sincere. Englishmen adulterate their goods, but not their conduct. If an Englishman makes you welcome, you feel at home ; and you know that, within reason, and often out of reason, he will look after your comfort, — that for your well-being while you are under his roof he considers himself responsible. Yet he does not thrust himself upon you, and you may do almost what you choose, and go almost whither you will. If he meets you and gives you two fingers, it means only two fingers ; if his whole hand grasps yours, you have his hand, and you have it most warmly at your parting. His speech is like his action. His social word is his social bond ; you may trust him for all that it promises, and commonly for more. If you do not understand him well, you may suppose at first that he is indifferent and careless, until something is done for you, or suggested to you, that shows you that his friend and his friend's welfare has been upon his mind.

In English society there are indeed people, and not a few of them, to whom social intercourse is a matter of calculation, a means to an end. But their like is to be found in all lands ; in Fiji, I believe; and of them I do not speak. Such professors of society are fewer in England than elsewhere ; and indeed it is better that they should be fewer ; for they do this business rather awkwardly. Social finesse is not the forte of the English people, although it is the foible of some Englishwomen. But their efforts in that way are stiff and heavy, and remind one of those of the German who practiced jumping over chairs that he might learn to be lively. One does sometimes wish that there was a little less rigidity in the social joints of England; but after all, in the long run suppleness is a poor substitute for solid strength. In the society of Englishmen you at least feel safe.

It is remarkable, in connection with this view of our subject, that, although the English manner in real life is quiet and undemonstrative almost to affectation, English acting is rude and extravagant; and that, on the other hand, while the French manner in daily intercourse is nervous and demonstrative, French acting is distinguished by delicacy, calm, and reserve. Each nation seems to seek upon the stage the complement of its daily acted life, as people whose existence is one of commonplace drudgery and of pinching poverty like to read descriptions of romantic adventure and of the splendor and magnificence attainable by the lavish use of fabulous wealth.

The manner of Englishmen to women is a happy mean between indifference and adulation, between hard mastery and abject submission. There is neither the effusiveness of the Frenchman nor the sad and voiceless slavery of the " American;" little bowing and flourishing, and not much flattery. But with a silent assertion of masculine mastery, and no readiness to yield everything to a woman's caprice or convenience merely because she is a woman, there is an exhaustless fund of tenderness and a never-dying flame of chivalry among these wife-beating men. The Englishman's bearing towards women is the Yankee's, wholesomely corrected by a tempering of common sense and not unreasonable selfishness. Frances Power Cobbe tells in the "Contemporary Review" a characteristic story illustrative of this point: how once she asked an elderly French gentleman, a M. de ——, with a ribbon in his buttonhole, to give some attention to a charming young lady who was going on the same train with him from London to Paris, and how he was " too happy to place himself at her service," and how he made himself very agreeable on the route ; but how when, on their arrival at Boulogne, there was serious difficulty about the lady's luggage, M. de ——, rather than lose a train to Paris, expressed himself as being *au désespoir*, and was whirled off, leaving his young charge to get out of her trouble as best she could. " The results," Miss Cobbe goes on to say, "might have been annoying had not a homely English stranger stepped in and proffered his aid ; and, having recovered the missing property, simply lifted his hat and escaped from the lady's expressions of gratitude. In this little anecdote, I think, lies a compendium of the experience of hundreds of ladies on their travels. The genuine and self-sacrificing kindness of English and American gentlemen toward women affords almost a ludicrous contrast to the florid politeness, compatible with every degree of selfishness, usually exhibited by men of other European nations."

The god of English social life next in dignity to mammon is propriety. Now propriety rightly worshiped is a very good god ; his rites are sweetness, order, decency ; and in their practice they involve that consideration for others which is the highest form of morality, and even of piety. But your average Briton makes propriety a Moloch, before whom he prostrates himself, and before whom he often makes his very children sacrifice some of the beauty of their youthful lives. The highest social aim, the greatest social law, to this sort of Englishman is to do the correct thing. Having attained this, he feels that he has absolved himself of every social duty, and clothed his soul in panoply of proof. Whether the correct thing be really the right thing he does not know, does not seek to know. That so it has been and that so it is are for him both logic and religion. In his mouth the greatest reproach is " unprecedented ; " the mere statement of the fact that an act has not been done before, that a word has not been spoken before, being to him its condemnation. Wherefore he lives his life surrounded by dead, shriveled forms, eyeless, brainless, bloodless, whose only voice is from the grave of a dead past. If he breaks away from this oppression, he is likely to run into extremes which violate all decency, all decorum, all propriety. Freed from his accustomed restraint, he is apt to add a grossness to vice which makes it more hideous, if not more harmful.

This general consideration of our subject, however, is likely to be of less interest and perhaps of less real instructiveness than some report of particular external manners among Englishmen. In this respect I was impressed at once, even before I had left the steamer, with the good behavior of the English people, from the lowest to the highest. I found them to be kindly, respectful, considerate, showing, with rare exceptions, that union of deference to others and self-respect which I have spoken of before. The custom-house officers, with three of whom I was brought into contact before I went on shore, seemed to me to have in perfection the manners fit for their position. They were quiet, civil, pleasant, considerate, and firm. They seemed to wish to do their duty as agreeably as possible, and they did not even give me a chance to offer a "tip." Such was their manner in general; but having reason to suspect one passenger, they searched one of his trunks thoroughly, and then, finding that he had several hundreds more of cigars than they thought a private gentleman should carry, they "went through him" without pity, yet with politeness. Just so pleasant and so worthy of respect I found the London policemen, whose quiet, good-natured ways, unpretending civility, and unofficious readiness brought me to look upon them as friends. Wherever and whenever I saw them in my wanderings over the great city, it was with pleasure and with personal interest. Their honest, cheery English faces and their English speech were the more grateful to me because of their unlikeness to Misther John Kelly's constituents, who, excepting those big, good-natured dandies, the Broadway squad, fill the ranks of the New York force.

I had been in England more than a month, going about everywhere in city and in country alone, and doing this, it should be remembered, as an English-man, before I had one uncivil or even one unpleasant word spoken to me; and when the word came it was from a 'bus conductor, and I was really in fault. Wishing to go to Hyde Park near Prince's Gate, I hailed a 'bus that was driving rapidly through Regent Street with "Hyde Park" upon its panels. Just as I was mounting to the top it occurred to me to ask the conductor if he passed Prince's Gate. "No, I don't," he replied, somewhat snappishly, "and a gentleman like you hought to know there's two sides to 'Yde Park, an' that they're a mile apart." I did know that as well as he did, and therefore asked my question. What I had not learned was how to distinguish the 'buses that ran on one side from those that ran on the other. I remembered that I had stopped him for nothing in full career, and when he was perhaps behind time, and I thought his fretfulness very excusable. Now this piece of mild incivility was not only my first but my only experience of the kind in England, where I found among those whose business it was to serve me not only general civility and a deferential demeanor, but a cheerfulness of manner and a pleasant alacrity to which an "American" is unaccustomed.

Not in omnibuses nor in any other public vehicles are you subjected to the incivility of being summoned to pay your fare as soon as you enter. There is no thumping upon windows or jangling of bells to call your attention to this duty. You pay just before you go out; or after a reasonable time a conductor comes and civilly takes your money. Nor does he then turn a crank and clang a great gong, or touch a spring and kling a little one, to announce to the world that you have paid and that he has received your twopence or threepence. The standing passenger rubbing against your knees and treading upon your toes is not the only familiar annoyance from which you will find yourself freed. Do not the companies lose some fares by this simple method of procedure? Perhaps they do. But the saving of money to common carriers is not regarded as the one great object to be attained.

The convenience and comfort of the passenger is the first consideration, and for that he pays. But to put him to inconvenience, or to subject him to unpleasantness, that he may thereby be made use of to correct the consequences of the possible dishonesty of the company's servants, after the New York fashion, is an imposition unthought of. Englishmen would not submit to it for a day.

It is pleasant, too, to be able to make a purchase at a shop and to pay for it on the spot to the person who sells it to you, and to go away, if you choose to do so, immediately. The system of checks by which, if you take a glass of soda-water or buy a paper of pins, you receive an order to pay five cents at some desk more or less remote, is unknown in England. So is the waiting for some trifle until a salesman makes three entries, and a cash boy makes as many, and a cashier as many, and your tiny parcel is wrapped up at the proper counter and "entered" there and numbered and what not, and then brought solemnly to you, or packed away to be sent to you at a certain " delivery." At the very eating-houses you pay the waiter who serves you, and he, if necessary, makes change for you out of his own pocket. For his general civility I will answer freely, but for his cleanliness I can say little. He is even in the morning discovered in a dress-coat and an untidy, dingy white tie, which makes him look as if he had been up all night. In his hand he carries a napkin, which even early in the day is so limp and smutched and unctuous that you dread lest he should wipe your plate or your knife and fork with it. He is very attentive, however, and at breakfast bustles about to find you a newspaper before he takes your order. And in so trifling a matter as a newspaper your minutest comfort is looked after. I remarked that in the coffee-rooms of hotels and in good restaurants the newspapers had a little triangular piece cut diagonally off the top of the middle fold. By this the annoying little wrinkle which otherwise is apt to form there and to prevent the paper from opening and shutting easily is avoided. The papers on the news-stands, too, are cut open. And all this is done not by a folding-machine or a cutting-machine at the newspaper offices, but personally by the people who serve you, and who do all that they can do to please you. The fashion recently adopted here of folding newspapers by machinery, when they are printed, in such a way that the reader is obliged to unfold and then refold them, is an example of a system of life and of manners the exact reverse of that which is practiced in England. But what matter to what inconvenience the American newspaper publisher puts the public, if by so doing he can save ten cents on a thousand copies! Does not the public in America exist for the benefit of railway companies and other corporations, of machine politicians, and of publishers of newspapers? Verily for little else.

In illustration of the stiffness and reserve of English manners, I was told by a friend who would be likely to know the truth, that the Athenæum Club had actually once undertaken to discipline a member who had spoken to another member without an introduction. But although the Athenæum is the highest and mightiest of all the literary clubs of London, and is so exclusive that strangers are not admitted within its doors, this story is probably an exaggeration of some trifling occurrence which has been caricatured

as a take-off of the haughty, " high-dried " manners
of the circle in which centres the loftiest intellectual
and social culture of London.   In fact, introductions
are at the present day almost disused in the best
company in England.   The fashion has its advantages, and is not without its comforts.   It protects
you against the annoyance of being dragged up and
thrust upon the attention of persons who may not be
so much in the mood to make your acquaintance as
they might be at some other time ; and it is a blessed
change from experiences in this respect which are
not easily to be escaped in the United States except
at the cost of unpopularity.   But it is carried, it
seemed to me, to an inconvenient and almost absurd
extreme.   People who are invited to meet at small
parties and at country houses are left to find each
other out and make themselves known one to another
as best they may.   The result is sometimes a degree
of awkwardness which perhaps is not quite out of
keeping with certain phases of English society.   But
I did not find that it interposed any real obstacles to
the pleasantest social intercourse ; and after all it is
better than the other extreme of promiscuous introduction, will you, nill you.   And it should be remembered that a person on entering a drawing-room
in England is always formally announced, and is
therefore known to all within hearing.

One trait of English manners was first brought to
my attention at the Birmingham musical festival.
As we went out after the morning performance, we
found at each door a nicely-dressed and pleasant-
looking young woman holding in her hand a plate
such as those in which collections of money are taken
up in churches.   This was to receive gifts for some

favorite charitable institution of the town, and as we passed the girls they rattled the money in their plates to attract attention. It was a new way to me of asking and receiving alms ; but what I chiefly remarked was that these young ladies for every addition made to the money in their plates said pointedly, " Thank you." Afterwards in London, on a certain saint's day, I found girls ensconced in chairs, and when it rained with umbrellas spread, in very public places, having plates before them to receive the alms of wayfarers for certain public charities ; and these also, I observed, for every gift said, " Thank you." In England there is always some one to say personally " Thank you " for a benefit conferred ; and this is the more easily and constantly done because there is in general a more direct personal contact than there is among us between all persons concerned in charitable works, whether as principals or as intermediaries. Not only, however, in return for alms, but for favor shown in any way, in making a purchase, or even in giving an order, this acknowledgment is made. It seemed to me that " Thank you " must be heard a thousand times a day in England for once that it is heard in America. I was thanked for my very cab-toll every time I crossed Waterloo Bridge.

Notwithstanding this trait of civility and considerateness in English manners, and notwithstanding the genuineness and, beneath its artificial surface, the heartiness of the English character, it has without doubt its repellent side. Englishmen themselves will hardly deny that too many of them are arrogant, insolent, and overbearing. And yet, as I write this, I am almost ashamed to do so, remembering what I never can forget, and should grieve and shame to forget, the kindness, the gentleness, the sweetness of nature, the almost tender thoughtfulness for others, that I have seen in so many Englishmen, not only in England, but here, before I ever met them on their native soil. It has been my good fortune to render some of them some very trifling services; and these were not only accepted in a way that enhanced greatly the pleasure of rendering them, but were ever afterward remembered and acknowledged in a way so frank and simple and charming that I was both delighted and ashamed at such a recognition. I therefore do protest with all my heart against Mr. Henry James's Duke of Green Erin as a type of his race, or (although I have known no dukes) as a fair representative of his rank. And yet, without doubt, he is a very possible Englishman, and a possible duke. His insolence does not pertain to his rank; it may be found in all ranks; but of course a duke who is by nature insolent may, and will, insult with greater freedom and impunity than is possible to a person of inferior position. Indeed, this trait of English manners manifests itself most readily and strongly in persons of rank and persons in authority. That it should do so is only to be expected. Such persons have more temptations than others have, as well as better opportunities, for the exhibition of an overbearing nature. This disregard of others does by no means always accompany a coarse and brutal organization. My captain was a coarse man; but my English friend who compelled me to bring him to book was one of the most refined and courteous of gentlemen. He merely took advantage of his position to rid himself of some trouble by setting quietly aside a man of whom he in fact knew very little. Perhaps this is not really an English trait. Not improbably there are just such men in France, in Germany, or in Japan. From what we know of Prince Bismarck, I am inclined to think that under like circumstances he would behave much in the same way. Mr. Trollope has admirably illustrated this unpleasant side of English character in his Duke of Omnium and his Marquis of Brotherton. It is not that these men were bad, but that they were deliberately insolent in their manner, so that in the case of the marquis we are all inclined to cheer when Dean Lovelace flings him into the fireplace.[1]

The influence of aristocracy and of the constant pressure upward of the inferior ranks is the cause of much of the forbidding manner of English gentlemen. They show this manner more among themselves than they do to others. The Marquis of Brotherton, because he was marquis and the head of his family, was insolent to his younger brother. And for this same reason Englishmen are suspicious of each other when they are not in the same rank of life. The meeting of two Englishmen who are strangers, knowing little or nothing of each other, and who have occasion to make acquaintance, — the doubt, the coldness, the holding out of hesitating hands, — is not a cheering sight. But if they find each other " all right," they will in a few days be mutually using their surnames without the Mr., or

[1] I mean not only the first Duke of Omnium to whom we are introduced, but the second, whom Mr. Trollope presents as an admirable person. But " Planty Pol's " behavior to Frank Tregedar when he first proposes for Lady Mary is very unbecoming a gentleman; and even to the doubtful Major —— (bidden to Gatherum Castle by the duchess, and asking of him nothing more than better men and men of equal rank had been asked before) his conduct is insufferably insolent. It awakens a desire to snub such a man to the quick, while treating him with the most deferential politeness

their titles without the "handle," and their intercourse will be much more hearty and informal than if they were "Americans" under the same circumstances. Their shyness of each other when they are strangers is most conspicuous in London, where there are so many people with money and fine clothes and passable manners that "one knows nothing about." Locality is no protection. Belgravia is almost as full of snobs as Fifth Avenue. If you doubt it, ask any snob who lives in either, and see if he does not admit it, deploringly.

The daily intercourse of families and friends in England is hearty and warm, although not effusive. They are not ready to give the hand to strangers; but very commonly all of a family, including the guests, shake hands on parting for the night; and on meeting in the morning the same greeting is hardly less common. It was charming to see two middle-aged men, who lived in the same house, meet in the breakfast room, and, shaking hands warmly, say, "Good-morning, brother." When I saw all this and was admitted to be a part of it, I wondered where the English coldness was of which we hear so much.

Salutation is so common, even between passing strangers in the country and while traveling, that I was reminded of the manners of New England in my early boyhood. Men on leaving a railway car, either first-class or second-class, will say "Good-morning" or "Good-evening," although they have exchanged hardly a word with you on the route, — which, however, is rare ; and this habit, which has come down from stage-coach times, and has been preserved on the railway by the small carriages, is one of the reliefs and pleasures of that unnatural mode of travel

The porter or guard who puts you into your carriage and hands you your bag, hurried as he is, yet finds time to say, " Good-morning, sir." If you are walking on a country road, those whom you meet salute you. The country folk, old and young, male and female, do so always. In Essex the rustic boys have a pretty way of waving their hands in the air by way of salutation as you pass. To see a knot of these little fellows execute this flourish is very charming.

One day, as I was walking in Sussex through a beautiful lane sunk deep between its green sides, where wild flowers grew at the feet of hollies with polished leaves, and of other little trees that stood so thick that they reduced noonday to twilight, I met a woman of the lower class, indeed the lowest. She was very handsome, in the prime of life, with a grand figure, and dark, bright, melancholy eyes. She looked more like a Roman than like an English woman ; and I do believe that her noble face and swarthy skin had come straight down to her from the loins of some Roman soldier, perhaps in Cæsar's legions. She had a child in her arms, and another walked by her side, holding her hand. As I passed her she paused in her walk, and, courtesying, said, " Good-morning, sir ; " and her sweet voice was English, although her face was not. I returned her salutation, and passed on, asking myself, Why should this woman, who never saw me before, and who is bearing doubly the burden of motherhood [for it could be perceived that the child in her arms would ere many months have to yield its place to another], — why should she, to whom every man owes deference, pause and courtesy to me because I am a " gentleman " ? For unmistakably there was deference in her salutation, and a recognition of the difference of our conditions. I was ashamed that I had not stopped and given her something that might have added a little to her comfort. Perhaps she expected the gentleman to do so. But she was too noble in mien and carriage, she impressed me too much, for me to offer her a trifling alms, lowly as her condition was. I turned my head, and if I had found that she was looking after me I should have gone back to give her more, perhaps, than I could afford. But I saw only her back, as she walked erectly and slowly on, with a grace which her burden and her condition could not repress, and which her poor garments rather revealed ; and at a turn in the lane she disappeared into its cool, clear twilight, and I only wished her health and happiness in her coming hour.

I have heretofore remarked that the dress of English gentlemen is very plain and simple. For although Macaulay bought many embroidered waistcoats, in which he arrayed himself with great delight, this personal trait must be regarded as one of the eccentricities of genius.[1] In its simplicity the Englishman's dress is not unlike that of gentlemen of corresponding condition in this country, but in his manner of wearing it there is a difference. Tidiness seems to be the most important point of dress in the

---

[1] This comparative sobriety of the English gentleman in external things seems to be a trait of race, and not a modern development. If we may believe Massinger, it manifested itself even in the days when rich dress was a mark of rank : —

> " *Viceroy.*   The slave is very fine
> *Cucuh.*   Your English slaves
> Are ever so ; I 've seen an English slave
> Far finer than his master.   There 's a state point
> Worthy your observation."
>
>   *A Very Woman*, IV. 2.

This of course is tenfold truer now.

eyes of a well-cared-for Englishman. Everything
about him is snug. He is like a horse well groomed
and harnessed. His morning coat, be it frock or
"cutaway," is never flying loose, but is buttoned
closely. This tidiness and completeness of apparel
is a sort of religion. I remember being in a railway
carriage with a young man who was very correct at
all points. The day, which had opened gloomily,
had suddenly cleared and become very warm. He
was dressed in a heavy brown tweed suit, and every
button of his coat was sent well home into its proper
button-hole. Another gentleman and myself relieved
ourselves by unbuttoning our coats, and I, as there
was no lady there, opened my waistcoat; for the air
was damp as well as warm, and we were sweltering.
But he would plainly have endured martyrdom rather
than be guilty of such looseness, and he sat impassible, bolt upright and tightly buttoned. He suffered
and was strong. I am sure that we all wished that
he had been less true to his religion.

The Englishman comes down in the morning completely dressed in this tight, tidy way. He does not
even indulge himself in the great luxury of easy life,
a slippered breakfast, but comes wearing, in addition
to his buttoned coat, stout, brightly-polished shoes.
While I was in England I did not see one gentleman
in slippers outside of his bedroom. This strait-laced-
ness has its merits. English gentlemen at all times,
unless they are recognized slovens, look trim, well set
up, presentable, and ready for service, whether business or pleasure. Nor do gentlemen in England of
good position look as if their clothes were all bought,
ready-made, at one "establishment," and as if they
had slept in them the night before in a "palace-car."

The same praise cannot be given to Englishwomen, who, although they dress elaborately for the evening, go about in the morning, too many of them, with hair and dress the reverse of snug and tidy.

Dinner is the great fact of English daily life. " Dine with me " is the Englishman's first request, if he likes you, or if he wishes to show you any attention. A letter of introduction is honored by an invitation to dinner, and that given, nothing more is regarded as necessary ; anything more depends on kindness and personal liking. To some " Americans " this dining, which is always formal, becomes oppressive. A Yankee friend of mine, a man of intelligence and charming manners, who, with ruddy cheeks and well-cut features, looks much more like the commonly entertained idea of a handsome Englishman than most of the Englishmen I met, went to England well provided with letters, and was soon so wearied with these inevitable invitations to formal dinners that he stopped the presentation of his credentials, and kept himself to himself. " I was bored to death," he said to me, " with the constant recurrence of the regular routine, and the dull succession of eating and drinking in full dress. I did n't want their dinners ; I wanted to see *them* at their houses, in an easy, informal way. As I could n't do that, I cut the matter short, and depended upon my own resources." As for myself, having taken no letters, I escaped these obligation dinners from strangers ; and in the half dozen dinner parties at which I was present I was more fortunate than he. Yet I saw enough of the heavy formality of these entertainments to be in some sympathy with him.

The habit of saying grace is gradually passing

away from the daily life of England, although if a clergyman is present he is invited to do his office; and even that of family prayers is beginning to yield to broad-church latitudinarianism, notwithstanding the influence of high-church altitudinarianism and low-church platitudinarianism. In more than one instance I was informed that attendance at prayers was not insisted upon. But I also remember more than one in which grace before meat was made more graceful by coming from the lips of a fair daughter of the house.

Table-talk at dinner is a much more formidable affair in England than it is with us. It is an "institution." Men prepare themselves for it as they do to make a speech. In some cases host and hostess arrange what subjects shall be started to bring out certain guests; and the table is hushed while this or that clever man discourses, in sentences sometimes rather too carefully constructed, upon a subject which is as slyly but as deliberately dragged before him as a cork and string before a kitten, and which he jumps at much as his feline prototype does at the mimic mouse. There is something of this kind with us among dinner givers of the more cultivated sort, but nothing to be compared with the formidable colloquies of the formal English dinner. In England is found, moreover, the dinner soliloquist, whom I cannot but regard as a dreadful form of the social bore. I remember one such man at a dinner party of some twenty people. He began to talk after he had spooned his soup for a moment or two, and as he talked very pleasantly, his sonorous voice, going forth to the whole table, was a welcome help over the threshold of our entertainment. But he went on, until his talk became a discourse. At each fall of his voice I supposed that he would stop; but he managed to link one sentence to another until he bound us all up in an endless chain of words. Although not aged, he was too old a man to snub, and also too good-natured and too well informed. And he was tyrannical in asserting himself. The sonority of his voice and the weight of his manner bore down all opposition and thrust aside all auxiliaries. There was no conversation possible except little fragmentary tête-à-têtes with one's next neighbor. Straight through dinner and through dessert did that dreadful man hold forth. How he managed to eat, how to breathe, was a mystery. When the ladies had retired, he resumed his seat with a sentence beginning with an "and," that connected it with what he was saying when our hostess rose; and he ceased not to pour down his flood of words upon us until we found refuge in the drawing-room. Such men are tolerated in England, perhaps, because they are useful in the performance of that most tedious and oppressive of all social solemnities, a formal dinner party. I was about to say that such talkers would not be tolerated here; but do we not listen to after-dinner speeches? Where, then, is the limit of our endurance?

Dinner, even daily family dinner, is such a religious rite in England that above a certain condition of life a special dress for it is absolutely required. Full evening dress at dinner is in England the mark of gentry. I once made a mistake in this respect. Being invited to a country house, some thirty miles from London, where I had time to stay but one day, and being a traveler, I thought that I might venture to go with only a small hand bag, and to appear at dinner in a dark frock. But I found that I might better have brought my portmanteau, my dressing-case, and my valet, if I had had one. It would be impossible for me to say how I knew this, but I felt it in a way that could not be mistaken. The very flames of the wax candles in the great silver cande-labra seemed to look askance at me, as I dared to sit there in my plebeian costume. The feeling amused me ; for I have little real respect for mere social con-ventionalities, least of all for those which concern dress. That a gentleman should be scrupulously nice in his person at all times, and that it is well for him to dress becomingly and appropriately, need not be said ; but that he, as well as the butler and the wait-ers, must, under pain of social damnation, put on such a queer garment as a black swallow-tailed dress-coat and a white neck-tie, and that a lady should make her-self uncomfortable by her full dress (for that it does make them uncomfortable ladies will hardly deny) because they are going to eat and drink together, as they eat and drink every day, is not with me an article of saving faith. Such, however, is the social righteousness of these English people that it was edi-fying to an unregenerate creature like me to see them at any time violate any one of their unwritten com-mandments ; and I took great comfort, one day, at seeing a belated honorable (that is, the son of a peer) come hastily in and sit down to dinner, like a pro-fane mortal, in his tweed coat.

I also could not avoid observing that men who were very scrupulous about evening dress were less fastid-ious upon other points of manners which could hardly be called conventional. I have seen a peer, who would almost as soon dine in his shirt and trousers as in a morning coat, sit after dinner in the drawing-room talking with a lady, and, taking his foot upon his knee to nurse, gradually run his hand half-way up his trousers that he might scratch his leg; and his was not a solitary instance of performances somewhat of this kind.   To me, "salvage man" as I am, born and bred in the wilderness of New York, and wont to roam with untutored mind from my native haunts over the waste places of New England, there did nevertheless seem to be some incongruity in the code of manners which prescribed swallow-tails, but permitted scratching, and which required buttoned coats and laced-up boots at breakfast tables at which there were no napkins.

In English society, however, the mere externals of manners, eating, drinking, dressing, and so forth, are much like those of "America" among well-bred people; and in these respects the countries seem to be approaching rather than receding.   But society there has yet a clearly defined form, which here it lacks. This is maintained by the influence of the great universities, of the cathedral establishments, of the country houses, of the county families, of Parliament, and of other long-established institutions in which the structure of society is involved.

CHAPTER XII.

SOME HABITS OF ENGLISH LIFE.

THE difference between manners — the subject of my last chapter — and habits of life is not great or strongly marked, and indeed the two things shade off into each with such delicate gradation that it is difficult to point out where one ends and the other begins. Soon, however, we reach from either side a line where we plainly see that one is what the other is not. This being the case, what I have to say now will seem in some respects a continuation of the foregoing chapter, but in others not so. If any of my readers are so bound to titles that this incongruity will disturb them, I am sorry ; but I beg them to remember that on this occasion and in this respect the fault is not with the writer, but in the subject.

Whether discipline in the British army is stricter than it is in the army of the United States I do not know ; I had no opportunity of making a comparison. In other departments of life it need hardly be said that rules are more rigidly enforced and authority is more absolutely maintained there than here. When Charles II. visited Westminster School, Dr. Busby, the head master, kept on his hat before the king lest the scholars might suppose there was a greater man than he. It would seem that the doctor might have taught deference better by showing it ; but his good-natured majesty allowed the plea. The

discipline of domestic life is insisted upon with an
exacting precision unknown to " Americans " of the
present day, and not, it seemed to me, disadvanta-
geously. I was much impressed and amused upon one
occasion of observing this difference. It was on a
visit to Knole, in Kent, — one of the most interesting among the remaining great houses of the Tudor
period. I was visiting for a day or two at a house
not many miles from Knole, and my host kindly
drove over there with me one Sunday afternoon. My
expectations of pleasure were very high ; for Knole
is in perfect preservation, and is built on such a
scale of magnificence that it contains, if I remember
rightly, no less than eighty-seven staircases. Its
oaken carvings, its corridors, and its bay-windows —
if we may believe prints and photographs — fully
justify the epithet " very noble " which Pepys so
often applies to his dinners, and as a whole are hardly
surpassed in England for their beauty and their character. It is indeed a perfect example of that admirable and truly English style of domestic architecture
which on the decay of feudalism succeeded the castle.

Our drive was delightful ; for the day was fine,
and Kent is called the garden of England. Our little jaunt was not without its little incident, which although trifling was significant, because my *cicerone*
was a nobleman of high rank, and of historic name.
As we were rolling along the smooth roads we met
a party of two or three taking a Sunday afternoon
stroll. When we drew near each other my host recognized them, and exclaiming, " Oh, there are the
——s ! " bade the coachman pull up. He sprang
out, and greeted them warmly ; and there was a lit

tle chat, with reciprocal inquiries and invitations. On resuming his place at my side, he apologized for the interruption, saying good-naturedly, " The ——s are very estimable people, and one does n't like to pass one's neighbors on a Sunday without a pleasant word." This would have been nothing worth remark had not I known the ——s by name and by reputation. They were very rich, and had recently established themselves in a country-seat in Kent; but according to English social gradation they were inferior in rank even to merchants; for they had grown rich, not by trade, but by a trade, and the family still carried on the practice of their art and mystery. Yet there could have been nothing simpler, franker, or heartier than my host's manner with them. It was altogether unlike the manner that, according to generally preconceived notions, might have been expected under the circumstances from a nobleman of his rank and position. I fear that as he was apologizing to me there was a snobbish note of exclamation in one of my eyes, and one of interrogation in the other; for, although I did not say a word or make a motion, he added kindly and simply, " I don't think it's kind or nice [nice is a great word in England] to treat such excellent people coldly when they are neighbors." It is only right that I should add that, because of his public position, in him popular manners were not only becoming, but might be serviceable, and that the ——s had a great establishment. But truly, I do not believe that he was influenced by this consideration; for when he was here in his younger days, he had been remarked by all who knew him well for simplicity of manners and thorough good nature.

We soon entered Knole Park, a place the very sight of which begat in my soul a serene and placid joy. It is grandly timbered, and is more undulating than any other park that I had the good fortune to see. It was manifestly open to the whole neighborhood on Sunday afternoons at least; for we saw groups, some of them very rustic in appearance and manners, walking over the greensward, or sitting under the great trees. And these people seemed to enjoy themselves much more heartily than any that I had ever seen in "America" on a similar Sunday or Saturday outing. The chief reason of this difference appeared to me that they did not stand upon their dignity, nor give their minds to being or to seeming as elegant and as fine as anybody else. If the old French chronicler found that the English people took their pleasure sadly, according to their custom, what would he say to the pleasure-taking of the English race under the elevating influences of democratic institutions! Whenever we approached these strolling parties near enough, they saluted us deferentially, but cheerily; and although my friend's equipage and his face were probably well known in the neighborhood, my general observation leads me to believe that the same would have been the case if we had both been strangers.

All through the park were fine beeches; and those which stood near the stone wall which shut in the gardens and private grounds, and over which the quaint but graceful gables of the great house peered, were the largest and grandest trees of the kind that I ever saw. Their roots, which, after the habit of the beech, began to spread well above ground, seemed sometimes to me like great buttresses of the majestic towering trunks, and at others like monstrous claws thrust savagely out to clutch the earth and bear it up into the air. The beeches at Knole, as I learned afterwards, are famous as being among the finest in all England.

We drove to the gate-way, descended, and pulled the bell by a chain ending in a knobbed handle, which hung by the door-post. A little door in the great gate opened, and a porter presented himself who was the very reverse of the "proud portér" of the old ballads. He was a fat little man, — so fat that he seemed to stick in the door-way. He wore a bright scarlet waistcoat, to the making of which there went much cloth. His face was beardless, sleek, and jolly, although it was sobered with evident effort to the decorum of his function; possibly also by the consciousness of a disagreeable duty which he knew that he must perform. He was much such a looking man as the late distinguished and rotund comedian, Mr. William Blake, would have been if he had got himself up in a scarlet waistcoat as a porter. My companion gave him good-day, and saying that we should like to see the house, stepped forward to lead the way in. " Beg pa'don, m'lud," said the little man, keeping himself directly in the doorway, " but Lord Sackville said that no one was to be allowed to come in wiles he was away. There's work goin' on; the 'ouse is a-bein' repaired." I saw my friend's countenance fall; but he brightened up in a moment, and said, " Could n't you let us in? I've driven over just to show my friend the house." " Very sorry, m'lud, that I can't let you come in, but his lordship's orders was very p'ticler : " and he stood in the door-way, deferential, very deferential — in manner, but a very firm, immovable, round little fact. My kind companion was evidently much disappointed; and seeing that the porter knew him he said, making another effort on my behalf, " I 'm sure that if my friend, Lord Sackville, were here he would let us in, and I wish very much to have this gentleman see the house. It 's his only opportunity." "No doubt, m'lud, his lordship would be most happy, if he was here; but my orders was very p'ticler, m'lud, — no one to come in wiles he was away." Apology and firmness could not have been more completely or more happily combined than they were in the face and manner and speech of this jolly little red-waistcoated porter. My friend looked ruefully in my face, and we got into the carriage again. As we drove off, after expressing his sorrow that I should have been so disappointed, he said, " I could have gone in, of course; for Lord Sackville and I are friends, and I saw the man knew me well. I could have easily pushed past him and have told him that I would make it all right with Sackville, as of course I could have done; but I did n't exactly like to show him the example of disobeying orders. Indeed, I 'm very sorry." As for me, I was sorely disappointed, but on the whole glad that the matter had ended as it did. It would have been a great pleasure to me to see Knole, with its eighty-seven staircases; but I don't know that it would have been greater than to see a nobleman of my companion's rank and position, a county magistrate too (a high position in England), yield gracefully and turn away from the door of his friend's empty house, which he had driven miles to see, rather than by a little gentle aggression lead a mere liveried servant into what would have been only a constructive disobedience of orders. My respect for the porter was great; but my respect for my friend was even greater than it had been before.

The mention of the careless and hearty enjoyment of their Sunday's pleasure by the rustic visitors of Knole Park reminds me that in London I came again and again upon little groups of children dancing in dingy courts upon the damp pavement. It might be drizzling rain, although not enough to wash their faces, yet they, poor hatless, shoeless, almost breakfastless creatures, danced, and danced merrily, without other music than that of their own little pipes, which they set up, unlike Chaucer's prioress, without entuning in their noses full sweetly. Such a sight could not be seen among the free and enlightened inhabitants of this country, except indeed among the children of German emigrants, who are often tempted into street saltation by brass bands, and even by hand-organs. But where among real "Americans" — the Yankees or the Virginians, for example — would you find hatless and shoeless boys and girls dancing in the open air in mere childish gayety of heart? Let us not boast untruly; the hatlessness, the shoelessness, the rags, and the dirt, we might find; but where the capacity of happiness which can despise rags, rejoice in bare heads and feet, revel in dirt, and set at naught falling water?

And yet these people work much harder than we do, and for less-wages. They do what I have never seen done in this country, — work in their gardens, if not in their fields, on Sunday. I have mentioned my surprise at hearing the cries of street venders in London on Sunday; it was even a greater novelty to me to see on my Sunday walks in the country, wherever I went, men, evidently respectable and in comfortable circumstances, at work with spade and hoe and rake among their vegetables. If I stopped to speak to them, which I did if I were near enough, they did not seem at all as if they were surprised in doing something of which they should be ashamed, or show the least shyness. Shyness, however, they would not be likely to show in any case, as I soon discovered. The existence of established ranks has the effect of causing a greater freedom of manner than is usual with us among people in any condition of life. They have fewer reserves ; they have need of fewer.

In illustration of this I recall a sight that I saw in Hyde Park one soft autumnal morning. I was to take luncheon at a house near the park; and as I was whiling away the latter part of the morning by a stroll through this noble pleasure-ground, I came upon two women, one sitting and the other reclining upon the grass. As I drew near them, I perceived that one was middle-aged and the other very young. Their likeness showed that they were mother and daughter, although the look of the girl's wan face and wistful eyes was very unlike the bright and rugged comeliness of the matron's. In a moment it was plain that the mother had brought her ailing daughter there for the benefit of the sun and air. The girl lay upon a shawl, with her body all in the sun ; but her head rested in her mother's lap, which was in the shade. I stopped and spoke to the mother. Her language was good, and the inflections of her voice, although hardly refined, were not coarse. They were evidently not what we should call poor people, but humbly well to do — so much so that I should not have thought of offering a gratuity (although the shilling-receptive faculty in England rises very high) ; but yet they sat out together in this way in such a very public place, and talked freely and pleasantly with a stranger, without any of that shyness and reserve and consciousness which would have been found among people of their condition in "America."

Most Englishmen of the lower-middle class and the lower class in cities have a way of walking which is a distinguishing habit of common life. I had observed it in Englishmen of this sort in the streets of New York, where I could tell them by it as far as I could see them. They lay themselves out in their walking, as if they were doing a day's work. They walk not only with their feet and legs, but with their hips and their shoulders and their arms, not swinging the latter, but arching them out more or less from their sides, and putting them forward stiffly as they step. Withal they look conscious of their walking, and seem well pleased that they are doing it correctly. This gait and carriage of body is most remarkable in the soldiers that one sees about the streets of London and of garrison towns like Canterbury, and in the cockney creature who has come to be known by the generic name 'Arry. You will meet two soldiers tightened up to the extreme of endurance in their scarlet shell jackets, with little flat caps so far down the sides of their heads that you cannot see why they hesitate at coming down all the way, and these two fellows, one of whom is pretty sure to carry a rattan with a jaunty air, will take up the room of three men by the set-out of their four arms from their four sides, and will walk as if their locomotion, instead of being by human muscles, were by

18

clockwork and steam. The number of their imitators cannot be told. An English gentleman has none of this toilsome swagger. He walks quite easily and unconsciously, and generally with a good, manly stride, just as a man of corresponding condition of life in Boston, New York, or Philadelphia walks. But in those places you will not see in persons of inferior condition that strange mode of locomotion which I have endeavored to describe.

On being measured by a London tailor whose custom was among the best people, I was surprised at the inquiry whether I would have a "pistol-pocket" in my trousers. It was the first time that I had had such a question put to me. But I found that this provision for carrying concealed fire-arms under the coat-skirts is quite as common in England as it is in that dreadful country which the British Philistine critic of society so constantly uses as a frightful example. Nor was I without confirming testimony on the subject. The inquiry reminded me of a passage in a story called "The Going Out of Alessandro Pozzone," which I read in one of the London magazines. An Englishman intends to investigate, and perhaps to avenge, the suspected murder of his father by an Italian, Pozzone; and at the end of the story are these two paragraphs : —

"When this was done, he put his hand under his coat-tails for a moment, as if to tighten the back-strap of his waistcoat; did not tighten the strap; went and got his hat; descended the steps from the dining-room into the garden, opened the garden gate, and went out into the lane."

He provokes an assault by his victim, and then —

"The Englishman drew himself up with a powerful ef

fort, shook himself clear of his assailant, slipped his hand beneath his waistcoat as though to loose its strap, drew out the hand —

" Bang ! "

Could there be a "higher-toned" proceeding than that, or one, according to British censure, more thoroughly "American"? The matter-of-course way in which the manœuvre and the preparation for it are rather hinted at than told is very significant. I will add that I saw more bowie-knives in London shop-windows during a few weeks' residence than I had seen in all my life in New York, although I found it not easy to get there or in Birmingham or in Liverpool a pocket-knife of first-rate quality.

Gentlemen in England have a very general fashion of wearing rings in what seemed to me a very lady-like way. Upon the hand of a man who can afford to keep it clean and out of danger of knocks and blows, a signet ring, engraved with a cipher, a crest, or a beautiful design, seems fit and becoming. Nor are we unaccustomed to see examples of annular gorgeousness — notably vast amethysts — upon hands which are not so cared for. But this is not the ring-wearing of gentlemen in England. There small rings set with stones are in favor. Diamonds set in heavy hoops, rubies as eyes in the heads of golden snakes which coil three or four times around the finger, diamonds and rubies, diamonds and sapphires, in alternation, are seen upon the fingers of most of the men who are above the lower-middle class, — noblemen, clergymen, army officers, university dons, hard-headed men of affairs, merchants. Not one ring only ; indeed, a single ring upon a man's hand is rather exceptional. You shall see a big fellow with big brown hands, or an elderly man of staid business habits, with three or even four jeweled rings upon his fingers; not unfrequently there will be two upon one finger. The turquoise is in great favor, — the most unmanly and woman-proper of all precious stones, in my judgment; most suitable to the fairest and daintiest of the sex. It is frequently alternated with the diamond on a heavy hoop, a wide space being left between the stones. The fashion impressed me as quite incongruous with manly dignity and simplicity. But perhaps this was merely because I was unaccustomed to it. I know that I saw a man whom I knew to be a gentleman, and had good reason to believe not unmanly, with a diamond ring and a plain hoop on one finger, a turquoise on another, and a ruby-eyed snake whose coils covered one joint of a third. If he and his beringed fellows had not been of my own blood and speech I should not have thought this habit remarkable; but thus it strikes a stranger who is yet not a foreigner.

Certain small exactions in England irritate the stranger, accustomed to the freedom from such petty taxation which prevails in the United States. For example, you are expected to pay for time-tables at railway stations, and for a bill of the play and toilet privileges at the theatres. The supplying of most of these needs is a little business which is farmed out to people in humble circumstances. The practice is not peculiar to England, but prevails upon the Continent. Englishmen, however, are beginning to fret under it, and to protest against it; and ere long 't will probably pass away, and England will be on one more trifling point " Americanized."

One sweet trait of English life I must not forget,

negative although it is.   During the whole of my
visit, neither in town nor country, north, south, east,
or west, did I see a spittoon, — not one.   I did not
miss the things, and it was not until my visit was almost over that I noted their absence, although the
difference of the two countries in this respect is a
very noteworthy fact in household economy.   For,
looking out of a back window this morning, did I not
count seventeen of them leaning against the house-
wall of my neighbor, Mrs. Hashitt, who takes a few
genteel boarders? — seventeen, so help me Santa
Cloacina, gorgeous in crimson and green and gold,
with their foul maws empty, and their great fuming
mouths turned up to the blessed sun!   She, being a
woman of elegant language, calls 'em cuspidores;
why, the genius of gentility who presides over her
establishment, including the seventeen, only knows.
But neither spittoon nor cuspidore saw I in England.

The absence of this unlovely utensil is due in a
great measure to the fact that in England a decent
man is as unlikely to chew tobacco as in America a
decent man is likely to wish the ladies of his acquaintance to know that he chews it.   (In vain, however,
are all his concealments and devices; for the breath of
a tobacco-chewer harbingers his approach before he is
visible.)   But it is also to be remarked that the natural tendency to spitting of any kind is much less in
England than it is here.   Our climate — meaning
chiefly the dry wind from west and northwest —
causes an irritation of the throat and the nostrils
which produces such a secretion of saliva and of mu-
cus as in England is almost unknown to those who
are in health.   It is nearly impossible for a man to
pass a day here, except in summer or in early au-

tumn, without relieving his mouth of some irritation
of this kind, at least — as Mr. Everett said that he
blew his nose — " in the privacy of me own apartment." But while I was in England I was quite free
from any such annoyance.[1]

In England everybody seems to have leisure time.
A gentleman is always supposed to have time to wait,
to sit down, to chat, unless he has shut himself up
that he may work. At an eating-house, unless you
dine *table d'hôte* fashion, *à la carte*, the time which
elapses between your sitting at table and the appearance of what you have ordered would be a sore trial
to most Yankees. If I had opportunity to look about
me and observe my neighbors, I did not mind it ; but
once or twice when I was shut up in a box all alone,
with no company but thoughts and memories, I fretted at my forced idleness, although I do not believe
that rapid movement is the greatest of all blessings. Perhaps it is because the Englishman moves
so quickly and so punctually when he does move that
he is able to take life leisurely at some time of day.
Your very railway traveling seems there a form of
leisure, a kind of rest, a soft, swift-passing silence.
You are taken noiselessly off at an appointed minute,
carried along with such nearly silent speed that you
seem to be sitting still to see the world glide past you,

[1] Our British kinsmen are, however, a little too " bumptious " in their
criticisms on this point. They talk and write as if this unpleasant habit
were unheard of in England, and should be set down as one of those Amer-
icanisms they are so eager to discover. They forget that Rosalind tells
Orlando that under certain circumstances " the cleanliest shift is to spit ; "
that in the same play we learn that "hawking and spitting were ever the
prologues to a bad voice ; " that George Brummell, that model of British
elegance, declared that " it was impossible to spit in clay," and had therefore a silver spittoon ; and that Miss Edgeworth tells us in *Patronage* that
English Clay paid a coachman to "teach him the true spit," to attain
which this peculiarly English gentleman sacrificed one of his front teeth

and you are set noiselessly down at the appointed
minute. You may not only read, but you may talk
with as much ease and comfort as if you were in a
library or a drawing-room, and indeed can write letters which may be read without difficulty. But as to
leisure, even the poorest man seems to have it, if he
quits his work at all. If an artisan takes a glass of
beer with a friend, they sit down to it, if they sit on
kegs with a barrel-head between them as a table.
Their beer seems to be drunk not merely to supply fluid waste and to furnish needed stimulant, but
rather as a festive accompaniment and garnish of a
brief time of leisure. The making of a mere gutter
of the throat is in England, I believe that I may say
in Europe, almost unknown. Indeed, there are other
things besides the star of empire that westward take
their way. The farther westward, the greater the
tendency to perpendicularity in potation. The Oriental squats at his sherbet or his coffee; the ancients
who dwelt around the Mediterranean Sea reclined as
they drank; the Frenchman sits at his ease over his
thin *limonade* or his *café noir;* the Englishman at
least plumps himself down upon bench or settle, and
sits there, even if in semi-silence, until his beer is
drunk; the " American," standing erect and solemnly·
announcing " My respects to you, sir," pours the fluid
into his person, sets down the glass, and silently
makes off about his business. Leisure would seem
to be almost undeniably a condition of mental ripe-
ness and of bodily grace. Wisdom and fine manners
have always come from the East.

One reason of the possession of leisure time by
Englishmen in so notable a degree seemed to me to
be that there is little time spent by them in seeming

to be what they are not. For the doing of this is a great consumer of time. The endeavor to be as fine as anybody, to live, or to seem to live, as luxuriously as those of much larger means live, is in itself, and quite apart from the question of income and outgo, a heavy draft upon all the forces, intellectual, moral, and material. In particular it uses up that part of time which, not being given to work or to the daily round of duties, would otherwise be leisure. That the tendency to this endeavor is favored and increased by a democratic form of society is the least that can be said. In fact, democracy urges, spurs, goads, all those under its dominion, except the few who are so independent in thought and in feeling as to be sufficient unto themselves, into this kind of social dishonesty, — dishonesty, because it is an imposition upon one's neighbors, and an attempted delusion of one's self. For in a democratic society, although there must be various conditions of life, the absence of established rank, and even of any perceptible and admitted distinctions of class, involves also the absence of the idea of fitness, of that which is becoming to the individual. In such a society money is the only standard of estimation the propriety of which is generally recognized. That is fit for a man which he can afford; and whether it is becoming is a matter of personal taste, — concerning which it is not to be disputed. Hence, the shocking and ridiculous incongruities in wealthy democratic societies. Probably in no other place since the world began has the jewel of gold been so often seen in the swine's snout as in New York, — New York, which with the elements of the finest society in the world has really nothing which may be rightly called a society; because, not

being a capital nor even a metropolis, not being the
centre of any interest, political, literary, artistic, or
even social, other than a commercial interest, it has
come to be merely a place for the speedy getting and
the speedier spending of money.

That a condition of things having some likeness to
this exists in England, and particularly in London, no
one who is even moderately well informed upon the
subject would think for a moment of disputing. But
notwithstanding the social tendencies of the time,
there are influences which greatly modify that condition and restrain its material manifestations. There
is the influence of the nobility and gentry, unavoid-
able, indisputable, irresponsible ; there is the influence of the great universities, a powerful and constant, although a silent force ; there is the influence
of the established church, and of the army and navy ;
and, moreover, there is the widely diffused sense of
subordination and of decorum ; all of which are checks
upon the aggressiveness of mere rich and vulgar pretension. To go no higher, the man who is " in holy
orders," or he who " serves her Majesty," although
he may not have two hundred pounds a year, has a
position which, notwithstanding the boasted omnip-
otence of money and its real power in society, mere
money cannot give in England. And although the
clergyman and the soldier may fawn upon Crœsus,
Crœsus knows this, and they know it ; and because
of it he lets them fawn, and pays them for their
fawning.

Indeed, social shamming is of very little avail in
England. The shamming must be very good to
make any impression at all ; and even then its success is short-lived. It is soon exposed, and quietly

put down.   The very country folk, the farmers, the villagers, and the farm laborers, will not put up with country-gentleman airs and old-family graces on the part of new landlords.   Lord A——, wealthiest of such raw country magnates, was openly snubbed by his humble neighbors when he took upon himself the gracious airs of a lord of the soil, and was given to understand that with all his money and his newly acquired acres he was only a rich Londoner.   And Mr. Disraeli could not use such a word as "after-math" to his rural neighbors around Hughenden, or speak to them of weather "which gives that brightness to the barley which farmers love to see," without being girded at by all the scoffing scribes of her Majesty's opposition.   In which they are hardly fair; for Mr. Disraeli, Hebrew *littérateur* although he was, inherited his little manor of Hughenden, and surely might have used any good English rural phrase with at least as much propriety as there was in his being an English earl.   But Englishmen are notably intolerant of any social pretension of this sort, and even the slightest exhibition of it is sure to provoke derision.[1]

The distinction between persons who are " in trade " and those who are not is insisted upon with constant vigilance.   This discrimination is perpetuated and deepened by the etiquette of the court.   If there are any " American " ladies who value their privilege of going to court (and at the United States legation it is believed that some such still remain), it would be well for them to remember this absolute

---

[1] I should say that the lordship of five thousand acres for three generations was requisite to the attainment of a well established, recognized position among the county families.

law when they accept the marriage proposals of British subjects. I knew of a case in which one of them was married to a wealthy British merchant, and, going to England, lived very luxuriously ; but as the wife of a British subject in trade she could not go to court ; while her unmarried sister, being what Pepys would have called a she-citizen of the United States, was solemnly and triumphantly presented. This distinction is carried to absurd extreme by some persons, generally women, who, although within the court circle, are of snobbish natures, and generally of new-born gentility. It has been told recently in a London newspaper of an English lady, whose married name is of most " base and mechanical " origin, that, having had one interview with a governess whom she thought of engaging, and having been much pleased with her, she on the second interview informed her that she was sorry that she could not engage her, as she had discovered that she had lived in a family the head of which was " in trade," — Sir Bache Cunard. The governess was the gainer by this manifestation of vulgar pretense and fastidiousness, for her services were soon afterwards engaged by a duchess. But in an aristocratic society, no less than in a barber's shop, a line must be drawn somewhere ; and the England of to-day draws it at trade.

Nor does the consciousness of the consequent distinction, ever present with those who are either above or below the line, imply arrogance on the one part or subservience on the other. It is recognized and insisted on by no persons more than by domestic servants, who, as I shall have occasion to remark hereafter, are great sticklers for rank and precedence A lady who was of rank both by birth and by mar riage, and who was the mistress of a great house, told me, as she was kindly explaining to me some of the details of such an establishment, that she had once seen a very nice-looking young woman who offered herself for service, and being much pleased with her appearance had expressed a wish to the housekeeper that she should be engaged. But after a quasi-competitive examination of the candidate, the housekeeper reported and said, " That girl is a nice girl, but she would not suit *me* at all, my lady. She has only lived at rich merchants' houses in town, and at their little trumpery villas ; and she knows nothing of the ways of great houses." The lady yielded ; for in such matters a person of her rank submits entirely to housekeeper and to butler, who are held responsible, and to whom all orders are generally given.

I have heretofore remarked that what is called an English basement house is, according to my observation, unknown in England. There is another little delusion very prevalent among us, — that tea only is drunk at English breakfasts, which consists besides chiefly of eggs and toast ; and we have " English breakfast tea " as we have English basement houses, and one with about as much reason as the other. I found coffee much more generally taken at breakfast than tea, although both were usually on the table. Eggs I saw rarely, and toast hardly ever. Indeed, I was offered eggs at breakfast only once while I was in England, and then I did not get them, although it was at a country house. I was sitting next my hostess, who remarked across the table to her husband that the lawn, which was in sight from the window, seemed to need trimming. Within so short a time that it seemed almost like magic, three men were at work with hand mowing-machines under our eyes. Just then she asked me if I would not have an egg. I accepted the offer, and she rang a far-off bell by pulling a little contrivance at her side. A maid appeared, and the order for boiled eggs was given. The maid quickly returned, and said, "Please, my lady, there are no eggs this morning." Here was an Englishwoman whose husband was lord of thousands of acres, and at her country house, although at a word she could have a company of gardeners to smooth her lawn to her liking, she had not an egg to her breakfast. If I had asked for a boiled cherub I could not have been told with more nonchalance that there were no cherubim that morning.

The talk at breakfast, and even at dinner, in such houses turns not unfrequently upon the estate and its management : what timber may be cut, what planting is needed, what farm leases are falling in, and whether the present tenants shall be continued, and how they manage their farms. In these consultations the ladies join and offer their opinions, which are received with consideration ; and the younger brothers, one or two of whom are almost always living at home, are looked to to take an interest and an active part in the management of the estate. This made the table-talk much more interesting and instructive to me than if it had been confined to politics, society, and "Shakespeare taste, and the musical glasses," although these latter subjects had their full share of attention. I was impressed, as I have heretofore remarked, with the wide range of topics upon which these sensible, highly educated women were able to give, in their quiet, modest way, sound opinions and suggestions. They were rarely "smart," but they were sagacious ; and they seemed to have the family interests much at heart.

The "unprotected female," who furnished John Leech with some of his happiest and most amusing subjects, I did not find so common as I had expected to find her ; but I met with one beautiful specimen on my way to Canterbury. She was beautiful as a specimen ; but the utmost stretch of gallantry would not allow me to predicate any kind of beauty of her as a woman. I had taken a cross-line from a little place which I was visiting, and I had some time to spend at the station, waiting for the train on the main line. As I walked the platform, there emerged from the booking office a short, dumpy, elderly woman in a loose gray dress, which did not conceal her fatness or lengthen her shortness. She wore large, round, silver-rimmed spectacles, carried a bulging umbrella, and her bonnet would have given a New York milliner, even in Division Street, a fit of nervous horror. But she was evidently a well-to-do person, and, although as fidgety and as confused as a weather-cock in a change of wind, quite able to take care of herself. She looked about for a few moments through her great glass artificial eyes, which seemed to have the effect of magnifying the unsatisfactory points in the condition of things before her, and then bustling up to a porter who was carrying an armful of parcels she exclaimed, " Where 's my things ? That 's mine [pointing with her elephantine umbrella to one of the parcels]. Put it down. What are you going to do with it ? I don't want to go by this train. I don't like this train. Where 's my tin box ? Miss ——, she 's a young lady at Riverhead, told me that if I came here at a quarter past twelve I should have a nice train to take me to Tunbridge ; and now I 'm to have a nasty train, and to wait till half past one." The man smiled good-naturedly, and, turning a half-winking eye to me, went on his way. She trotted after him, expostulating, and clamoring for her tin box. Presently she trotted back, and went about pottering and cackling and stirring things up like an old hen in a muck heap. My time to go soon came, and I left her waiting for her nasty train.

I suppose that this old lady traveled second-class, as the phrase is in England. She would not have felt at home in a first-class carriage, and would besides have grudged the extra shillings ; and a third-class carriage she would surely have regarded as very nasty, that is, unpleasant. Between second-class people and first-class people there is less sympathy and good fellowship than there is between third-class and first-class. I remember hearing a peer and an Oxford don discuss the economy of railway traveling ; and they agreed heartily that it was pleasanter to travel third-class than second-class ; third-class people were not so disagreeable as second-class. Now the third-class carriages are very cramped and uncomfortable, and the passengers are of the humblest and coarsest sort. But thus it ever is : we are more annoyed by the unpleasant peculiarities of those who are most like us, and yet are not of us, than by the stranger and perhaps more offensive habits of those whose remoteness from us relieves us from any implication with them or their affairs.

Sharply as classes are defined in England, in comparison with the uniformity in this country (for of course they shade into each other there, and the shading becomes year by year broader and more ob-

literative of the established lines), first-class people
are not always distinguished from their inferiors by
English people of dull perceptions. The friend at
whose house I was going to lunch, when I saw the
mother with her invalid daughter in Hyde Park, told
me with much amusement of his being mistaken for
a shoemaker. He is the second son of a distinguished
man "with a handle to his name," and is himself a
man of mark. A friend of his, quite inferior to him
in social rank, had ordered a pair of shoes of peculiar
make of *his* shoemaker, and by mistake they had
been sent to *his* house. He was about calling upon
his friend, and being a very easy-going man, and not
at all fussy about his personal appearance, he took
the shoes in a parcel with him. And by the way,
to do this in London a man must be very easy-going
indeed. For to carry a parcel, however small, or
however elegantly wrapped, through London streets
is something which a " gentleman " would not think
of doing much sooner than he would think of walking through them in his shirt-sleeves. The tiniest
purchase, which would not make your waistcoat
pocket bulge, is solemnly sent home to you as a matter of course. But you may carry a book, if it is not
too large and is not wrapped up. A book is a book;
but a parcel may be a pound of cheese, or a pair of
shoes. At his friend's door my shoe-carrying friend
asked to see Mr. ——, and was understood by the
servant to ask for Mrs. ——, to whom he was directly taken. The lady, who had never seen him before, looked up, and asked curtly, "What have you
there ? " " Mr. ——'s shoes," was the reply. " Oh,
yes ; quite so, quite so. It 's all right. Mr. —— is
out, but he 'll be in soon, and if you want to see him

you 'd better take a seat in the hall, and wait till
he comes." "But, madam " — began my friend.
" Never mind, never mind ; it 's all quite right. Step
out in the hall, please, and wait for Mr. ——." The
gentleman appreciated the situation at once, and had
much too keen a sense of humor to spoil it by an explanation. He therefore did step out into the hall,
intending to give the shoes to a servant and go on his
way rejoicing in his joke. But he met his friend
coming in, and, being too considerate of his friend's
wife to put her to the blush and enjoy her confusion
by returning, he gave the shoes to their owner, and
after a few words upon the occasion of his visit bade
him good-morning. If he should chance to read this
chapter, I hope that he will pardon me for repeating
a story which in all respects is a most characteristic
manifestation of English habits, and not the least so
in his modest carelessness about the lady's mistake,
and his thoughtful care to protect her against the
consequences of her blunder.

19

CHAPTER XIII.

"NOBILITY AND GENTRY."

THE word "gentleman" is peculiarly English. In other languages it has counterparts, but not equivalents. Although its application has been widened even in England during the last century, the core of its meaning has not been changed. To this, rather, there have been made additions, as the suburbs have been added to old London; but the city is the city still. It is in the English of England only that the word has this inner steadfastness; for, as I have had occasion to say before, when writing upon another subject, in "America" this word is entirely without meaning unless we know the person who uses it; and generally, too, we must know the occasion of its use and the persons before whom it is spoken.

A gentleman is properly a man of gentle, or genteel, birth and condition; and this sense remains fixed in the word in England, although it has there, besides, other varieties of meaning and of use, as it has in the United States. When the gentlemen of the county are spoken of, or the gentlemen of England, not every man is meant, nor even every respectable, educated, and decently behaving man. There is implied a certain condition in life, a certain social position, which may or may not be accompanied, but which generally is accompanied, by a certain degree of wealth. But an English gentleman in his completeness is much more than this, even if he is lord of thousands of acres upon which his forefathers have lived for centuries. Earl Dudley, writing to the Bishop of Llandaff in 1821, said of Mr. Stuart-Wortley (a political opponent) that on an occasion of much public importance he " spoke as became a great English gentleman ; " and the Emperor Nicholas said that to be an English gentleman was his highest ambition. Now both the earl and the emperor had in mind something much more than the visible position of a man whose forefathers had been " spacious in the possession of dirt." It was an idea of a man of independence, of probity, of a high sense of honor, of courage, of personal dignity, of good breeding, and of some knowledge of the world and of books. The ideal English gentleman adds all these to the position which is given him by his birth and his estate; and it is because it is acknowledged that, in theory at least, gentle birth in England, and the condition of life by which gentle birth is usually accompanied there, tend to foster all those fine qualities of manhood, and because they are expected of a man in that position, that the word "gentleman " has come to be, of all words that can be applied to a man, the most gracious and the most comprehensive of all that is admirable and lovable and of good report, and that it has come to mean something that is not always found under the coronets of earls or the crowns of emperors.

A complete English gentleman is thus one of a class composed of the most admirable and enviable men that can be found or imagined. It is not in human nature that the whole of a large class, or even the great majority of a large class, should be men of such completeness; but such is the model which the man aspiring and honestly striving to be an English gentleman has before his mind's eye.

Besides this name and notion of the individual gentleman, there is in English, for the class or body of which he is one, a name, a word, which has neither counterpart nor equivalent in any other tongue, — gentry. This word means, first, the condition in life of a person gentle by birth and breeding; as when Mrs. Page says to Mrs. Ford, in regard to Falstaff's love-making, "And so thou shouldst not alter the article of thy gentry." Next, and as now most commonly used, it means the whole body of those who are distinguished from people below them in rank by being of acknowledged gentle, or (to use again an old-fashioned word) genteel, birth and condition, and from those above them by not being noble according to the English rating of nobility. For in England nobility is a dearer possession and is more charily bestowed than it is in other countries that have an established aristocracy. English literature is thorny with slighting allusions to French and Italian counts and German barons; and the sharpness is not the mere sprouting of prejudice or of arrogance.

In England nobility means very much more than it does on the continent of Europe. Not that English nobility is more ancient, more important in history, or more splendid in associations than the nobility of France, of Spain, of Italy, or of Germany. On the contrary, any one of the latter countries can show a roll of nobles who, in the antiquity of their titles, the grandeur of their positions, the importance of their actions, and the vastness of their possessions, far surpass the existing nobility of England, which.

with few exceptions, is comparatively of recent origin and of minor historical dignity. The superiority of English nobility consists, first, in the fact of its limitation to peers of the realm, who have a seat and a voice in the House of Lords ; and, next, in that this rank and position are the accompaniments, the tokens, the splendid witnesses, of large landed possessions and correspondent political and social influence.

An English nobleman is a great landlord. The tillers of thousands of acres, the dwellers of half a dozen or a dozen of villages, occupy their land and their houses by his sufferance, — because they pay him rent. The exceptions to this rule are so few that they are of no significance. Macaulay and Disraeli are the two most eminent examples of comparatively landless men who have been ennobled in England. For Marlborough and Wellington great estates were bought. And as to Macaulay and Disraeli, it may be safely assumed that if they had had children, or expectation of children, they would not have been made peers. Peerage merely personal and not hereditary is scouted by the House of Lords, — hardly less by English commoners ; and an hereditary lordship without an income to support the dignity, and without landed property, is abhorrent to Englishmen, or, what is worse, ridiculous.

In the history of England, one fact is remarkable in regard to its social aspect : there has never been that hatred of the nobles by the common people which has been so often manifested in other countries, and which in other countries has been the cause of so much political disturbance. The common people of England have always been proud of the no-

bles ; and they may even yet be said to be proud of
them.   The liberals, the very radicals, are opposed to
nobility rather in a theoretical way.   I did not hear
a word among the lower classes and the lower-middle
classes of disrespect toward the nobility as a class, or
of dislike of noblemen as nobles.

It should be said, however, that I saw less of the
lower-middle class, that is, of small shop-keepers and
of artisans, than of any other, — much less than I
saw of the peasantry and of the corresponding classes
in the towns.   This is natural.   A stranger, not in
the condition of the former, is by force of circumstances thrown among the upper-middle classes, and,
if he happen to have made such acquaintances, among
people of rank.   Among the farmers and the peasantry he may go if he will ; but dissimilarity of habits
makes intercourse with the classes just above them
constrained and without interest, and even access to
them difficult.   And these people, — the lower-middle class, — notwithstanding their great numbers, are
of the least importance in the organization of English
society.   They have no apparent influence upon it,
and do not represent it in any way.   This will be
apparent from the consideration of the fact that they
furnish neither private soldiers nor officers to the
army, and, with very rare exceptions, no scholars to
'he universities, no members to the learned profes-
.'ions, and it need hardly be said, with exceptions of
like rarity, no members to Parliament.

This lower-middle class, however, shares with the
lower classes — the lowest — a feeling toward the
aristocracy which is the result of a peculiarity in
the constitution of English nobility, — a peculiarity
which is as old as England itself.   The commoners

of England have never been overridden by an army
of nobles. In other countries all the sons of noblemen have been and are noblemen, and the land has
swarmed with landless counts and barons, who assumed the bearing and had the privileges of nobles,
who held themselves aloof from all intercourse with
those of inferior birth, and disdained to give themselves to any useful occupation. It is not so in England, and, for centuries at least, it has not been so.
There the son of a nobleman of the highest rank is
a commoner before the law ; and, except by courtesy,
he has neither title nor privilege. He has the advantage of his connection, which is of course very
great, and which gives him position and opportunities the value of which can hardly be overestimated.
But before the law he is only a commoner, like a
shop-keeper or an artisan ; and any one of these may,
if he will, enter upon the unequal contest with him
for any of the good things of life, or even for its high
places. And unequal as the contest is, men from
the lower classes have risen, as we all know, to the
highest places in the English social scale, — to the
bench, to bishoprics, to the woolsack, to the peerage.
It is the consciousness of this possibility, the consciousness of the limitation of nobility and its privileges, the consciousness of the established rights and
recognized power of the commons, which has kept
the nobility of England so long in its eminent and
(with allowance for evils and defects almost inevitably consequent upon an aristocracy) its admirable
position. English landlords are generally respected,
often liked, and not rarely loved by their tenantry.
English noblemen are looked up to and treated with
willing deference by all below them in rank, unless

by their own conduct they forfeit respect and deference. No Englishman hates them because they are noble.

Because, however, there are no nobles in England except the peers, the members of the House of Lords, it does not follow that there is no other aristocracy. An English gentleman — using the word in its proper English sense, already set forth — is noble. The gentry of England correspond to the *petite noblesse* of other countries which have an aristocratic society. Many an English gentleman, a mere commoner, whose forefathers have been commoners time out of mind, is tenfold a more important personage in every respect than hundreds of Continental counts and barons are. He has birth of which he is as honorably conscious, perhaps as proud, as any count or baron of them all; he bears arms which his forefathers have borne for centuries; and, more than all, he lives in the house and is lord of the acres which have been in his family for generations. In the observation of English society, it must be constantly borne in mind that, although only peers are noblemen, the English gentry are a kind of nobility, and that in any other country having an aristocracy they, or at least the greater part of them, would be ranked as nobles. Mr. Stuart-Wortley, whom Lord Dudley wrote of as a great English gentleman, was soon afterward raised to the peerage as Lord Wharncliffe. By this he gained a step in rank; but he hardly gained in importance in Yorkshire, where his family had been seated as great English gentlemen for five centuries. He was rather made a peer because of that very importance, and because of his course in Parliament.

The present nobility of England, as I have before

remarked, is not an old nobility. Very few English peers bear titles which have been in their own families more than three hundred years.[1] This is through no fault of theirs ; nor is it by reason of any incapacity of England to breed a grand and enduring race of noblemen. But nobility is, after all that may be said, only a matter of hereditary landed wealth, and of the importance and the opportunities given by such wealth. Therefore, where inheritance fails, no less than where wealth fails, nobility, dependent upon the union of the two, is extinguished. The noble Norman possessors of England, and such Englishmen as they had gradually admitted to their order, killed each other in the Wars of the Roses. If they had been " Americans," and each party had regarded the other as " Indians," they could not have more thoroughly improved each other off the face of the earth. Consequently, the Tudor kings of England had to make an almost new nobility. But it was not until the second Tudor king, who was so afflicted with wives, took into the possession of the crown all the

[1] This has striking illustration in the fortunes of one very great and important barony, that of Northumberland. The recent Dukes of Northumberland have assumed the name of Percy ; but their family name is Smithson. A great Yorkshire baronet, Sir Hugh Smithson, married the heiress of the Northumberland estates, and was invested with the title which had lapsed for lack of a male heir. A Yorkshire gentleman spoke to me with some disapproval of the assumption of the Percy name by Sir Hugh, who he said was "just as good as the Percies," — his own name, by the bye, ended in *son*, which is a sign of the Danish origin of many families in the North of England. What he said was measurably true, indeed ; because the family into which Sir Hugh Smithson married themselves not really Percies. The very Percy of Chevy Chase was not a real Percy; the family of the original Percies having come to an end about a century after the Conquest. And in fact these Percies never were Earls of Northumberland. The real family name of Henry Percy, who was created Earl of Northumberland in 1377, was De Louvaine; a gentleman of that name, a younger son of the Duke of Brabant, having married the heiress of the fourth Baron Percy and assumed her name.

land of the abbeys and monasteries throughout the kingdom that the new royal family had on hand a good stock of the material for new noble-making. It must be confessed that they were not allowed to be slack in the labor of their vocation. Would-be noblemen fell upon their monarch like robbers upon an unsinging traveler. Favorites, courtiers, soldiers, eminent lawyers, asked for land and for titles, for abbeys, for priories, for manors. They begged for them ; they importuned, they intrigued, for them ; they offered themselves souls and bodies in exchange for them. The lands and the houses most of them got, and many of them got the titles. Such a swarm of human harpies was never let loose upon a country as that which ravaged England from 1540 to 1600. It is to this rapacity, this gathering of the vultures over the carcass of the Roman church, that most of the oldest noble families in England owe their possessions and their peerages. Some of those highest in rank owe their coronets to the efforts made by that estimable monarch, Charles II., with the aid of Barbara Palmer, Louise de Quérouaille, and Nell Gwynn, to increase the nobility of the kingdom. Those three ladies (the first two were made duchesses, respectively, of Cleveland and of Portsmouth, poor Nelly remaining simply " the Protestant ——" which she declared herself upon a memorable occasion) did their best to prevent the race of dukes from dying out in England ; and verily their representatives have done likewise unto this day.

Many more modern noble houses owe their rank to the needs of Sir Robert Walpole and other ministers for votes in the House of Lords. Many peerages were bought, outright, from James I. and his suc-

cessors. Nor has the fashion of getting them by
some such influence entirely gone out, it would seem,
even in the present day. Baron Stockmar tells of
an application to him by a man eminent in the literary world, who offered him a very large sum of
money if he would support his petition to be made a
peer. The baron gave the application such a reception as it deserved. A man in his position in the
court of Henry VIII., Edward IV., Mary, James I.,
or the earlier Georges would have taken the bribe,
and perhaps have obtained the title.[1] Clarendon,
who recorded what he knew, tells us that even poor
Charles I. in the extremity of his distress, and Charles
II. when in exile during the Commonwealth, were
tormented by importunities for titles. It is not thus
that the untutored mind imagines the growth of an
old nobility. But it is thus that the greater part of
what is called the old nobility of England came into
being. To this rule there are sóme admirable and
many respectable exceptions, to specify which would
be both superfluous and invidious.

Admitting, however, that the origin of few — comparatively few — noble houses in England could be
remembered by an honorable man with pleasure,
does it follow that the English nobility is to be regarded and estimated from the point of its origin?
I think not. The ancestors of most of these noblemen got their lands and their lordships in the man-

[1] Here is the story as it is told in the *Memoirs of Baron Stockmar*, vol.
i. p. lxxv: "A rich Englishman, an author and a member of Parliament,
called upon him one day, and promised to give him £10,000 if he would
further his petition to the Queen for a peerage. Stockmar replied, 'I will
now go into the next room to give you time. If upon my return I find
you here, I will have you put out by the servants.'"

Was there in Stockmar's time (1830–1850) more than one man made a
peer who was rich, an author, and a member of Parliament?

ner which was the fashion of their day. The matter would not be at all bettered if the old Norman nobility had survived. In the eleventh century the fashion of getting lands and lordships was by conquest; in plain words, by forcible robbery. Then the great man was the strong man. In the condition of society at that time, it was inevitable that the strong should take and keep. Dugdale [1] quotes from the record of an old trial, or examination, in which a certain baron of Norman descent is asked by what title he holds a certain manor. Whereupon *produxit in curia gladium suum antiquum et evaginatum*, etc., — he produced in court, unsheathed, his ancient sword, — and said that this was his title; that his ancestors had come to England to conquer it for themselves and for their children, and that they had conquered it, and that their children meant to keep what their fathers had taken. Plain speaking, but the simple truth. These men got their manors, in virtue of which they were summoned to Parliament as barons, by seizing them violently, slaying or driving out their old owners, and holding the land by force of arms. Those of some hundreds of years later got theirs by the arts of courtiers, by favoritism, by importunity, by intrigue, or as soldiers or lawyers, in reward for services which would not be thought very admirable by Englishmen of to-day, or even perhaps tolerable, unless they were performed in India or in Africa. Some of those of a century or so later got theirs because some half dozen women bore illegitimate children to a king of England; those of yet

[1] Or perhaps Camden. It is many years since I read the passage, and I have not the book now, nor time to look it up. I am quite sure as to the passage, and it makes little difference whether the authority is Camden or Dugdale.

another century because they served the ends of an unscrupulous prime minister.

However this may be, it happened long ago; and the present fact to be considered is that their descendants are in possession — legal possession — of the lands and the titles. This being the case, they must be regarded, and they will be regarded, as to their estates and their rank, just as if they had bought the one with money, and won the other from a grateful king and people by an exhibition of all the ennobling virtues in the service of their country. As to personal character and conduct, it is they, not their forefathers, who must be judged by the standards of to-day. What does it matter to an anxious mother that the man proposing for her daughter is descended from a pretty unmarried actress? It is not unlikely that among his married ancestresses there were women far less estimable than she in every way; and the present fact is that he has forty or fifty thousand acres, and is a duke, and that he is just as likely to be a decent man and a good and loving husband as if all his foremothers had been she-dragons of chastity. Of what moment is it to his friends, his political associates, his tenantry, how his ancestor got his title and his lands two hundred or three hundred years ago, or what were the personal traits of that ancestor's character? Hardly more than whether his ancestor was tall or short, or whether his lady-mother's nose was snub or aquiline. He has full possession of his rank and his estates, and it is not his ancestor or ancestress whose personal character concerns us, and who is to be tried by our moral standards. If we are to go into the origin of titles to possession which are centuries old, we shall oust more than half the peoples and governments of Europe and America. A consideration of these facts may modify the views of some who seem to think of nobility as if it were born full-grown out of the chaos of the dark ages, and of others who regard every nobleman as a robber and an oppressor, because he did not buy his estate at an auction.

The relative degrees of rank in the English nobility, and the position of the members of noble families and of commoners who bear titles, are so frequently misapprehended by people in general, and even misrepresented by accomplished writers, that I shall venture to set them forth succinctly, even at the risk of seeming to offer needless instruction to many of my readers.

The various ranks of noblemen now in England are, beginning at the lowest, baron, viscount, earl, marquess, and duke. Every peer is a baron, and every baron is a peer. The House of Lords is, and has always been, an assemblage of the barons of England. A baron being in the old feudal sense of the word a man who is lord of certain manors, and who, upon the summons of his sovereign, must take the field at the head of a body of retainers, the title is a generic one for noblemen of all ranks. Thus Magna Charta was extorted from King John by certain barons; but they were the most important and powerful noblemen in the kingdom. A man summoned to Parliament by writ was summoned as baron of a certain lordship in land which gave him his title, or one of his titles; and a man who in modern days is raised to the peerage is made a baron, whatever other and higher rank may be bestowed upon him. But the title baron is never used in England in ad

dressing a peer. On the Continent it is used in
speech and in writing; and barons are baroned from
morning till night by every person who addresses
them, not exclusive, I believe, of such citizens of the
Republic of the United States of America, male and
even female, as are obliged to endure the company of
a nobleman. In England the word used is simply
" lord ; " and this is applied to all peers below the
rank of duke, except in formal addresses or other
documents, or " in print," when there is some reason
for particular distinction.

The next step in nobility is to the rank of viscount, which, however, is not an old title in English
nobility, and, like marquess, is not regarded as particularly English. A nobleman raised from the rank
of baron to that of viscount still retains his baron-
age. Thus if a gentleman were raised to the peerage as Baron Stratford, he would be called Lord
Stratford ; and if he were afterwards made Viscount
Avon he would be called Lord Avon, but he would
still be Baron Stratford as well as Viscount Avon.
This adhesion of the inferior titles (except in certain cases of limitation by patent) continues as the
nobleman rises, if he should rise, to the highest rank ;
and if our supposed example were made Earl of Kenilworth, then Marquess of Coventry, and finally
Duke of Warwickshire, he would be baron, viscount,
earl, and marquess, as well as duke ; and he might
also be a baronet ; and all his titles would be mentioned in an account of his rank in the peerage.

Earl is the oldest of English titles, and of all titles
is the most thoroughly English. There are barons,
viscounts, marquesses, and dukes in other countries,
but earls only in England. I am sure that I cannot

be alone in finding a peculiar charm and attractiveness in the position and title of an English earl. He has the rank which was once the highest in the land, and which is still high enough to be of great distinction, while it is not one which must be kept up with a great deal of splendor, and his title is one peculiar to his country. I know that if I were an English earl I should not receive with any great thankfulness an offer to make my wife into a "female markis," especially if my earldom were one around which was a cluster of pleasant historical associations; for example, the earldom of Warwick, or that of Derby.

Marquess, which means lord of the marches (that is, borders), is a title unknown in England before 1385. The first English marquess, Robert Vere, had an Irish title, Marquess of Dublin, which was bestowed upon him by Parliament at the pleasure of Richard II. It was rarely bestowed afterwards, until the last century. Its chief advantage seems to be that it affords the crown, or the crown's advisers, a degree of nobility to which they may raise an earl without making him a duke. Dukes are intended to be very rare birds indeed. To be raised to a dukedom, a man must be enormously rich, and have very great connections. A marquess, although next him in rank, may be a long way behind him in these respects.

Duke, the title of the highest rank next to that of the princes of the blood royal, is the third in antiquity in England as a title of honor and dignity. As the name of an office, *dux*, it was used in very remote times all over Europe; but the first English duke was Edward the Black Prince, whom his father made Duke of Cornwall; whence the oldest son born to the reigning monarch is born Duke of Cornwall, but not Prince of Wales, the latter title being afterward conferred upon him.

A duke is the only English noble who is usually addressed by his title. It is proper, in addressing him at the beginning of a conversation, or after a break in it, to say, for example, " Duke, will you be kind enough ?" etc.; at other times, it is almost needless to say, he is addressed as "your grace," in the use of which title much want of discretion and self-respect may be shown. But no other nobleman is commonly addressed by his title, as marquess, earl, or viscount. All from baron to duke are addressed simply as " my lord ; " and in the use of " your lordship," although it is legitimate, there is a peril similar to that in the use of " your grace."

This phrase, " your grace," is called "the style " of a duke, who is formally addressed on letters and otherwise as His Grace, the Duke of, etc. The style of a marquess is the Most Noble ; that of earls, viscounts, and barons, the Right Honorable. But, except in the case of a duke, who is supposed to be a very awful and inapproachable person, friends, in writing to each other, usually omit these styles, and address the marquess or earl of ——, or, more generally, use simply Lord.

This is an end of nobility, except that nobility which comes of office, as in the case of bishops, the lord chancellor, and certain judges, which, except in the case of the lord chancellor, is not nobility at all. All other titles are merely what are called courtesy titles borne by commoners, or titles of knighthood, the bearers of which are also commoners. The son of a duke, a marquess, or an earl bears the second title of

20

his father, by the courtesy of the crown. A duke, as I have already remarked, is also an earl, a viscount, and a baron, and generally, but not always, a marquess; a marquess is also an earl and a viscount and a baron, and so on. The eldest son of a duke bears, therefore, as his courtesy title, that of his father's marquessate or earldom. For example, the Marquess of Hartington is a commoner, just like John Smith; and he is a member of the House of Commons, which he would not be if he were really a marquess. But by courtesy he is called by the second title of his father, the Duke of Devonshire. The Duke of Norfolk's eldest son, however, is not by courtesy a marquess, but an earl, — Earl of Surrey; because the dukedom of Norfolk is older than the day when the fashion of making English marquesses came into vogue, and his second title is Earl of Surrey, which he would not have made marquess for any sum of money that could be offered him. The younger sons of dukes and marquesses (although of course commoners) are called Lord, and their daughters Lady. Thus the eminent statesman who for forty years and more was known to all the world as Lord John Russell was only a commoner, and would have been described in a legal document as the Honorable John Russell, commonly called Lord John Russell. His "lordship" came to him merely by courtesy, because he was a younger son of the Duke of Bedford. He was made a peer in his own right, as Earl Russell.

It should be mentioned, however, that there may be and have been lords in the House of Commons who are noblemen, bearing their titles not by courtesy, but by inheritance or patent. These are Scotch or Irish peers. To sit in the House of Lords, a peer must be a peer of Great Britain, or of the realm, as it is called, unless he is chosen as a representative peer from Scotland or Ireland. All English peers are peers of Great Britain; but Scotch and Irish peers are not so, unless in addition to their Scotch and Irish peerages they have an English peerage. Thus, the Duke of Argyll, a Scotch peer, sits in the House of Lords as Baron Sundridge and Hamilton in the peerage of Great Britain, and the Marquess of Drogheda, an Irish peer, as Baron Moore of Moore Park, Kent. Lord Palmerston was an instance of a nobleman's being in the House of Commons. He was third Viscount Palmerston in the peerage of Ireland ; but he was not only English (he was of the family of Sir William Temple), but the most English of Englishmen. He was elected member for the Isle of Wight in 1807, and sat in the House of Commons for nearly fifty years, during which time he was twice prime minister. He was one of the most powerful of British subjects : he made peers of Great Britain, and bishops and archbishops ; but he himself never rose in rank, nor even became a peer of the realm, but passed his political life in the Commons.

The presence of a Christian name after the title Lord is in itself evidence that the bearer of the title is not a nobleman, not a peer, and also that he is a younger son of a duke or a marquess. And so also Lady Marys and Lady Sarahs are not peeresses, but the daughters of earls, marquesses, and dukes. For the sons and daughters of viscounts and barons bear no courtesy title, but are styled Honorable. This title Honorable, which is made ridiculous in the United States by its bestowal upon every man who fills, or has ever filled, one of our million public offices, however petty, is little used in England, except as a token of noble descent; and it pertains, as I have remarked, as well to women as to men, which is also true of Right Honorable in case of peeresses or the daughters of dukes and marquesses. This is shown by an old poetical satire, "The Metamorphosis of the Town," 1731, upon the fancy costumes worn then on the Mall : —

> "Look, yonder comes a pleasant crew
> With high crowned hats, long aprons, too,
> Good, pretty girls, I vow and swear;
> But wherefore do they hide their ware?
> Ware? what d' ye mean? What is 't you tell?
> Why! don't they eggs and butter sell?
> Alas, no y' are mistaken quite.
> She on the left hand, dressed in white,
> Is Lady C——, her spouse, a knight;
> But for the other lovely three
> They all Right Honourables be."

This Lady C——, although she was my Lady, was a commoner, and the wife of a commoner. A knight baronet, or a simple knight, who may be an alderman, a painter, or a musician, is called Sir, and his wife is called Lady, just as any peeress is, under the rank of a duchess.

Baronets are peculiar to England. They are commoners; and yet they have an hereditary title. The title was originally sold by James I., who invented it for the purpose of raising money by its sale to quell a rebellion in Ulster; whence all baronets bear the red hand of Ulster in their shields of arms.

Knighthood is not hereditary; because it is always conferred upon the bearer for services or qualities personal to himself. It was originally a very high honor, and one which noblemen did not always bear, but, bearing, always greatly prized. The Black

Prince himself, the heir apparent to the throne, did not "win his spurs," the token of knighthood, until the battle of Cressy.[1] If conferred upon the field of battle, knighthood was a great distinction, and gave its bearer precedence before other knights not so created. But gradually it sank in estimation, because of the reasons for which it was bestowed. In Shakespeare's time it was given "on carpet consideration," and from that time it became more and more common, until now it is the lowest and least regarded of all tokens of social distinction. It has, however, one remnant of its original value: it belongs to the person, and must be won. But one of the acknowledged gentry of England would not receive with pleasure a proposal that he should be knighted, except, indeed, in the form of being made, for conspicuous merit in the public service, a Knight Commander of the Bath; for that a simple gentleman should be made a Knight of the Garter is quite inconceivable. The garter is reserved for noblemen of high rank; and during the last century and a half it has been worn by many dull and sordid and even base creatures, who had no claim to it but large possessions and great parliamentary influence.

Baronetcy, however, and even simple knighthood are prized for one reason, — precedence. There is in precedence a fascination which even the sturdy manliness of the so-called Anglo-Saxon mind seems unable to escape. To have the right — a right recognized on all formal occasions — to take place before some one else is one of the most highly-prized privi-

[1] I have found so many intelligent persons in error upon the point that I am sure I shall be pardoned for mentioning that Edward of Woodstock was a fair, blue-eyed man, with light hair. It was his armor that was black.

leges of rank. It cannot be regarded as the object of a magnanimous ambition ; and to see how much it is thought of tends greatly to diminish respect for an aristocratic organization of society. The disputes in regard to it which are recorded here and there in history ; the bitter heart-burnings about the right to certain seats or places in court ; the painful consideration of the grave question as to whether a royal or a princely personage is to take two steps forward or three in receiving a certain guest, or in what exact order some half a dozen others are to be placed at table, or which of two ambassadors is to be received first, and with what ceremonies, and so forth, and so forth, seem to be the magnification of the merest frivolity and fiddle-faddle. Courtesy is the flower of good-breeding, the rich, fine bloom upon the fruit of the highest culture ; but between courtesy and etiquette the difference is so great that they have really nothing in common. Courtesy is perennial, immortal ; but etiquette is but an artificial manufacture of social pedantry, and changes not only from generation to generation, but sometimes from one year to another.

The etiquette of precedence in England is a puzzling and intricate subject, which is in the hands of heralds and masters of ceremonies. It is regulated with an elaborate minuteness which is ridiculous, I am sure, even to many of those in whose favor it is established. That the royal family should have precedence of all others ; that dukes should have precedence of marquesses, marquesses of earls, and so forth ; and that a line should be drawn somewhere, from below which people cannot go to court, seems sensible and right in an aristocratically constituted society. But when members of the same family are broken up into classes of precedency, and separated, and we are told that the eldest sons of dukes take precedence of earls, while the younger sons of dukes (all the sons being commoners, it should be remembered) come after earls and the eldest sons of marquesses ; and when we find a specific place assigned to the eldest sons of the younger sons of peers, and another much lower to their brothers, the younger sons of the younger sons of peers, we must feel a little pity for grown men who are pleased at walking about in such filigree go-carts.[1]

The complication resulting from this minute dissection and distribution of precedence has its liveliest illustration in the case of the female members of noble families, who generally take this matter of precedence most to heart. Thus, all the daughters of a peer have the rank of their eldest brother during the life-time of their father. All the daughters of a duke, therefore, rank as marchionesses ; and this rank they retain, unless they are married to peers, in which case of course they take rank as peeresses. But if some of them should thus become countesses, viscountesses, or baronesses, and one of them should marry a commoner, whether a baronet or a coachman, she, as a duke's daughter, would still rank as a marchioness, and, although a commoner, take precedence of her peeress sisters. Her marriage to a commoner does not lower her in the scale of precedence, or raise him. Tittlebat Titmouse thought that when he married the Lady Cecilia he would be Lord something or other ; but he found that it was not so ; and

---

[1] And yet Carlyle tells us in his Reminiscences that Mrs. Wordsworth was an insignificant little woman, chiefly remarkable for her anxiety in regard to her proper seat at table, — *her* precedence !

other Titmice have been similarly disappointed. And can we forget "The Countess of Warwick *and* Mr. Addison"?

Precedence in England extends even into the servants' hall and the kitchen. This is manifested every morning. At family prayers all the house servants attend, just as they used to do here in families in which that domestic discipline was kept up. A row of chairs is placed for them in the breakfast room, and they enter and take their seats. The head of the house reads prayers and the lesson of the day, or some other part of the Bible. I observed that the servants in each house always entered in the same order, the housekeeper marching at the head of the line, and taking the seat farthest from the door. And it was, I am sorry to say, rather funny to see some dozen or more of them pound solemnly in and plump stolidly down upon their seats. After prayers are over, they of course rise and go out. But I saw that they did not do this in reverse order, the one nearest the door going out first, as would have been natural and convenient. They rose, stood in a line, and then the housekeeper went out first, followed by the servant next her; and thus the line doubled upon itself, the file telling itself off, so that the one who entered the room last left it last. The order of entering and leaving was the same.

On speaking of this, I was told with smiles that precedence was strictly observed among them; that in the servants' hall the housekeeper took the head of the table, the butler the foot, and that the servants, upper and under, had places strictly assigned to them according to the dignity of their positions. What is the order of their sitting or of their going the lord

of precedence only knows; but I suppose that the
my lady's maid sits on the right hand of the butler,
and my lord's own man on that of the housekeeper.
At dinner they sit together at the common table
down to cheese; then the upper servants only rise
and go in state to dessert in the housekeeper's room.
The upper servants are those who have servants under them; an upper servant never wears livery.
When visitors at a great house bring servants with
them, the guests in the servants' hall are formally
assigned places strictly according to the rank of their
master or mistress. I learned also that servants do
call each other by the titles of their masters and mis-
tresses, and that this incident of "High life Below
Stairs" is no fiction. A nobleman told me, with much
enjoyment of the joke, that when he was going about,
a young heir expectant, and by courtesy Viscount
———, he often heard the servants at the country-seats
of his friends address his valet by his own title. He
also heard something which he thought much "jol-
lier:" —

There was a certain lady, a dowager peeress, no
longer young, but rather youngish, who had an own
man, a confidential servant, who was her factotum.
One day, she being on a visit to his house, my friend
heard some of his own servants call out to this man
by his mistress's title, and ask him to go somewhere
or do something with them; to which he replied with
a languid air, "Oh, I can't. I've got to take my
old woman into the city to look after the stock-mar-
ket You know the old girl likes that sort of thing."
He intimated with much glee that if Lady ———, who
was very airy and coquettish, had heard the words
"old woman" and "old girl" she would have taken

measures to have that man speedily poisoned. He told the story with so much mischief in his eye that I wonder that he refrained from telling it to the lady herself; but that would have been inhospitable and unkind; and that he should be either unkind or inhospitable it is quite impossible to believe.

This same gentleman also once unconsciously illustrated to me one trait of English aristocracy which is in many respects admirable, — independence of the opinion of others. He is of a family eminent for ability as well as for rank. When he was in New York, some years ago, I had the pleasure of knowing him well, and one day I took him to see Miss Hosmer's statue of Zenobia. After we had looked at it for a while in silence, he turned to me, and quietly said, "Who was Zenobia? I don't know." Another gentleman of the same rank passing a day or two at my house, I had occasion to tell him that he would do well to change his drawers for a thicker pair on a walk we were about taking. "Drawers!" he replied, "I never wear them;" at which I was somewhat surprised; but he continued, "People tell me that it 's not a nice habit not to wear drawers; but I can't see that it is n't nice; and as I don't like them, I don't wear them." Although I could not sympathize with my guest in his taste, I could not but like his independence of Mrs. Grundy. But what matter is it to a man who is an earl and a deputy-lieutenant of his county, with two seats, a townhouse, half a dozen livings, and the control of a seat in Parliament, if Mrs. Grundy does whisper and sniff! He can afford to set her and her cackling at naught. The immunity of such a position has, on the other hand, its evil tendencies with evil men; but it leads, on the whole, to independence of personal character, which is an English trait.

Outside the circle, and just below the rank, of the recognized gentry of England is the large, respectable, and all-powerful body known as the upper-middle class. Of this there is of course a considerable number who are members of the various professions ; but the greater number are merchants or manufacturers, or are connected with trade in some way. Those of them whom I had the pleasure of meeting did not in any way justify the pictures of them that we find in plays and novels, which, according to my observation, are not truthful representations of a class, but caricatures of individuals. I found these gentlemen, as a class, so intelligent and so well informed that I should hesitate at placing the merchants of New York, or even of Boston, as a class, in comparison with them. Many of them live in great luxury and with a splendid display ; but very many who have wealth live, although in the height of comfort and elegance, more modestly, as, in their opinion, becomes their station. One of these, who lived in a cluster of spacious, elegant villas, with fair grounds about them, said to me, as we strolled past a very large house, " Mr. —— has offended the taste of his neighbors. He has built himself entirely too great a house for a man who does n't keep horses. A gentleman in England is a man who has horses and hot-houses." Now he himself had neither horses nor hot-houses, although he could well afford to have both ; his plate bore a crest to which his right was undoubted, and he was a man of importance in an important place ; besides which, he was certainly one of the best read and most thoughtful men I ever met, and a man of sterling character and highly respected. But, being all this, he yet recognized with content his well-defined place in society.

This cheerful recognition of place, even by those who are inferior, seemed to be remarkable. I spoke one day to a lady of high rank in regard to what I had heard from some of her friends of the feeling of certain members of the royal family about the marriage of the Princess Louise. "To be sure," was her reply, "how could it be otherwise? I suppose they feel very much as we should feel if one of our own rank should marry an upper servant." And this of the heir of MacAllum More, whose rank and family had been far above her own for centuries![1] It illustrated the same point that one day a peer replied to his wife, who said that a certain estate that was for sale would hardly find a buyer at the price asked for it, "Oh, my dear, you may be sure that the price will be paid by some opulent shop-keeper." If my host had brought out his coronet and set it solemnly on his head, he could not have more impressively asserted his rank; and the succession of *ops* in the last words of his reply seemed to give him great pleasure.

---

1 We may be sure, I think, that the lady had not in mind the following passage from Heywood's *King Edward IV.*, in which the situation and the feeling expressed by her, and almost her very words, will be found. The Duchess of York is censuring her son for marrying a woman so far beneath him in rank as the Lady Elizabeth Gray, and the Queen reminds her new mother-in-law that, like the Marquis of Lorne, she comes of an ancient ducal house.

> "*Duchess.* There 's no such difference 'twixt the greatest peer
> And the poor silliest kitchen-maid that lives
> As is betwixt thy worthiness and hers.
> 　*Queen.* I do confess it: yet my lady York,
> My mother is a duchess, as you are,
> A princess born, the Duke of Bedford's wife."
> 　　　　　　　　　　　　　　　　　(Act I. Sc. 1.)

They lingered upon his lips, and were uttered with unction.[1]

· Briefly, although the government of Great Britain is practically republican, and although the complaint there is, that year by year their institutions are becoming more and more "Americanized," rank and precedence are still the coveted prizes and the paramount influences of English society.

English peers are, on the whole, a noble race of men, worthy of the honor in which they are held. So far as my observation extended they are notably simple in their habits of life and unassuming in their manners, not narrow in their sympathies, and conscious of the duties imposed upon them by their position. True, they stand by their order; but do we not all stand by ours, even when it is disorder? Of course there are some within the pale of nobility who might better be without it, — men, and women too, who disgrace their rank by frivolity and by brutality. An eminent churchman, himself of a noble family, speaking to me of the brutality of some noblemen, said of a certain earl of ancient family, recently deceased, that he was a perfect reproduction of the rudest of his ancestors, " just like Front de Bœuf." And on the other hand one meets among the gentry and in the middle classes men who in character, in dignity, in ability, and in public spirit would seem to deserve to have no superiors in rank, and to

[1] A year and more after the publication of this paragraph in the *Atlantic*, the following passage appeared in an article in the *Saturday Review :* "Social dignity is greatly valued in England, so valued that we shall not be ridiculous if we bring our argument to a crucial and absurdly extreme test. It would be worth the while of any millionaire with two millions to give one for Knowsley, or Longleat, or Dalkeith Palace, or Floors Castle, with the lands attached, even if the lands did not return one shilling per annum interest on the money." Five millions of dollars!

be more worthy of lordship than many of those who are born to titles. But it is also to be said that there are many sad examples of that crass snobbishness and toadyism which might be regarded as the peculiar fruit of an aristocratic society, if we did not find the same snobbishness and the same toadyism in society in which wealth suddenly acquired, and often ill-gotten, is the only recognized title to distinction. But notwithstanding the unadmirable origin of many peerages and the vicissitudes of families, the English nobleman of to-day is not unfrequently a fair representative of his ancestor, who was thus described by an old French poet, Ronsard, —

> " Autour de son palais je vy ces grands milords,
>   Accourt, beaux et courtois, magnanimes et forts."

So early did Frenchmen call an English lord a milord.

CHAPTER XIV.

TAURUS CENTAURUS.

THE umbrella that I bought in Burlington Arcade came to an untimely end. Going to pay for it, I had taken it in my hand, not because of rain or that the sky was lowering, but because one always carries an umbrella in England, whether one uses it or not. Indeed, a Lancashire friend of mine, who was with me when I bought another umbrella in Liverpool, said, as I was picking and choosing, " Find a good stick ! An umbrella serves chiefly as a walking-stick. Get a good one for that, and you 're all right." As I walked away from the Arcade, at the very first crossing, — at Sackville Street, I believe, — I was suddenly conscious of a horse and a rushing of wheels. I had just time to draw back when a hansom cab dashed past me so close that I smelled the horse's breath. The great wheel caught my umbrella, which was twisted out of my hand in a twinkling, like a foil from the hand of an unwary fencer, and thrown upon the ground, where the wheel passed over it. The cabman took not the slightest notice of me as he turned the corner and dashed down Piccadilly. I picked up my wounded water-shed, and returned with it to Burlington Arcade, where it was found that, although stick and ribs were uninjured, every gore of the silk was cut through in two or three places, and that never having been used it would yet have to be completely new covered. I could not but remark the plainly unaffected concern of the sales-woman from whom I had bought it. As she opened gore after gore, and found them all destroyed, her countenance fell, and she looked ruefully in my face, as if she and not I had lost twenty-five shillings, and as if she, not I, would have to pay for a new cover. I remarked her manner, although it was undemon-strative and perfectly simple. It was one of many manifestations of like feeling from trades-people to-ward their customers to which I was witness in Eng-land.

My adventure with the cab, happening on the sec-ond day after that of my arrival in London, gave me timely warning of a fact which I found to be both characteristic and important, — that in England the man on horseback is master of him that goes afoot. He who walks is expected to give place to him who rides and to him who drives. He is, for the mo-ment at least, the inferior person, the subject of the mounted man, whose convenience or whose pleasure he is expected to consult at loss of his own pleasure, or of his own comfort, or of his property or his limbs, or, it would almost seem, of his life itself. A sign or token of this in London, and if I remember rightly in other cities, is the contrivance called a "refuge," which is placed at intervals more or less convenient in the roadway of the street. These refuges are formed of stout stone or iron posts about a yard high, which stand some two or three feet apart, half-way from curb to curb, making a sort of pen or pound, into which persons who are timid or not agile may flee as they cross the street, and where they may rest in safety until the way is clear for them to complete their crossing without the risk of broken bones. If it were not for this contrivance there are many women, and, I suspect, some men, in England who would never get quite across some of the thronged thoroughfares. The man who undertook to swim across a mill-pond, and who, having got half-way over, instead of going on, turned round and swam back again, might, if he had found a place for a moment's repose and reflection, have seen that it was as well to go forward as to turn back; and thus the timid wayfarer in the streets of London is enabled to pause amid the clattering of hoofs and the whirl of wheels, and, taking courage from offered opportunity, complete his half-made transit. The refuge seemed to me a very characteristic thing. It is a sign of that thoughtfulness of the personal safety and comfort of the general public which is a much more constant and impelling force in England than it is in the United States; but it is also a sign of that deference to the horse and to his rider or driver which is one of the most striking of English traits.[1]

---

[1] The following paragraph appeared in the London *World* some months after the first publication of this chapter: —

"It has been calculated that the yearly average of persons killed by accidents in the streets of London is greater than the annual total of persons massacred on all the railways of the United Kingdom. During the last decade the victims of the thoroughfares of the metropolis have reached an aggregate of 2195, while in 28,071 cases more or less serious injuries have been inflicted. These statistics are startling, and they signify in reality more than at first appears. Only the known instances are enumerated under the published categories. There is a considerable percentage of casualties which does not find its way into print; and when it is said that last year the killed and wounded in the London streets amounted to 236 and 3699 respectively, it must be remembered that the estimate is reduced to a minimum."

This is astonishing, and reveals a condition of things peculiar to England. Even in the thronged streets of ill-governed New York there is not the hundredth part of this number of street casualties.

My horseless English friend who told me that in England a gentleman was a man that had horses and green-houses was nearly right in his jocose definition. But the first half of it is the more significant. The importance of the horse in England, and the importance which he gives to his possessor — even his temporary possessor — is not easily overrated. The feeling from which this springs is traditional, and comes down from the time when, in peace as well as in war, nobles, gentlemen, and men-at-arms were mounted men, and rode over the common people. When coaches came in, their use was for a long time, of necessity, confined to the great and wealthy; indeed, they were such a sign of high social position that among inferior persons many even of those who could well afford them did without them, lest they should subject themselves to the charge of presumption. It is amusing to read Pepys's debates with himself on this point; his doubts being not whether he could afford a coach, but whether his position was such as warranted him in appearing before the public with his wife in his own vehicle. It need hardly be said that a private carriage is everywhere an evidence of a certain degree of wealth in the owner; but although the grandson of the man who first set up his carriage in New York is yet living, the possession of such a "leathern conveniency" conveys to the public mind nothing of that feeling which still lingers in England in regard to the man who (for pleasure, not for business) has a "stable," great or small. Mrs. Gilpin, on her only holiday in twenty years (how cruel she was to poor John in saying "these twice ten tedious years"!), did not have even her hired chaise and pair brought to the house, but had it stayed three doors off, "lest folk should say that she was proud."

It is partly because of a great liking for horses, but partly also because of the survival of this feeling, although in a much modified form, that the first desire of an Englishman, when prosperity begins to come to him, is to be the possessor of a horse. Chiefly, his desire is to ride; and if he is a weak-minded, pretentious creature, he sometimes makes false pretenses of having ridden or of being about to ride. In England the stirrup is the first step to gentry. The phrase "in the saddle," as an expression of readiness for work, is a peculiarly English phrase. We use it because we are of English blood and speech; still it has not with us the full pertinence and significance which it has in England. An English "gentleman" who cannot ride reasonably well, and who does not ride, is an exceptional sufferer from some hapless disability, physical, moral, or pecuniary. Englishwomen not only walk more than their American cousins do, but they ride very much more. Ten to one of them, compared with women here, are accustomed to the saddle. Girls as well as boys begin to ride early; indeed, before they begin to learn to dance.

I was walking one morning in the weald of Sussex, with a friend, to call at the house of a kinswoman of his. And, apropos of my subject, this gentleman, although he had a stable on such a scale that, seeing it first by chance in the twilight, I thought that it was another country house, and although he was a grandfather, proposed as a matter of course that we should walk the three miles between the two houses. Notwithstanding it was a warm September day, I was very glad that he did so, and that I did not lose one bright moment of the smiling beauty of that morning, or one of the ever-varying phases of the view across the weald to those grandly reposing downs, that couch like headless sphinxes before the sea.

We had walked about two miles, when we saw, a few hundred yards off, what might at first have been taken for a great doll mounted upon a great dog coming rapidly toward us. It was a little girl riding a shaggy-maned pony, whose back was not nearly so high as a donkey's. Little miss, although she certainly could not have been more than eight years old, came tearing along at a pace that turned back her short skirts in a flutter, and made her long curls stream out in the air behind her. " Oh, uncle," she broke out, as she pulled her pony up to a sudden jog-jog-jog, which I thought must pitch her out of the saddle, but which did not, — " oh, uncle, what an awfully nice pony this is! He goes like lightning. Papa says he thinks there is n't a match for him in all the weald," — pronouncing the last word, by the way, quite perceptibly as two syllables, yet with the suggestion that this was only the effect of a full and rich enunciation of the letter *l*. Her eyes were dancing, her cheek glowed ; and after a kiss and a few more hurried words from her fresh little mouth, off she dashed again, at the same headlong pace. Soon we met the maid who was out in attendance upon her, and to whom, as I found, it was her wont to ride back, after she had gone about a quarter of a mile, and take a fresh start.

Although she had a pony and a maid, the girl's dress was as simple and as uncostly as it could possibly be consistently with cleanliness and comfort

Nor was her father a man of wealth. My host, who was his landlord, told me that the rent of the pretty house, at which we soon arrived, and which looked much like a villa at Brookline, or Dorchester Heights, and some thirty acres of park land, was but two hundred and forty pounds a year, and the furniture and the upholstering were far less gorgeous than those which are found in the houses of thousands of New York men whose daughters never saw a pony, and who could no more keep a seat upon such a tempestuous little beast as that than they could ride a whirlwind. But *per contra*, as their fathers might say, their *toilettes* would, in their splendor, altogether eclipse the homely garb of this unmistakable little gentlewoman. Ponies like this one of course we all know; but I saw more of them during my visit to England than I had seen in New England and in New York in all my life.

The number of ladies that one constantly sees in England on horseback, in the parks, public and private, and on the rural roads, is a distinguishing feature of the country. They ride in parties, with gentlemen, of course, and often alone with a groom in attendance, but oftenest, it seemed to me, in pairs, with the inevitable tidy groom just out of ear-shot behind them. There is not a more characteristic representation of English life, nor one more pleasing to a man's eye, than the sight of two fair, healthy English girls, well mounted, their blue riding-habits full of health and their faces full of good-nature, cantering easily through a wooded park. I remember meeting such a pair on a visit to —— Hall, in Lancashire. I had chosen to walk, as I often did, and I met these young ladies in the park, about three quar-

ters of a mile from the house. They were walking
their horses, and I had opportunity to make good
view of them. Their faces were beaming with the
delight of life; the indefinable charm of the spring-
tide of existence seemed to radiate from them, and to
take me within its influence; they sat their horses
with an ease and grace which Englishwomen do not
always show on foot; and their dark blue habits
made, with the bright bay coats of their black-maned,
black-hocked horses, sharply shown against the rich,
green sward, a combination of color which was grateful to my eye. It was a sight worth seeing for itself,
and the most English thing that could be seen in
England. I saw that they were the daughters of the
house, or at least that one of them was, and raised
my hat as I passed them, and got a pretty blush and
half a bow in return. After I had walked on a while,
I thought that I might venture to turn and look again
at such an attractive spectacle; when to my surprise
I found that they had anticipated me in my exhibition of inquisitiveness, in which their groom stolidly took no share. I could not see them blush again,
but I could see their white teeth as they smiled
at this mutual detection of our common curiosity. I
am sure that should they chance to see this page
they, who added so much to the pleasure of my visit
to —— Hall, will pardon this reminiscence of our
meeting.

The Egyptians mummied all sorts of sacred brutes,
including bulls, cats, and crocodiles. If Englishmen
should ever take to embalming beasts, I am sure that,
notwithstanding the national name and the place
which roast-beef holds in English song and story,
they would pass by the bull, and swathe the defunct

horse in muslin and spices. For if the horse be not a god in England, at least the cult of the horse is a sort of religion. There are tens of thousands of English gentlemen who have horse on their minds during the greater part of their waking hours. The condition of the animals; their grooming; the cut of their tails and manes; the way in which they stand, or step, or stride; the fashion of their harness; the build, the look, the dress, of coachman and groom, — these are matters to them of deep concern, of uneasy anxiety. And this is so not once a year, or once a quarter, or once a month, but every day, and two or three times a day; every time, indeed, that they ride or drive.

Nor do I mean only those who are called "horsey" men, gentlemen drivers of mail-coaches and the like, who are grooms in everything except taking wages, and some of whom, I was told, will carry their coachmanship so far as to take a "tip." Apart from these, there is a very large class for whom the perfection, to the minutest point, of their equestrian "turn-out" is a question of the major morals. When one of this class feels sure that his horse, his "trap," and his groom will bear the criticism of his friends and rivals, the ineffable air of solemn self-sufficiency with which he sits the saddle or the box is very amusing. These men criticise each other's equipages as women criticise each other's dress, as pedants criticise unpedantic scholarship. Indeed, in England there is a pedantry of the stable.

In a lower condition of life there is of course less expense and less display, but not a whit less of the hankering after horses. On the roads in the suburbs of London, a frequent sight in the afternoon, when it

does not rain, is a sort of light cart or buggy with a
smallish horse driven furiously by a coarse man, who
sometimes has a coarse companion, male or female.
I rarely took an afternoon's walk within five or ten
miles of London without meeting a dozen of these
Jehus. They tear along the road at a mad pace,
and evidently expect everybody and everything not
bigger or stronger than they are to make way for
them. When I remarked upon this one day to a
friend who was walking with me, and who lived in a
little suburban town, he told me that these were
mostly small tradesmen or farmers of "horsey" pro-
pensities, who used in this way at every opportunity
the horses which in the morning were used in their
business. A light cart or buggy takes the place in
England of our ugly contrivance, the trotting wagon;
and I must confess that it seemed to me much the
more comfortable vehicle. Certainly, its drivers appeared to enjoy themselves much more than our
trotting men do. They do not sit in stolid silence,
pulling at the reins with gloomy determination.
They give the horse his head, and drive with a free
rein and an easy hand, and chat and laugh as they
bowl along the smooth, well-packed road. Indeed,
these fellows appeared to me really to have more
pleasure in their horse exercise than their superiors
had. They were without the conscious, anxious look
of the others, and did not seem to sit in fear of criticism. And yet I have no doubt that they did criticise each other as they met or passed, and made
remarks upon each other's "tits," or harness, or
driving. For when an occupation or an amusement
becomes a cult this is inevitable. But I never saw
them race. If they were overtaken or passed by one

of their own sort, they kept their pace and seemed
to enjoy their drive for the drive's sake, without
running the risk of taking off each other's wheels,
and without anxiety upon the important question
whether they " did " the last mile in 2.40 or 2.39, 30.

English riding did not, however, awaken in me all
the admiration which I had expected. The horses
and their riders were indeed in all respects admirable ; nor did the boldness and self-possession of
the latter in the saddle, and their calm mastery of
the situation, leave anything to be desired, at least
so long as the pace was not very rapid. But the
English seat did not seem to me easy, or even quite
safe ; although it must be so. And yet to see men
rising to the horse, as they commonly do, and alternately sitting in the saddle and standing in the stir-
rups, awakened in me a feeling of anxiety and distress, which, superfluous as it must have been, I
found not infrequently reflected in the countenances
of the riders. Accustomed as I was to see men who
were accounted good horsemen sit in the saddle or
on bareback as if they sat in a chair, although the
horse was at full career, it did not please me to
see riders bobbing up and down so that a good ar-
tilleryman could send a round shot between pig-skin
and buck-skin at every stride. In this feeling, however, I must have been wrong. English riding is
far beyond such criticism as I could bring to bear
upon it. The matter must be one of mere habit and
fashion.

I had not the good fortune to see a hunting field,
— only some cub-hunting ; but even that was made
a pretty sight by the horses, and the light crimson
coats of the riders, and the action of the hounds.

But I did not mourn my loss greatly in this respect; for I shall not hesitate to sink myself very low in the estimation of some of my Yorkshire friends by confessing that the only interest a fox-hunt would have for me would be the show, and that, fond as I am of riding, I should enjoy it in any way better than in risking my neck in the chase of a little red beast with a bushy tail. The excitement and the pleasure of hunting tigers, or bears, or wolves, or boars, I cannot only understand, but sympathize with heartily; but that twenty or thirty grown men on horseback should follow a pack of hounds in chase of a little creature about as big as a cat seems to me a proceeding so essentially absurd and preposterous that I cannot think of it with patience. Still worse, and with the addition of most inhuman (I wish that I could say unmanly) cruelty, seems the coursing of the hare. That men should go out with hounds to find pleasure in the flight, in mortal terror, of the most timid and harmless of dumb creatures is to me quite inexplicable. Shooting hares is one thing, coursing them quite another. I know that there are no wild beasts left in England but hares and foxes, and that field sports are delightful and invigorating. If country gentlemen must have field sports, and there are only foxes and hares left for them to hunt, I suppose that foxes and hares must be hunted. But it would seem that men might get open-air exercise and excitement in a more humane and reasonable way.

As to fox-hunting, however, with all that we read about it in English novels and other books, we have hardly a just appreciation of its importance as an English "institution." It also is a religion. It comes next to the British constitution and the Church of

England. Hunting men talk of the sport with a solemn earnestness which is infinitely amusing to an "outsider." To hunt well, or, as the phrase there is, to ride well to hounds, is an accomplishment, like the mastery of an art or of a science, or a like distinction in literature. I do not believe that there are ten men in any thousand in England, whatever their success or their distinction in other respects, who would not prize, if they could attain, the added distinction of being good fox-hunters. Hunting has even a moral significance. Years ago an English lady, a Yorkshire woman, writing to me of Louis Napoleon, after telling me this and that of him in terms of admiration, added, "And he rode well to hounds; and somehow if a man rides well to hounds he is pretty sure to be a good fellow." I could not see the *sequitur*. But perhaps if I had been born and bred in Yorkshire I could have discovered the connection between good-fellowship and a good seat in the saddle, — between a sound heart and bold and wary riding.

To hunt something to death or to shoot it seems to be a sort of necessity with the "average" Englishman, with whom it is a creed, an article of faith, that certain animals are created by a benign Providence to be hunted and killed in a certain way.[1] For the

---

[1] "It is a melancholy fact that English people are apt to be intensely bored with themselves on summer afternoons. They cannot spend the whole of every day in killing something, even after the 12th of August; and when they are neither slaying, eating, nor sleeping, the fever attacks them with great virulence. . . . . In the country we are brought up to consider two occupations as comprising the whole duty of man. These are the destruction of life and playing at ball; and when we are deprived of the former resource we have no choice left but the other. . . . . You may even have a Prime Minister, an archbishop, a monsignor, and a free-thinking contributor to a monthly magazine staying in your house, and yet your ntertainments will give no pleasure whatever to the average Englishman

way in which it is done is all important. A man who would shoot a fox is little better than a heathen; far worse than a publican and a sinner. And the feeling pervades all classes. In "Joseph Andrews," as the hero, his sweetheart, and Parson Adams are on the road near Squire Booby's, a hare, pursued by hounds and huntsmen, interrupts a passage of love between the two younger folks, and Fanny exclaims, "with tears in her eyes, against the barbarity of worrying a poor innocent, defenseless animal out of its life, and putting it to the extremest torture for diversion." Fanny would have protected the hare, but he fled from her. The end is told in the following paragraph : —

"The hounds were now very little behind their poor, reeling, and staggering prey, which, fainting almost at every step, crawled through the wood, and had almost got round to the place where Fanny stood, when it was overtaken by its enemies, and being driven out of the covert was caught, and instantly tore to pieces before Fanny's face, who was unable to assist it with any aid more powerful than pity ; nor could she prevail on Joseph, who had been himself a sportsman in his youth, to attempt anything contrary to the laws of hunting in favor of the hare, which he said was killed fairly."

This passage is remarkable, first, because it shows that, although Fielding was the son of an English squire and soldier, his good sense saw and his tender heart felt the cruelty of the sport which he describes ; although, with an eye to the prejudices of his fox and

unless you give him something to kill or a game at ball." — *Saturday Review*, September 14, 1878.

This brings to mind the story of the Massachusetts butcher, who, waking on a very fine night, exclaimed to his spouse, "O Miss ——, dew look at that beautiful moon! I mus' git up an' go to slarterin."

hare hunting readers, he puts his own thoughts into
the breast of a young woman and expresses them by
her lips.   Next, we see that this careful delineator of
contemporary manners makes Joseph something of a
sportsman in his youth, although he had been brought
up in the humblest condition of life.   Finally, the
hero, whom Fielding sets before us as a model of all
that is good and kind and gentle, refuses to protect
the hare, even to stop the tears of his sweetheart, but
lets it be torn to pieces before her eyes, because, according to the laws of hunting, it was killed fairly.
The establishment of laws, which it is unsportsman-
like if not ungentlemanly to violate, but according to
which a poor dumb, timid creature may be driven
wild with terror and to death's door with fatigue during a very appreciable part of its little life, and at
last torn to pieces for the amusement of those who
make the law, may not be peculiar to England; for
the laws of venery have prevailed in all lands ; but it
is safe to say that in none are they so religiously observed as they are in England, and that their application there to hares is a peculiarity due probably to
the lack of larger game.   The combination of a strict
regard for the laws of hunting with an utter disregard of the sufferings of the hare, resulting in a kind
of implication that the poor beast itself should be
quite satisfied if it were chased and worried and torn
to pieces "fairly," is an exquisitely perfect manifestation of a feeling, not confined to field sports, that
pervades society in England.   This feeling is embodied in the phrase, so common there that it has
become cant, " May the best man win."   It would
seem that it is in the spirit of this phrase that John
Bull looks upon any strife.   He says not, May the

right man win; not, May the right put down the
wrong; but, Right or wrong, may the best man
win, — "best" meaning strongest and boldest. The
very sympathy which he shows sometimes for the
weaker, and on which he prides himself, is but another manifestation of this feeling. If the little fellow can go in and win, and kill his antagonist, or beat
him, "fairly," let him do it; may he do it! "Hoo-
ray for the little 'un!" But the little one, for all
that he is little, may be utterly in the wrong; he may
be so foully and so aggressively in the wrong that he
ought to be trodden out of existence, like a venomous creature. But let him show "pluck" (favorite
word in England, but hideous, as Professor Newman
has said), and he is sure of John Bull's cheer, if
he were as wicked as Satan and as venomous as a
viper.[1]

This feeling has its spring in a quality of the John
Bull nature (by which, be it remembered, I do not
mean the best or even the characteristic English nature) to which I am extremely loath to apply the
only word that will describe it, — brutality. And in
brutality I imply nothing of the wild-beast nature,
nothing of cruelty. I mean an admiration of brute
force, a deference to it, a contented recognition of it
as the rightful title to the possession of all things.
Strength must indeed be the *ultima ratio ;* and civilization means that strength is on the side of society.

---

[1] I remember a case in which I was tempted to interfere, because I
thought a big fellow was bullying a little one; and indeed he was beating
him soundly. It turned out that the little fellow was an ungrateful, malicious thief, and that the beating he was getting was from a benefactor
whom he had robbed and vilified, and who was thrashing him in vain to
make him restore the stolen property, which was afterwards found on his
person. He was so determined to keep his booty that he took the thrashing without flinching, and almost in silence.

But between the first reason and the last reason there is a long series of stages in which brute force may at least be kept out of sight. In England, however, it is kept constantly before men's eyes, and they are taught to worship it from very children. The little boy goes to school to run the errands, pick up the balls, and black the shoes of the big boy; to be tyrannized over by him; to have his ears boxed by him; to be flogged by him, — not merely to be "licked" in a boyish fight, but to be solemnly flogged, whipped with a rod, or "tunded" with staves as punishment. "I had the honor," writes Thackeray, "of being at school with Bardolph before he went to Brasenose; the under boys used to look up at him from afar off as at a god-like being. . . . . When he shouted out, 'Under boy!' we small ones trembled and came to him. I recollect he once called me from a hundred yards off, and I came up in a tremor. He pointed to the ground. 'Pick up my hockey stick!' he said, pointing towards it with the hand with the ring on. He had dropped the stick. He was too great, wise, and good to stoop to pick it up himself." A small boy may free himself from tyranny by beating his tyrant "fairly" in a fight. But this is only another manifestation of the worship of brute force. He is free not because it is right that he should be free and strength is on the side of right in his little society, but simply because he has had the "pluck" and the luck to beat his tyrant.[1]

---

[1] "If a boy persistently shirks fagging, he is sent for by the prefects, and a hint given to him that he had better come and fag in future. After one or perhaps two warnings, he would get a "licking." There is a very little fagging except this, and what there is is done in no regular way. For instance, when a prefect wanted his study swept out, he would catch any small boy that was handy to do it; in consequence of which the fags

It is commonly sought to dignify this feeling by showing that it is no respecter of persons. But what a story is that of the boy who, on his first appearance at an English public school, was asked by the bully head-boy, " Who are you ? " and on his answering, " I am Lord ——, son of the Marquess of ——," was greeted with the reply, both in words and in action, " Well, there 's one kick for the lord and two for the marquess ! " I have heard this story told by men of rank as well as by middle-class men, with an expression of delight in it as a manifestation of English manliness. " Did the boy good, sir, — took the nonsense out of him." But what sort of nature must that be which needs, and takes kindly to, one kick for itself and two for its father, by way of taking the nonsense out of it ! And what a school of manners is that which thus welcomes a stranger, young, weak, friendless, ignorant yet of his surroundings ! I for one refuse to believe that the English nature requires this brutal discipline to bring it to that manliness and dignity and that solicitous consideration for others which it exhibits in its highest perfection. I believe that this worship of brute force is merely a traditional cult preserved in a spirit of Philistinism, and that without it more Englishmen would attain a full development of all the highest English virtues and

rather eschew the study side of the quadrangle between breakfast and ' second lesson.' . . . .

"The chief punishments are ' extra school,' lines, flogging by headmaster, and ' prefect's licking.' This latter is not such a great matter for ordinary cases, such as shirking fagging; but for any grave offense it is serious. There is always an appeal to the head-master. In case of grave offenses by a ' prefect,' he would be degraded or sent away, but not flogged. All the Upper VIth are *ex-officio* prefects, and some of the Lower VIth, by appointment at the head-master's discretion, to supplement their numbers." — *London Examiner*, August 9, 1879.

graces than now do so with it. Were it otherwise, in discriminating between the two peoples I should be obliged to say that brutality was one of the things which Yankees left behind them in the old home.

Next to the horse in England is the gun. Accustomed as we are to see Englishmen who have crossed the Atlantic to visit America, and whose idea of that tour of observation seems to be to go two thousand miles westward into the wilderness among Indians and frontiersmen to shoot, we yet have no adequate appreciation of the importance which shooting as one of the grand occupations of life has in the minds of tens of thousands of Englishmen. Hunting and shooting in England are not mere recreations, forms of casual pleasure, to be enjoyed now and then, leisure and weather serving. In the hunting season hunting men are not content, as I found on talking with some of them, to go out with the hounds once or twice a week. They hunt three or four times a week, and even every day, except Sunday, if possible. I wonder that they except Sunday. For if a man in the country may work in his garden, and a woman in London may cry water-cresses on Sunday, out of church hours, I can see no reason why these gentlemen should refrain on that day from laboring in their vocation. Their vocation and calling it surely is. It is the business of their lives; and to hear them talk about it one would imagine that it had the importance of an affair of state.

Shooting is hardly less thought of, and is more general because it is less costly. The pheasant, the partridge, and the woodcock are sacred birds provided for solemn sacrifice. "Does he preserve?" is a question that I have heard asked by one country

22

gentleman about another with as much interest and
seriousness as if the inquiry were whether he had a
seat in Parliament.   An engagement to shoot is paramount to all others ; an invitation to shoot, like an
invitation from the President at Washington, sets
aside all others.   Englishmen will go from one end of
the country to another for a few days' shooting; and
shooting means, nowadays at least, not a morning's
walk with dog and gun in a fine country and the
bringing home of a few well-earned birds and rabbits,
but mere gun-practice in a park at birds as flying
marks.   It has lost its connection with the enjoyment
of nature and invigorating exercise.   The "sports-
men " take their stands, and the birds are roused
from the gorse by the gamekeepers' helpers, and are
shot down, or missed, as they come within range.

As I was in England during the shooting season,
I had some invitations to take my chance at the
pheasants.   But I accepted none.   I could use the
little time I had to spend there in other ways, more
to my advantage, and also to my pleasure.   As to
shooting birds in such a business-like fashion, I would
as soon take trout out of a tub.   And that, I suppose, will be the way provided erelong for the practice of the contemplative man's recreation.   The
next thing to it seems to be the going to a fishing-
hotel and angling from a boat in a mill-pond.   Why
not fish and shoot by telegraph as well as in this
way ?   The charm of field sport is the field, — the
early start, the sharp, clear morning air, the sunrise,
the walk over hill and through meadow, the country
through which the game leads the seeker, the midday rest and luncheon with a companion or two by a
clear, sheltered spring, whose cool water is tempered

by the contents of flasks which counteract the unmitigated effect of that dangerous fluid, the renewal of the search for game by wood-side or brook-side, and the pensive walk home to a hearty dinner, a pleasant evening's languid chat, and a long dreamless sleep. Compared with this, preserve-shooting and pond-fishing are tame mechanical occupations.

"Does your ladyship hunt?" Sir Harcourt Courtly asks of Lady Gay Spanker, in the most brilliant comedy of English life that has been produced in the last thirty years and more. "Does my ladyship hunt?" ironically replies that wily she-centaur; and then comes that description of the hunting field, which, given with spirit by a pretty woman, always brings down the house. Lady Gay has always seemed to me one of the most forbidding female characters upon the modern stage, because she is one of the most unfeminine, and her hunting speech, a mere clap-trap deliberately set for what it always catches. Here, however, I remark upon her and it only in the way of the illustration of my subject. It need hardly be said that the number of hunting women in England is comparatively small; but it must be positively large. Now while so many women hunt in England, it seems somewhat strange that Englishmen and Englishwomen should find occasion of criticism in a tendency which they discover in their American sisters to usurp the places and the occupations of men. Riding itself is not the most feminine of accomplishments. A horse's back is not exactly the place for which nature has fitted woman. Neither in body nor in soul is she peculiarly suited to the saddle. But of all occupations hunting belongs, on every consideration, peculiarly to man. Now "American" women don't hunt. I never even heard of one who hunted, — except for that sort of wild beast of which every woman hopes to capture and tame one in the course of her life. While this distinction in the sex obtains in the two countries, it seems at least perilous for the countrymen of the hunting ladies to be censorious on the point of womanliness. Nor are these criticisms back and forth either pleasant or profitable. The customs of both countries are such as have been imposed upon peoples of the same race by the conditions of life in which they respectively live. Either transplanted to the other's soil becomes in a few years as if he were "native and to the manner born." I have no doubt that with practice John Bull might learn to sit still in his saddle, and thus become truly Taurus Centaurus.

CHAPTER XV.

PARKS AND PALACES.

In the present chapter I shall record memories of a miscellaneous character, some of which I shall present just as I find them in the letters that I wrote home while I was in England. These will at least have the value and possibly the interest which generally attaches to descriptions and relations written upon the spot. It should be remembered that these letters were written hastily, in the midst of the multitudinous avocations of a traveler (I wrote them in bed in the morning, and even on the railway when I was alone in the carriage), and were intended only for the members of my immediate family. But I give them just as I find them, only suppressing names.

" I walked from Twickenham to Hampton Court. J. H. went with me. We had walked a few miles, and were skirting a brick wall, which did not attract my attention by being unlike other brick walls that I had seen, when H. said suddenly, ' Here we are ! ' and we turned into a gateway. What a sight ! — a sight of trees such as I had never even imagined. I found myself in an avenue about two hundred yards broad, which stretched on before me for what proved to be a mile and an eighth. On either side were gigantic horse-chestnut trees, standing five deep at

regular distances, which had given them ample room
to spread. They looked as if they were a hundred
feet high. Even as they stretched on before me into
the distance I saw that every tree was higher than
the roof of any dwelling-house in New York. And
such majesty of foliage! There is nothing finer,
even in this country. The great avenue at Windsor
Park is longer, but when a roadway is a mile and a
furlong in length, what matter as to its effect at any
one point how much longer it is or might be!

"This is the famous avenue of horse-chestnuts at
Bushy Park. It is much praised for its beauty when
the trees are in blossom; but I was glad that I found
it clothed only in green. There is in rural nature
hardly anything equal to, surely no other thing quite
like, a lane between two orchards of apple-trees in
bloom. In tint and in perfume, the concentrated
expression of all the beauty, material and spiritual,
that accompanies our idea of spring finds there its
perfect and absolute embodiment. And there is
about the apple-tree a homeliness and a home-keeping character which make it fit to don this daintily
beautiful and somewhat womanish garb of welcome
to the returning year. It is not too grand nor too
dignified to wear a chaplet of blossoms. But I have
always felt that the horse-chestnut was far too lofty
and elegant a creature to be beautified by floral decoration. It seems to me like sending bouquets to a
big, bearded man. I should as soon think of crown-
ing a statue of Washington or of Wellington with
a chaplet of roses. Horse-chestnut trees must have
blossoms, or there would be no chestnuts, and the
trees would come to an end, — just as a man who
marries must figure in the absurd position of bride-

groom ; but I would rather see Benedick a month or two after the wedding, and the horse-chestnut tree after it has cast its blossoms.

" When this avenue has run its mile and its furlong it opens out suddenly into a circle more than a quarter of a mile in diameter, from which stretch avenues which are like transepts to a nave. In the midst of this circle is a vast basin with a fountain. Then come the lawns and the gardens around Hampton Court palace ; the former of such closeness and fineness of turf that it seems as if it is the velvet carpet that should be likened to *them ;* and all about such old, old yew-trees ! The garden is made by formal beds cut out of the turf and filled with flowers and plants with richly colored leaves, which are arranged in patterns. The extent of all this is greater than you would imagine. There is a broad canal that stretches up from the Thames to a terrace in front of the palace. It was used in former days for barges that brought visitors from London. Its functions, but not its beauty, are now assumed by the railway. Old ' Ego et Rex Meus ' may have been a man of unbounded stomach, but beyond dispute he had fine taste in palaces ; for you will remember that this noble seat was of Wolsey's planning and building. The first sight of the palace itself is very disappointing ; for the principal front which it presents shows at a glance the hand of the architect of the cathedral of St. Paul's ; but the part built by Wolsey is very fine, — old Tudor brickwork in excellent preservation. The roof of the great hall — openwork in wood — is beautiful both in outline and detail ; but the stained windows seemed to me of dubious date, and to be lacking in richness of tone and simplicity of design.

"Almost all the royal apartments have been turned into picture-galleries, which contain a mixture of the good work of great men with not a little rubbish. The Sir Peter Lelys, — portraits of the beauties of Charles II.'s court, — about which there is so much talk, are poor, flimsy, meretricious things. Even the flesh tints, which are the best part of them, are weak and washy ; and the drawing is very bad. The eyes are, I think, the worst that I ever saw in paintings of any pretension. The shape of the eye, which is exactly the same in all the beauties, is much like that of an Assyrian statue ; and the under lids would be costly if the lot were sold at a dollar a pound. All this is much modified and improved in the engravings by which these portraits are generally known. Notwithstanding the presence of the work of some greater men, I was chiefly impressed — no, not chiefly, but very greatly — by some heads by Bassano, which for strength and vitality surpassed any that I had ever seen, except some by Velasquez, and some of Titian's and Holbein's which I know only through copies or engravings. Perhaps I was the more impressed by them because the painter was new to me.

"A great surprise was the portrait of Madame de Pompadour, by Greuse, — an exquisite painting, with all the signs of being a good likeness. It is full of life and character. But to my surprise I found her fair, with bright blue eyes and a retreating chin, — a very manifest double chin, too, although she is in the bloom of early womanhood. Her complexion is divinely fair, and her figure shows the perfection of womanly beauty. But I had always thought of the haughty, brilliant, scheming favorite of Louis XV as a tall, dark-eyed, dark-haired woman, with a firm, well-rounded chin, and a face of great spirit; it was hard to accept in place of my ideal this soft, blue-eyed, simple, almost rustic-seeming beauty. It was only one more added to a thousand lessons from which I should have learned before the truth that Shakespeare makes the disappointed Duncan utter, —

> "'There is no art
> To find the mind's construction in the face.'

"After we had spent a long morning in the palace and its grounds, we went to the Greyhound Inn, just outside the gates, for a little luncheon, — some cold beef, of which a huge joint was set before us, the whole of which we might have eaten, if we had chosen, at the same price that we paid for our not very moderate inroads, and some beer, of which we each easily disposed of an imperial pint. We were punctiliously served by a waiter who did not look like a live waiter at all, but just as if John Leech had drawn him.

"The walks in the country around Twickenham are idyls. On Sunday evening, as the west was reddening, H. and I went out, and walked three or four miles leisurely, returning just after sunset. It was like living Gray's 'Elegy.' From the old church towers in the distance came the chimes of bells, soft, sweet, irregular, making a gentle clamor. Everything is soft here; mellow and tender upon the surface, although it may be rich and strong within. We talked when we first set out; but gradually we gave ourselves up in silence to the enjoyment of a sense of harmony that stole alike through eye and ear, and which, like the enjoyment of all beauty of the higher kind, produced an almost sad, submissive feeling.

"A few days afterward I took with the same companion a walk of some twenty one or two miles, which led us through some of the Thames villages, Kew Gardens and the museums, Richmond and Richmond Park. We started at half past nine in the morning, were on our feet all the time except when we stopped at a little ale-house in Isleworth for a bite and a sup of beer, and we came in at such a pace that it was remarked, as we passed through Twickenham, and I was good for five miles more at the same pace; which, as Pepys said of his dancing, I did wonder to see myself do, particularly when I found that I was as fresh as ever the next morning. Now in the atmosphere of New York or New England, neither my companion nor myself could have done that with such comfort and ease, — indeed, such pleasure; for we were both out of all training, not having walked five miles on any day within three years.

"What we saw was greatly gratifying, chiefly owing to the Thames, which we skirted frequently and crossed three times.[1] Of the beauty of this

[1] One of these three crossings of the Thames was at Twickenham ferry; the ferry consisting merely of a little skiff and an oarsman. The embarkation, the passage, and the disembarkation occupied about one minute, and the fare was one penny; and yet it was so charming and picturesque an incident of that day's enjoyment that I shall never forget it. Only a day or two ago I happened to see at Schirmer's, for the first time, this song: —

TWICKENHAM FERRY.

"O hoi ye ho! ho ye ho! who's for the ferry?
(The briar's in bud, and the sun's going down.)
And I'll row ye so quick, and I'll row ye so steady,
And 't is but a penny to Twickenham town."
The ferry-man's slim, and the ferry-man's young,
And he's just a soft twang at the end of his tongue,
And he's fresh as a pippin and brown as a berry,
And 't is but a penny to Twickenham town.

"O hoi ye ho! ho ye ho! I'm for the ferry.
(The briar's in bud, and the sun's going down.)

river from this distance above London to its upper water we have no type in any one of the United States with which I am acquainted. At Richmond it is hardly as wide as the Mohawk where travelers usually see it ; but the land lies around it in such a way as to give it a certain graceful dignity. The banks do not so much slope as gently curve down to it, and everywhere they are covered with the soft, richly green turf which seems to be the natural clothing of this island. This is darkened here and there all along the banks by beautiful trees, singly, in clumps, and in rows, that are to my eye a never-ceasing surprise and delight.

[Nevertheless, the notion generally prevalent about trees in England is erroneous. I have seen larger oaks and elms in New England and in New Jersey than I saw in England. Except some shells of

> And it 's late as it is, and I have n't a penny ;
> And how shall I get me to Twickenham town ? "
> She 's a rose in her bonnet, and oh she looks sweet
> As the little pink flower that grows in the wheat,
> With her cheeks like a rose and her lips like a cherry.
> " And sure and you 're welcome to Twickenham town."
>
> "O hoi ye ho ! ho ! " you 're too late for the ferry.
> (The briar 's in bud, and the sun 's going down.)
> And he 's not rowing quick, and he 's not rowing steady :
> You 'd think 't was a journey to Twickenham town
> O hoi ! and O ho ! ye may call as ye will ;
> The moon is a-rising on Petersham hill ;
> And with love like a rose in the stern of the wherry,
> There 's danger in rowing to Twickenham town.

Now the existence of this ferry and of this song is highly characteristic of the difference between the two countries. For centuries, ever since there was a Twickenham, and probably longer, the Thames has been crossed at that spot in just the same way; and far be the day when it shall be crossed there in any other. Hence, and because of the beauty of the river there, this song is possible. But here I do not know one ferry about which such a song could be written; not one which even the writer of *Barclay of Ury* and *Barbara Frietchie* could hope to make successfully the subject of a ballad song; nor can there ever be one.

trunks, I saw no oak so great in girth as that noble tree lately cut down at Tory Corners, near Orange, in New Jersey, the first branches of which were like large trees, and which, although they were rather less horizontal than is common with the oak, had a spread of more than one hundred feet. Nor did I see anywhere in England elms with the tower-like trunks and domes of green that are to be found in not a few New England villages. It is the multitude of very large trees, and the strong, rich, juicy green of their foliage that is so impressive. Oaks and elms with trunks four or five feet in diameter are common. They stand alone, or in ranks by the roadside; they nod to you over high brick walls; they gather together in great groups upon the meadows, where they do not push and crowd each other, but remain somewhat aloof with a becoming mutual respect. I soon gave over measuring their trunks; early in my walks a circumference of from sixteen to eighteen feet became too common to attract my special attention.]

" The view from Richmond Hill is of such a grand loveliness, like the beauty of some of Titian's women, that you wonder how nature could accidentally dispose forms and colors so as to give such delight to the eye and the mind of man ; and the moist air, because of the light which it holds in solution, marks the distances by a distinct but very delicate gradation. But of this view I have spoken before. From it I went directly to Richmond Park. Everything of note that I have seen here, excepting Stratford-upon-Avon, I have found more beautiful than I expected to find it ; but in many cases it has been smaller. Richmond Park, however, is not only more beautiful, but much larger, than I expected, — on a much grander scale. Compared with it, or indeed with any great park that I have seen, our so-called 'Central Park' at New York, admirable as it is in many respects, is slight and fanciful. Olmsted is the ablest man in his profession that I know; but even he cannot contend successfully with time and space and nature. I shall never forget the companies of great solemn oaks that I saw brooding over the earth in this park. I shall never forget seeing a gentleman and a lady come cantering out of a stretch of wood, that seemed more than half a mile off, right down upon us, until at about half their distance they turned at right angles, and we could hear them talking — his manly tones and her sweet, clear Englishwoman's voice — back and forth, but no sound of their horse's hoofs upon the turf; and they were so far away that they looked like toys. On that stretch of sward there might have been a tournament of giants."

Some requests which I have received, both in person and by letter, with regard to certain phases of life in England, cannot be better complied with than by the following extract from a letter, — which, like the foregoing, is a literal transcript except in the suppression of names : —

" Now I will tell you a little — it can be but a little — about life in the 'great houses,' as they are called here. When you are asked to come to one, a train is suggested, and you are told that a carriage will be at the station to meet you. Somehow the footman manages to find you out. At ——, which is a little station at which few people get out, I had hardly left the train when a very respectable-looking person, not a footman, stepped up to me and said, ' Lord ——'s carriage is waiting for you, sir.' The carriage and the footman and coachman were of course on the other side of the building. My drive from the station to —— took quite as long a time as it took me to come down by rail from London, although we went at a grand trot. The country was beautiful, stretching off on both sides in broad fields and meadows, darkened in lines by hedges, and in spots by clumps of trees. The roads were very narrow, — they seemed rather like lanes, — and this effect was increased by the high walls and hedges on either side. Two carriages had hardly room to pass in some places, with careful driving. Being in Lord ——'s well-known carriage, I was quite in state, and the country folk, most of them, bowed to me as I went on ; and of course I followed the apostolic injunction, and condescended unto men of low estate. And, by the way, yesterday afternoon (for a day has passed since I began this letter, and I am now at ——) Lady —— drove me through their park and off to ——, the dowager Lady ——'s jointure house, and I had the honor of acknowledging for her all the numerous bobs and ducks she received from the tenants and their children. So you see I shall be in good training when I come into *my* estate. When and where I entered the park, either here or at ——, I could not exactly make out. There were gates and gates, and the private grounds seemed to shade off gradually into the public. I know that the park extended far beyond the lodge. The house at —— is very ugly. It was built by Inigo Jones, and, never handsome, was altogether spoiled by tasteless alterations in the last century. The ugliness of English country houses built at that time is quite inexpressible.

"I ought to have said that the ——s are in mourning; . . . . and it was very kind of them to invite me. I was met at the door by a dignified personage in black, who asked me if I would go up to Lady ——'s room. She welcomed me warmly, said that Lord —— had been called away for a few hours, and offered me tea from a tiny table at her side. And, by the way, you are usually asked to come at a time which brings you to five-o'clock tea. This gives you an opportunity to rub off the rough edge of strangeness before you dress for dinner. Lady ——'s own room was large and hung with tapestry, and yet it was cosy and home-like. The hall is large and square, and the walls are covered with old arms. The staircase is good, but not so grand as others that I have seen; that at ——, for instance, where there was an oriel window on the first landing. This one has no landing; it is of polished oak, but is carpeted.

"Lady —— is a very attractive and elegant woman, sensible, sensitive, and with a soft, gentle way of speech and action, which is all the more charming as she is tall. Her tea was good. She talked well, and we got on together very satisfactorily. Presently a nurse brought in her two little daughters. I thought she must have approved of her savage Yankee guest; for she encouraged them to come to me and sit upon my knees; and all mothers are shy about that. Soon in popped Lord ——, and gave me the heartiest welcome that I have received since I have been in England. He has altered somewhat since he was in New York; is grown a little stouter, and a very little

graver, but is just the same frank, simple fellow as
when you saw him. About seven o'clock I was asked
if I would like to go up to my room. He went with
me, — an attention which I found general; and 'directly he had left me,' according to the phrase here,
a very fine-mannered person, in a dress coat and a
white tie, appeared, and asked me for my keys. I
apprehended the situation at once, and submitted to
his ministrations. He did everything for me except
actually to wash my face and hands and put on my
clothes. He laid out everything that I could need,
opened and laid out my dressing-case, and actually
turned my stockings. Dinner at eight. I take in
Lady ——. Butler, a very solemn personage, but
not stout nor red-faced.[1] I have seen no stout, red-
faced butler since I have been in England. Dining-
room large and handsome. Some good portraits.
Gas in globes at the walls; candles on the table.
Dinner very good, of course. *Menu* written in pencil
on a porcelain card, with the formula in gilt and a
coronet. Indeed, the very cans that came up to my
bedroom with hot water were marked with coronet
and cipher. I was inclined to scoff at this, at first,
as ostentatious; but after all, as the things were to
be marked, how could it be done better?

"After dinner, a very pleasant chat in the drawing-
room until about eleven o'clock, when Lord —— sent
Lady —— to bed. She shakes hands on bidding me
good-night, and asks if half past nine o'clock is too
early for breakfast for me. I was tempted to say
that it was, and to ask if it could n't be postponed

---

[1] The "swellest" butler that I saw in England was a tall thin man, pale
with gray hair and side-whiskers closely cut. He was quite like the
Bishop of ——.

till ten ; but I did n't. The drawing-room, by the way, although it was handsome and cheerful, was far inferior in its show to a thousand that might be found in New York, many of which, too, are quite equal to it in comfort and in tasteful adornment. Lord ——— and I sit up awhile and chat about old times and the shooting on Long Island, and when I go to my room I find that, although I am to stay but two days, my trunk has been unpacked and all my clothes put into the wardrobe and the drawers, and most carefully arranged, as if I were going to stay a month. My morning dress has been taken away.[1]

"In the morning the same servant comes, opens my window, draws my bed curtain, prepares my bath, turns my stockings, and in fact does everything but actually bathe and dress me, and all with a very pleasant and cheerful attentiveness. At a quarter past nine the gong rings for prayers. These are generally read by the master of the household in the dining-room, with the breakfast-table laid ; but here in a morning-room. After breakfast you are left very much to yourself. Business and household affairs are looked after by your host and hostess ; and you go where you please and do what you like.

" On Sunday I of course went to church with the family : a charming old church ; tower of the time of Edward III. ; some fine old monuments. We merely walked through the park a distance of about the width of Washington Square, passed through a little door in the park wall, and there was the church just opposite. It was Harvest Thanksgiving day, a festival recently introduced in England, in imitation

---

[1] To be carefully brushed, examined, and, if it is found necessary, put in order otherwise. You are not consulted upon such trifling matters.

23

of that which has come down to us from our Puritan
forefathers. There was a special service ; and the
church was very prettily dressed with oats, flowers,
grass, and grapes, the last being substituted for hops,
as it was too late for them. The offerings were for
the Bulgarians ; for everything now in England is
tinged with the hue of ' Turkish horrors.' After
service Lord —— took me to the chantry, where the
tombs of the family are. It was to show me a famous
statue, that of a Lady —— and her baby, at the birth
of which she died, it dying soon, too. The statue is
very beautiful, and is the most purely and sweetly pa-
thetic work in sculpture that I ever saw. It had a
special interest for me because I remembered reading
about it in my boyhood ; but I had forgotten the
name of the subject, and I had no thought of finding
it here in a little country church.

"Much the same at —— Place, or rather ' The
Place,' as it is called simply, in the phrase of the
country. I found there another ugly house, but the
most beautiful park I had yet seen. The sweep of
greensward before my bedroom window, the grand
march of stalwart, high-crested trees, and the stately-
terraced garden gave me great delight. In the middle of the house is a great square hall with a polished
oak floor, and columns supporting a corridor which
runs all around the hall on the next floor, and upon
which some dozen or fifteen doors of bedroom suits
open, all alike, — a perilous similitude. Floor of the
corridor oak also, very rich in color ; and this and
the staircase and the hall below so polished that you
could slide on them like a boy on ice.

"There are three drawing-rooms, one of which,
that which is used as sitting-room or parlor, has

at one end an organ ten feet wide and six deep, showing nineteen pipes in front, of which six are large; and yet it does not look too large for the room, in which besides are a library table of the largest size, a grand piano-forte, a round table that might have served King Arthur and his knights, a divan that would seat a harem, and a dozen great chairs with welcoming arms, and 'nary one alike,' — but, by the way, no rocking-chair; at the absence of which pest you know I must rejoice. The organ was once the Duke of ——'s, Lord ——'s uncle, who got tired of it and gave it to him. It must be pleasant to have uncles who get tired of organs. The great Oxford musician —— was down here and played on it admirably; and on the piano-forte, too, very well. But English organ-playing seems always better to me than English piano-forte or violin playing. The latter is at best a little cold, tame, and precise. I have not, however, heard Arabella Goddard.

" The blue drawing-room, or West Room, has some fine pictures, among which are the best Canalettis — views in Florence — that I ever saw. In the dining-room is the finest Sir Joshua I have yet found anywhere, in public or in private. It is the portrait of a former Lady ——, and is the perfection of the expression of grace and elegance; sweet and silvery in color, and yet not pale. A very interesting and peculiar picture is on the staircase. It is a copy by Gainsborough of a half-length portrait by Vandyke of the Duke of ——, an ancestor of Lord ——. The subject, the original master, and the copyist make it a very singular and valuable painting. Lord —— is very much absorbed in science, and has a laboratory and workshop in one wing of the house, where he and I spent some interesting hours; but this did not keep us from playing lawn tennis with the ladies.

"This is the way life passes from day to day in these 'great houses;' in which, by the way, except at dinner, and when you dress in the morning and in the evening for dinner, you rarely see a servant, unless you ring for one. There is a movement, which I am glad to see, to introduce the custom of having none but women servants *inside* the house. Lord —— mentioned it to me, and at —— I found it in practice. It seemed to work admirably. And certainly it was pleasant to see a comely kind of female butler and four tidy, comely maid-servants, in white gowns and blue ribbons, drawn up in row at the head of the table when we entered the dining-room; and it was far more agreeable to have them serve us than to have three or four great hulking he-creatures, in black coats and white chokers, attend to the little wants of the table, when they should have been doing man's work of some kind.

"At all these 'great houses' my host has, at a hint from me, kindly taken me through all the offices, even to the laundry, etc., and has told me all about the management of such a household, which I wished to know by actual observation. I have managed to get the same information in the same way in regard to middle-class houses as well; and have thus seen the domestic economy of England from that of the peasantry to that of the peer. I have seen nothing of such great establishments as the Duke of Omnium's at Gatherum Castle; but what I have seen is enough. In households such as those of which I have been speaking, there are between twenty-five and thirty servants *inside* the house; that is, exclusive of those ın the stables, the gardens, and the grounds. And yet it was funny to hear two of my hosts, when I asked the functions of these servants, begin the list with, 'There's the odd man.' The place of each servant is very strictly defined, and they are all very punctilious about doing nothing that does not belong to their several places. This has caused the introduction, lately, of a functionary who is called the odd man, whose place is like John Wesley's parish, and who is about the most important person in the household. Tell —— that Du Maurier is right, and that ladies here *do* wear mob-caps at dinner."

Here the extracts from my letters end. What follows is the mere expansion of brief memorandums.

Our British cousins twit us " Americans " (for they " lump " us all, Yankees, emigrants, and children of emigrants, together) with a liking for high-sounding names. On my walk from Twickenham to Hampton Court I passed "Devonshire House," " Bolton House," " Claremont Villa," and some other private residences with like names, which were written on their gate-posts. It might be reasonably supposed that these houses were at least pretty villa residences ; but no, they were scrubby little roadside cottages, with a neglected patch of earth or grass before them by way of court-yard, — cottages that did not rise even to the height of the shabby genteel. And, for my particular benefit, I suppose, a wretched row, the worst of them, the eaves of which were not ten feet from the ground, was styled " American Buildings." Every English house which is not in a town has a name ; and all over the country these names are either ambitious or sentimental to a degree that is somewhat absurd.

Mammon is worshiped in England quite as much as in the United States; but there are other gods there of nobler mien which we have not. One difference in this respect is worthy of remark. There is in society no talk, or very rarely any talk, about money or about business, using the word in its trading sense. I was at the houses of men of business of various sorts, " city men " and others, where, among half a dozen or a dozen male guests, I was the only one not connected in some way with commerce; I was for some days at the country house of a London banker, where guests were coming and going, and we sat from eighteen to twenty-five at table; and not once, in the dining-room or in the drawing-room, did I hear these men talk of pounds, shillings, and pence in the way of business, or as a topic of conversation, or any mention of stocks, or consols, or principal, or interest: — nothing of the sort. I could not but think, at one of these informal entertainments, of the last dinner-party that I had attended in New York, where the company was supposed to be of the higher sort; and indeed we had at least a dozen very " prominent gentlemen " there, including two ex-cabinet ministers. And yet the fish was not removed before all around me the table buzzed with the sound of "dollars," " bonds," " five-twenties," " legal tender," " principal and interest." Before they reached the *pecus* they began to talk about *pecunia*. This subject, with a slight admixture of party politics of the narrowest and most personal kind, furnished the only topics of conversation. In England everybody that I met had something else to talk about; the very " city men " showed themselves able to leave the city behind them when they came home to their families and friends, and to be only too glad to do so. There seems to be, even for the trader, the manufacturer, and the artisan, a richer and more varied life in England than the same classes have in "America." They love money there, perhaps even more than we do here; but they do not appear, the great mass of them, to love money-making so much for its own sake. At any rate, they have interests beyond it, — I will not offend Wall Street and Mr. John Sherman by saying above it; and when you see two men chatting together in England over a chop, or an oyster, or a glass of ale, even if they are elderly men of business, you may in most cases be pretty sure that their talk is not of pounds, shillings, and pence, or any subject thereto pertaining. If social, moral, and literary topics fail them, or are beyond their ken, they have at least Ireland, and India, and Turkey, and Africa, and disestablishment, and burials, and ritualism, and game laws; and failing these, the "Court Circular."

The careless confidence of people generally, in England, soon attracted my attention. There seemed to be no fear of thieves and burglars. At hotels it is common to leave the doors of bedrooms open, and the housekeepers smiled incredulously when I suggested the danger of the custom. I saw many front doors in London and in smaller towns left open or ajar. A friend to whom I mentioned this said that I was quite right, and pointed out to me that the windows of the large and handsome houses in the suburban place through which we were walking were absolutely without shutter or blind. It was true. The windows of these houses, all of them residences of wealthy merchants, were without such protection of any kind, inside or outside; and when I, with my friend, who lived in one of them, reached his house, we found his own front door ajar! And this in the country which produces the London cracksman, who is the terror of the police the world over.

At Rockfort, near Birkenhead, in Lancashire, I observed what seemed to me a remarkable manifestation of that determination to active resistance of wrong which is a distinguishing trait of English life. It seems that somehow, no one knew how, a report had got about that there was small-pox in Rockfort. Wherefore the authorities of the place had set up posters all about the neighborhood, in which they formally and officially denied the truth of the report aforesaid; and not only so, but threatened the parties originating and circulating this slander with prosecution at the law. Such a poster here would not be thought of; and if set up it would only excite laughter; but perhaps there is a question whether the determination and the ability to resist injurious misrepresentation have a moral and social aspect which is quite ridiculous.

As I was on the rail from Birmingham to Liverpool, I found myself in a carriage with a woman, the charm of whose presence I shall never forget. She was very handsome; a fair-skinned, dark-eyed, dark-haired beauty. She was approaching the maturity of woman's years, and her tall figure had ripened into a large and noble loveliness. A boy about ten years old called her " mamma; " and yet her sweet lips and her sweet face were fresh, — as fresh and sweet as her voice. She was one of those women who bestow a blessing upon the world every time they come forth into it. So far she might in all respects have been a Yankee. But horrors, the dress of her! It might be called heterogeneous; but that would imply that it was somewhat geneous. Her gown was of a great plaid of purple and gray; around her neck she had a silk kerchief of bronze and brown; over her plaid gown was a short embroidered velvet sacque; and all this she had surmounted with a light blue velvet bonnet in which flaunted a white feather!

Differences in custom, in fashion, and even, it would seem, in natural objects, distinguish places in England which are only a few miles apart, — a remarkable and characteristic trait. For example, observing, as I walked in Sussex, a peculiarity in the forms of the tops of some chimneys, the lines being more complex than usual, I remarked upon it to a Sussex gentleman who was with me, and he told me that all chimneys in Sussex were finished at the top in that way. I found that this was true. I saw no chimneys built otherwise in that county, and I saw none of this form in any other county. And yet more, all the pigs in Sussex were black. Those I saw elsewhere were white, — as white as conscientious pigs could consistently be; but, great or small, the pigs in Sussex were as black as crows.

That such peculiarities should be limited by the narrow boundaries of counties is very noteworthy evidence of stability, of individuality, and of self-assertion. It is difficult for us, whose local traditions go back little farther than two hundred years, and have been disturbed and almost obliterated by the mobility of the whole civilized world within that period, to imagine how such peculiarities originated among people of the same blood living within a few miles of each other. They are, doubtless, of very remote origin; and their preservation is the consequence of the immobility of rural life in England. Clarendon records that Charles II. was very near being discovered on his flight from the defeat of Worcester, because it was remarked by a smith at an inn where he stopped that " his horse's four shoes had been made in four several counties." Think of a way of putting shoes on a horse peculiar to the farriers of one county, and noticeably unlike that of the farriers in counties on either side ! But the variety was limited only by the capacity of the beast. If Charles had traveled upon a centipede, the English counties could have furnished him with peculiar shoes for every foot. We may laugh at this; but is it not better that a man should be himself, that a community should be itself, than that either should be a mere imitation, a duplicate, or, it may be, a centuplicate, of some other man or some other community? Better county fashions in horse-shoes than shoes turned out in packages by machinery, *in usum totius mundi ;* to say nothing of the possible service of the county fashion in preventing the escape of royal fugitives from justice.

In the climate of England I remarked the greater effect of the heat of the sun and the less of his light. I used to write most of my letters in bed before breakfast. At the end of October, the sun would shine into my window so warm that, although the room was large, I more than once had to get up and pull down the shade. The rays which fell upon the bed did not hurt my eyes with glare, but I could not bear the heat ; and yet it would afterwards rain almost all day. We never have the sun with us so hot in the middle of October that we cannot bear it through a window ten feet off. At first I thought that the climate was cooler than ours at the same season; but that was because there was a "cold snap;" only there was no snap at all in it, but a dismal, cheerless, uncheerable dankness. It is this ever-present moisture that makes a little heat oppressive. Its effect seems to be all pervading. Excepting champagne, nothing in England is ever quite dry, not even humor.

CHAPTER XVI.

ENGLISH IN ENGLAND.

THE worst English that I have ever heard spoken I heard in England. There, however, I also heard the best that could be spoken, — not better, indeed, than is spoken in New England, New York, New Jersey, and Pennsylvania; but of this best English I must acknowledge that I found much more among my British than among my "American" acquaintances, in proportion to their numbers. The standard of comparison in all cases is a British standard; for it is a postulate in the discussion of this question that the best English is that which is accepted as the best by people of the best education and social standing in England. What is accepted by them; not necessarily what is spoken by them. For, as we shall see, they are somewhat remarkable for variation by individuals from their own undisputed standard.

Almost all "Americans" who live in cities have opportunities now and then of hearing English spoken by natives of Old England, which, however, is not therefore necessarily the best English. For, as many Frenchmen, even many Parisians, speak very bad French, so many Englishmen and many Londoners, in fact most Englishmen and most Londoners, speak bad English. I think that the vilest French that I ever heard was from a Parisian born and bred; and a *sociétaire* of the Théâtre Français agreed with me in my opinion of it. It would seem superfluous to say this, were it not for the common assumption that a Parisian must speak good French, and for the assumption by many Englishmen, who speak in the vulgarest way, that because of their English birth they are competent to criticise and to censure the speech of men born elsewhere, who are as thoroughly English in blood as they are, and whose education and training have been far superior to theirs. Nor is mastery of idiom so absolutely a matter of race, or even of early education. Whose English surpasses in clearness and in idiomatic strength that of the German Max Müller, first as an English writer among all contemporary philologists?

Among home-keeping Yankees who had never visited England, I was, I am inclined to believe, somewhat exceptional in my opportunities of observing the speech of Englishmen of various ranks, which began when I was a boy, and went on increasing in frequency until I crossed the ocean. There was therefore nothing very new to me in the average speech around me when I found myself among my kinsmen in the old home, and nothing at all new in the English that I heard from the friends that I found there, and from their acquaintances. How should there be? This, too, would seem a superfluous remark, were it not for the assumption and assertion by some fussy and insufficiently informed purists and pedants that there are important differences between the language of the two peoples, due in part to the preservation in this country of phrases and pronunciations which are obsolete or obsolescent in England, and in part to changes which have taken place here, some of which are attributed — Heaven help us! —

to the influence of the aboriginal "Indians" upon
our habits of mind and body !

Many Yankees who speak with unconscious freedom the language of good " American " society must
have encountered with amusement the complimentary
expressions of surprise at their " pure English," with
which they were favored in England. A friend of
mine, a lady, met one of these with a whimsical and
characteristic reply, of which she told me with great
glee. She was on both sides a Yankee of the Yankees ; but her mother bore a name which stands high
among the historical patronymics of England. She
was as fair, golden-haired, blue-eyed, and buxom a
young matron as you would find in New England,
or between the Tweed and the Channel ; and being
once where there were many portraits of members of
the family in question, her likeness to some of them
was so striking that it was remarked upon. Nevertheless, a gentleman, an officer in the British army,
thought it necessary not only to compliment her upon
her English, but to ask her if she was not peculiar in
this respect among her countrywomen. " Oh, yes,"
she immediately replied ; " but then I have had unusual advantages. There was an English missionary
stationed near my tribe." His captainship subsided
at once into silence, and seemed to be revolving the
matter in his mind in a more or less dazed fashion,
which afforded her great amusement.

Between the majority of Englishmen and the majority of Yankees there is a difference of pitch and
inflection of voice. The English pitch is generally
higher ; the inflection is almost always more varied.
The "average American's " voice is comparatively
hard and monotonous. But upon this point, and

upon the general superiority of the Englishwoman's voice in its quality, — a soft, rich sweetness, — I have said enough elsewhere. Nor would any remark upon this point be on this occasion either requisite or pertinent. It has nothing to do either with the substantial part of language, the vocabulary, nor with pronunciation, which varies more or less from generation to generation, which differs more or less in different circles, and which is not quite alike in all individuals in the same circle. This of course is true of both countries.

The first peculiarity that attracted my attention in the speech of Englishmen was a thick, throaty utterance. It was not new to me, but I was struck by its general diffusion. The effect is somewhat as if the speaker were attempting to combine speech with the deglutition of mashed potato. This peculiar utterance, in which a guttural *aw* seems to prevail, is, however, far from being universal. It is not high-class speech. Yet it begins to manifest itself somewhat high up in the social scale, being perceptible just below what may be called the Oxford and Cambridge level. Then it broadens down from precedent to subsequent, until, when it reaches the lowest level, it is broad enough and thick enough for the foundation of a very substantial theory of peculiarity in national speech. It manifests itself chiefly in the utterance of some of the sounds of *a*, *o*, and *u* in combination with *l* and *r;* for example, in such words as *ale*, *pale*, *people*, and *royal*, which are spoken by Englishmen of the lower and lower-middle classes much as if they were written *ayull*, *payull*, *peopull*, and *ryull*, the *l*'s being gobbled low in the throat with a turkey-like gulp. The tendency to this mode of speech seemed to be strongest in those who were short-necked and corpulent. I remember one obese, red-faced shopman who gulped at " Royal Wilton " in such a strangling fashion that I should hardly have been surprised to see him fall down upon the spot in a fit of apoplexy. General negative assertions are unsafe ; and I shall therefore not say that this gulp is never heard among educated English gentlemen and ladies ; but I am sure that in such society I never heard it.

The ill treatment which the letter *h* receives from a very large proportion of the English people has long been known to the most superficial observers of their speech. It is the substance and the point of a standing joke which never loses its zest. Mr. Punch's artists, when hard put to it for the subject of a social sketch, can always fall back upon the misfortunes of the aspirate. *H* in speech is an unmistakable mark of class distinction in England, as every observant person soon discovers. I remarked upon this to an English gentleman, an officer, who replied, " It 's the greatest blessing in the world ; a sure protection against cads. You meet a fellow who is well dressed and behaves himself decently enough, and yet you don't know exactly what to make of him ; but get him talking, and if he trips upon his *h*'s that settles the question. He 's a chap you 'd better be shy of." Another friend said to me of a London man of wealth, and of such influence as comes from wealth and good nature, " The governor has lots of sense, and is the best fellow in the world ; but he has n't an *h* to bless himself with." And there seems to be no help for the person who has once acquired this mode of pronunciation. Habits of speech, when formed in early life, are the most ineradicable of all habits ; and this one, I believe, is absolutely beyond the reach of any discipline, and even of prolonged association with good speakers. I have had opportunities of observing many English persons of both sexes who came to "America" in their early childhood, who were educated here, and who had attained mature years, and yet they could not utter the initial *h*, but, for example, would say *ee* for he. If they did, by special effort, sound the *h*, it was with a harsh ejaculation, and not with that light touch which, although so distinctly perceptible, is but a delicate breathing, and which comes so unconsciously to good speakers in England, and to bad speakers as well as good — to all — in "America." In England I observed many people in a constant struggle with their *h*'s, overcoming and being overcome, and sometimes triumphing when victory was defeat.

The number of *h*'s that come to an untimely end in England daily is quite incalculable. Of the forty millions of people there cannot be more than two or three millions who are capable of a healthy, well-breathed *h*. Think, then, of the numbers of this innocent letter that are sacrificed between sun and sun! If we could send them over a few millions of *h*'s a week, they would supply almost as great a need as that which we supply by our corn and beef and cheese.

There is a gradation, too, in the misuse of this letter. It is silent when it should be heard; but it is also added, or rather prefixed, to words in which it has no place. Now the latter fault is the sign and token of a much lower condition in life than the former. The man who puts on a superfluous *h*, and says *harm* for arm and *heyes* for eyes, will surely

drop the *h* from its rightful place, and say *ed* and *art*
for head and heart; but the converse is far from being true. The superfluous *h* is a much graver solecism
than the suppressed. It is barbarous. To hear it
you must go very low in the social scale. But, on
the other hand, the suppression of the *h* is a habit
that creeps up towards the very highest ranks, diminishing in strength and extent as it rises, until it
wholly disappears. For example, only Englishmen
of the very uppermost class and finest breeding say
home and hotel; all others, *'ome* and *'otel*. And the
latter are so unconscious of their slip, so sure that
they do say home and hotel, that if they are charged
with dropping the *h* they will deny it, and make des-
perate efforts to utter the sound, which result only in
throwing a very great stress upon the *o*.[1] These two
words are the last and most delicate test of the *h* mal-
ady. Past that line English speech, when not impaired by individual incapacity or tainted by affectation, is perfect, "express and admirable."

Widely spread as this incapacity for managing the
h is, it seems to have attracted little other attention
in England than that which manifests itself in ridicule. No English orthoepist or phonologist whose
work I have met with has made it the subject of examination, or of more than a mere passing remark.
Nor does it seem to have been even laughed at until
very lately, — hardly before the beginning of this
century. Until that time there is no evidence which
I now remember that it had ever been taken note of.
The Elizabethan dramatists make the English speech
of Frenchmen and of Hollanders the occasion of

---

[1] This assertion I make upon competent concurrent testimony. I tried
no such experiments myself.

laughter; and among their own countrymen, Welsh-men, and even English rustic folk, do not escape. The dramatists of the Restoration ridicule the Irish speech till we are surfeited with their Teagues and their "dear joys." The speech of English clowns is also imitated, and in general ridiculed, not only in plays but in ballads, and at last in novels, from the first of these periods to the close of the last century. But in all this mass of low character painting there is not a touch of fun that depends upon a misplaced or a displaced *h*. Even such personages as Lord and Lady Duberly, Zekiel and Cicely Homespun, in "The Heir at Law," and Old Rapid and Young Rapid, Farmer Oatlands and Frank Oatlands, in "A Cure for the Heart Ache," although their "cacology" sup-plies no small part of the fun in the performance, are not represented as maltreating their *h*'s. Sheridan, who belongs to the last quarter of the eighteenth cent-ury, leaves this trait of speech unridiculed, although he has low characters and made a Mrs. Malaprop. It would be hardly possible to find such personages in a play or a novel of to-day who were not made the butt of laughter on this account.

That English writers on language should have made no remark upon this trait of English speech is in itself noteworthy. For it is peculiarly English, or rather South British. The Lowland Scotch, who are as English in blood as the people of England them-selves, and whose speech is an ancient and important English dialect, are entirely without this *h* trait; and so are English people of Irish birth, the descendants of them of the old "English pale." Men of English blood and American birth, New Englanders, Vir-ginians, and the like, are also without it entirely

Yet it so pervades England that it might be regarded as a trait of normal English, but for the fact that it is entirely absent from the speech of those who speak the best English, and is to them a cause of aversion and an occasion of ridicule. It is remarkable, too, that this trick of speech is not at all the consequence of any inability with regard to the proper utterance of *h*. Quite the contrary; for the man who threatens to " punch yer 'ed " will also " blarst yer heyes." [1]

These facts seem to me to point to a conclusion which yet cannot be accepted as established, because of a fact which points another way, and which cannot be set aside, although it may be explained. The absence of any allusion to the *h* difficulty by English dramatists and humorists of the seventeenth and eighteenth centuries can hardly be accounted for except by the supposition either that it did not exist, or that it was not then peculiar to a low condition of life. The fact that it does not exist and never has existed in the speech of the English people of Ireland or of " America " almost compels the conclusion that it was unknown in England in the fifteenth and sixteenth centuries, when (as to Ireland mainly, and as to North America absolutely) the English language was translated to those countries. The sudden outbreak about the beginning of this century, of ridicule provoked by the dropping and adding of the *h*, would seem to indicate either that the habit had been formed or had come into vogue with the lower classes during the eighteenth century, or that, having until

---

[1] A deliberate use of this pronunciation raised a laugh one day. At luncheon a gentleman found a stew rather too warm for his mouth. After a moment of condolence, another said, "Oh, it has always been so with English cooks. Does n't Gray say,

" ' Even in 'heir hashes live their wonted fires ? ' "

that time prevailed among all classes, it was dropped and stigmatized as vulgar by the upper classes about the end of that century.[1]

To the former of these inferences there is opposed the very stubborn fact that there is evidence in old English literature that what is now called the vulgar use of *h* was in past centuries the common and received pronunciation of English. This is not the place for a purely linguistic discussion ; but I will mention that in the " Lay of Havelok the Dane," written about A. D. 1280, and existing in a manuscript of about that date, eye is written *heie*, earl *herle*, old *hold*, eat *hete*, ate *het*, ever *hever*, and English *Henglishe*. There is a great deal of such evidence. Moreover, there is the evidence given by the presence of the full form of the indefinite article *an* before words beginning with an accented syllable now aspirated : as, for example, " an household," " an habit," " an headache," " an history," " an hundred." This continued until a recent period, and has not yet entirely passed away, although it is passing. For example, Mr. Trollope, in his " Three Clerks," writes, " If the Board chose to make the Weights and Measures *an* hospital for idiots, it might do so. . . . . He would never remain there to see the Weights and Measures

---

[1] It is worthy of remark that *h* suffered in the speech of certain Romans in Catullus's day, not by being dropped, but by being added, as we see by his epigram on Arrius : —

> " Chommoda dicebat, si quandò commoda vellet
>   Dicere, et hinsidias Arrius insidias ;
> Et tunc mirificè spectabat se esse locutum,
>   Quum quantum poterat, dixerat hinsidias.
> Credo sic mater, sic liber avunculus ejus,
>   Sic maternus avus dixerit, atque avia.
>   .   .   .   .
> Ionios fluctus, postquam illuc Arrius esset
>   Jam non Ionios esse, sed Hionios."

become *an* hospital for incurables." The presence of the *n* in such cases shows pretty clearly that the *h* was silent; in which case there is evidence that it was dropped by the best English writers of the last century in many words in which it is now *de rigueur* that it should be heard.

The change in some words is not yet quite perfected. Mr. Thackeray spoke of the English *h*umorists; and that pronunciation is given by Phelp of Cambridge in Stormonth's dictionary, the most convenient and trustworthy handbook of English speech that I have found; but I heard Cambridge dons talk of "Every Man in his Umour." In this, however, they merely preserved the pronunciation of the last generation, as certain English clergymen do, who offer "'umble and 'earty thanks" in the church service every Sunday. Walker gives the pronunciations, hospital *ospital*, humble *umble*, humor *yumer*, in all of which Phelp calls for the sound of *h*. Mr. Trollope's "an hospital" is merely a remnant of old-fashioned pronunciation, which, if I remember rightly, will not be found in his later novels.[1]

The question is one which it is not safe to undertake to decide without a careful and thorough examination of the whole range of English literature; but

[1] In the English Bible such instances as the following are countless: "and set *an hedge* about it" (Mark xii. 1); "and when ye come into *an house*, salute it" (Matthew x. 12); "and there was a good way off from them *an herd* of swine feeding" (Matthew viii. 30). The best writers of Queen Anne's reign use *an* in this way before *h :* "that no person below the dignity of a Roman knight should presume to write *an* history." (Addison, *Freeholder*, No. 35.) The following passage from Taylor's translation of the *New Cratylus*, A. D. 1793, seems to have been written when the writer's ear was distracted by a changing pronunciation: "*Soc.* What, .hen, if I should call anything in such a manner as to denominate that *an* horse which we now call a man, and that a man which we now call *a* horse?" (Page 3). But on page 19 we have "*a* horse" six times.

I venture the conjecture, which, however, is somewhat more than a conjecture, that the suppression of *h* was once very widely diffused throughout England among all speakers, including the best, during which time — a very long one — the function of *h* was to throw a stress on the syllable which it ushered in, as it is, for example, in the Spanish word *hijo ;* that the widely diffused suppression of the breathing among the lower classes of modern England is, like many other so-called vulgarisms, a mere survival among them of what has perished among their "betters ; " and that this suppression of the *h* was so general, even among the upper classes so late as the middle of the last century, that it provoked no remark, — indeed, attracted no attention from the social critics and satirists.

This theory, however, leaves the correct pronunciation of the *h* by all classes in Ireland and in "America" unaccounted for. But that remarkable fact may possibly be the result of a predominance in the emigrants to those countries of people from the north of England. For the dropping and the adding of the *h* is even now, after forty years of railway intercourse, so much more common in most of the southern counties of England than in the northern as to be remarkable on that account. It is sometimes called a "cockneyism." No view of it could be farther from the truth. Some of the most marked cases of it that I have ever met with were in Cornish people from near Land's-End, who had never been in or near London.

Nor do all London people of the lower orders have this trouble with their *h*'s. I observed this in many instances. One particularly impressed me. On my

way from Rochester to London I left my own seat,
and entered a third-class carriage, on a visit of observation. Taking my seat next a woman, I soon fell
into talk with her, which before we had gone many
miles became somewhat confidential on her part.
She was, I found, a commercial traveler; in a word,
a female bagman. But although she was born and
brought up in London, and was quite in her proper
place in a third-class carriage, I observed that her
pronunciation was perfectly correct, and that she
never dropped an *h*, much less added one superfluously. Her language also was good, although her
manner of speech and the tone of her voice revealed
the lowness of her origin. She was very intelligent;
and although she talked with a strange man thus
freely, her behavior and her manner were perfectly
modest.

One pronunciation, which has been called a Yankee
trait, I was surprised to find diffused all over England and among all classes, — *aou* for *ou*. I had first
observed this some years before in the case of an
English gentleman, an author of some note, whom I
met in New York, and who said very plainly *paound*
for pound. I thought it might be a trick peculiar to
him ; but when I was in England I found quite to
the contrary. Paound was the rule ; pound the exception. In Liverpool, the next morning after my
arrival, I went to look at a house which was to let ;
and the young lady who was kind enough to show it
to me (the daughter of the tenant, a physician, and
of repute, as I learned) told me that it was "a beautiful haouse," which indeed it was. A railway porter, on my asking him how long I should have to wait
for a train, replied, "Nearly a haour, sir." I was at

breakfast in London at the University Club with an author of distinction and a Fellow of his college, when a friend of his, evidently a member of the club, came up and said, "Haou d' deaou?" At Westminster Abbey, at the door of which I presented myself at a certain time in the service, a verger said to me, "You cawnt pahss in neaou, sir." In a first-class carriage on the South Eastern Railway I had as fellow passengers two men, who were quite well dressed, and one of whom was nicely gloved. Their talk was bucolic. "Osses are bad to git." "They *are* bad to git; 'igh prices." "Haou abaout caouws?" "Caouw cattle are very good at Aylesbury." These men said "*di*-rectly" and "sheootin" (shooting); and one of them, "Must n't we alleaow [that is, confess] that?" On my walk from Canterbury to Harbledown I asked direction of a boy whom I met, who said, "Ther 's an old church up aour way that they call Hairbledaoun church," just like a rustic Yankee boy that I might have met in the remotest parts of New Hampshire. In Kent the farmers and the peasants spoke warmly of the goodness of the "graound."

One instance of this pronunciation produced an odd effect. At Warwick Castle, as I walked across the greensward of the base court on my way to the great tower, I picked up a large, handsome gray feather, which I still have. I asked the man who stood at the foot of the tower to take my shilling, what bird had dropped this feather. Looking at it a moment, he said, "It 's an auk." Of course I knew that he did not mean the bird called the auk, and I showed him that it could not be a hawk's feather, when he exclaimed, "Oh, it 's a haowl, it 's a haowl!

We 've got a big haowl 'ere, and 'e 's dropped one of
'is feathers." Two or three days afterwards I was at
a performance of "King Lear" in Birmingham by an
actor of reputation. In the last act, as the poor old
king is coming in with the dead Cordelia, he cries,
"Howl, howl, howl!" These words are heard from
behind the scenes before Lear actually appears; and
they were on this occasion so very nearly "Haowl,
haowl, haowl!" that they brought the Warwick
"haowl" instantly and vividly to my mind; and the
result was far from being in keeping with the feeling
proper to the scene.

These examples, it will be seen, come from all
quarters and from all classes. This rueful note is,
however, uttered with a difference in the two countries. In England the *aou* has none of that nasality
which often enters into its composition in "America," and makes it, not lovely in itself, certainly one
of the most offensive sounds that can be uttered
by the human voice. But among the better class of
speakers in "America" this *aou*, either compounded
with nasality or pure and simple, is never heard.

There is, in fact, in the pronunciation of the upper
classes in England no marked difference from that of
well-educated, well-bred people in the Northern and
Eastern States of the Union. I observed, however,
on the one hand a stronger tendency to the full, broad
ah in some words, and on the other to the English
diphthongal *a* (the name sound of the letter, *aee*) in
others. At Westminster Abbey I observed that the
officiating canon said "comm*ah*ndment" and "*re*-
membr*ah*nce," trilling the *r* as well as broadening
the *a*; and at King's Chapel, Trinity, Cambridge,
where I sat next the reader, my ear was pleased

with his "power and commahndment." I heard the
same broad *ah* sound of *a* in transplant, past, cast,
ask, and the like from three distinguished authors,
one of them a lady, whom I had the pleasure of
meeting in London. At the debates among the young
men at the Oxford Union, I heard the same broad
sound, — grahnted, clahss, pahsture, and so forth.
But at St. Paul's, in London, a young deacon who
said, "Heah beginneth the tenth chaptah of the book
of Kings," yet said, "And it came to păss," and
even worse "păth," clipping his *a*'s down to the
narrow vowel sound of *an*. On the whole, however,
the broad sound very greatly prevailed among the
university-bred men.

The name sound of *a* attracted my attention
chiefly in proper names, mostly classical. It seemed
somewhat strange to hear a Cambridge don say Cleo-
paytra and Coriolaynus; and not the less so because
he did not say Aythens. But I remember that By-
ron (somewhere in Don Juan, I believe) by a rhyme
requires the pronunciation Sardanapaylus. This use
of the English *a* is carried into Latin; and at Oxford the prevailing pronunciation of Baliol is Bayliol.
Yet at the Union debates and elsewhere I heard the
Continental *i* insisted upon strongly in calibre, — pronounced caleebre, — although the accepted pronunciation is calĭbre, as in "America."

In words like "institute," "duke," and "constitution," in which *u* follows *d* or *t*, the English *u* (io-
tized *u*) is generally uttered with very unmistakable
clearness by the best speakers. Some of them are so
very particular on this point that they suggest the
spelling institewt, constitewtion, which seemed to me
somewhat extravagant and affected. It is well to

avoid insti*toot* and *dook ;* but still one need not *tew* the word, like a rustic Yankee saying *too*.

From a clergyman in Kent, the rector of one of three parishes, which, lying together, are called " the three Graces," because the living of each is a full thousand pounds, I heard the old pronunciation of *were*, making it a perfect rhyme to *ware* and *there*. This pronunciation, which prevailed for centuries, and which is correct (if in pronunciation there is any correctness other than a conformity to the best usage of one's time), had passed out of vogue before Walker's day, more than three quarters of a century ago. From the same reverend gentleman I heard the old pronunciation of *mercy*, *earth,* and *virtue*, — not *murcy*, *urth* and *vurtue*, — but a sound of *e* like that in the first syllable of *error*, which I had heard from well-educated old people in my boyhood. And yet this gentleman was not an aged man. He had merely preserved the pronunciation which he had learned in his youth. The fact is worthy of remark chiefly as it is an illustration of a certain independence, or rather individuality, of speech which is not uncommon in England. English people do not fear to maintain a little singularity even in their language.

Among clergymen I observed a general retention of the final *ed* of the participle, as belov-ed, betray-ed, observ-ed, and the like. To this I had been accustomed, of course, in the reading of the Liturgy and of the Bible ; but in England I heard it even in sermons, in the delivery of which " American " clergymen, according to my observation, always use the contracted form. In other respects the delivery of the clergy of the two countries seemed to me quite alike, making allowance, of course, for merely indi-

vidual peculiarities on both sides. And when I speak
of clergymen in America, I do not mean such men as
he who preached the sermon on " a harp of a thousand strings," but men like Dr. Dix, Dr. Potter, and
Dr. Schenck in the Episcopal church, and Dr. Adams,
Dr. Bellows, and Dr. Chapin among the Presbyte-
rians, Unitarians, and Congregationalists. It is, however, true, I believe, that in England more than in the
United States clergymen read the service, the Bible,
and their sermons not only with a more settled emphasis, but with a perceptible cadence, which in some
cases approaches a see-saw inflection, and which has
somewhat the effect of a measured chant. I heard this
from one old clergyman here in my childhood, — Dr.
Milnor, of St. George's, where I first went to church.
I was only six years old when I last saw him in sur-
plice and bands, but I can now hear the regular rise
and fall of his silvery voice, the measured inflections
of which seemed to my childish ears to have a certain
sanctity in them in keeping with the place and with
the religious function which he was performing.[1]
But after that time I never heard it until I went to
England, and there not from all clergymen.

This style of delivery is a survival of the old style
of elocution. The late Hon. Luther Bradish told me
in the later years of his life that in his boyhood he
was at a country house in England, not far from
London, and that Mrs. Siddons used to be there

[1] This venerable and most estimable clergyman always read prayers and
preached in black silk gloves, as indeed my own grandfather did ; for it
was the fashion then among clergymen of the Episcopal church who were
at all particular about clerical costume. The forefinger and thumb of the
right-hand glove were slit open to enable the wearer to turn the leaves of
Prayer Book and Bible. A fine line-engraved portrait of Dr. Milnor in
the pulpit, and thus decorated, is in my possession.

often, and would read poetry to the ladies as they sat at needle-work in the morning parlor. He spoke with great admiration of the beauty of her voice and the nobility of her manner. I asked him what was the style of her reading, — whether it was free and natural. He replied, "Not quite. She read with a measured cadence. As I remember it now, there must have been a good deal of sing-song about it; and there was the same in her delivery of long speeches on the stage. But still it was very fine, and in her it seemed to my boyish taste angelic."

The conversion of final *ng* into *n* is notably common in England, even by speakers of the highest classes; far more so, I should say, than it is in "America;" certainly much, very much, more so than it is among our best bred people, who indeed are very rarely guilty of this slovenliness. But in England members of Parliament, Fellows of colleges, dukes and dandies, farmers, philologists, say doin', bein', seein', and even line for lying. I heard an absurd little swell (and yet I believe he was at bottom a good fellow) say, "Oh, yeth! But you thee, I bein' tho vewy fond of 'untin' and thootin', I cahnt be thtoppin' in London in the autumn." And yet I'll be bound that little chap thought great scorn of the "American" way of speaking English. I observed, by the way, that impediments, or rather incapacities, of speech are much commoner in England than they are with us. A lisping man here is a very rare bird; but in England, especially among the upper classes, he is not uncommon. As an affectation the fashion is not very new. Chaucer's wanton and merry friar lisped "to make his Englissch swete upon his tunge." There is the same comparative common ness there and uncommonness here of men who have trouble with *r*, and who say, like my little friend, " vewy." It was amusing to hear an officer in the Guards talk about his " wedgment."

Of pronunciations which were evidently deliberate variations from the standard, I observed, in addition to those which I have already mentioned, *know*-ledge, which I heard only from the lips of educated men, first from a barrister of unusual scholarship and accomplishments ; — oppo-*zite*, which I heard not infrequently from speakers of all classes, and which I first heard in this country from an English clergyman who was visiting at my father's house, and who produced a pocket Greek Testament at morning prayers and followed in it my father's reading, somewhat, as I discovered, to his amusement ; — tor-*toys* (tortoise), in which the last syllable was pronounced just like the plural of *toy ;* but this, though not a low-class pronunciation, was uncommon, the general pronunciation of the syllable in question being, not as the dictionaries give it, either *tis* or *tus*, but an abbreviation of *toise* which is quite inexpressible by letters. In Chester the *l* in *half*, *walk*, *talk*, *balk*, and the like words is still sounded. Those from whom I heard it were neither rustic nor uneducated speakers.

One of the most characteristic and striking speeches that I heard was from a young gentleman, an author, and the son of an author and editor of some distinction (neither of them is now living), who in the course of talk about Lord Beaconsfield, then Mr. Disraeli, exclaimed, " Wot 'n igstrawnry man ! " I could make no mistake about it, for he repeated the remark soon after, — " Wot 'n igstrawnry man ! "

Of quite a different sort was the noteworthy pronunciation of a little fellow who officiated as " buttons " at a house in Essex where I was visiting, and who said to me, as he came into my room one morning, " I 've took your dress trousis to the tiler's, sir." Now if he had taken my hat to the tiler's, it would not have been so surprising. But in fact he had taken my trousers to the tailor's ; and his pronunciation of the title of that functionary was a, to me, charming survival of the old sound of the word. For English *i* is *ah-ee*, and *tiler* is simply *ta-ee-ler* (with the *a* broad); that is, the French *tailleur*, in which form our modern name for the old "sempster" came into the language.   And by the way, whatever uncertainty there may be about other words of like termination, there is no doubt that this is an English form of the French *tailleur ;* and yet neither Johnson himself, nor the most bigoted of Johnsonian etymological spellers, has insisted upon spelling the word *tailour*. The Doctor and his followers have remained content with *tailor*, although, unlike *honor* and *favor*, it has no Latin original. This little fellow also told me that it was "foive minutes past aight."

Of words new to me I met with only one. (I of course am leaving out of consideration the dialect and the folk phrases of remote rural districts.   And indeed of that I had little opportunity to hear anything. In the counties in which I took my rural walks I found few dialectic peculiarities worthy of special remark, either in vocabulary or in pronunciation.) This word was *singlet*, which came up to me printed on my first washing bill in Liverpool. I had never seen it before ; but its suggestion of *doublet* of course instantly showed me that it must mean an under-vest, as it did, — a merino under-shirt. I never heard it spoken, nor did I meet with it in any other part of England ; nor is it in any English dictionary. It is a Lancashire word. And yet of course it is not dialectical, which being Romanic it could not be. It reminded me that in one of Ford's tragedies a woman passing from one chamber to another in the night speaks of herself as going "thus singly," meaning plainly, and as the context shows, not that she went alone, but that she was covered with a single garment.[1]

Of familiar words used in a somewhat peculiar sense I found a few.

Ever is frequently heard in composition thus : "Whoever is it?" "Whatever can it be?" This usage is mostly confined to ladies, and is not regarded as good English.

Tiresome is used for disagreeable. "Those tiresome Brighton people." "Do be quiet : why will you be so tiresome?" "That cross, ill-natured, tiresome woman."

Mind, as a verb, not uncommon in "America," has its function stretched to an extreme which is sometimes laughable. There is not only "Would you mind handing me the milk-jug?" for "Would you take the trouble," etc., but "I don't mind that," meaning, don't find it unpleasant. I heard a lady, a peeress, say to a very swellish fellow who had just taken honors at Oxford, "A—— is a very good fellow, — so pleasant ; don't you think so?" "Ah — yes," was the slow reply, "I — don't — mind him."

---

[1] The curious reader will find the passage in *Love's Sacrifice*, Act II. Sc. 1.

This brought to my recollection that in one of Charles Reade's novels a young gentleman, also a swell, proposes in this fashion : " Would you mind our getting married ? I should n't."

Nasty. This word, of unpleasant suggestions, is used much more commonly in England than it is in the United States. An ill-natured speech is called " a nasty speech," a stormy day " a nasty day ; " and I even heard an English lady call an awkward step " a nasty step." Therefore, when Lady A—— said here at a dinner, where she sat at her host's right hand, speaking to her husband, who sat at the hostess' right hand, and who thought it proper not to touch his soup, " Do take some, A—— : it 's not at all nasty," she did not mean to be so rude, that is, quite so rude, as she seemed to those who sat with her. But some ladies have told me that her cuffs and collars might have had the word applied to them with fitness, if not with propriety.[1]

Jug is universally used for *pitcher.* I did not hear the latter word once in any part of the country, or from speakers in any class of life, while I was in England, but always the " water-jug," " the milk-jug." This usage is of very recent origin, and the

[1] How constantly this word is applied in England by well-bred people to other people who are also well bred, but disagreeable or much in the way, may be inferred from the fact that I met with all these examples in reading one novel of Mr. Trollope's, *Is he Popenjoy?* The lovely Mary Lovelace exclaims, in a fit of jealousy, "Nasty creature! wicked, wicked beast! Oh, George, she is so ugly." (Chap. xxxii.) "But she is a nasty, vile creature; and I will never speak to her again." (Chap. xl.) "He is so nasty. Don't you see that his face always shines?" (Chap. xlix.) "What a nasty, false, wicked old woman she was!" (Chap. l.) "Nasty, fat old woman. I 'm sure I did n't want to hear her." (Chap. lx.) "Oh, George! dear George! you have made me so happy. . . . She is a nasty, hardened creature; and I do hate her. . . . How a woman can be so nasty I can't imagine." (Chap. lix.)

word itself is comparatively new. According to all evidence of English literature and lexicography, a jug is a coarse vessel with swelling sides, usually made of stone-ware or brown clay, — a thing that never would be brought upon a nicely served table. A pitcher, on the contrary, may be large or small, gracefully shaped, and of porcelain, of china, of crystal, of silver, or of gold. The word *jug* is unknown to our earlier literature, and is not found in the Bible, although *pitcher* and *bottle* occur there frequently; and *pitcher* has been known for centuries as the equivalent of *ollula*, *urna*, *amphora*.

Merchant is widely misused. You shall not find a grog seller who does not call himself a spirit merchant, or a man in a little black den of coals who does not call himself a coal merchant. The word is misused in this way among us of late years, but not quite to such an extent. Still, however, there is in England a standard and a tribunal before which such bad usage has no force. I heard of a man who had been in trade, and in a large way; but his affairs had gone to utter ruin, and left him old, poor, and helpless. He was respected and personally liked, and there was an effort to get him into an asylum founded for " decayed merchants." The trustees, although they had the kindest feeling toward him, and wished to give him help, decided that they could not admit him, because he was not a merchant. He had never been engaged in foreign trade, — had never owned or even chartered a ship.

Tidy is strangely used to mean good of its kind, pretty. The misuse, however, does not, according to my observation, rise above the lower-middle class. Among them a tidy girl means a pretty girl, and

particularly a girl with a good figure.   Indeed, I
have often heard *tidy* applied to a young woman of
whose person and clothing tidiness, according to the
true meaning of the word, could surely not be predi-
cated ; for the untidiness of the lower-class Englishwoman, unless she becomes a chamber-maid or a bar-
maid, passes man's understanding.   *Tidy* is also used
for *pretty* in a metaphorical sense, as thus, by a distinguished novelist : " The alcohol we consume every
day would be a tidy sale for a small public-house." [1]

Do is made a word of all work.   Women do their
back hair, and do everything that they arrange.   " I
have got these flowers to do," meaning to arrange
in a vase.   " Tom," said a lady at luncheon, " would
you mind changing seats ?   I can't do this beef,"
meaning that she could not carve and serve it.   On
my way from Birmingham to London a lady got out
of the carriage at a small station.   She was one of
the women who take responsibility heavily ; for she
faithfully tried to shut the door of the carriage, and
after struggling with it a moment she broke out, "Oh,
dear! you must call some one.   I can't do this door." [2]

Just so, just so, is the most common phrase of general assent ; *Fancy, now!* a very common expression
of surprise ; and among men, especially among young
men, a greater degree of surprise, with an added implication of protest, breaks forth in *Oh, I say!*

Immediately and *directly* are strangely used for

[1] Of *tidy*, in its primitive sense, timely, I remember this singular exam-
ie : "With good olde wine, and good, fat, and *tidie* flesh or byrdes."
(*The Byrth of Mankinde,* by Thomas Raynald, 1540, M. i. *a.*)   That is,
flesh or birds in season.

[2] That clever writer, Harry Quilter, in the London *Spectator,* says,
" I want to take hold of my little friend in the red-morocco slippers, and
give him a good shake, and make him *do his hair* like other men.
(March 6, 1881.)

" when " or " as soon as." This usage is not regarded as the best, and has not the sanction of the
best writers; but in every-day speech it prevails
widely, and it is even found in the books of writers
of repute. The following passages, from the pages
of a novelist of distinction, furnish examples of this
queer and widely prevalent misapprehension and
misapplication : " Directly he entered the room,
Mrs. D—— formally introduced him." " Immediately N——'s arrival was heard of, Mrs. W——
hastened up to town." " 'Are you ill?' said G——,
directly she saw him."

" Different *to* " for " different *from* " is in general
vogue, except among the most careful speakers. Although it is in almost universal use in England, it is
not defensible, and is not English. It is, however,
no novelty. Baker, in his " Remarks on the English
Language," 1770, justly censures it, as well as " different *than*," which is also in common use. " Different *to* " has, however, the support of Addison.

Awfully. I cannot say that the misuse of this
word in England struck me as peculiar, for it is misused in the same monstrous way here. But there I
was amazed by the high quarters in which I heard it
maltreated. We all know what *awful* means in
Shakespeare, in the Bible, the Prayer Book, in Addison, and in Macaulay; but when I heard a Cambridge don, who was engaged in earnest scientific
talk with another, say, " That 's an awfully good experiment," and when I heard the president of the
Philological Society say to a lady who sat next me,
in the most matter-of-course, unconscious way, " Oh,
yes, she 's an awfully nice girl," I came to the conclusion that, whatever it may have once meant in

the speech of England, in the language of Philistia *awfully* means "very."

My horror of horrors, however, was the hearing at Oxford — at Oxford of all places, and at the Oxford Union ! — a member of the university speak of "events which are daily *transpiring* under our very eyes." After that I gave up observing, or even caring about, the misuse of English in England. What was it to me that they had not escaped the loathsome contamination of which I saw evidence in the sign, "Wine Office and *Sample Room*," at 95 Regent Street Quadrant !

I was surprised, indeed, to meet with that disgusting Americanism, of New York origin, in London ; but I was none the less amused at the fastidious shudder with which a lady in a first-class railway carriage said to her daughter, who had declared that something or other was "not worth a row of pins," "My dear, I do wish that you would not use that low American slang." American slang ! Oh, Lady Philistina, how I longed to quote to you the passage from the sad scene in Richard II., in which the queen, apprehensive of her coming woes, says, —

> "But stay, here come the gardeners :
> Let us step into the shadow of these trees.
> *My wretchedness unto a row of pins*
> They 'll talk of state."

Indeed, what simile would better fit a woman's mouth, queen although she was ? This passage, by the way, is of interest as showing that pins were put up in the same way three hundred years ago as now.

The general pronunciation of French in England is remarkably bad. As good French as I ever heard came from English lips ; but in England generally, even among educated people, there seems to be a difficulty in the mastery of the French tone and inflections which does not exist in the United States. A Frenchman first called my attention to this fact. The French commonly heard in England, even among the higher classes, is well represented in "Punch" by Mrs. Jones, *née* De Topsawyer, who, on being shown by an old French seneschal the tomb of William the Conqueror, says, "C'est trays anterressong poor mwaw, voos savvy; parsker je sweez oon descendong de Gilyome le Conquerong." The seneschal bows and says, "Et moi aussi, madame." I was amused at hearing an accomplished actor, on being asked the pronunciation of *chevalier*, reply with a lofty glibness, "shove-alley-ay." In the same way he gave "amusemong" as the pronunciation of the French *amusement*. The reason of the greater facility of "Americans" in French, which is undeniable, it is not very easy to discover.

I must pass over not a few minor points in regard to the English of England which I hoped to touch upon, and close this chapter of my English experience with a story of a little talk I had with a man on the Surrey side of London Bridge. I was passing a hatter's shop, and seeing the shop-keeper himself, as I supposed, at the door, and thinking that he looked like the sort of man I should like to talk with, I stopped, and, entering, asked the price of a hat. "Seven and six, sir, that style. Them, nine shillin. But if you 'd like to 'ave sumthink werry helegant, 'ere 's our tiptop harticle at ten and six." I thought 't right to tell him at once that I did not intend buying, but that I was attracted by his hats, and wished to know the price. He was perfectly civil and good-natured, as I always found London shopmen, whether

I bought or not; nor did I ever encounter among them either servility or browbeating. He answered, with a rueful little *h'm* and smile, "Hi thought so. Hi see your 'at was too new for you to want a hother. *Would* you be so good as to let me look hat it, sir?" I doffed and handed it to him. "H'm! Lincoln and Bennett! Hi thought so. Hall you swell gents goes to them, 'cos they 've got a big name, an' so they gits big prices. But there 's hother people knows 'ow to make a 'at as well as Lincoln and Bennett. Look a' that 'un," handing me one of our tiptop harticles. Then, with a burst of enthusiasm, "*Would* you be so good as to put on that 'at, sir?" I complied. "There! Hi do think that sets you hoff, helegant. Hanythink nobbier Hi never see." As the hat was decidedly too small for me, to say nothing more, I did not agree with him, and set it down in silence. "That 'at, sir, 's a harticle Hi 'm proud of, an' I 'll set it agen hanythink that hever come hout of Lincoln and Bennett's shop." "I beg pardon," I said, "but you call *at* an article; I thought it was a preposition." The temptation was irresistible; but I did not know what might come of my yielding to it, and I prepared for a quick retreat. But I was safe in the density of his mental faculties. "Proposition, sir?" said he, after a moment. "I 'ave n't 'eard hany; but I shall be 'appy to 'ave one, though I could n't put it hany lower to you than wot I 'ave." To tell the truth, I felt a little ashamed of myself. The man's ignorance was not his fault. Putting my own preposition on my head, I bade him good-day; and as I turned the corner — it was the next one — I saw him looking after me with the bewildered air of one vainly struggling at apprehension.

CHAPTER XVII.

A CANTERBURY PILGRIMAGE.

MOST of my readers probably know that the head of the Church of England is the Archbishop of Canterbury; but I have been led to believe that many intelligent and generally well-informed people, even in England, do not know why he is so. By the head of the church, I mean the sacerdotal head, — the Primate, as he is called. The nominal and secular head is at present her most gracious royal and imperial majesty Victoria, who holds this position as the successor, although not the descendant, of that long-suffering and tender-conscienced monarch, Henry, the eighth of that name, who was so sorely tried by the sex through which came death and all our woe, — an assertion for which I hasten to say that Moses and Milton are alone responsible. And as the afflictions of that exemplary monarch in the matter of wives form an important part of the history of the Reformation, about which it is becoming to all people who would seem well educated to be exact, I venture to offer a little rhyme, not generally known I believe, which will help to keep the facts in mind, and be at any time convenient for reference — to those who can remember it: —

> "King Henry the Eighth to six spouses was wedded:
> One died, one survived, two divorced, two beheaded."

This is not thoroughly original; it being manifestly

framed on the model of "Thirty days hath September," etc. ; but like that most frequently repeated of all English stanzas, to which I confess that I am obliged to recur for much-needed assistance at least twelve times in every year, it may save many worthy people from being put, by ignorance, to open shame.

The reasons why the Archbishop of Canterbury is the priestly head of the Church of England are the very reasons why I was particular to visit the little city from which his see takes its title. Canterbury is the cradle of English Christianity ; and not only of English Christianity, but of the Christianity of the whole Teutonic race, — that great race which has done more for morality and for freedom than any other known to history, and more for literature and for philosophy, although not for the fine arts, than any other since the decadence of ancient Greece. It may be worth our while to glance at the events which gave this place a position so elevated and so extraordinary.

Almost all names of places in England have the admirable quality of a meaning. They were given for a good reason : and that reason, if not apparent in their modern clipped and curtailed form, may be extracted by a little patience. Very little patience is needed in the case of Canterbury, which is merely a condensed form of the " Anglo-Saxon " Cantuarabyrig ; that is, the burg, or stronghold (" Eine feste burg ist unser Gott "), of the men of Kent. Kent is the part of Britain which first became English. Its position would naturally make it so ; it being that part of the island which is nearest to the continent of Europe, from which the English or " Anglo-Saxon " people came ; and such history as we have of their migration from the country now known as Schleswig-Holstein tells us that in Kent Hengist and Horsa made their landing. But the Angles and the Saxons did not bring Christianity into Britain. They were heathen; and soon extinguishing a little flame of Christianity, of Roman lighting, that they found there, they worshiped for centuries the gods whose names are upon our lips almost hourly, because they are embodied and embalmed in the English names of the days of the week, which were respectively consecrated to their service.

The interesting story about the English captives, whose fair faces, blue eyes, and long golden hair caused the monk Gregory to say of them, " Not Angles, but angels " (*non Angli, sed angeli*), — to which story I have already referred, as early evidence of the beauty of the English race, — has a direct connection with the christianizing of England, and therefore also with our present subject. Gregory, learning that these beautiful Angles were heathen, earnestly desired to convert them to Christianity, and set out on a mission himself for that purpose; but he was stopped on his way to England, and he turned back to Rome, to become afterwards known as Pope Gregory the Great. But the Pope did not forget the benevolent scheme of the monk, and he sent as his apostle a priest named Augustine, who was afterwards known as St. Augustine; albeit he was not a very saintly personage. Augustine, if he should make converts, and succeed in establishing a Christian church in England, was to be the first English bishop and archbishop. But Gregory also intended that there should be another archbishop in England, one at York. (He knew about as much of Kent and

York, and of their relative positions, we may be sure, as most English bishops nowadays seem to know of New York and Chicago, and probably supposed them to be a few miles asunder). And this double intention of his produced an ecclesiastical complication, which brought much trouble to England, ecclesiastical and other. His intention in regard to York was the consequence of the fact that the young Englishmen by whom he was so captivated came from Deira, in the then great province or kingdom of Northumbria, which included what is now Yorkshire.

It was in A. D. 597 that Augustine set out upon the mission that was to have such important results, not only in England, but on the continent of Europe and in North America. He landed with his ecclesiastical suite on the Isle of Thanet, then as now the extreme eastern point of Kent, but then, as not now, really an island; being made so by an estuary formed by the sea and the river Stour, upon which the land has so encroached during the succeeding centuries that it has almost disappeared. The Italian priest and his followers disembarked, as Hengist and the Danes had disembarked before them, at a place called Ebbe's Fleet, a little southwest of Margate. The word *fleet* is Old English for a creek or small shallow water, where boats can float. It is preserved in the name of Fleet Street in London ; that street having been so called because it coasted Fleet ditch, a little water-course which in old times had the place now held by the Thames, as the chief receptacle of the city's sewage. Nor has the name Ebbe's Fleet disappeared in thirteen hundred years, notwithstanding that the water which gave it its name was long ago displaced by land. Just where Hengist and the

Danes and Augustine landed, on a strip of high ground which rises out of the marsh, and was plainly once a little promontory, is a farm-house, known as Ebbe's Fleet.[1] In such records of the past is one of the charms of England.

All students of early English history know that at that time Ethelbert, the king of England, had a Christian wife named Bertha, the daughter of the king (so called) of Paris. There was then no king of France, nor for centuries afterward. Ethelbert allowed Bertha to live as a Christian; and she worshiped at a little chapel which stood just outside the town of Canterbury, and which had been used as a place of worship by British Christians. Whether she persuaded her husband to receive Augustine favorably is not known; but he did so receive the missionary, and, after a conference with him in the open air at Thanet, gave him an old heathen temple near Canterbury for temporary use, and at last permitted him and his followers to worship with the queen at her chapel, which was even then called St. Martin's. Erelong Ethelbert yielded to the power of precept and example, and received baptism; and before the year was over, on Christmas Day, 597, ten thousand Englishmen were baptized, two by two, in the Swale, the couples reciprocally immersing one another, at the word of command from St. Augustine. How many forefathers of those who now call themselves "Americans" thus dipped each other at once into the Swale and Christianity it may not be beyond the

---

[1] I make this statement on the authority of Dean Stanley. I did not visit Ebbe's Fleet. Dean Stanley, now of Westminster, was once Canon of Canterbury, a fact to which we owe his interesting *Historical Memorials* of the place.

power of statistics and the law of chances to discover. The royal convert now gave Augustine his own palace in Canterbury as a dwelling, and an old pagan temple hard by for a church, building himself a new residence a few miles off, at Reculver. Christianity was thus planted in England, and Augustine, the first bishop, established his see in Canterbury, where it has remained from the year 601 to this day. Thus it is that the Archbishop of Canterbury, as the lineal successor of St. Augustine, is chief priest of the Church of England.

Not only did English Christianity take its rise in Canterbury, but, as we have seen, hard by, in that part of Kent, was the very beginning of the English nation in the first landing there of the Saxons. Moreover, its great cathedral was the scene of a political murder which was of graver consequence to England than any other, even of a royal victim, recorded in her annals, — that of Thomas à Becket, Archbishop of Canterbury, who was slain by partisans of Henry II. for his resistance to the king's encroachments (in the interests of law and of justice) upon the privileges of the clergy. Within the walls of this noble church lie the remains of the Black Prince, whose name and whose glory are known to all school-bred people of English race, even to those who are ignorant of his history and of his real character. To Canterbury went that train of pilgrims whose figures were wrought into an immortal life by the first great English poet, in one of the greatest of English poems. To Canterbury came Oliver Cromwell, England's last real king and last tyrant, and bore away from the Black Prince's tomb the sword which had pointed the way to victory at Poictiers.

There is no place in England, excepting London and Westminster, which is so enriched by memories and by memorials of the past. And yet I found intelligent, well-educated men in London and elsewhere, not three hours away, who had never seen Canterbury and its great cathedral. I can understand this; for I was myself in England six weeks before I made my Canterbury pilgrimage; and if I had been born in England to live there, I too might have postponed the journey indefinitely.

I went to the Rose inn, because I had heard that it was clean, comfortable, unpretending, and old-fashioned. It deserved all those praises. No place open to the public could be less like the "American" notion of a hotel. In the principal street, which is narrow, and which was meant to be straight, but which happily neither street nor road in England is but for a very short distance, the snug hostelry stands, distinguished in no way from the other old but not antique houses of the neighborhood except by a lantern over the door and the name of the inn. I went in, and found sitting by an inner window of a room that opened on one side into the passage-way, and on the other into the kitchen, a pleasant-faced woman of years between youth and middle age, who asked if I would like to have a room. On my answering Yes, she said, "Please walk up-stairs, sir, and the chamber-maid will show you one." I did so, and the maid met me at the first landing, and took me to a snug, clean, comfortable room, where my trunk was soon brought, and where she quickly returned with warm water; and that was all. Oh, the ease and comfort and privacy of these English inns! — where you are not called upon to write your name and ad-

dress in a big book for any curious idler to read, and
any reporter to copy and publish, and bring upon you
calls when you would be private; where you do not
perform all the offices of life, except sleeping and
dressing, in the eyes of all your fellow lodgers, and
of half the loungers of the neighborhood; where you
do not feel as if the house were a mere continuation
of the street, except the paving-stones and the carts
and horses! They would be improved by "coffee-
rooms" a little more bright and cheery, — for the coffee-room of an English inn on a dark, damp day is
not a place of enlivening and inspiriting influence, —
and by a little parlor or modest receiving room (as
unlike as possible that concentration of glare and vulgarity known to us as a hotel parlor), in which lodgers
who have not a sitting-room could receive those whom
they do not wish to ask into their bedrooms. But
these are comparative trifles. A man in health who
could not be contented at the Rose must have in himself the causes of his discontent.

The city of Canterbury (city in virtue of its bishop's see) is a small town, irregular in every way, and
old-fashioned without being very antique. It lacks
the effect produced, for instance, in Coventry and in
Chester by houses of the sixteenth and the seventeenth century. Dwelling-houses which are, on their
outsides at least, more than a hundred or a hundred
and fifty years old are comparatively rare. But
nearly the whole town seems to be composed of
houses of about that age; and mingled with these
are the few which are older, and an unusual number
of old churches and other buildings more or less
ecclesiastical. These old towns in England had a
never-failing charm for me; not because of their an-

tiquity, of which I am no blind worshiper, nor because
of their beauty, for of that they commonly have very
little, but because of their naturalness. They have
manifestly grown, and were not made to order. Even
the streets most nearly straight were plainly once
paths; and natural paths, physical or moral, are never
straight. One house was built in a certain place and
in a certain way, because its builder chose to build it
there and in that way; another was built in another
place, in another way, because at another time another man so chose to build it; another was built between these in yet another way, perhaps because its
builder could do no better. The town does not look
as if it were put up in sections by contract. There
is no air of pretense, and the place seems like an ag-
gregation of homes. The resulting difference between these towns and one in the United States is
like the difference between a crowd of men, each one
of whom has his individuality of feature and of expression, and an array of puppets or lay figures all
cast in one mould.

Over all in Canterbury rise the three towers of the
great cathedral church, which dominates the city and
the surrounding country. Seen from a distance, this
great building seems larger than it does near by. It
dwarfs the whole city, like a great growth in stone
rising from amid a little bed of rubble. It is an
architectural expression of the ecclesiastical suprem-
acy which it embodies.

As soon as I could do so I went to the cathedral,
approaching it through a short, narrow street called
Mercery Lane, which has its name from the little
shops which have lined its sides for centuries. I entered the nave, and walked its whole length beneath

26

its lofty roof all alone. At once it took me captive; it swallowed me up in its immensity. The effect of grandeur is much increased by the elevation of the choir to a great height above the floor of the nave, from which there is an ascent by a lofty and broad flight of steps. As I walked slowly up the nave and mounted this majestic stairway, the tones of the great organ and the voices of the choristers chanting the morning service fell upon my ears, seeming to come from the dusky void above my head. I found that I could not enter the choir: the grated gates were closed. I stood and listened. The singers were invisible who were taking part in the worship from which I was shut out. Was it only by the gate? Should I have worshiped if I had been within? Could I have worshiped even in that sacred place as I should have done if I had come there when I was a child?

Moved by the solemn strains within and the thoughts which they awakened in me without, I forgot for the moment why I was there. The music rose and fell; it swelled and soared, and died away among the lofty arches. Breaking forth anew, it became a cry for mercy and for salvation, a passionate entreaty to be received into the joys of heaven. As I leaned against the iron barrier between me and the holy place within, the tones of the unseen singers pierced my heart and seemed to cleave it in sunder. But my soul did not answer to them. I knew that I was moved only by a sensuous thrill, by the vast and solemn gloom, and by the charm of sweet association. I felt that there was more between me and those sacred rites than the iron which stayed my steps. Alas! those bars only figured to me the hard and stern realities which stood between me and the rites which I had been taught were pledges and a foretaste of the heavenly life. I might stand and look across the threshold of that paradise; but from its enjoyment, except as an intellectual and sensuous pleasure, almost as an exhibition, I was shut out forever. At every note my heart grew sadder, and the music became to me only the requiem of a buried faith.

Turning away with a sense of self-inflicted banishment, I descended the steps and wandered through the nave, musing, and oppressed even more by my thoughts and by thick-coming memories than by its grandeur, or by the sense of loneliness that came upon me in its vast silence, until the service was ended. The gates were opened. A few commonplace people came out: maiden ladies with umbrellas; matrons with chattering children, already familiar with that which was so strange and impressive to me; a nondescript man or two, one of whom was pale and damp and peevish. They had performed one duty, and now they went forth to others. I watched them as they passed through the door-way into the world, and then turned back to make the tour of the great church.

The choir of Canterbury cathedral is more imposing than that of any other ecclesiastical edifice that I ever saw. It combines in a rare degree those two great elements of architectural effect, extent and elevation. It alone is very much larger than our largest churches. Its length is one hundred and eighty feet. From the steps of the altar you look down the nave through a vista of arched stone, which stretches before you for more than five hundred feet. The grandeur of the elevation of the choir above the nave is repeated and enhanced within the choir itself

by the elevation of the altar, which rises before you
with a majesty which is almost oppressive. From
the first entrance into this noble religious building
the eye is led upward, and again upward, in long
reaches of solemn beauty. The light comes to you
only from above, softened and enriched by the marvelous hues of the stained-glass windows of the clear-
story. With the light Caen stone of the walls and
piers and arches is mingled another of a dark, rich
color, which, warmly tempering the somewhat cold
gray hue of the former, produces an effect of color all
the more admirable because it is not excessive and
does not seem to be elaborate.

As I stood upon the steps of the altar, I observed
that a few knots of people here and there in the choir
began to draw together; and presently a verger in
his gown, whom they were following, stepped up
to me and asked if I wished to see the cathedral.
The other visitors joined themselves to us, and we set
off upon our round. I shall not describe what I saw,
nor tell what I was told. To do so would occupy at
least all the space that I could ask for my whole
chapter; and then I should have told no more than
may be found in a good guide-book. Nor do I hold
such descriptions in high estimation. They are useful to those who are just about to see the objects described; and to those who have seen them they serve
as aids to recollection. To all other persons they
have really little value.

In the course of three quarters of an hour I had
stood by the tomb of the Black Prince, and had seen
hanging over it the surcoat, the helmet, and the
gauntlets that he wore at Poictiers; I had seen
Archbishop Chichely's strange two-storied tomb, on

one slab of which he is represented in health, clothed in his archiepiscopal robes and wearing his mitre, while on the other he is, by his own directions, represented in his dying state, attenuated to a skeleton ; I had looked with a sentiment of retrospective wonder and pity at the stone staircase to à Becket's shrine, worn in hollows by the knees of the pilgrims who were obliged to ascend it painfully, in the humble attitude of prayer ; I had followed the course of the murderers of this arrogant and tyrannical priest to the place where they struck him down, and had stood over the spot where they scattered his brains upon the pavement ; and I had peered through the dim light upon the sombre beauty of that crypt, distinguished from all others even less by its varied architecture than as the scene of one of the most extraordinary and yet most characteristic transactions of past ages.

For here, in 1174, two years after à Becket's slaying, Henry II., in whose interest, although not by whose command, the deed was done, did a second penance in expiation of that crime and sacrilege. After having lived upon bread and water for some days, and after walking barefooted to the cathedral, where he knelt in the transept of the murder (called the martyrdom), he was led into the crypt, where à Becket's tomb then was. Upon this he bowed his head, and, his lower garments having been removed, the king of England, a Plantagenet, received five strokes from the rod of each bishop and abbot who was present, and three from each of the eighty monks ! After this he stood the whole night barefooted upon the bare ground, resting only against one of the rude stone pillars of the crypt ; and thus he passed the whole night, fasting. A belief in the efficacy and the merit of such performances did not die out for six hundred years; and it shows us the arrogant, ungainly figure of Samuel Johnson standing in the streets of Litchfield, bareheaded and exposed to the weather, for hours, in "expiation" of an act of disrespect to his father. Perhaps even yet, among enlightened people who are freed from the sacerdotal tyranny to which Henry II. succumbed, there may be some who believe that a wrong that they have done may be atoned for by suffering on their part which can do no good to the person they have wronged. To them I would recommend a meditation in the crypt of Canterbury cathedral.

I was pleased with my verger, and I found that he was not displeased with me. He was a middle-aged man, with a fine, intelligent face and a very pleasant manner, and he talked well as he led us from one spot of interest to another. If he had introduced himself to me as the dean, I should have accepted him as such without a doubt, and have been perfectly satisfied. And yet this man expected a shilling. Had it not been for my previous experience, I should as soon have thought of offering him broken victuals.[1] He evidently was pleased with the great interest in the cathedral which I could not conceal (and why should I have concealed it?), and plainly rejoiced in the questions which I asked; and when I requested

[1] We should not, however, judge him and such as he by our standard in this matter. These gratuities are looked upon in the light of *honoraria* or fees, and are reckoned as a part of the regular income of the places to which they pertain. A verger receives his shilling just as Mr. Barnum receives twenty-five cents for seeing one of his shows, and with no more feeling of obligation or dependence. And as to the possible independence of a man in such a position, I had an example of that in my Windsor Castle warder.

him to tell me where I could find three little arches, two of which were pointed and one round Norman, he led me to the spot with alacrity and a face lighted up with something like gratified vanity. Well might he be proud of his cathedral. But when, on passing a stately, elevated seat, half pulpit, half pew, he said, " The archbishop's throne when he attends service," although I knew that the Archbishop of Canterbury is a great ecclesiastical prince, the word throne grated on my ears, as I thought of Him who had not where to lay his head; and I thought, too, of the murder done in that very church seven hundred years ago, which was the bloody end of a strife to determine whether — whoever might be king *of* England — Henry Plantagenet or Thomas à Becket should be king *in* England. But as the king came in the end to penance of scourging in the crypt, well laid on by priestly hands, perhaps throne is the proper word for the seat of à Becket's successor.

After my guide and I had parted at the choir entrance, I went alone through the precincts of the cathedral, wandering at my will, inquiring my way, and asking information as I needed it; and always receiving the kindest attention, often from persons more or less ecclesiastical, to whom I should *not* have ventured to offer a shilling, although I did not tell them my name nor ask theirs. In these extensive precincts, beautiful buildings in perfect preservation are mingled with ruins which have been ruins for centuries: there are pillars and arches which form aisles that now are roofless and lead no whither; grand gateways, the only remnants of buildings to which they were once the mere entrance, and which are now put to humble uses; libraries now in use, and the houses of the dean and chapter.

As I wandered about I came suddenly upon an object with the forms of which I was familiar, and the sight of which had been one of the expected pleasures of my visit, the Norman staircase leading up to the building known as the King's School. I thought that I knew it too well to find anything surprising in it, notwithstanding my admiration; and yet, seeing it unexpectedly as I turned a corner, I felt a little shock of delight. And why? Why does that small structure give the eye such joy? It is but a porch of three round arches resting upon heavy columns, and a succession of some five or six small arches supported by graduated pillars; the detail shows little fancy, and the workmanship little finish; but the whole is such a beautiful imagination that among lovers of architecture it is as well known as a perfect poem is in the world of literature, or as a masterpiece of musical composition, like Beethoven's "Moonlight Sonata" or the Andante of Mozart's quartett in C, is to lovers of music. Description of it is quite in vain; for a description which should be quite correct might, like a similar description of a musical composition, apply equally well to a work the design and the informing ideas of which were utterly without beauty. That which constitutes the real charm in any work of fine art, although its effect may be expressed, can never be described by words.

My next visit was to St. Martin's church, the mother church of England, the oldest ecclesiastical building in that land, the memories of which go back thirteen hundred years, and which bears in its walls memorials of a time yet earlier. St. Martin's I found perched on a little knoll on the outskirts of the town. The knoll has been cut down around the old church, which is left standing upon a slight elevation supported by a stone wall. Around it are ancient yew-trees ; and its tower is so covered with ivy as to be almost wholly concealed. The stem of this gigantic parasite is like the trunk of a large tree. I found the same great growth at other places. We have no notion of the size to which this " vine " attains in England. The chancel end of this little church is evidently much older than the tower end ; and here it was plainly that Bertha worshiped : — not necessarily within even this older part of the building, but where that portion of it stands, and not improbably between the foundation walls. The British chapel is gone ; but in its place and on its site was built the little Early English church which now forms the chancel of St. Martin's. Its walls are composed in part of the material of the walls of its predecessor ; red Roman tiles being built into it freely with the rubble and shale and mortar.

After I had looked at the outside of this venerable memorial of English Christianity alone to my content, I made inquiries for the key, and was directed to one of a row of small houses not far off. Thither I went, and found a kindly woman with two or three children around her, who each accepted a penny with round-eyed joy. The eldest was sent off after the goodman, while I sat talking with the goodwife in the little parlor. She was such a comfortable, cheery, simple creature, so far from pretending to be anything but what she really was, that I liked her, and homely as she was in feature, I did not think her husband was long in coming with the key. The interior of the church contains little to gratify the eye. It has none of the charms of St. Andrew's, near

Windsor, or even of the characteristic evidences of antiquity which I found at the old church at Harbledown, which I visited also on this day. In appearance it is the least interesting of these three churches, which are the oldest in England, and of which it is the senior. There is a clever but shabby attempt, by a rude stone coffin and a Latin inscription, to produce the impression that Bertha's body was entombed there; but it lies in the great cathedral. A rude font is shown as that in which Ethelbert was baptized. It is certainly of very great antiquity; but I observed that the upper part of it was certainly Norman work, although the lower seemed to me to be Saxon; an opinion in which I afterwards found that I had but coincided with others much better able to form an opinion on such a point; and indeed I could have expected nothing else. Even the lower part, however, I am inclined to think is of a period much later than Ethelbert's reign. Moreover, I suspect that he, instead of being baptized in full dress and from a font, as the friends of Voltaire's Ingenu expected that their young convert would be, received the rite in the waters of the Stour in that perfectly natural and unadorned condition in which the Huron (who had read only the New Testament) awaited it on the banks of a similar rivulet, while his priest-taught friends and sponsors fretted for him at the church in their best bibs and tuckers.

The modern pilgrim to Canterbury, if he is at all interested in ancient ecclesiastical architecture and in the early history of England, should not neglect to visit Harbledown. It is but two miles away, and the view of the cathedral from the road on the return is alone well worth the little journey. The old village, apparently no larger than it was twelve hundred years ago, lies in a hollow, and is now seen by the traveler and now hidden from him, as the road rises and falls with the undulation of the country. Chaucer's pilgrims passed through it; and this effect of its position is the origin of the whimsical perversion of its name by which the poet refers to it.

> "Wot ye not wher there stont a litel town,
> Which that i-cleped is Bob-up-an-down,
> Under the Ble in Canterbury way?"[1]
>
> (Prol. to the Maniciple's Tale, l. 1.)

[1] The origin of this perversion has not been pointed out, I believe, by any of the editors of Chaucer. Indeed, one of the latest and most eminent of them gravely remarks, "I cannot find a town of that name in any map; but it must have lain between Boughton, the place last mentioned, and Canterbury." The only place between Boughton and Canterbury is Harbledown, the name of which is easily, naturally, almost inevitably, corrupted into Hobble-down, a form of it which I heard there, and which is itself suggestive of a jocose perversion. But besides this, Hob is one of the nicknames of Robert, the other being Bob. With these suggestions it would have been strange if the little town which seemed to rise and fall had not been called Bob-up-an-down by rustic wits six or eight hundred years ago. The Ble is the wooded hill of Ble or Blean which rises just above Harbledown.

This note brought me the following interesting letter from a far-away writer, whom I have not the pleasure of knowing. My readers, I am sure, will thank me for giving them the opportunity of reading it.

CALLAO, PERU, *June* 6, 1880.

DEAR SIR, — I have just read your *Canterbury Pilgrimage* in the April number of the *Atlantic Monthly* with a great deal of interest, — the interest of one who knows every inch of the ground.

My object in dropping you this note is to say that as far as verifying the locality of Chaucer's Bob-up-an-down I believe I am the only one who ever attempted practically to solve the difficulty: I have *walked* all the old roads between Faversham and Canterbury in search of Bob, and (I believe) I found it under the name of *Up and Down*. In these days of blockade and frequent bombardments I have no books within reach, but if you can refer to the *Athenæum* of December, 1868, or, better still, to the temporary Preface to the Chaucer Society's Six-Text Edition of the poet's works, you will find a short account of my ramoles. I hold that Chaucer's pilgrims did not pass through Harbledown at all! Excuse me pointing out the existence of "Up and Down," as your note on page 532 seems to take it for granted that Bob-up-an-down is a perversion of Harbledown.

Yours with much respect,   J. M. COWPER.

Here Lanfranc founded a lazar house or hospital, and the hospital is still there, although it has been twice rebuilt; but the old church or chapel, where service is performed once a week, stands nearly as it was originally built, somewhat dilapidated by time, but little injured by restoration. As I neared the village I asked one or two persons that I met for the old church there (I preferred to go about thus, inquiring my way and talking with the people), and I was directed to a church upon a little hill, which was indeed an ancient and an interesting building; but after a brief examination of it I was dissatisfied both with its appearance and its position, and I learned afterwards that, venerable as it was, it lacked six hundred years of the age of that which I was seeking!

The ground about here is very irregular, and at one place the road is split into two parts, one of which, used only by wayfarers on foot, passes over an elevation, from which there is a steep descent to the part used by carriages. As I walked along the lower road, a carpenter, with his tools over his shoulder, called down to me, and asked me to please to tell him where Mr. Pelburn lived. With malice prepense I made him repeat his request; for I always enjoyed these inquiries put to me in places where I found myself for the first time, — places three thousand miles from that where I and my kindred had been born and lived for more than two centuries. They began, these inquiries, before I had been on English soil two days. In Chester, the day after my arrival, I was driven, by a heavy shower, under an old pent-house, where I was soon joined by a man who was evidently a gentleman, and one who I con-

jectured from the cut of his jib was a " horsey "
squire. We chatted as the rain poured down ; and
when the clouds began to break a groom came down
the street on a fine spirited horse, which he checked
and irritated by his impatient handling. My temporary companion, who had received with favor a remark that I made upon the horse's clean fetlocks and
the fine fall of his haunches, and who fretted almost
as much as the poor beast did under his rider's irritating hand, presently broke out to me, " Now, sir,
if that was my horse, I should dismount that fellow,
and discharge him on the spot ; would n't you ? " I
assented. By this time the rain had stopped, and he,
preparing to go on his way, said, " And now, would
you be kind enough to tell me the way to " — I forget where. I answered, " I would with pleasure, sir,
but I 'm an entire stranger in the country. I arrived
from America but yesterday." He turned upon me
a look of puzzlement and wonder, hesitated a moment, and then bade me good-morning. It was an
early beginning of a series of similar experiences.
— But I am far away from Harbledown.

I found the hospital and the old church sooner than
I fear my carpenter found Mr. Pelburn. An old man
was at work in a sort of garden in front of the hospital. I asked him where I should find the key of
the church. He looked me full in the face, but without any expression of intelligence, and bawled out,
" I can't hear a word you say ! I 'm as deaf as a
stone. But I know what you want. Just knock at
that door," and he pointed to one of two or three in
the hospital.

I remark here that I found many more deaf people
in England than I ever met in America. I have re-

marked before upon the greater number of rheumatic and otherwise disabled old people that I saw there. I was soon in the old church. It is no larger upon the ground than a good-sized country school-house, but it is very interesting. The pillars and arches on one side are Norman; on the other, Early English. The roof is open timbered, like that of St. Andrew's, but much ruder and heavier. Some pillars are round, some square, and the capitals have ornaments which brought to mind those in Saxon missals. On the wall on one side are the shadowy remains of an ancient painting, in which the ghostly figures, life-sized, of a king and a bishop may be discerned. No place that I saw in England took me quite so far back into the past. Here, indeed. I seemed to have got before the Conqueror, and among my forefathers whom he found in England when he and the rabble of fierce robbers whom he had sharked up landed there and fought and took possession. How did I know but that upon the floor where I was standing some man or woman whose blood was flowing in my veins had knelt a thousand years ago? It was more than possible.

In the hospital are some relics; but in those I felt little interest, and I was soon on my way back to Canterbury, where I passed the rest of the day in wandering from one old building or quaint nook to another. I did not undertake to " do " the town systematically; and here as elsewhere I avoided professional guides and eschewed guide-books.

As I was walking about the town at night, I came upon a strange sight. I stood upon an elevated street, and looked down upon one lower; which, indeed, was rather a small open place than a street. There I saw an assemblage of large wagons, most of

them covered; and there were some booth-like stands,
built or in building. Here and there were lights;
and figures were moving about in the darkness with
lanterns. As I leaned against a railing and looked
down upon this theatrical little spectacle, I turned to
a man who had taken a place beside me, and asked
him what this was. He told me that it was the beginning of the preparations for a fair, which was to
take place in a day or two. The fair used to be an
important event, but its interest had diminished, and
only the lowest orders of people took any part in it.
By his speech and his manner, and a fustian coat he
wore (I could not see his face, the night was so dark;
and, besides, he kept looking straight before him), I
discovered that he was a respectable artisan, or person in that condition of life, and we soon fell into
talk together.

I found him intelligent and even thoughtful. The
hoarse voices of men and the shriller tones of women
speaking in strange accents came up to us from the
lights and the wagons. I asked him who these people were, and where they came from. He did not
know. They were n't Canterbury folk; they came
from the country around, no one knew whence; some
of them from far enough away. "It's sad to think,
sir, that there must be such people in a country like
ours; that they must live, and that they will, one
way or another." The tone of his voice was more
monotonous than that of most Englishmen: it was
the monotone of sadness. He seemed willing to talk,
and I led him on. He was evidently oppressed by
desponding thought, and his voice and manner suited
the gloaming, gray-hued darkness. He was well
enough to do himself, he said, and was always com-

fortable, and had a pound or two laid by for a rainy
day; but he plainly brooded over the condition of
those who were not comfortable, and who had no
pound or two, and could n't get even shillings.
"What is to become of them, sir?" he said. "There
are so many of them; and there are more every
year." He always said "them," as if he were not
thinking of himself or of his own. "It's something
that gentlemen like you, sir, know nothing about, except what you see in the newspapers; but I'm nearer
to it, and I see it for myself. They call 'em dangerous classes; but they're dangerous because they're
poor; and if there were n't people, many of them, so
much richer than they, there would be nobody to be
in danger." I asked him if he thought there was any
danger to the government. "Oh, no, sir; how could
that be in England? The government 's well enough.
It 's a good government; and an Englishman 's a free
man, and always has the law on his side. And there
must be rich people and poor people; and lords, too,
for the matter of that. I don't mind there being
lords. And I know that what a man gets honestly
he 's a right to keep, little or much. But what 's to
become of the people that get nothing, — not enough
to eat? And there 's so many of them, — so many."
I asked him if he thought the matter would be helped
by taking the land from the great land-holders and
giving it to the people. "Lord bless you, sir, no;
leastways only for a little while. Some people *will*
get poor; and if a man has a little land and no
money, he 'll sell his land; he must; and the men
that have land and money too will buy more land.
You can't stop that." Alas! I thought, as he uttered
this truism; this poor, sad-hearted fellow sees the one

inevitable law, — to him that hath shall be given, and from him that hath not shall be taken away even that which he seemeth to have; and remembering that those who had least money always, as a class, had the most children, I could say nothing to encourage him. I suggested emigration; but he replied, " Yes, sir, that 's all very well, although it 's a hard thing for a man to go away from the place he was born in. But to emigrate, a man must have *some* money; and I 'm thinking about the people that have n't enough to last from day to day; and England 's full of them, and is getting fuller and fuller every year." He had never heard of Malthus or of Ricardo, and Mrs. Besant's little book was not yet published; but he was plainly in sympathy with them all. Our talk became more desultory, and it was growing late. I bade him good-night. We had touched the gravest question of the day for England, the crucial question of the time, and we parted without having seen each other's faces. We were one to the other only a voice speaking out of the darkness.

The next day I went again to the cathedral. The gloomy sky of the night had harbingered a heavy mass of clouds which were now descending in a copious but fine and gentle rain. The cathedral was deserted. Even the verger was not there. He was represented by his daughter, a pretty, slender girl. He had evidently remembered my interest when he went home; for she stepped up to me, and asked with a little emphasis, " Would you like to see the cathedral again, sir?" I said yes, of course; and she went with me to the gate of the choir, which she opened. All at once the wish arose to be there without even her attendance (there was not another person in sight), and I asked her, with no expectation of consent, if she could not let me go in by myself. She looked at me a moment with sweet, steady blue eyes, and kindly said, " I think I may let you go, sir." She shut the gate behind me. As I turned away I heard the key creak and the bolt shot. Then a great silence fell upon me ; I walked slowly on until I stood before the high altar ; and there I was, alone in that dim magnificence.

I made little use of my liberty. I was not there to mouse among antiquities, nor to study architecture. Details seemed petty to me, enveloped in that vastness, and whelmed in the flood of those associations. I did go to the Black Prince's tomb, and, although I am no relic-monger, as I stood by it I longed to touch one of those gauntlets. To clasp even that glove would have done something toward bridging the gap of five centuries, and placing me by Edward's side at Poictiers. I wish that I had asked that blue-eyed girl if I might do so. I verily believe the good creature would have helped me to a ladder. But I soon wandered back to the great altar, and sat down upon the steps. The day was dark, and notwithstanding the pale color of the walls the vast space was filled with the dusk of twilight. I did not people this grand gloom with figures ; and indeed I doubt if that is ever done by any one ; but I did think, as on the day before I could not have thought, of all the much good and the little ill to me and mine of which that noble church was a sign and a witness. Here Chaucer's pilgrims came ; but what was their pilgrimage to mine ? They made a three or four days' journey to do reverence, for their own profit, to the tomb of a crafty, ambitious churchman : I had come three thousand miles to stand upon the spot where my people were born to civilization and baptized into Christianity. But for what happened here and hard by I should have been, not a savage, indeed, nor a heathen, because the world has taken all men on in the course of thirteen hundred years, but something other than I am; and I fear not something better. For me there might have been no Alfred, no Chaucer, no Wicliffe, no Sidney, no Bacon, no Shakespeare, no Milton, no English Bible, no Bunyan, no *habeas corpus*, no Bill of Rights, no English law; and what a man is, who does more than eat and sleep and wear apparel out, depends hardly more upon the nature that he has inherited from his forefathers than upon what they did for him. A man is a result, — result of forces which were tending toward him centuries before he appeared; a result over which his own will and his own work have but a modifying influence. And, thus sitting alone in Christ Church at Canterbury, I felt that I was near what was for me, except as a mere animal, the beginning of all things, — certainly the beginning of all things good.

But I was to leave the town that afternoon, and calling my pretty portress I walked with her for a little while under the gray arches, and then said good-by. At the Rose, when I told my friend who sat by the window that I was going directly, and by such a train, she said, "Oh, I'm sorry; our 'bus does n't go to that train." I then asked her to get me a fly. "Oh, no, sir," she said, "no need of that. I'll send to the —— [naming another inn] and get them to send their 'bus here for you. Cost you only sixpence, sir." Did any one of my readers ever have his sixpences, or even his dollars, looked after so carefully at a hotel in "America"? After a cheery good-by from this good housekeeper, I got into the rival 'bus, and was soon at the station. Not until I had bought my ticket, did I discover that I had left my hat at the Rose. I had put on my traveling hat in my room, and in my haste had forgotten my chimney-pot. It was the identical preposition which had excited the professional jealousy of the Surrey hatter. I could not do without it. Looking at my watch, I found that I had twelve minutes before the arrival of my train. I hailed the fly with the best-looking horse, and told the driver, "Double fare to get me to the Rose and back again, for the next train." We dashed through old Coventry at a pace that would have astonished Chaucer's Prioress, and did somewhat alarm some good Kentish women. At the inn my hurried entrance caused great surprise; but I had hardly said what brought me, when the chamber-maid flew past me, and, shooting up-stairs like an arrow feathered with petticoats, in an instant she met me with the hat in her hand. She had no shilling to expect, and I no time to think of giving her one. I jumped for my fly, and was set down at the station just as the train was coming in; and in five minutes I was steaming off to Rochester.

CHAPTER XVIII.

JOHN BULL.

As I was taking luncheon at a London club, and trying to fix my attention upon a soup for which its kitchen has a singular reputation, I was conscious that a gentleman who was passing my table paused; a hand was lightly laid upon my shoulder, and I heard the salutation, "How are you?" with that up and down and up again inflection of the voice upon the three words which makes the greeting so cheery from English lips. I turned my full face to the speaker, and for a moment we looked straight into each other's eyes; then he stepped back, saying, "I — I beg pardon; I was mistaken." In that moment of mutual scrutiny, although I had never seen him before, I had recognized the fine, sagacious face of Sergeant ——, one of the leaders of the British bar; but in his face there was only blankness, astonishment, and confusion.

The incident impressed itself upon me not only or chiefly because a like mistake in regard to me had been made twice before in England, but because Sergeant ——'s face was familiar to me from a good photograph I had had for several years at home, and because in considering it I had been struck with its conformity in feature and expression to a common New England type. And yet a more thoroughly English face could not be found between John o'

Groat's and Land's-End. It was not round and rosy, nor was it at all bluff, but rather long or longish; the cheeks not full and with little color, but that healthy; the nose aquiline; the mouth not small, but well shaped, with mobile lips; the chin firm; the forehead high, and rather narrow than broad. In brief, it was a face as unlike that of "John Bull" as a human face could well be; and yet, as I have already said, one more thoroughly English could not well be found. And here was a typical Englishman taking an unmitigated Yankee, not one of whose forefathers had been in England for two hundred and forty and odd years, for another Englishman, his familiar friend, and the latter recognizing the typical Englishman's face as one known to him for its New England form and favor. As types will survive long under strange skies, and even after disappearing for some two or three generations will break forth again, this was not at all out of the natural course of things. The significant fact in the incident was that this New England face on a London barrister's shoulders was the typical face that has ruled, although it has not reigned, in England for centuries, and yet that it is absolutely unlike the face which (who can tell why or how?) has been thrust upon the world, nay, accepted by Englishmen, as the characteristic English face, — the face of "John Bull."

Now it is with careful consideration and after examination of the subject that I say that one of the rarest men in the England of to-day is John Bull, and that in the England of the past he was almost unknown. But we all know him well. He began to appear in caricature about a hundred years ago; a huge, broad-backed, big-bellied, uncouth, stolid, beef-witted animal, as incapable of thought or high daring, not to say of poetry, philosophy, statesmanship, or chivalry, as a fatted calf. Nevertheless such has been the creature set up as the type of the people which has produced Sidney and Spenser and Shakespeare and Bacon and Cecil and Newton and Nelson and Napier, — men who were only the first among a throng of others of their kind, and "John Bull" is soberly regarded by half the world, England included, as the type of the people which has assumed his name. There was never a more absurd misrepresentation, except in the typical Yankee of the British stage, which our own caricaturists — if we have any who may be rightly called our own — have in like manner adopted, thereby giving to a ridiculous libel a semblance of authority and perpetuation.

John Bull may of course be found in England, but his appearance there, like that here of him who is strangely called the typical "American," always occasions remark, and of a character somewhat jocose and disparaging. I have observed that if one Englishman speaks of another as "a real John Bull" it is generally with a smile, and that the real John is sure to be in a somewhat lower social position than the speaker. Whence comes this coarse, obtrusive figure, elbowing his way before his betters, to thrust himself forward as the most English of Englishmen? He has no place in England's history, even in the history of the English people. His face and figure do not appear in the throng of those whose lineaments, either because they were men of mark, or in many cases, perhaps in most, merely because they were possessors of English land, have been handed

down to us on canvas. John Bull's face does not look
upon posterity from England's long gallery of portraits until within the last century ; and even in that
period he appears but rarely. Turn over the copious
collections of engraved portraits of Englishmen from
the times of the Wars of the Roses, in the throes
of which modern England had its birth ; wander
through the oak-carved rooms and raftered halls
from which ancestral Englishmen gaze down in still
amazement upon their successors, not always their
descendants, and you will see that John Bull, unlike
Napoleon, was not an ancestor. Nor does the type
of which he may be accepted as the caricature appear ; except, indeed, with such rarity of occurrence
and vagueness of conformity as might be found in
the pictured memorials of any people. John Bull as
we hear him described and see him represented now
is a production of the coarse caricaturists with pen
and pencil of the last century, and he has been
thoughtlessly adopted by their successors and by the
public for which they have worked ; the adoption
being favored by the fact that it took place at a
period when England was reaching the pinnacle of
her military, naval, and commercial eminence, and
when her lower-middle classes, in which J. B. is
found, were rising to political importance.

This I know : that in no English home into which
I was admitted, whether a peasant's cottage or a
"great house," did I find John Bull, either as
host or guest. I met him neither at Oxford nor at
Cambridge, as don or undergraduate, nor at the Inns
of Court. He never brought me my chop in London
nor waited on me at a country house. I did see
him, however, from time to time, but very rarely. I

met him on the top of an omnibus, in a grill-room,
as one of the magnates of a knot of suburban villas,
in the coffee-room of a provincial inn, and once in
the pit of a theatre, where he was accompanied by
the dreadful female of his own species, for whom he
went out and brought in food, as became an animal
ferus naturæ : and very odd he and she looked there
in full evening dress.

As to his make and his manner, who needs to be
told them ? He is ungainly, with too much solid fat
for ease of movement ; grace is beyond his apprehension ; he knows not what it is. He is red of
face, and often of whisker ; and his big mouth is
oftener open than shut, even when he is not engaged
in the serious occupation of putting something into
it, or in the rarer employment of speaking. His
reason is an oath or a bet ; his wit a practical joke ;
his merriment a horse-laugh ; his most powerful argument a clenched fist. In John Bull there seems to
be embodied a certain element of rudeness which has,
by time and circumstance and change of clime, been
bred out of the English blood in this country. It is
that element of character which makes some Englishmen not only use force brutally, but even submit to
it when it is so used with effect. John Bull will
thrash you if he can, and make you do his dirty
work ; but if you can thrash him, he will submit
and do yours, shake hands, and bear no malice. He
fights to try who is the best man ; and the best man,
not right, is to rule.

It is this element of character which is the stable
foundation of fagging at the public schools. The
small boys and the new boys must submit to the
big boys and the old boys, and fag for them, simply

because those are small and new, and these are big and old. Hence the cruel floggings and " tundings " which make the blood of other folk to boil within them. The female Bull is not without this trait of coarseness. Flogging seems to be the most dearly cherished privilege among parents, even the mothers, of the John Bull class. Some years ago, when there was a protest made in the London papers against flogging girls, sundry British matrons, glowing with virtuous indignation, rushed into print, and to the rescue, and told with unction how they had stripped and flogged their daughters, marriageable girls, and with what good effect ; for, marvelous to tell, the girls submitted. And an English lady whom I know well told another whom I know better how her uncle, a peer, came one morning into her bed-room, as he was going to ride to hounds, and making her get up, flogged her with his hunting-whip as she stood in her night-gown ; and this because she would let her cousin, his son, make love to her, to the prospective peril of some family arrangements. She was an orphan and brotherless ; and therefore let us hope, and be willing to believe, it was that this coroneted Bull had not his nose brought to the ring.[1]

[1] This story, on its first publication, was made the subject of indignant and incredulous comment in England. It was told to one of my own family by the lady herself, who added that one cut of her uncle's whip left a weal still visible when she was in evening dress. Moreover, she added that her husband (the cousin for whom she was whipped, and to whom she had clung) himself beat her before she had been his wife one year, and while she was bearing his first child. It died, and its father also died, soon after its birth; and she, who would have been otherwise well provided for as its mother, was left in a state of poor dependency. In the Contemporary Review, Frances Power Cobbe writes as follows: " Wife-beating exists in the upper and middle classes rather more, I fear, than is generally recognized; but it rarely extends to anything beyond an

As to the cruel and indiscriminate flogging in public schools, Fielding's wise head and kind heart protested against it more than a century ago. "Discipline, indeed!" says Parson Adams. "Because one man scourges twenty or thirty boys more in a morning than another, is he therefore a better disciplinarian?" True, scourging is a very ancient and much-honored form of educational discipline; for have we not Butler's protest against innovation in this respect? Parson Adams himself scourged boys who could not say the catechism. It is the acceptance of this rule of life by the scourged as well as by the scourgers, and the willingness of fathers that their boys should be beaten by any one who is able to do it, from master and usher down to the school bully and the town bully, which is particularly John Bullish. The father would be delighted if his boy could and should thrash the bully; but the right of the bully to thrash if he can, and to have his own way because he is the best man, he rarely ventures to dispute. The right of might and the laws which might establishes are not to be denied.

The laws of the hunting-field are too much those of English society. It was perfectly in keeping with this spirit that recently an anti-vivisection meeting was broken up by two or three hundred medical students, and such like, who marched into the lecture-room of Mr. Spurgeon's Tabernacle, yelling, blowing trumpets, ringing bells, breaking the chairs and the

occasional blow or two of a not dangerous kind. In his apparently most ungovernable rage, the gentleman or tradesman somehow manages to bear in mind the disgrace he will incur if his outbreak be betrayed by his wife's black eye or broken arm, and he regulates his cuffs and kicks accordingly." — It is not with pleasure that I remark upon this distinguishing trait of John Bullish — I do not say English — character.

chandeliers, and at last fighting with the police. They were presumably educated men, students of science; but because the call for the meeting spoke of vivisection as cruel and demoralizing, they broke it up by brute force, and gave a high finish to their proceedings by lighting their pipes and cigars and puffing the smoke into the faces of the ladies who were present. John Bull was present in large force on that occasion.

On the other hand, the same sort of Englishman bears himself with a deference to rank and wealth which is unknown not only here, but on the continent of Europe, except perhaps in Germany. John Bull, it has been said, "loves a lord;" but to be loved the lord must have lordly belongings and surroundings. The respect is for gross material advantage, of which the title is a sign and token. A peer may become poor, but poor men are not raised to the peerage. The rich lord rules not only the land but the heart of England. At this very day and under the last reform, which distributes the suffrage so widely, even the liberal London "Spectator" tells us that the "constituencies decline to send up young men unless they are eldest sons." [1]

The diffusion of knowledge and the political elevation by which that has been followed seem to have increased rather than diminished the numbers of the abject worshipers of mammon. True, the worship is merely a manifestation of selfishness ; but in England it takes on the form of a religion, and seeks to invest itself with a sort of social mystery. The "Saturday Review," apropos of the loathsome Bagot will case, says that one point brought out by it is

[1] May 9, 1878.

" the slavish adulation accorded nowadays to mere wealth." " If," the reviewer continues, " a man attains to the dignity of a ' nugget' his roughness is pardoned, or lauded as an absence of affectation ; his vulgarity treated as naturalness or eccentricity; and his vices slurred over, or attributed to defective education." But this is nothing new in England ; it is no peculiar mark of nowadays. In the very book and in the very chapter from which I have just brought Fielding to witness, he makes Joseph ask, " What inspires a man to build fine houses, to purchase fine furniture, pictures, clothes, and other things, but an ambition to be respected more than other people ? " Nor indeed is this particular kind of respect peculiar to the English or to any other people, or to any period. The Apostle James, in rebuking the early Christians for showing respect to a man who came among them with a gold ring, in goodly apparel, and disrespect to the poor man in vile raiment, merely touched a spot of moral weakness which seems to have appeared at the earliest stage of man's development, — possibly before ; for is there not a snobbishness in dogs ? And yet the dog may have caught this from his human companion. The wolf, who we are told is his ancestor, is pure from it. In his eating he is no respecter of persons. The only peculiarity of English society in respect to this feeling is a sort of declarative pompous deification of material wealth, without any of that attempted graceful mitigation of the grossness of the adulation which appears more or less among almost all other peoples.

But in England, more than in most other countries, riches impose duties and responsibilities. There a man of wealth, especially of hereditary wealth, can

not hold up his head among men unless he makes
some use of his money that will benefit others, —
at least "the county" and "the parish." He may
do it in a reasonable and benevolent way, or he may
keep hounds, or at least subscribe to the hunt; but
something he must do, or be set down as a shabby
fellow. To pass over the more serious responsibilities of this kind, he is expected to give with his own
hand, if he is anything less than a duke. In England, *noblesse. oblige* means that he who has pounds
must give shillings. *Largesse* has dwindled into
the less mouth-filling *tip;* but the duty remains. I
sought in vain the line that defined the man who did
expect a shilling from him who did not. It was easy
enough to find those who did not, although much
easier to find those who did; but to discover exactly
where the expectation began was very difficult. And
a repetition of the silver sweetener, corresponding to
the barrister's "refresher," is expected to be more
frequent than I was prepared to find it. There is a
butler in Lancashire who, after much not unrewarded
attentiveness, parted from me with a cold, reproachful stare of ducal dignity, which when I had got a
little distance from the house I felt sure was because
of some neglect of what was becoming on my part.
I was almost tempted to turn back and beg his for-
giveness with the acceptance of a half-sovereign. In
my lonely moments and waking hours that man's
lofty look of disappointment troubles my memory.
In truth, I believe that he was more disappointed in
me than in the loss of a "vail." He had thought
better of me. As to the two classes, of expectants
and non-expectants, it would perhaps be safe to assume that tips are not looked for by peers and per

sonal friends; but — safest rule of all — when in doubt give the shilling.

Perhaps one element of John Bullism is that self-assertion, personal and national, which is certainly a very marked trait of English character. It is not new. Sir William Temple says somewhere that no people so abounds in originals as the English. Doubtless time and the drift of modern society have somewhat done away with this tendency to eccentric excrescence in England; but it exists there now to a degree which makes Sir William Temple's remark still hold good. They have "characters" in England. Everywhere they may be found; but they naturally come to the surface more in small communities, — provincial towns and villages. In these places, characters — men who dare to be peculiar, eccentric — are known to almost all the townsfolk, and are allowed to have their way, if their way is harmless, even if they are poor; if they are rich, whether or no. We have not these characters. There used to be some in the New England villages, but they have mostly if not entirely disappeared, and we are all now ground down into the pulp of average.

It is this element of self-assertion that makes John Bull a grumbler even when he is good-natured at bottom. He does not shrink from letting you know just what he wants, and that what he wants he expects, particularly if you have taken his money. This is so general a habit and so well established a privilege that those who do give anything for money look for some grumbling, not only as a matter of course but as a guide. I had been little more than a week at my lodgings in London, where my breakfast was served to me by the lodging-house keeper, at her dis cretion, when the maid said one morning, as she went out with the tray, " I 'm afraid we shan't satisfy you, sir, with your breakfast." I told her that the breakfasts were very good; that tea and eggs and bacon and fish and muffins and marmalade were a breakfast good enough for any man, and quite all I wished to pay for. " Yes, sir," she replied, " but you never grumble about anything you have, and so we don't know how to please you." Could this trait of character have had better illustration than in such a disappointed groping for it as a guide by this good girl, who seemed to study my slightest wishes, and who generally did anticipate them?

Characteristically English conduct was that of a very eminent man of letters, of whose performance I was told. He was visiting two old maiden ladies, who were co-heiresses of a small estate, and were of the rank of gentry, but did not keep a very large domestic establishment. They had been brought up when the fashion of " tubbing " every morning was not so common as it is now. What was the horror of the household — wholly female — at the appearance of Mr. —— at the head of the staircase in the morning, more thinly and lightly clad than became a middle-aged bachelor among spinsters, and bawling out, " I should like to know how I 'm to take my bawth with this little can of water!"[1]

This individual self-assertion takes form in customs peculiar to families, which are adopted very easily and retained firmly. In some cases they have been kept up for generations. In one country house at

[1] This word *bath* has three sounds in England among " the best speakers:" some of whom pronounce it as this gentleman did, *bawth;* others, *bahth* (*a* as in *father*), which is most common ; and others, *băth* (*a* as in *an*).

which I visited it was the custom to breakfast in the library, dinner being of course in the dining-room. On Sunday morning I went as usual to the library at breakfast time, but although I was a little late there were no signs of breakfast. I took up a book and began to read. Erelong a servant appeared, and asked me into the dining-room to breakfast; and there my host informed me, with apology, that on Sunday the custom of the house was reversed, — breakfast was in the dining-room and dinner in the library. At a time of some domestic confusion in days past this had happened to be convenient; it was continued for some unknown reason for a while, and had then hardened into a family custom which became a part of the religious observance of Sunday. The free and independent American citizen does not do so. He is not free and independent enough to dare to be eccentric, and to be so, as in this case, it would seem, chiefly for the purpose of having some custom peculiar to himself and to his household. But it was not unpleasing.

Coexistent, however, with this strong individuality and the license accorded to it is a disposition to resent any attempt to introduce social changes, particularly if the attempt seems to imply any reproach. The sensitiveness on this point is very great, — so great that it becomes touchiness. *Nolumus leges antiquas Angliæ mutare* expresses the spirit of the rulers of society now as well as it did that of the rulers of the state centuries ago. It is not the general custom to use napkins at luncheon in England, although at "great houses" luncheon is in reality a small dinner; as it may well be when "ta muckle dinner hersel" is at eight o'clock, and on great oc-

28

casions at nine. An " American " lady was visiting
at one of these houses, where she found the usual
absence of the napkin at midday. She knew her
hostess so well that she could venture to ask her
why it was that napkins were not used at luncheon.
Her grace (for she was a duchess) replied simply and
briefly that it was "not the custom," and with an
air that signified that that settled the question.
But her guest had taken luncheon with the queen
more than once at Balmoral, and there she had found
napkins. This she told her friend as a sort of jus-
tification of her inquiry. " Indeed ! " replied the
duchess. " The queen had better be careful. She
will make herself unpopular if she undertakes to
change the customs of the country." The Philistinism of John Bull does not even stop short of napkins.

Herein is manifested the feeling which takes another form in the dislike of anything foreign and in
the assumption that nothing out of England can be
quite so right as it is in England, — nothing moral,
mental, or physical. This is a genuine feeling, and
not an affectation, nor the result of arrogance, as it
is generally assumed to be. It is often exhibited
with a simplicity which is at once laughable and
charming. On the Tichborne trial, the last one
which condemned the impostor to penal servitude,
Major F——, of Roger Tichborne's regiment, said,
in giving his testimony, that " Roger was very much
of a Frenchman, *but* a perfect gentleman." Nothing
more natural or unconscious ever was spoken ; and
the speaker would probably be very unwilling to
insult a Frenchman, or to wound his feelings. And
so the candid London " Spectator " said of the hero of

a book that "he lived in a perfect bower of Dresden china, wore blue satin clothes, and told falsehoods with all a *foreigner's facility.*" [1] And yet if there is a journal in the world guided by a spirit of justice so fine that it passes into a noble generosity, it is the " Spectator."

It would seem that " a foreigner " is and always has been the subject of doubt and wonder and laughter in England. " But Lord ! " writes Pepys, when the Russian ambassador comes to London, "to see the absurd nature of Englishmen, that cannot forbear laughing and jeering at everything that looks strange ! "

But notwithstanding the protest that naturally rises at this British assumption, and the arrogance that springs from and accompanies it, the simple truth is that it is not without reason. Of all gentlemen, an English gentleman is the most complete and admirable. His probity is the most absolute, — so firm and well settled that it needs not to assert itself ; his courtesy is the most genuine, for it unites with a manner which is so simple as not to be a manner a thoughtfulness for others and a hearty benevolence that stops at hardly any self-sacrifice ; he is a dignified embodiment of manliness and truth. His weak point is apt to be in tact; a deficiency which results from a radical lack of sensibility, and from a hardy superiority to the little things of life. But in fine specimens of the class this is supplied by breeding ; and the result is a type than which nothing could be more " express and admirable."

It is somewhat strange to see a people so marked by national egoism, so arrogant and self-asserting,

[1] November 27, 1862.

so bound up in a sense of the excellence of their race
and of their own institutions, that their insolence is
chiefly a result of consequent moral insulation, ready
to adopt and even to claim the product of other lands
and other races as their own. Let any man live in
England, and take up English ways and prejudices,
and he will soon be reckoned among Englishmen.
The more surely will this be if he has any special
gift in the arts. Thus, for example, it is not a little
amusing to hear Englishmen reckoning Händel as an
English composer, and Alma Tadema as an English
painter, because of their English domicile. For not
only were they born and bred in other countries and
of other races, but the cast of their minds and the
nature of their productions are thoroughly un-English.
In like manner, Mrs. Billington, born and bred in
Germany, is much vaunted as an English singer, because she was married to an Englishman and lived
and sang in London. And this same self-centred,
self-asserting people is ruled nominally by a family
of Germans, whose habits and tone of thought, and
whose daily household speech, even after generations
of life in England, are German; and ruled really when
I was among them—this downright people—by a
crafty Hebrew whom their German queen afterwards
made into a grotesque semblance of an English earl.

One result of the egoism and self-assertion which
pervades all classes of Englishmen is admirable and
much to be desired. This is the maintenance of
personal rights, of whatever kind. It is absolute,
beyond all reach of wealth, or power, or rank; practically even beyond, it would seem, the vaunted om-
nipotence of an act of Parliament. This absolute-
ness is a genuine outcome of the English character.

It exists nowhere else. Liberty, fraternity, and equality will not secure it; rather the contrary. I have already defined England as the land where every man has rights which every other man must respect,— can disregard only at his peril. He may incur the danger of disregarding them if he chooses to do so; but in that case the chances are ninety-nine in the hundred that, whatever his rank or his influence, he will suffer for it, even if he accomplish his purpose; and even that he will not do without a fight. The rights are not the same rights, and those who would rather have identity of rights with the constant risk of having them disregarded with impunity by "the public," or by rich corporations, or even by an assuming individual who takes on the form of a corporation — perhaps physically as well as financially — will probably prefer some other country.

CHAPTER XIX.

OXFORD AND CAMBRIDGE.

THE title of this chapter of my wanderings in England misrepresents my course, for I went to Cambridge first; but custom has so firmly settled that in speaking of the two towns together we shall give precedence to that which is the seat of the elder university that it would seem strange to reverse this order. I set out from London in the company, almost in the charge, of a Cambridge don, a friend who, having met me in the great city, took me off with him, and quietly made himself my host as well as my guide and counselor. I was doubly fortunate, nay, *ter quaterque beatus*, in having such a companion, for he was one who could have made a journey to Newgate in a prison van agreeable; he knew everything about Cambridge, where his official position gave him access and his personal distinction secured him welcome everywhere; and he had a pride in his university, and just enough good-natured jealousy of her rival to act as a pleasant stimulus in the discharge of the friendly office which he had assumed.

Apart from the colleges, there is not much to be said of Cambridge by way of description; for it has no other distinguishing features or marked character. And yet I found it — I mean the town itself — attractive, pleasing, almost charming, in every way. I know no place in the United States to which, even eliminating the colleges, it can be compared by way of illustration. Although, like its New England namesake, its only apparent reason for existence is that it may contain a university, there is no other resemblance between the two places. The Cambridge of New England is elegantly rural and is sparsely built; whereas the Cambridge of Old England is urban and compact. We fondly call the seat of Harvard Old Cambridge, — and indeed it is one of the oldest towns in the country; but compared with the other Cambridge it still has upon it the gloss of newness, not to say the rough edge of rawness, although the latter, except in its colleges, is not antique or even venerable in appearance. Nevertheless it is one of the charms of the town that, being more than a thousand years old, and having been for centuries a place of the first importance in England, it yet has only thirty thousand inhabitants, — an increase of hardly thirty a year since it has been known to history. No signs of traffic, no thronged streets, no hurry, no bustle, no clattering, jingling street railways, no omnibuses, disturb its quiet; no dirt, no new-built ranks of costly houses in hideous brown-stone uniforms, mar its decorous charm.

The people are not idle, and yet they all seem to have time to go about their business leisurely; and from their look as you pass them in the streets, and from the whole air of the town, it is plain that it is not the Cambridgian's chief desire and occupation to get quickly somewhere else. To him a railway is not a Jacob's ladder leading to heaven, with angels ascending and descending upon it. At nine o'clock in the morning, near the end of October, I found no one in the streets, and few shops open. Yet its people seem comfortable and happy, and the place has an air of solid, steady prosperity. But this combination of prosperity and quiet is not unusual in England. At a quarter past nine I found Oxford streets yet unpeopled. A few shop-boys and shop-girls and a few coster-mongers with their carts were all the visible signs that the day's business was begun. A few shops in "the High" were just open, and boys were rubbing the windows and sweeping. So I found it at Warwick; and not only there, but even at Birmingham, on both my visits; and it was much the same in London west of Charing Cross. Indeed, nothing impressed me more constantly and more pleasantly in England than the absence of "drive." Everybody seemed to take life easily; nobody seemed to be very hard worked. And yet the amount of effective work of all kinds done in England, whether with hand or head, is very much greater than that which is done in "America."

Be this as it may, Cambridge seemed to me to be a place in which a man whose happiness does not consist in living in a big town (of which, by the way, however big it is, he can never see more at one time than he could if it were little) might live comfortably, and as elegantly as his means and his taste would permit. Indeed, the presence of the university makes a provision for elegant life and cultivated tastes an important part of the business of the traders. For example, I found in a Cambridge shop some water-color drawings of English scenery which were of a higher quality than any that I happened to see for sale in London. It is characteristic of England that I, having looked at these on the afternoon of one day, on going the next morning at half past nine to make a selection from them (as I was to take a morning train for Oxford), found no one in the shop (which a lad was then opening), and had to wait some time until the shop-keeper could be summoned from the domestic recesses of the floor above.

I went, as I was advised, to the Bull Inn (for of course my bachelor friend could not lodge me at his college), and I found the advice good. Nothing more unlike a hotel, even in a small town in " America," could well be imagined. From its outside, a stranger would not be likely to take it for a public-house. Yet it was the best hotel in the county town of Cambridgeshire, the seat of one of England's two great universities, — a house frequented by the best and wealthiest people in that rich country; and well fitted I found it for their comfort. The door passed, the most unobservant eye could see that the house was not as private houses are; but here the unlikeness to an " American " hotel in a similar situation was even more striking. A passage-way, on one side of which was a " coffee-room " [1] of moderate size, turned at right angles to a kind of office, which was like a sitting-room with a broad half-sashed window; and this room was nearly filled by half a dozen people, some of whom seemed to be guests, who were chatting with the landlord and with each other. A respectable-looking, intelligent woman was attending to the business of the place. The walls of the passage-way were thickly hung with a great variety of prints, the subjects of which were various, — portraits, college views, sporting scenes, and so forth, — and the paper and frames of which were mellow, not to say dingy, with age. My bedroom and bed were

[1] This name for the dining parlor or eating room is general in England.

the perfection of comfort, and were much like those in a small private house; but they were without ornament of any kind. My bill shows that one breakfast was the only meal I was allowed to take there in three days; and I remember it as a very satisfactory performance, not only as to the viands but as to the way in which they were served, which was not the formation in front of me of a lunette of small oval dishes, half filled with half-cooked, half-cold, and wholly "soggy" food of half a dozen different kinds, but the bringing to me warm and fresh-cooked what I ordered when I came down. To satisfy the demands of a first-rate appetite in this way cost me three shillings (seventy-five cents), the usual price of a coffee-room breakfast in England, except in the rural districts, where it diminishes to two shillings, or even to eighteen pence, without deterioration in the quality of anything, except perhaps that of the fish; for, strange to say, I found in London the best fish that I ate in England, although they all come from the north.

The architectural interest of Oxford is so great that Cambridge is too much neglected in this respect. Its college buildings are very beautiful, — so beautiful that only to see them would be worth a journey from any part of England. To describe them is no part of my purpose. I shall only say that I found their chief attractions in quarters not likely to meet the eye of the casual visitor; in views of the buildings from old gardens and greens and tennis courts, and from the walks in those silent grounds behind the colleges, on the other side of the Cam, where the aisles of lofty lime-trees make green arches high overhead, through which the eye is led to rest upon a stately tower far in the distance. One entirely private and secluded place I remember well: an old bowling green it was, or something of the kind, with old walls and gate-ways, shaded by old trees and by shrubs that, fresh and green as they were, had yet plainly never committed the indiscretion of being very young ; and this was looked down upon by wise old windows in the rear of an old but hale and hearty gabled building, which, although merely of red brick, diffused about it the soft influence of a quaint and dreamy beauty. I never saw another place — I did not find one at Oxford — which so captivated and soothed me and allured me to linger, lulling me as if I had eaten lotos with my eyes.

Trinity College, although it is not one of the oldest Cambridge houses, it having been founded by Henry VIII., in 1546, is of preëminent distinction in this university. It has given great men to the world ; among them him whose name stands with Shakespeare's and Bacon's as one of the greatest three among the immortals of the modern world. But Trinity is rich and strong in every way. It has sixty fellowships, and the presentation to no less than sixty-three livings and to four masterships. Its revenues are larger than those of any other college, — much larger than those of any other except Corpus Christi, called "Corpus." Its library is celebrated for its treasures in print and in manuscript. Among them I saw the great Capell collection of the early quarto editions of Shakespeare's plays, and the manuscript of Capell's own notes. I noted with interest that these grotesque but learned and thoughtful comments were written in a singularly clear, neat, and precise hand, and with few erasures or interlineations.

Between my visit to Trinity library and one to be made to the Fitzwilliam Museum, I went to luncheon with my friend at his rooms in Trinity. On our way from the gate to the quadrangle from which his stairway ascended, we passed the " buttery hatch," and my host, pausing a moment, said to a man in attendance, " Send a stoup of ale and a manchet to my room, please," and was going on, when he checked himself, and changed his order : " No, send a plate of ale." The term *buttery hatch* may possibly need explanation to some of my readers. It means the hatch, or half door, of the buttery. There are old houses in rural New England in which such half doors or hatches may yet be found. Their purpose was to close the door against entrance by ordinary methods, and yet to permit speech between those within and those without. To get over the hatch was to effect an irregular and indecorous entrance. Shakespeare makes the Bastard Faulconbridge reply to Queen Elinor, when she says that she is his grandam, —

> "Madam, by chance, but not by truth; what though ?
> Something about, a little from the right,
> In at the window, or else *o'er the hatch*."

The buttery hatch is much the same as the buttery bar, which the saucy Maria mentions in " Twelfth Night," when, meaning to tell Sir Andrew Aguecheek that his hand is dry, she says, " I pray you bring your hand to the buttery bar and let it drink." The modern bar (as in " bar-room ") is a remnant of the buttery bar ; and its name is a mere abbreviation of that of the place where ale and wine used to be served out in great houses of old. The term *plate* as applied to ale was, my host informed me, in constant use to mean a vessel of two quarts. If a stoup of ale were ordered, a quart pot would be sent; if a plate, a great tankard containing two quarts. Although he was a man well "up" in all such questions, he said that constantly as the word was so used, and had been used from time immemorial, no one now knew why two quarts of ale were called a plate. It occurred to me that possibly it was because the large tankard was, from its size, brought on a salver of silver or pewter; and he was kind enough to receive my hasty conjecture with favor.

However this might be, the ale — brewed by the college — was excellent, and I enjoyed it so much, and in his judgment, it would seem, with such discrimination, that he declared I should have some "audit ale." This ale is peculiar to Trinity, and one of the privileges of a Fellow of Trinity is that he is entitled to six dozen of it every year.[1] It has its name from being served to the farmers and other tenants of the college when they come to the audit of accounts and the payment of rent. The farmers, he told me, preferred it to any wine that could be given them. And well they might do so; for on a bottle's being brought and broached, I found that such a product of malt and hops had never passed my lips before. It was as mighty as that which Cedric found at Torquilstone, as clear as crystal, and had a mingled richness and delicacy of flavor as superior to that of the best brewage I had ever before

[1] G. O. Trevelyan, in his memoirs of his uncle, says, "I never remember the time when it was not impressed upon me [by Macaulay] that if I minded my reading, I might eventually hope to reach a position which would give me £300 a year, a stable for my horse, six dozen of audit ale every Christmas, a loaf and two pats of butter every morning, and a good dinner for nothing with as many almonds and raisins as I could eat at dessert." These are the perquisites, or some of the perquisites, of a Fellow of Trinity

tasted as that of Château Yquem is to ordinary Sauterne. It would have justified the eulogy of the host in " The Beaux Stratagem : " " As smooth as oil, sweet as milk, clear as amber, and strong as brandy ; . . . . fancy it Burgundy, only fancy it, and 't is worth ten shillings a quart." As I absorbed it I began to think that it is because " they who drink ale think ale " that Trinity produces Newtons and Macaulays. I afterwards found that, like some of the more delicate kinds of wine and finer growths of tea, it was somewhat impaired by transportation across the ocean, even when it was allowed a fortnight's quiet to recover from the effects of the voyage. And yet perhaps it rather owed some loss of its supreme excellence to the absence of the circumstances under which I first made its acquaintance : those still, booklined chambers, the very air of which seemed saturated with the aroma of elegant scholarship ; that noble old quadrangle upon which they opened ; and the mingling of common sense, wit, and learning in the discussion of subjects in which we had both been long interested, with which my host had before beguiled our walk and then seasoned our repast.[1]

Our afternoon was spent in visiting the Fitzwilliam Museum and other places of interest, and in strolling by what I suppose I must call the banks of the classic Cam, which gives this town its name. But what a thing to be called a river ! It is a long ditch, hardly as wide as an ordinary drawing-room. The

---

[1] So Persius says : —

> " Tecum etenim longos memini consumere soles,
> Et tecum primas epulis discerpere noctes ;
> Unum opus, et requiem, pariter disponimus ambo,
> Atque verecunda laxamus seria mensa."
>
> (Sat. V. 74.)

water is turbid, of a tawny tint, and so sluggish that its motion is imperceptible. How the feat of rowing is performed upon it I did not have an opportunity of seeing, and cannot imagine. I should as soon think of yachting in a beer vat. And yet what oarsmen the Cambridge under-graduates are! It would seem as if difficulty did really perfect endeavor. However, they are absolutely secure against one peril, — that of drowning. Even to bathe in the Cam would not be an easy nor, I think, a very cleanly operation.[1]

We returned to my host's rooms to rest, and to make a little preparation for dinner; and as we sat chatting in the early twilight his gyp entered and said, "Hall, sir!" This is the customary announcement that dinner is served. They speak there not of going to dinner, but of going to hall. The attendance of under-graduates at hall as well as at chapel is noted; and a customary absence from either is one of the minor offenses against college discipline. Under all circumstances dinner is an important fact in England. A student of law is said to "eat his terms" at the Inns of Court. And here I will add that our afternoon's inspection of the college precincts ended with a visit to the offices, including the kitchen, which my thoughtful host timed so that I saw the latter in full operation. It was a vast, ancient, arched stone chamber, full twenty feet high.

[1] Upon the original publication of this chapter, the *Pall Mall Gazette*, springing, like insulted Naaman, to the defense of its native rivers, mentioned an instance of a Cambridge scholar's drowning in this something, which, whatever it may be, can hardly be called a stream. I confess with shame my slanderous error. It must be admitted that such a casualty is possible; for does not Faulconbridge say to Hubert that he might drown nimself if he would "put but a little water in a spoon"?

But the strange and striking part of it was the principal fire-place. This was a shallow recess in the wall, some seven feet high, and a foot or two wider, before which there was an iron grating. In this huge, upright range was burning a perpendicular fire of glowing coals, in front of which was a complicated system of upright jacks on which no less than twenty-eight legs of mutton in rows, one above the other, were turning and roasting at once. The sight and the savor were anything but appetizing. I wondered if those cooks, of whom there were not a few, ever ate roast meat, or whether they took their nourishment by absorption of the fumes of steaming flesh through the pores of their skins.

At hall the under-graduates sit at tables which run lengthwise of the great room, the walls of which are decorated with portraits of distinguished Trinity men. The table at which the Dons and Fellows sit stands upon a dais, which runs transversely across the upper end of the hall. My friend had put on his gown and taken his square cap when we were summoned, and I found that all the others were attired in like manner. This full dress is constantly worn in public at the universities. My seat being next the Vice Master's, who of course sat at the head of the table, I happened to stand, before we took our places, close by the officers — for there were two — whose duty it was to say grace. An attendant presented a small wooden tablet on which was pasted a printed paper. One of them held this; and in a style something like intoning they half read, half chanted, the grace in an antiphony of alternate lines. It was in Latin, of course; but if I had not happened to stand just behind them, where

I could see the paper, I should not have been able to make out one word of it, because of the peculiarity of their pronunciation, which was like nothing that I had ever heard before, either from Continental or from English scholars. I afterwards learned that this pronunciation had been recently introduced by an eminent Latinist and professor of the university; but that it was by no means common, even at Trinity, of which he was a member.

I had the honor of being introduced to this gentleman, and the pleasure of sitting next him at table, and I ventured, conscious of my temerity, to ask him some questions as to the Cambridge pronunciation of Latin, in which, as I have mentioned before, I had noted the marked and bald English sound given to the vowels, — the unmitigated English *a*, *e*, and *i*. He replied very kindly to my inquiries. But one little passage between us seemed to me characteristic. To get a clear apprehension of the vowel sounds, I asked him in regard to the nominative and genitive cases of nouns of the first declension, — *musa, musæ;* " Do you say mu*sah*, mu*say*, or mu*say*, mu*see ?* " He hesitated a moment, and then said with a tinge of sadness, not to say of solemn reproach, " I hope that under no circumstances do you say mus*ah*." With perfect gravity, I believe, and I hope with the utmost respect, I replied that under no imaginable circumstances would I be guilty of saying *mŭsā* but *mūsă*, and that I had accented the last syllable of the word in my question merely by way of discriminating emphasis. My apology and explanation were courteously accepted ; but I felt that I had narrowly escaped condemnation, perhaps commination or the major excommunication, for a very gross example of

29

what in any form is a crime at Oxford and Cambridge, — a false quantity.

My learned neighbor then asked me how we pronounced Latin in "America." I replied that recently, I believed, various new modes of pronunciation had been introduced (I dropped no hint as to the grace), but that I had been taught a pronunciation which I illustrated by speaking a few words. "'M ! — ah ! — yes ! — I see ! — quite so, — a sort of Sc-o-tch pronunciation." His words dropped slowly from his lips, and he was very long in saying Scotch ; and I thought of the Bishop of Oxford in the "Fortunes of Nigel," who, although he was loyally silent beneath gentle King Jamie's censure of his Latin as compared with Scotch Latin, was as ready to die for his pronunciation as for any other part of his creed.

When we had dined, the butler laid out a long napkin before the Vice-Master, and placed upon it a tall silver vessel containing, or supposed to contain, rose-water ; whereupon we all stood up, and the Master, bending his head, said, "*Benedicatur*," which he pronounced bene*diecay*tur. The under-graduates then went out ; but a few of us who sat on the dais, taking our napkins in our hands, marched down the hall together, and went up-stairs to a smaller room, in which a dessert of fruit and wine was set out upon a noble mahogany table, the dark brilliancy of which reminded me of the tea-tables of my boyhood. And indeed, Spanish mahogany is your only wood for such uses ; walnut and rosewood are poor, pretentious substitutes. This custom of withdrawing to another room for dessert is a remnant of a very old fashion. We now loosely call a feast from beginning to end a banquet ; but *banquet* originally meant a second course of dainties after the principal meal, and it was the custom of old to take this at another table, and generally in another room. The custom died out long ago in general society; but it has been preserved among the dons at the universities. As to what passed at this banquet, I shall only say that a more delightful social hour could hardly be imagined, and that a possible assumption that the talk was confined strictly to subjects of a scholastic nature would be somewhat at variance with the facts. But further than to say that the port wine was worthy of the reputation of the college I shall not go. Hall was public; not so this brief symposium.

On one of the evenings that I spent at Cambridge there was special service in the chapel, in honor of some obscure saint whose name I forget. I attended, and was fortunate in the occasion. The professors and resident Fellows and the under-graduates appeared to be present in a body, and as they were all in surplices, the masters of arts and the doctors of law and of divinity wearing their colored hoods, each of a peculiar tint, the sight was an imposing one. The great chapel was filled with this cloud of white-robed worshipers; and when they rose and sat at the various stages of the service, the soft rustle of their flowing raiment swept past me like the sound of wings. But I fear there were not so many angels among them as there seemed to me in this unaccustomed vision. The spectacle was impressive because of this sacred garment and of the numbers of those who wore it. The trappings that are worn by various orders of men, sacred and secular, the stars and the garters and the crosses, seem to me to be only fit to please children; and to see a dozen or a score of mature men within a chancel or on a dais tricked out with these trinkets provokes me to sit in the seat of the scorner. But here the simplest garb possible concealed the tight, angular ugliness of our daily dress by flowing folds of luminous drapery; and of these white-robed witnesses to Christianity there were hundreds gathered beneath my eye, as I sat in an elevated stall. To them it was the mere routine performance of an ecclesiastical function; to me it seemed for a moment supramundane. The service was divided, part of it being read in one place, part in another; and a verger, or some such officer, brought the huge, gilded books now to one, now to another. My stall was next that of the reader of the epistle, and nearly opposite that of the reader of another part of the service. I have heretofore recorded the excellence of their reading, and some marked traits of their pronunciation.

One great beauty of this service was the music. The body of singers was large; but the volume of tone was not more remarkable for quantity than for quality. It was very rich and delicious, and the performance, although lacking a little in *nuance*, was not without intelligently graduated expression. But above all the mass of sound there rose one voice, the counter-tenor of a man, that most ravishing of all voices when it is of fine quality and is delivered with purity and feeling, — a voice compared with which even the finest female *mezzo-soprano* is tame and pale and bloodless. The musical cry of this singer pierced me to the very soul with its poignant beauty. I could not see him, and I am glad that I could not; for I am sure that nature could not have been so doubly beneficent to him as to give him a face becoming such a voice.

The service ended, the congregation and the singers in their shining raiment went slowly out. But alas! hardly had they reached the door when they broke headlong for the robing-room, flung off their surplices as if they were tainted garments, and rushed out pellmell into the streets, shouting, laughing, and careering with the spirits of youth set free from tedious confinement. And this is my last memory of Cambridge.

The next morning I went to Oxford. The country between the two towns is the most uninteresting that I saw in England. It presents no features of any kind to attract the eye. It is not even flat enough to have a character of flatness. A fitter country to pass through by railway could hardly be found; and for almost the first time in my life I wholly approved of that way of traveling.

Oxford is the most beautiful place that I saw in England, and I am inclined to think that it is the most beautiful town in the world. I need hardly say that it is made so chiefly by the colleges. For here in a place of only fifty thousand inhabitants are more than twenty colleges and halls, most of them impressive by their extent (and mere size is a just cause of admiration in architecture, although not in countries or in pictures), and all of them more or less beautiful with a beauty unknown in our country and unattainable; for it is a beauty that comes not by command, nor by purchase, but by growth. These colleges are built around quadrangles, and their gateways admit you not to the interior of the building, but to the quadrangle. Some have two quadrangles, an outer and an inner. Their style is what is generally known as Tudor Gothic. Very few exhibit any remains of an earlier school of architecture. Their effect, consequently, is not that of grandeur or even of solemnity, but of dignity and repose, with a suggestion of domestic comfort. As one looks upon them, it seems that, although it might be possible to live in them and be dull, or even ignorant, it would hardly be possible for their inmates to be ill-mannered or vulgar. To pass four years in their halls, their courts and quadrangles, their closes, their greens, their walks and meadows, must be in itself an education, if education is anything but the getting of knowledge out of books. Here I had the good fortune to be expected by a Fellow of Queen's, a scholar whose name is known and honored the world over. It is needless for me, however, to recount an experience of college hospitality which repeated that which was so pleasant at Cambridge. I will only mention that as we were walking through a gallery in which were many portraits, my host naming one and another to me, I recognized Henry V., and mentioned his name myself. "Ah, yes," said my guide, in a by-the-way tone, " he was an under-graduate of this college ; and so was the Black Prince for a while."

I was not allowed to miss anything that was of interest; but I am not writing a guide-book, and I shall pass by the show places without mention. But I cannot refrain from advising every one who visits England with a desire to see its characteristic beauties to give at least two or three days to Oxford. Besides the colleges themselves, the views around them are of a peculiar and an enchanting beauty The view across Merton fields, behind Merton college, off to the tower of Magdalen, is perfection in its kind. The wide expanse of vivid green coming close up to the college walls, the noble old trees, the gabled roofs and mullioned windows of Merton, and Magdalen's noble tower closing the vista, the forms of its strongly outlined buttresses and pinnacles softened and enriched by the distance, make this view seem rather like the ideal composition of an imaginative landscapist than the unpremeditated result of man's seeking for his own comfort and convenience.

And Magdalen has a deer park, to which and about which I walked three times in my visit, approaching it through quaint and irregular ways more or less public. Skirting its stone wall, I came one morning upon a little chapel, whose tiny bell was clamoring sweetly for some half a dozen maids and matrons to come to service; — the cleverest scene-painter that ever wielded brush never devised anything half so pretty. Then not far beyond I found a great old double-roofed stone barn, which on examination proved to be a part of some ancient ecclesiastical building, which had been saved from absolute destruction and converted to farming purposes. More than once I walked past Baliol and St. John's down St. Giles's Street, where the martyrs' monument stands at the head of a double row of trees, to a beautiful place on the edge of the town, where Oxford park lies on one side of the road, along which stretches a noble row of trees for almost half a mile. Here I found a cluster of villa houses that filled me with longing to come and live in one of them, such was their union of comfort and unpretending elegance as they stood there looking out upon the park, and yet within twenty minutes' walk of the High Street, where a man could obtain everything that he could crave for the delight of mind or body. I found in three days no end to the beauty of Oxford.

At the Taylorian museum I looked over not only a selection of water-color drawings by Turner, in which he appears at his best, but a collection of original drawings by Raffael and Michael Angelo, of such interest and value that they would be cheap at their weight in diamonds. But after all I believe that a head, a portrait, by Masaccio, who preceded Raffael and even Leonardo, most impressed me by its large simplicity of style and purity of color. It had a red hat, which was a crown to the painter, if not to the wearer.

In London a distinguished Dublin professor and author had asked me somewhat dubiously, as I was breakfasting with him at the University club, if I would care to know an Oxford under-graduate. "Why not," I replied, "if he is a good fellow, know an under-graduate as well as a don?" — whereupon he gave me a hearty commendation to one of his former pupils. I did not deliver this letter; for on inquiring for the gentleman's rooms I was directed by mistake to those of another under-graduate of the same name. Him I found, and when I presented my letter to him in person (for I was sent straight up to his rooms, which were not in college but in lodgings; scholars living thus are called oppidans, I believe) he smiled, and explained the mistake; but he received me most courteously and kindly, and at once offered me such attention and such services as were in his power. I did not find in all of England that I saw one specimen of the surly, "grumpy" Englishman of whom we hear so much.

As I was walking back briskly toward Queen's in

the twilight (for it was almost time for hall) I was conscious of some one overtaking me and keeping pace with me for a moment or two, and then I heard my name spoken with an inflection of inquiry. I turned, and saw a scholar of Baliol whom I had met at his father's house in London. After welcoming me to Oxford, he asked me if I would not like to go to the Union (a university debating society and club), where there was to be a debate that evening. Of course I was glad to do so; and he also invited me, with needless but attractive modesty, to take luncheon with him and some other under-graduates at his rooms next day, — an invitation which I gladly accepted.

After hall at Queen's he called and took me to the Union. The floor of a large room or theatre was filled with under-graduates. There was a Speaker sitting at an elevated table, a secretary, and another officer of some sort. Before the Speaker was an unoccupied table. The audience, among whom I took my place, thronged a gallery which ran round three sides of the theatre. The question for debate that evening was (as nearly as I remember it), "Is the foreign policy of Mr. Disraeli and the government entitled to the confidence of the country?" The proceedings were conducted in the most parliamentary manner. The speakers went up to the head of the room, and, placing their hats, which they took with them, upon the unoccupied table, faced alternately the Speaker's chair and the audience. They always referred to each other as "the honorable membah," "the honorable membah who had previously addressed the house." Indeed, parliamentary etiquette was strictly observed; and it was (I hope I may be pardoned for saying) a little amusing and not unpleasing to see them lift up and set down their hats, and put their hands behind them under their coat-skirts to cock them up in a manner which perfected the illusion. The debate itself was conducted with an ability that made it highly interesting. The speeches, without being too formal, yet had form, and were remarkable for a happy arrangement and development of the views which the speakers presented. But what chiefly commanded my admiration and caused me some surprise was the readiness and fluency of the speakers. None of them used notes, and all the speeches, except the first, were in reply. In a word, it was a real debate. Yet the hesitancy, the fumbling for fit phrases, the unreadiness, of which Englishmen are accused, and of which they even accuse themselves in comparison with "American" speakers, were in no case apparent, but on the contrary the ready command of a full vocabulary. The " honorable members " on the floor cheered their favorites, cheered ironically, and groaned, all in true parliament fashion. The debate was summed up with marked ability and great spirit by a gentleman who was evidently a favorite with the whole house, even with his opponents, and justly. I think I never listened to an abler speech of the kind in a deliberative assembly, least of all in a state legislature or in Congress. The Speaker's name was Bowman or Bauman, and I venture the prediction that if he should obtain a seat in Parliament he will be heard of there and elsewhere. When the question was taken, it need hardly be said that there was a large majority in favor of the government; for the Tories are strong at Oxford. But it was delightful, immediately upon adjournment, to hear cheers for Bauman called for and given with a hearty good-will by all the house, his opponents taking the lead. This is a sort of English fairness of spirit the manifestation of which it is pleasant to contemplate.

After the debate we went to the Union refectory, and passed half an hour in chat over cigarettes and coffee. No spirits, wine, or even ale are " licensed to be drunk on the premises," — a sensible provision at which I found no disposition to grumble. And I noted the modest and sober fitting up and furniture of this apartment. There was no display of polished wood or gilding ; no bright colors, either on the walls or on the floor. All was simple, but comfortable and cheerful. My luncheon at Baliol was very pleasant, but furnished no occasion for particular remark. There were two other under-graduates besides my host, — sensible, manly, modest fellows, with the careful dress and polished manners of high-class Oxford men. It would have been impossible, I think, to find any difference between them and three under-graduates at Harvard of like social position. And how and why should any difference exist ?

The next day I had a luncheon of quite another sort. As I was walking in " the High " it occurred to me that my inner man needed a little restoration, and having seen a pastry-cook's shop with ' Boffin " over the door, I decided, for the name's sake, to go there. As I approached it I saw a card in the window announcing that chocolate was to be had, and entering I asked if I could have chocolate and rolls. " Oh, yes, I could 'ave them, but not there. Would I be kind enough to step up to their other place, which was only a little way up the

street?' This struck me as rather a curious result
of the advertisement in the window; but I was happy
to comply. I had before observed the other place,
and wondered that Oxford, among its manifold excel-
lences, should be so happy as to possess two Boffins.
(I may remark here that I found in London and
elsewhere some of Dickens's oddest names, which I
had supposed were of his own fabrication.) On
reaching the duplicate Boffin's, I again asked for
chocolate, not this time to be sent elsewhere.
"Would I please to walk up-stairs?" I was politely waved to a "dark backward and abysm" of the
shop, in which I dimly saw a small winding stairway.
Up this I slowly screwed myself, my mind revolving,
as my body turned, this singular way of dispensing
chocolate to the public. For the affair was of so
strictly private and, so to speak, recondite character
that I was somewhat embarrassed. I felt as if when
I reached the top of the stairs, and before I could
unwind myself, I must certainly intrude upon some
homely family arrangements which I should be loath
to disturb. I did not know but I might break in
upon Mr. Wegg engaged in declining and falling off
the Roman Empire.

At the top of the stairs I found a small dark room,
sombre of hue and of furniture, in which were two
or three tables formally laid, as if for hot joints, at
one of which I sat myself down in meek expectancy.
I was kindly allowed some time for reflection. At
last, after I had ruminated a while without my cud,
there appeared a short, serious, middle-aged man in
black, with black hair which had not a perfectly
natural look, but seemed as if it were of that color
to be in keeping with his general appearance and

manner, which was that of a respectable, conscientious undertaker engaged in professional business. He had something like a dirty white halter round his neck, and he saluted me with so much gloom and so much consideration that I should not have been much surprised if he had asked me if it were perfectly convenient to me to step out and be hanged. But no; he only said that the weather was very pleasant for the young gentlemen coming up, — plainly meaning the under-graduates, and brought me my luncheon. Yet he shut the door so carefully and silently when he went out that he left me not without suspicions that the name over the portal bade me leave all hope behind, and that instead of Boffin it should have been Coffin. Immured within this twilit cell, I felt shut off from human kind. I have not yet been in prison; but when I do go, I am sure the sensation will not be new to me. In solitude I drank my chocolate, feeling that it should have been cold water. I ate my roll and butter conscious that it should have been a mouldy crust. I felt guilty, — guilty of some nameless crime. Erelong my attendant stole into the room again, bearing on his arm a damp, limp napkin, with which he solemnly approached me. But he did not throw it over my face; he only asked me, very respectfully, if I would " 'ave hanythink else." I did not choose to have anything else; what I had had already sat heavy on my soul; and I left Boffin's with the mingled feelings of joy at release and consciousness of moral ruin which become a discharged convict.

They keep early hours at Oxford, and, taking a hint from Charles Lamb, make up for late rising in the morning by going to bed betimes at night. At ten o'clock Oxford streets are silent and almost deserted, and at nine they begin to lose their life. A dim light hangs within the gateways of the colleges; and the quadrangles are grayly seen, only by the help of the moon, when she shines in the pale, shy, shame-faced way with which she does her duty in England, where it cannot be said of her,

> " Cold and fair
> Sits she there,
> Calling the tides."

For the moon of England seems fitted only to rule the ebb and flow of such waters as the Cam; and yet, so deceptive is very nature, the tides in England, as we all know, are grander and mightier than any that our bold, bright Cynthia controls. I found a charm in the sight of these old scholastic buildings at night, and went again and again from one to the other, loitering in and about the quadrangles and cloisters, and contrasting the dim confusion of the architectural forms below with the sharp, irregular lines of the turrets and gables against the sky. More than once some belated Fellow stared at me inquiringly, as he found me sauntering near his own particular precincts; but I was never questioned.

The night before I left Oxford I was walking through a narrow lane, near Queen's College. Stone walls were on both sides of me. As I walked I heard the sound of music. I listened, and distinguished the tones of an organ and the voices of a choir. I walked on a little way, the music becoming clearer, till I came to a door, one which appeared not to be in use and not to have been opened for a long time. I laid my ear against it, and thus heard the music very plainly. How good it really was I shall not undertake to say, for in my mood then I was not a trustworthy critic ; but suiting my temper, and veiled by distance and by obstacle, it seemed to me beautiful, ravishing, divine. I could not hear a word, but I needed no word to tell me its sacred character; it seemed indeed less ecclesiastical than celestial. At once I was borne back by swift-winged memory to the boyish days when things were as they are not now, and I was as I shall never be again. Once more I stood, as at the gate of Canterbury Cathedral choir, shut out from the place whence I heard the songs of Paradise. I remained leaning against the door until the last tones had died away, and then, loitering no longer, went to my hotel. I did not learn what and why this music was at that late hour ; for early the next morning I left Oxford for the north.

CHAPTER XX.

A NATIONAL VICE.

In that scene of "Othello" in which Iago betrays Cassio into drunkenness, he sings a clattering drinking song, of which he says to his victim, "I learned it in England, where, indeed, they are most potent in potting : your Dane, your German, and your swag-bellied Hollander . . . . are nothing to your English." But remember, complacent brother Yankee, that this description of English manners concerns you directly. You cannot say that the galled jade in England may wince, but your withers are un-wrung. It is your forefathers whom Shakespeare thus describes by the lips of that jovial soldier and prince of good fellows, "mine ancient." You have just the same concern in the picture that your British cousin has : no more, but not a whit less. *You* may have followed Falstaff's advice to himself to leave sack and live cleanly ; but if any one is at all impli-cated in the potting of Englishmen between two and three hundred years ago, you are the man. Never-theless, there is at the present day a very manifest difference between the two great divisions of the English race in this matter, although the amount of wine and whisky and beer consumed in "America" seems to increase year by year, rather than to dimin-ish.

What may be called domestic drinking has, how-

ever, much fallen off among us within the memory
of living men. In the days of the fathers of the
present active generation, some forty years ago, it
was the custom here to offer cake and wine to ladies
at morning calls; and not long before that time wine
and spirits were in use even at funerals. These customs have happily passed away, and although they
may have been succeeded by others not less objectionable in the same respect, the use of alcoholic
drinks in the household, except at dinner and on
festive occasions, has diminished so greatly that the
change is one of the most notable that has taken
place in our society. In England, however, although
wine is not offered, as a matter of course, to callers,
wine, beer, and spirits are drunk freely at all times
in households of a grade and a character which here
would be a warrant that nothing stronger than coffee
or tea, or, of late years, on extraordinary occasions, a
little "lager" beer, would be seen upon the table.
For, in England, not only do people who live generously, not to say freely, and with a respect for
creature comforts, draw regularly upon the cellar or
the tap, but, with very few exceptions, all of that
large class — it is almost equally large in both countries — which unites narrow means, frugal living,
and a strong religious and ascetic feeling are constant
drinkers of malt liquor, and most of them of spirits,
although in a moderate and truly temperate way.
With this class in America it is both virtuous and
economical to substitute, for cakes and ale, pie and
water.

The free use, not only of wine and beer, but even
of spirits, by all classes, and by both sexes, among
people of the highest respectability and the most dec-

orous life, was the very first of English habits which attracted my attention. My readers may remember the mention of my observation of this habit at the morning performance at the Birmingham musical festival, where, at midday, between the parts of the concert, sandwiches and biscuit were accompanied by highly fragrant draughts from silver and gold-mounted flasks, which were freely drained by ladies in all parts of the immense hall, even by those in the "president's seats," where the nobility and the "swells" in general were carefully roped off from the rest of the audience, and where there was an archbishop who might have said high grace over what his friends around him were about to receive. They may remember, too, that fair and delicate woman with whom, the next day, I was shut up alone in a first-class carriage between Birmingham and London, and who astonished me by filling her horn, not exactly as Diana fills hers, with a fluid that made our compartment as highly odorous as a cellar in Cognac.

The impression made upon me by these incidents was deepened every day that I spent in England. In London I saw respectable-looking women coming out of tap-rooms, wiping their lips, at ten o'clock in the morning. They were not "ladies," but they were women of decent dress and demeanor, — women of a sort that here would be frightened at the thought of entering a bar-room.[1] At restaurants I saw the

[1] "I suppose that no one likes spirits when he first tastes them. But when once the habit of drinking them is acquired a craving for them is speedily developed. This is more particularly the case with women; and the number of women that step into a public house to treat each other to gin is greater than even that of the men." — London *Truth*, May 1, 1879.

The following paragraph, quoted from some British journal, recently appeared in the *New York Herald:* —

"An Edinburgh gentleman recently counted in confectioner's ladies

same freedom on the part of women of a much higher grade. I mentioned this to a New York woman who had gone over in the same steamer with me, and who was with her party for a few days at the same hotel. She, who had been in England two or three times, had, nevertheless, been newly impressed in like manner; and she told me that only the day before, when her party, which consisted of her brother-in-law, her sister, her nephew and niece, and herself, after some fatiguing hours of sight-seeing, had gone to a restaurant to take a hearty luncheon, in the order for which ale and brandy and water had been included, to her amazement the waiter placed the ale before the gentlemen, and the brandy, by no mistake, but deliberately, before her. The waiter, when he was requested to change the arrangement, made no apology, and did not seem to think that he had been guilty of a blunder. She enjoyed the joke too much to be offended.

I hasten to say, however, that I did not see, in any part of England, in any society to which I had the pleasure of being admitted, a single instance, even among men, of perceptible excess in drinking. And I venture to add that I am so far from being squeamish upon this point myself that I respected a friend, a man not only of character and high social standing, but of strong religious feeling, when he said to me one morning, "Last night, when I was talking with you, I was somewhat excited by wine " (I had hardly observed it), " and perhaps was somewhat vehement. Some people are ashamed to own that they are, or

room twelve ladies drinking spirits, porter, or ale, a girl of fourteen taking a bottle of stout. At the counter two misses in their teens were paying for three brandy-and-sodas. School-girls, he says, also take nips of cherry brandy."

have been, excited by wine. I am not." I could not but reflect, however, that a similar confession by an American of his years and character would quite surely never be made.

This gentleman, moreover, was a man of active benevolence, and was one of a few who had undertaken the establishment, in one of the large towns, of chocolate houses for the benefit of the laboring people, to win them away if possible from the alehouse, the tap-room, and the gin palace. I visited one of these chocolate rooms with him, and was pleased to see the simple earnestness with which he made inquiries of the person in charge as to the favor with which they were regarded by those for whose good they were established, and the satisfaction with which he received information that the number of visitors was increasing. But the result of my observations on the whole did not lead me to look for much social amelioration of England by this well-meant and possibly wise project.

The Englishman, and particularly the Englishman of the laboring class, is wedded to his beer. He feels that it is the great comfort, and one of the very few enjoyments, of his life. And not only is the chocolate room or any other like contrivance " slow," but there is about it an implication that he is taken in hand and managed by his betters, like a child, which he not unnaturally resents. Rightly or wrongly, he feels more ashamed of being treated in this way than he does of being drunk once a week ; once, however, being here a word of wide signification. For in these cases " the same drunk " often extends from Saturday night to Monday and not unfrequently into Tuesday. The result of this habit, which may almost be called a custom, is deplorable and socially injurious to a degree of which we in America have a very imperfect idea. The beer of England is not like the light German beer which has come so much into vogue here of late years under the name of "lager," and of which a man of any stability of brain and knee might drink enough to swim in without feeling any other effect than that of unpleasant distention ; it is heady, strongly narcotic, and apparently not exhilarating, but depressing. Drunk in large quantities, after a short period of excitement, it dulls the brain and fills the drinker's whole bulk with liquid stupefaction. He becomes not intoxicated, but besotted. Not only laboring men and men who ought to labor but do not give themselves up to this debasing habit of beer-drunkenness through two or three days of the week, but skilled artisans, men whose work is of a kind and of an excellence which is worthy of respect and admiration. I was more than once told in regard to an artisan of this class, a man whose work was always in demand at the highest price, and who could with ease have kept himself and his family in perfect comfort and have laid up money, that he would not work for any man nor at any pay more than four days in a week. Blue Monday is a recognized "institution" in England ; and, as I have intimated, the blueness of it not unfrequently tinges Tuesday, and this among the very best of the skilled artisans. One bookbinder told me that his two best men, "finishers" to whom he gave his finest work in perfect confidence that it would be done unexceptionably both in workmanship and in style, never "made any time," that is, never got really to work, before Wednesday. Like stories were told me of other equally accomplished workmen. This is not only ruinous to the men and to their families, but the aggregate industrial loss to England must be very great.

Such steady, besotted drunkenness seems to be at the bottom of much of the distress and most of the crime of England. A clergyman whose work lay chiefly among the laboring classes told me that he felt utterly powerless before this vice, which was a constant quantity in the problem that he was called upon to solve. I knew a lady who was a district visitor in a suburb of London, one of those ministering angels who in England, more, it seems to me, than in any other country in the world, give themselves up to the work of helping and bettering the most wretched and degraded of their kind, and who carry purity and grace and Christian love into dens of filth and sin and suffering which, if they did not see them, would be beyond their chaste imaginations; and I asked her one day if she met with any encouragement, and if she thought she had been able to do much real good. With a sad, sweet smile she answered, " Very little. The condition of these people seems hopeless; and *they* are hopeless. All that we can do is to help them from time to time; and we find them always where we left them, or, if possible, yet lower, more degraded, more wretched. And at the bottom of it all is drunkenness. The men are always more or less drunk, and the women are almost as bad. They earn a little money, and they get drunk. Husband and wife get drunk together; they quarrel; they fight; and the children grow up with this before them. They are never really quite sober unless they are starving or ill

What can be done for such people? How can they or their condition be made better?" The tears fell from her eyes as she spoke. I knew that it was so. My own observation, very small and of little worth as compared with hers, had yet shown me this. And I was struck with horror at the besotted condition of so many of the women, — women who were bearing children every year, and suckling them, and who seemed to me little better than foul human stills through which the accursed liquor with which they were soaked filtered drop by drop into the little drunkards at their breasts. To these children drunkenness comes unconsciously, like their mother tongue. They cannot remember a time when it was new to them. They come out of the cloud-land of infancy with the impression that drunkenness is one of the normal conditions of man, like hunger or like sleep. Punishment for mere drunkenness, unaccompanied by violence, must seem strange to them, one of the exactments which separate them from the superior classes, from whom come to them, as from a sort of Providence, both good and evil.[1]

[1] Not unreasonably some of my readers might suppose that this picture was highly colored; but a few days after this page was first sent to the press, I found in a New York newspaper the following extract from the London *Telegraph*: —

"No substantial progress can be made in the laudable enterprise of grappling with the curse of strong drink in this country until the fact is more largely and more candidly recognized that women as well as men are accustomed to get outrageously tipsy. Although the proportion of women sots is not so large as that of men, a female drunkard may be more mischievous than a male one, because the home, when the wife and mother drinks, must inevitably be broken up, and the children, in the majority of instances, take after the drunken habits of the parent of whom they see the most. A very painful illustration of this recently came under the notice of the magistrate at Marlborough Street, when a married woman, who was brought up on remand as a 'drunk and disorderly,' herself applied, under the Habitual Drunkards' act, to be sent to

Those superior classes themselves, however, seem to have been, not very long ago, at least as much given to intoxication as their inferiors are now. The adage "as drunk as a lord" is indeed obsolescent, and with good reason; but its existence is proof of the habits of the class which it makes a basis of comparison. The adage, however, is, I am inclined to think, not a very old one. I know no instance of its use more than one hundred and fifty or two hundred years ago; and I am inclined to the opinion that it witnesses a condition of society which did not obtain until after the Restoration, and which was most fully developed in the last century. English literature, even dramatic literature, of an earlier time, affords no evidence that Englishmen of the higher ranks were notably given to intoxication. Had they been so, this evidence could hardly have been lacking

a home for inebriates. The poor woman had been married twenty-three years, and had brought up a numerous family, but latterly she had taken to drinking to excess, had turned her two daughters into the street, and threatened to tear her boy's tongue out and to set fire to the house."

Read, too, this deplorable confession, and the accompanying description of a scene the horrors of which are almost incredible : —

"A picture of the social habits of some of the poorer classes in this country is afforded by the evidence given at an inquest, held on Monday at Stafford, on the body of an old woman named Mary Devellin, found dead under the following horrible circumstances. A daughter of the deceased, on returning home last Friday night, found her mother absent, and proceeded to the house of an Irishman, named Mahoney, in search of her. On opening the door of the room, she saw five or six men and women lying on the floor in a state of intoxication. 'They were all piled together like dead bodies,' and on a bundle of sacks in a corner of the room was the body of her mother. Her face was frightfully swollen and discolored. The daughter tried to awaken her, but in vain. The old woman had drunk herself to death, and was lying there a corpse among her unconscious boon companions. A post-mortem examination revealed the fact that the internal organs of the deceased were nearly 'eaten away by the effect of alcoholic liquors,' and the verdict of the jury was in accordance with the medical evidence." — *Pall Mal. Gazette*, May 12, 1879.

in the plays of Dekker, of Heywood, and of other playwrights. We all know, however, the habits in this respect of a large proportion of the men of rank in England at the end of the last century and at the beginning of this. The evidence upon the subject is so strong, and shows such a condition of society in this respect, that the change to the present admirable temperance and decorum, which I have already mentioned, is not only to be admired but to be wondered at, as having been effected in so short a time.[1]

It is safe to assume that, in the last century, among English people who were able to live generously and who were not under the restraint of religious asceticism, the large majority of both sexes were more or less fuddled every day after dinner, which then among such people was at about three or four o'clock, afternoon. This fact affords an explanation, and to me it is the only admissible or conceivable explanation, of the behavior of the elegant people of that

---

[1] The following whimsical caution given to young ladies by a clever but now forgotten writer of the last century, an elegant man of "society," is apropos here: —

> "But ever let my lovely pupils fear
> To chill their mantling blood with cold small beer.
> Ah, thoughtless fair! the tempting draught refuse,
> When thus forewarned by my experienced Muse.
> Let the sad consequence your thoughts employ,
> Nor hazard future pains for present joy.
> Destruction lurks within the pois'nous dose,
> A fatal fever or a pimpled nose."
>   SOAME JENYNS, *The Art of Dancing*, 1795, Canto II.

As to the common people the same writer bears the following testimony: —

"Now whoever has been present at a fair, a sermon, a horse-race, an assizes, a cricket match, or a visitation, or any other numerous meeting in the country, must know that on the most enlarged computation the number of sober cannot exceed the proportion of those who are drunk. — *Works*, 1795, vol. ii. p. 158.

century and the early years of this at the theatre,
and even in the drawing-room when there was sentimental singing, like Tom Moore's. Men as well as
women would weep openly ; and at the hearing of
tragedies, the very reading of which now would make
us yawn, damp handkerchiefs were waving all over
the house, especially in the boxes. At very affecting
passages ladies would swoon or shriek, and be carried
out in hysterics. When Tom Moore sang, in his little voice that could hardly be heard over a large
drawing-room, ladies of the highest rank hung over
him at the piano-forte, and gave way to their emo-
tions in the most effusive and engaging manner, so
that there too they not unfrequently were faint or
hysterical. The men were hardly behind them.

It is difficult to believe that these are the manners
and customs of the same race, only two generations
removed, in which now the mark of good breeding is
the restraint of all expression of emotion, particularly
that of a sentimental kind. To believe it would be
impossible, were not the change accompanied by one
with regard to ebriety by which it is explained. At
those theatres and in those drawing-rooms it might
have been said, as the Reverend Mr. Stiggins remarked to Brother Tadger at the Brick-Lane Branch
of the Ebenezer Temperance Society, " the meetin 's
drunk." Doubtless a large majority of those present
were, if not intoxicated, maudlin with drink, and
ready to be affected with that which would not have
stirred them a jot had they led constantly sober lives.
Only on such a supposition as this can the impression which was produced by " The Beggar's Opera "
be accounted for. How such words and such music
could have set the town wild, and caused lords to

fall in love with the actresses and ladies with the actors, is otherwise quite incomprehensible.

Even now, however, the consumption of wine and beer in the higher ranks of life in England, although it rarely, I believe, leads past the bounds of a decorous hilarity, is very great when compared with that of well-to-do people in the United States whose grandfathers were born in the country. Unmitigated water is rarely drunk, and is generally regarded with mingled aversion on the score of taste and dread on the score of health. "What is that you are drinking, G—— ? " said an elderly gentleman to his nephew as we sat after the ladies had withdrawn; and he peered curiously down the board at the young man's glass. "Water, sir," replied the young fellow. "Hm-m-m! wa-ater," and then a puzzled silence. He did not say, as his most gracious majesty William, the fourth of that name, is reported by Greville to have been graciously pleased to say on a like occasion, "I 'll be damned if any man shall drink water at my table;" but evidently he was very royally minded upon the subject. I should have remembered the occasion, even if my host had not emphasized it by speaking to his nephew; for it was, I believe, the only one at which I saw pure water drunk at a dinner-table in England. I do not remember even one lady who confined herself to the simple element; and I am speaking now not of dinner-parties, or of occasions at all festive, but of the daily habits of families in which I had the honor and the great pleasure of being received without ceremony and made quite at home. Upon this point there is a corroborative passage in the very amusing "Court Etiquette," by Professor Fanning, of Toronto, Canada, who speaks, we are informed, with the authority of one who has received instruction in the Lord Chamberlain's office. He say that at family dinners "young ladies are limited to three glasses of light wines, while married ladies are accustomed to drink sometimes six." A matron in France may go to the Palais Royal; in England her privilege is six instead of three glasses of wine at dinner. Then there is the wine and the beer which is drunk at luncheon, which is a substantial meal at about two o'clock, with a joint and a pudding, and not unlikely a glass of sherry and water before bed.[1]

But the constant and somewhat free drinking of wine on the part of the ladies was not all that attracted my attention. I was astonished at a certain disregard of simplicity in their potations. Their drinking was multiform, and in what was to me a somewhat disturbing way. I have seen English ladies, after having had their full allowance of sherry, champagne, and claret at dinner, drink down a tumblerful of beer, or even of black porter! The first time I saw this done the performer was an actress; and as some of the ladies of her vocation are said to be not quite so scrupulous as to certain social matters as, let us say, the leading ladies of the Baptist and Methodist "persuasions" are, I supposed that I might set down the porter to this slight professional eccentricity. None the less, however, was I puzzled to account for the unfastidiousness of palate which

[1] "The public has been disgusted this week by the story of a number of married women in Birmingham getting drunk and causing a street row at noonday. The exposure revealed the fact that a certain number of these females, *belonging to what is called the respectable classes,* have been in the habit of meeting at a certain public house for the purpose of drinking to excess." — Frances Power Cobbe, *Reëchoes.*

could desire, and the stoutness of stomach which, after sherry, champagne, and claret, could retain, a great glass of porter with a tawny head upon it, at the mere sight of which even my masculine, and I had thought very submissive, gorge rose in rebellion. But as to my former supposition I was entirely wrong; for I saw ladies of position and of rank, after dinner was over (not regularly, but occasionally), drink off a glass of very strong beer, so strong, indeed, that one glass of it alone would turn the heads of most "American" women. My fair friends in England were, however, not disturbed by it; or certainly they were not before they retired from the drawing-room.[1]

This looking upon wine or beer as a necessity of life gives to the condemnation of malefactors, public and domestic, to a diet of bread and water, which is so often referred to in our literature, a severer significance than it has to us in "America." I remember that when I used as a boy to read and to hear of this aggravation of punishment, I supposed the deprivation to be, as it was in my own case, when under corrective discipline, of milk, of tea, and of coffee, — but the privation which it really did impose was that of beer and wine; and indeed the form of the sentence dates from a time when coffee and tea were unknown. But to an "American," or I should rather say to a Yankee, who does not belong to the drinking

[1] A lady who had lived many years in England expressed to a friend of mine her gratification at these remarks about English ladies, because they would tend to relieve some of the latter from misapprehension on their visits to this country, where their mere continuance of a custom common among women of their condition at home would be likely to subject them to unpleasant and unjust remark. And yet I have known New York women of the best position and the highest character drink off the larger part of a pint bottle of champagne just before going out to a party in the height of the season, to keep them up and make them brilliant.

classes, the deprivation of wine, beer, and spirits during imprisonment would not add appreciably to his discomfort. Not so with Britons of any class.

A short time ago a gentleman of my acquaintance, an officer in the army, received a letter from a friend in England, introducing an actress who had come here with intentions of pursuing her profession. He called, and as he was taking leave he asked the lady if there was anything that he could do for her, meaning any service that he could render her as a stranger. " Oh, yes," she at once replied, " do send me a case of table claret; for in this dreadful place I 'm expected to drink wa-a-ter or some nasty washy stuff they call lager, and I 'm so famished for some wine that I think I shall die. Do send me some, please." I am sorry to say that my friend did not send the case of wine, and was so taken aback by such a request on a first interview that his first call was his last; and indeed the lady, disgusted, I suppose, with a country where she was expected to drink water, went back to England without making an engagement. He was a little too shy and suspicious. Such a request from an actress to a British officer would not startle him as being much, if at all, out of the way, and almost any officer would have so heartily sympathized with this lady in her privation that he would have been glad to supply this deficiency in her commissariat.

In London streets I myself had similar requests made to me, although on a much smaller scale. These requests were altogether new to me, and caused me some astonishment. They were made as I was strolling in New Bond Street or in Regent Street. I declined compliance at first; but one evening, as I was returning to my lodgings from dinner at a restaurant, a youngish woman dressed plainly in black, not at all pretty, but with a modest and pleasant manner, stepped up to me and said in a sweet voice, " Please, sir, would you kindly give me a glass of wine ? " I reflected that I was a perfect stranger there, and might do with impunity what I should not think of doing at home (as English and " American " ladies go to the Mabille in Paris), and wishing to see how the thing was done, I said, Yes, and asked where we should get it. " There 's a wine-room, yonder," she replied, pointing across Regent Street. I went with her ; and surely there could not be a place less adapted to lure man or woman to mirth or pleasure. It was a small room not more than twelve feet square. The floor was of deal boards, not positively dirty, but not too clean. The walls were of a dingy nondescript color, and without ornament or decoration of any kind. Across one side, opposite the door, was a deal counter or bar, also dingy. On the floor were a chair or two and two or three small casks, upon which men were sitting. Behind the counter were other small casks with taps. So utterly doleful and forlorn a drinking place I had never seen. But the men were decently dressed, and were chatting pleasantly ; their manner was decorous, and they were plainly not roughs. I asked my fair friend what wine she would have. She said, Port ; whereupon two glasses with stems, but with straight sides, holding about as much as a small champagne glass, were filled from one of the casks and placed upon the counter. I gave one to her, and touching my lips to the other as she took a draught, I paid for the wine, and setting down my glass bade her good-evening and went out.

I had not gone far before I heard the pattering of feet and the rustling of skirts behind me. She laid her hand gently upon my arm, and said in a tone of distress that went to my heart, "Oh, sir, sir, how could you treat me so? To take me there and leave me to drink my wine alone! You might have waited. I was so ashamed." Her manner was perfectly simple and decorous; and she was evidently hurt. I apologized and explained to her that I was a stranger, quite unfamiliar with the etiquette of such places, and that I supposed she merely wanted the refreshment of a glass of wine, which I gave her with pleasure. "Well, well," she answered, "I suppose you meant no harm; but it was awfully hard. Thanks, sir; good-night!" and we went our several ways. I was truly sorry; but I had not supposed that a woman who asked me for wine in the street would mind much how she got it, or under what circumstances she drank it. Familiar as I have been from my boyhood with the streets of New York, at all hours of the day and night, this was my first experience of the kind; and it was my last in England, although the same request was made of me again and again, by day as well as by night.

Applications of this kind to a "gentleman" are of the commonest occurrence in England. Any information or assistance that I asked was generally given to me with good-natured alacrity, and without any intimation that a "tip" was expected; but in the case of persons of inferior condition, I always found that sixpence was accepted with pleasure, and as being quite in order. More than once, though, when my inquiries had extended into something like conversation, I found an answer to my last query rounded off with, "And I should be very 'appy to drink your 'elth, sir." Of course I produced the means of securing such disinterested wishes for my well-being.

Once, however, I was tempted to say, "Oh, my health is so good that it does n't need drinking;" but I was not reviled, as I had expected, and I may almost say hoped, to be. There was only a bewildered stare, and a silent turning away. The only sign that I saw of a ruffled temper from the absence of an expected fee was from a French waiter at a first-class restaurant. The little account which he presented had across the top, printed in large letters, "Attendance charged in the bill," which is common in England. Determined to see what this meant, when the waiter returned with my change, I put it all into my pocket; whereupon this Frenchman, who had been all bows and smiles and pleased alacrity, instantly became so insolent in his manner that I was tempted to make a complaint against him and test the question as to attendance. But I reflected that I was "only a passenger," and merely retaining in my pocket the sixpence that otherwise would have found its way into his hand, I went out.

To return to the subject of drink. It is generally expected that when a "gentleman" goes among men of lower classes, and talks with them, he will, in the common phrase there, "stand something," which means pay for beer for all; and as a pint may be had for twopence, the tax is not very heavy. If he remains while the beer is drunk, one spokesman says for all, "Your very good 'elth, sir." The beer is drained off and the drinkers wipe their lips with the backs of their hands, and the backs of their hands

31

upon a remote and invisible part of their trousers.
I observed the pronunciation of *'elth* in these cases.
It is not merely *health* with the *h* suppressed, but a
gulping of the syllable low down in the throat.   Indeed, this pronunciation of *l* is as much a distinctive
mark of lower-class English as the suppression of *h*
or its superfluous addition.   The higher classes give
it with exactly the same sound that it has in the
speech of educated Yankees.

Men are, however, not alone in expecting a gentleman to stand something.   As I was walking through
a narrow street in Birmingham, I saw a comfortable-
looking dame of decent mien at the door of a little
house, and, asking her some trifling question, fell into
talk with her.   She soon invited me in, with that
freedom of hospitality which I found common wherever I went.   I entered what proved to be her kitchen
and living-room.   It was very tidy and orderly.
There was a fire in the grate, and the kettle was
singing and puffing upon the hob.   There were two
other women of her sort there, chatting (everybody
in England seems to have time and inclination to
talk), and they kindly allowed me to enter into conversation with them.   But erelong one of them said,
" Per'aps the gentleman would like to treat us."   I
was startled, for it was my fourth day in England;
but of course assented.   When the question was put,
" Shall it be beer or gin ? " I announced to my entertainers that I was perfectly indifferent on that point,
and taking out half a crown gave it to one of them
and bade them good-morning; for I must confess that
in my inexperience upon the subject of gin and beer
in England, I felt very doubtful into what hands I
had fallen.   The probability is that they were per-

fectly respectable people of their class. What was so strange to me was merely a custom of the country.

Of quite a different sort was an equally novel experience I had in London. One night about ten o'clock, as I was passing through a street which crosses the upper part of Regent Street, a door suddenly opened and let a flood of light upon the pavement, and down a flight of stairs came, in some disorder, a little troop of men and women who were hilarious with some potation more subtle and exhilarating than beer. They were plainly all flown with wine. To my great astonishment one of the fair bacchantes rushed up to me and, flinging her arms around my neck, broke forth into expressions of admiration and affection, the genuineness of which it would have been cruel — to both parties — to doubt. Nevertheless, I was coy and shrank away ; and I am sure that if I ever blushed, I blushed then. True, it was dark, and my confusion was concealed ; but what of that ?

> "Nocte quidem ; sed luna videt, sed sidera testes
> Intendunt oculos."

I gently disengaged myself, and a few steps set me free from the first and only encounter that I had in England with a woman whom drink had carried beyond the bounds of decorum. Need I say that the conduct of this young person and that of some others whom I have mentioned does not in any way implicate that of any respectable woman in England, however lowly her condition ? As to the special " evil " of which she was a signal illustration, I shall say nothing more than I have said before in passing allusions. I found it most rife in London, in Oxford, and in Canterbury. This incident is told of here because it is characteristic and distinctive; for familiar as I am with town life in "America," by night as well as by day, I never before, either in my own experience or in that of another, knew of any occurrence like it.

As to the disposition to drink intoxicating liquors which has made drunkenness a national vice in England, it is to be said that there are reasons for it which do not exist in other countries. England lacks good water, and produces no wine. Although I drank much less water while I was there than I ever did during the same length of time before, I did drink much more than I am sure any native of the island does in thrice that time. But only twice did I have a draught of pure "soft" water. Nor in my walks and drives did I see one spring. It needs hardly to be said that there are springs enough there; but I think that in the southern part of the country, at least, they must be much less common than they are in New England and in the Middle States, where one can hardly take a country walk without coming upon one of these clear, cool, over-brimming cups of pure refreshment offered by the hand of Nature. Many people cannot drink the water of England unqualified without being made ill. Then the climate itself makes stimulants more welcome, if not more necessary, there than elsewhere; and it also increases the ability to bear stimulating drink. Hence, we may presume, the opinion of Addison's innkeeper ("Freeholder," No. 22), although it is open to the objection of being professional and somewhat interested, that "for constant use there was no liquor like a cup of English water, provided there was enough malt in it."

I was surprised not only at the quantity that I could drink at any time and at all times with impu nity, and with apparently good effect, but at the eagerness with which my whole body seemed to imbibe it. I shall never forget a certain place — it was in Fleet Street, I believe — where porter was to be had at a penny a pot. It is well known for the quality of its tap, and a friend took me to it one day, saying that he would " stand tuppence " and give me a treat. We had just had a hearty breakfast ; but as I turned up my glass of this black fluid I seemed to absorb a good part of it on its passage down my throat. It was of delicious flavor, cool without being cold, and of an inexpressible lightness, notwithstanding its thick, heavy look. There was a stream of people going in and out, and I was told that the stream of people and of porter did not cease from morning till night. In " America " I should as soon think of drinking pure alcohol directly after breakfast as a glass of porter.

These material and consequent physiological conditions should always be considered in judging English habits of drinking. Moreover, there is the traditionary custom. Time out of mind beer has been the common beverage in England. It has not been so in " America." The establishment of public breweries requires time and capital, which the early colonists had not to spare for that purpose; nor had they in their small households the means of supplying themselves with home-brewed malt-liquor. Consequently the stimulating beverages of this country were until lately rum, cider, whisky, and imported wine. The first was nearest at hand in the West Indies, and was afterwards made in New England ; the second came into use soon after the apple orchards reached maturity; whisky began to be made after there was grain enough to spare from making bread. Wine was a luxury. Hence in the early colonial days women and children commonly drank no beverage of this kind, except a little cider, wine being a luxury for the wealthy ; and this custom, coming of necessity, and strengthened in New England by puritan asceticism, extended a gradually diminishing influence even to our own day. Beer, although not unknown, was rare, and was regarded, perhaps not altogether without reason, as a very coarse drink. For example, I can say that although not unfamiliar in my boyhood with cider and good wine (including, by the way, such Madeira as I did not taste in England) I had not drunk four pints of beer before I left college. In England a boy might drink four pints in a day, although he might not do so every day. There the custom of brewing beer at home is still kept up at many of the great houses. I expressed surprise at this, as brewing is such a troublesome operation, particularly when performed on a small scale, and as such excellent beer may be had by the cask or the dozen, left at any door, even in the country. The reply was characteristic. It was that experiment having shown that the cost of the home-brewed beer and the public brewers' beer was about the same, those who had large households chose to keep up their old custom. Plainly, if home-brewing had been a little more costly, economy would have kicked the beam, and old custom would have gone up into the air.

The outcome of all this is that water as a fluid for internal application is treated with very little respect in England. Possibly so much is applied by nature to the inhabitants externally that they think they

have quite enough of it in that way. Of every other
thing drinkable you see a plentiful supply all around
you; of bitter-beer pint pots in rows, of fat ale vats,
of claret tuns, of crusted port good store; but Dives
did not beg Lazarus for wine; and if you have that
thirst upon you that nothing but cold water can slake,
you must needs, like the rich man in the parable, put
up your special petition for it. And if you ask a
butler for a glass of water at the dinner-table, not
improbably he will receive the request with such a
look of fish-eyed wonder as he might put on if a
chance whale should wallow into the dining-room and
ask for the material for a spout; and then you may
see him turn to a footman — lower means suit lower
ends — and say, " Tubbs, ah, ah, gloss of — ah —
wa-a-ter."

Notwithstanding the enormous quantity of beer
and wine and spirits now consumed in England, — to
the value of nearly one thousand millions sterling
(£987,320,660) in the seven years preceding 1879, —
and the besotted condition of so large a number of the
lowest class (and the largest class) of the people, the
consumption and the drunkenness are gradually diminishing; not positively, but in proportion to the
population. Those who had observed society there
for many years assured me that the change for the
better was appreciable, although not great; and a
lady who was the mistress of a house in which the
family consisted almost entirely of men, and in which
dinner-parties, mostly of men, were frequent, told me
that she, who controlled the whole household sup-
plies, had remarked a steady but slow diminution
during the last fifteen or twenty years in the quantity of wine required, although the number of the en-

tertainments and of the guests at each had somewhat increased. England seems, therefore, to be gradually freeing herself from the vice which for so many centuries has been regarded as national in her. It will be long before she is able to cast it off completely; for the subject is involved with one of the most important principles of constitutional liberty, the freedom of individual action, the liberty of the subject or the citizen. Moreover, in England the brewers and the licensed victuallers are a great power. Nor is abstemiousness so easy or so desirable as it is in "America;" and hardest although most desirable of all things everywhere is, not abstemiousness, but temperance.

CHAPTER XXI.

THE HEART OF ENGLAND.

It was on a bright Sunday morning in October that I set out from Warwick for Stratford-on-Avon. Autumn was more than half gone; and yet the almost cloudless sky was one of a succession of smiling welcomes which, meeting me in the southern counties, had gone with me to Cambridge and to Oxford, and now followed me into Warwickshire, the heart of England, for so this most midland shire is called.

I see that I have just spoken of southern counties and a midland shire. It cannot be strictly said that those two parts of the country are thus distinguished; but although " shire " and " county " are synonyms to a certain extent, there is a difference in their use which is in a certain degree distinctive. Although *shire* is the older and the truly English word, all the shires are counties, but all the counties are not shires. Kent, Sussex, Essex, Surrey, Norfolk, and Suffolk are not called shires; and their people speak of going to or coming from " the shires," meaning the rest of England. I observed evidences of some little local pride in these people who " did not belong to the shires." Whence is the origin of this pride I do not certainly know; but I am inclined to think that it has two causes quite unsuspected by the people who have it, the feeling being traditional, while the facts from which it sprung are long forgotten. These are, first, that these regions have been English longer than any other part of the island. The eastern and southeastern shore of the country, from its position, was that on which the Saxons first got foot-hold; and the names there show the simple early distinctions made between themselves by the new-comers : Norfolk = north folk, Suffolk = south folk, Essex = east Saxons, Sussex = south Saxons. The other reason for the local pride is that these counties make up the larger part of the country which was not thoroughly conquered by the Danes and completely subjected to Danish influence. Evidence of this original English condition appears in the fact that these counties are not named from their county towns, as is the case with the large majority of the counties : for example, York, Yorkshire ; Derby, Derbyshire ; Oxford, Oxfordshire ; Warwick, Warwickshire ; Chester, Cheshire. But of Essex the county town is Chelmsford, of Sussex Chichester, while in Kent the county town might be said to take its name from the county, — Canterbury, the town or borough of Kent. When the Danes were driven out, it became necessary to reform and make again thoroughly English the counties in which they had for many generations subverted the English government, even to the obliteration of the old names ; and in doing this it was convenient to name the counties from their chief towns. It is not in the ordinary course of things for counties and county towns to have the same name, as may be seen by comparing those of New England, New York, and Virginia, for example, even although the names there are of such very modern origin.

But to return from names to places. My bright

Warwickshire day was not so pleasant as it might have been, or as some other bright days, or even as many cloudy days that I had seen in England. For the east wind was blowing, and had blown steadily for forty-eight hours. Now an east wind in England is not at all like an east wind here. To us it brings clouds, and, if long continued, a heavy, driving rain. The dreaded east wind of England corresponds to our northwest wind, the wind with which our sky clears after a northeast storm. And, like that wind, it is, to me at least, the most dreadful of the skyey influences. It blows pitilessly, steadily, and pierces you through and through with a dry, rough-edged blast; it aggravates its essential qualities by exposing you to the glare of sun and sky unveiled by any cloud, unsoftened by any mist; it deludes you with a show of brightness, and then stings your cheeks and grinds your joints together, and rudely takes liberties with your hat, your hair, and your clothing. And yet the weather that our northwest wind brings is what many people, merely, it would seem, because the sun is visible, praise as beautiful and bracing; uttering their eulogies with watery eyes, dripping noses, red, tingling cheeks, and a scowling brow, as they face the pitiless glare of the unmitigated sun.[1]

Warwick is reckoned a Shakespearean town; but I did not particularly care for it on that account, my liking for Shakespeare not taking the form of relic-worship or house-haunting. But Warwick has intrinsic interest for every student of England in the past, for every lover of architectural beauty, or of

[1] This wind is called by Crevecœur, in his *Letters of an American Farmer*, "the tyrant of America."

that beauty of reclaimed nature which is found in perfection in great English parks and around English country-seats and farm-houses. And my visit to Warwick was marked by one of those quiet, unostentatious acts of attention of which I met with so many, and from entire strangers, that I am sure that they were merely a mainfestation of characteristic kindness and hospitality in English people. A gentleman living in one of the beautiful suburbs of Birmingham, hearing accidentally that I was in England, searched me out by post and telegraph, and offered to show me Warwickshire, of which I found that he knew not only all the great places, but every by-path and every nook and corner. He sent me full and particular directions as to all that I ought to see, and asked me where he should meet me, if I did not choose to come first to Birmingham. It was more convenient for me to go there last, and I took him at his word and asked him to meet me at Warwick ; and there he came, we seeing each other for the first time in that venerable town. He, a busy man, gave up three days to guiding me through his county. I met with so much of this kindness that I never can forget it, but shall cherish the memory of it gratefully while I live.

Warwick is one of those towns, of which there are not a few in England, for the existence of which it is difficult to account. Why people should have gathered their dwellings together at this spot in sufficient numbers to make a large town is not easily discoverable. It has no trade, no manufactures, no cathedral, no schools, no centralizing attraction. How the people live there is a mystery. For visiting strangers can do little to support the inhabitants of such

a place; and whence do the Warwickers get the
money wherewith to pay each other? The castle,
part of which was built before the Conquest, must
be the nucleus around which the town slowly gathered through centuries, until it stopped growing. For
there is nothing new about it. On the contrary, it
has a charming air of having been finished long ago,
of having got its growth, and fulfilled its purpose.
I did not see a house in it, except in one street, that
did not seem to be at least a century old, and many
of its dwellings were thrice that age. These English
towns of from five to fifteen thousand inhabitants,
which have the respectable air given by an appearance of stability and comfort not of yesterday, and
which have no ragged outskirts where cheap and
showy houses are going up, and land lies waste, waiting for improvement, while it changes hands yearly
from bankrupt speculator to bankrupting speculator,
and into which even a railway cannot bring the nine-
teenth-century bustle, seem to me, next to a genuine
country house, the most perfect places imaginable for
human habitation. You can walk out of them from
any point, through clean, well-paved streets, in fifteen
minutes; and then you are in the midst of green
fields, great trees, and pretty hedges, on roads which
are neither dusty in dry weather nor muddy in wet.
Unless you live in London, or in one of three or four
other great commercial or manufacturing towns, you
are within easy reach of a country ramble; and even
in London you are within easier reach of the next
best thing of the kind, a walk through great parks,
where the velvet verdure under foot and the majestic trees above your head both seem to have prepared their beauty for you centuries ago, and in

which, although they are well kept, you are not
warned to keep off the grass. You do not have to
stand up in a street-car and hang on by the straps, or
be squeezed flat on the platform for half an hour before you can get to the nearest entrance of your only
ground for quiet, healthful recreation. Of all the old
towns in England that combine convenient smallness
of size with a certain civic dignity and that air of
being finished which I have already mentioned, and
with the attractions of easily accessible parks and
gardens of exquisite beauty, Oxford, as I have already said, is the most admirable. But as one cannot reasonably ask always for the beauties of Oxford,
a man must be very exacting if he cannot be pleased
with those of other places, even of one so very inferior as Warwick.

To Warwick Castle, the gate of which is within
a stone's-throw of the main street of the town, I
went alone, my self-elected guide having not yet arrived. It was very strange to turn out of a paved,
gas-lit street, lined on either side with shops and
dingy brick houses, into a gloomy causeway cut deep
through the solid rock, shaded with great trees, and
winding gently up an acclivity to a grim gray mass
of feudal masonry; and such is the approach to Warwick Castle. The buildings, which stand around a
large grassy base-court, are of various periods, but all
of great age, one of the towers having been erected
in Saxon times. I pulled the handle at the end of
a chain hanging at the principal entrance, and was
admitted. Within I found some half a dozen persons, decent English folk of the middle class, waiting
their turn to go through the apartments. It is the
custom in these great show places for an attendant to

make the tour as soon as a sufficient number of sight-
seers have assembled to make it worth while to do
so; and at Warwick Castle this happens usually
about every hour or two during daylight, when the
family is not in residence.

Hardly had I glanced at my companions when a
large and ₁elderly woman advanced toward us and
began to speak. She was a hard-featured female,
with a slight, ragged, stiff mustache and big, stony
teeth. She was dressed in black, and wore a formidable cap. She began her office immediately, without the slightest greeting or preface, plunging directly
in medias res, and not addressing herself particularly
to us, but sending out her voice into the great room
as an owl might hoot in a barn. It was somewhat
startling to find one's self in a strange place filled
with armor and other relics, and to have a stout
human female in mustaches begin thus as if she were
touched off like one of the old firelocks : " The hold
baronial 'all ; this is the 'all that was destryd by fire ;
hancient harmor ; Guy of Warwick's 'elmet ; hetruskin vawzes," etc., pointing with a large emphatic
forefinger at each object which she named. Her pronunciation of " vase," *vawz*, one of the extreme affec-
tations of the extremely elegant people at the end of
the last century and the beginning of this, was in
amusing contrast with her ill treatment of the letter
h, and the sounds which she gave to other words.
People in her condition of life in England not uncommonly have some well-preserved affectation of
this kind in speech or in manner, to which they hold
as a sign of superior position.

As we went through the rooms I could not but observe in my companions what had impressed itself on

me before at Windsor Castle and other grand show
houses, that the English people who visit them do so
chiefly to see the state in which majesty and nobility
live ; to look at the grand furniture, the gilded cor-
nices, and other splendors of the apartments, with
little or no interest in architecture or historic associations, and with the density of stocks and stones as to
the beauties of the objects of art which are generally
found in such places. A queen's or duchess's state
bed, hideous and ponderous, and overwhelmed with
stuffy embroidered curtains, attracts more attention
from them than the surcoat and gauntlets that the
Black Prince wore at Poictiers, or a masterpiece of
Titian or Vandyke. As far as the average native
Briton is concerned, these visits are pilgrimages of
prying snobbery. In Warwick Castle are some noble
pictures by the great masters of the sixteenth century ; but these, pointed out by the tremendous forefinger, and set forth as to subject and painter in a
somewhat amazing style both of speech and criticism
by our guide (as, for example, " Ed of a hox by Bug-
gim," meaning Berghem), were hardly glanced at.
One gentleman did ask, " Oo 's the hold fellow
hover the door ? " but suddenly corrected himself
with, " Ho ! it 's a woman." When, however, we
came to a gorgeous table, the top of which our guide
informed us was " hall of preshis stones," there was
an eager looking and a pricking up of ears ; and as
the pudgy, strong-nailed thumb with which she chose
to point out its splendors moved over its variegated
surface, and paused on one spot and another, as she
explained in a voice husky with importance, " hagate,
hamethyst, honyx," etc., she was attentively followed
and when she closed her description with the an-

nouncement, " This table cost two thousand paounds," she evidently awakened a feeling of delighted awe. What was chain armor that had gone through the first crusade, what were Raphael and Titian and Rubens, to that !

Among the paintings at Warwick is a portrait of strange impressiveness. It is that of a gentleman in the costume of the middle of the sixteenth century, standing with his left hand resting near the hilt of his sword, and looking out of the canvas straight into your eyes. Upon a plinth against which he leans is an inscription in Spanish, telling that he was one who feared nothing, not even death.[1] There have been other men who were as fearless ; but no such portrait of any one of them, as I believe. I never saw a painted face of such vitality and character, never painted eyes that seemed so plainly to have a thinking brain behind them, never painted lips that so seemed as if they could speak but would not. Then the perfect simplicity and ease of the position, the faultless drawing, and the color, of which the mere harmonies are a perpetual delight, unite with its other merits to make a picture the sight of which is worth a pilgrimage. I had seen Vandykes and Rubenses and Sir Joshuas almost by the acre, and it was with a memory of the best of these, and also of what Raphael and Titian and Velasquez and Holbein have done in this way, fresh in my mind, that I felt that this portrait by Muroni, a painter almost unknown to me, is one of the greatest in the world. Certainly I never saw one, or the engraving of one, that is its superior.

As we passed through one room our guide said

---

[1] Aqui esto sin temore y della muerte no he pavor.

with an affable air and a condescending wave of
the hand, " The view of the park from these windows is thought to be one of the most beautiful in
Hengland." I stepped forward into the deep em-
brasure and looked out. She had spoken truly. The
beauty of the scene in its kind could not be overrated. Bright, rich greensward was shadowed with
clumps of oaks and gigantic cedars that spread
broad, sombre fans, almost like roofs, high above the
grass. The soft, sweet blue of the sky was filled
with fleecy clouds full of light, and here and there
the verdure seemed to blaze like a pavement of
emerald. Through all the little Avon, here a brawl-
ing, freely flowing stream, wound from dark to light.
The park stretched away, mingling with the distance,
till it seemed as if all England must be a park, of
which Warwick Castle was the centre, the very heart
of the heart of England. And just below was the
castle mill, whose turning wheel prettily suggested
that union of the practical with the beautiful, and
even with the ˙stately, which is a characteristic trait ˙
of English country homes, whether they are castles
or granges.

After making the tour of the apartments, including the chapel, where we were told that " there was
service hevery day by their hown chaplain when the
family was hat the castle," we retraced our steps,
and my companions went out. I remained ; and a
slip of paper given me by a friend procured me the
privilege of going through the rooms again alone and
looking at the various objects of interest which they
contained, at my leisure. I lingered so long, chiefly
over the paintings, that a new party of visitors had
gathered while I was still making my solitary round.

And then I heard, far off in the distance, but distinctly, the same sound with which I was greeted, " The hold baronial 'all — hancient harmor — hetruskin vawzes — hagate, hamethyst, honyx — this table cost two thousand paounds," and so forth, word for word, letter for letter, haitch for haitch. And when I reflected that this good woman went over the same ground, day after day, and many times a day, pointing out the same objects to knots of gaping sight-seers, I reproached myself for my criticism of her style of explanation, and bethought me of the Jew clothes-dealer's reply to Coleridge, who asked him, " Jew, why cannot you say old clothes instead of old clo'? " — " Christian, if you had to say old clothes as often as I do, you would be glad to say old clo', or anything else to shorten it." Nevertheless, this obtrusion of housekeepers and vergers and warders and sextons is the great drawback to the enjoyment of the places under their care. I was fortunate in being able to free myself from it on other occasions.

One of the most interesting places in Warwick is the Leicester hospital. It was founded by Robert Dudley, Amy Robsart's Dudley and Queen Elizabeth's Earl of Leicester, for twelve old men, who are called brethren, and a master. It is a fine and well-preserved specimen of the domestic architecture of the time; many-gabled, and with dark oak beams showing on the outside, the interstices being filled with plaster,— suggesting a man whose skeleton has struck through his skin. I think that it is the finest example of this style that I saw, except Speke Hall in Lancashire, which is peerless, outside and in; in which the walls and the ceiling of the dining-room are rough

with rich carving in dark oak, and where one of the
bay windows is of such a size that it has on one side a
larger fire-place than I ever saw here, even in the
kitchen of an old New England farm-house. It is
of architectural celebrity, but it is so remote from
the line of travel, and so jealously guarded, that it is
rarely visited by strangers. When I saw it, and
others of its kind, I could understand Mr. Halliwell-
Phillips's remark as to " America," that he " thought
he could n't live comfortably in a country where there
were no Elizabethan houses." In their union of the
expression of simple domesticity with quiet stateliness, these houses have a charm which is unique.
One could not comfortably live in a castle unless one
were a wealthy peer ; but any man whose notion of a
home is not limited to " a brown-stone front" might
long to live in one of these Elizabethan houses.

The brethren of the Leicester hospital wear, on
state occasions, long gowns or cloaks, which have
upon them metal badges formed of the device of the
Bear and Ragged Staff ; and these badges are now
the very same that were worn by the first brethren
three hundred years ago, so carefully have they been
preserved. The eldest of the brethren showed me
about the place, and in explaining to me the nature
of the institution, or the " foundation " as it is there
called,[1] said to me, among other things, " Th' Herl o'
Leicester d'ow'd this haouse for twel' hold men an' a
master ; an' th' brethren comes out o' three parishes,
and none can come into 't but on'y they." Of a little house that I pointed out, he said, " That doant
belong to we." This is a fair representation of the
speech of a Warwickshire man of his condition. I

[1] " God save the foundation."— *Much Ado About Nothing*, V. 1.

went with him into the kitchen, where the brethren sit and drink ale before the enormous fire-place, and there he showed me an old three-legged oaken chair which had but lately been discovered in some nook or corner of the building, and which I saw from the carving upon it was made by a Saxon craftsman, and probably antedated the Conquest. There, too, he showed me a little piece of embroidery worked by poor Amy Robsart. It was framed and hung up against the wall. The frame, he told me, had been paid for by "a gentleman in America," of whom I probably had never heard, " one Mr. Charles O'Conor, a great lawer." Mr. O'Conor had seen it " laying araound loose," and for Amy Robsart's sake had furnished a frame for its proper preservation.

The house stands upon a declivity, the road which leads to Stratford descending rapidly there; and the chapel is built upon an arch over the street. The effect of this, as you approach Warwick and look up the hill, is pleasing and impressive, the tower rising into the air almost with grandeur, although the building is comparatively small. This is worthy of remark as an example of the effect produced by the converse of that leveling and straightening mania which possesses all builders and that sort of folk here. Not a little of the beauty of the old towns and buildings in England is owing to the fact that architects used their art to conform their structures to the natural features of the places in which they were erected, instead of making the places conform themselves to the buildings.

Warwick has a church, the chief interest of which to me was the Leicester chapel and the crypt. In the former are the tomb and effigies of the great Earl of

Leicester, as he is called, and of Fulke Greville, the
founder of the present Warwick family, upon whose
tomb it is recorded by his own wish that he was
" servant to Queen Elizabeth, and friend to Sir Philip
Sidney." He might have served a better mistress
than that vain, vacillating, lying, penurious termagant, who drove Cecil, the real ruler of England in
her reign, almost mad, and whose one merit was that
she knew a man when she saw him; but he could not
have had friendship for a nobler or more admirable
gentleman than Sir Philip Sidney. But this struck
me as I looked at the tomb: Who now would deem
it a distinction to have it recorded upon his tomb
that he was the friend of any man? Is it that there
are no gods among us, or that we have lost the faculty of worship, except for two idols — Me and Mammon?

It was pleasant to see in this church two mural
tablets set up in memory of two of the housekeepers
at Warwick Castle. One of them recorded the fact
that the subject of the inscription had held her position for sixty years. Faithful service seems rarely
forgotten in England.

In the crypt, the mighty ribbed arches of which
spring from one enormous pier, there is an article
which has long gone out of use, — whether advan-
tageously or not I shall not venture to say, — a duck-
ing-stool, made for the public discipline of scolding
women. This is one of the only two, I believe, that
remain in England. It consists of a strong oaken
frame on low wheels, from which a seat rises upon an
inclined beam that works upon a pivot or axle. The
scold was lashed into the seat, and then the "institution" was drawn to the river-side at a convenient

deep place, and rolled in until the patient sat just above the water. Then the land end of the beam was tipped up, and consequently the other end with its lading went down under the water, where it was allowed to remain not too long, and was then raised for breathing time. This process was repeated as often as it was thought beneficial to the lady under treatment, or necessary for the peace of her family and neighborhood. Whether husbands ever interceded for wives thus disciplined, as wives do now sometimes for husbands who are unreasonably interfered with in the gentle sport of blacking their eyes or kicking their ribs, is not recorded.

After dinner I asked for a hint as to the way of passing the hours before bedtime; but in vain. No one could tell me what to do: " Warwick was a quiet place, with nothing going on." As I knew no one there, I was thrown upon my own resources, and sallying forth, I wandered about the town. I met hardly a human creature; nor did many of the houses show lights to cheer my lonely loitering. Erelong, however, a sense of bustle stirred my ears, and following their guidance I soon came upon an open place which was fitfully lit up by the flaring light of many large petroleum lamps, or rather torches; for they were without shades or chimneys. One side of the place was filled by three or four large booths, on the outside of which were signs and transparencies; and within each was a noise of hand-organs and of brazen instruments of music, so called. On some half a dozen stands in the open air various articles were exposed for sale. In the midst of all this some hundred people or so of the humbler sort were moving quietly about. I had plainly fallen upon the Saturday fair of Warwick and its neighborhood. The people offered little occasion of remark, being generally of that sober, respectable sort which is always uninteresting. The shows proved to be equally dull and decent; and even the vociferations of the showmen at the doors of the booths were remarkable only as evidence of an untiring strength of lungs. Soon, however, I was attracted by the performances of a dealer in crockery, who was disposing of his wares by the process known in England as a Dutch auction. A long, broad deal board, set upon two trestles, and covered with teapots, plates, tumblers, bowls, and piggins, formed his whole establishment. Before him a dozen or two of men and women were gathered in little knots. As I came up he was crying out at the top of his voice in praise of a huge and hideous teapot, which he held aloft. "Two shillins for this helegant harticle! Honly two shillins. You wouldn't get one loike it in Lunnon for arf a crown; not for three shillin. Wouldn't you like it, ma'am? It 'ud look helegant on your tea-table." Silence. "Eighteen pence, then, for this lovely tea-pot! Look hat it!" and he whisked off the lid, and held it and the pot abroad high in air in either hand. "Eighteen pence," — silence, — "and no one wants this splendid tea-pot at one shilling. Wouldn't you like it, ma'am, for ninepence?" turning to an old woman wrapped in a huge rough shawl. He had found his purchaser. The ninepence went into his pocket, and the tea-pot disappeared under the shawl. He then went to a pile of plates, of which he took up two, and set them whirling on the tips of his fingers like a conjurer. "Look at them plates; as fine as any one ever eat a dinner off of. Who'll have a dozen of 'em? Only two shillins the dozen." He shouted a while, but no notice was taken of his invitation. Then he caught up two or three others, and shuffled them back and forth in his hands as if they were cards, making a great clatter. He flung them up into the air and caught them again. He dashed them down upon the board in seeming recklessness, calling attention to their soundness and strength. "The children couldn't break them plates." But I saw that the skill and dexterity of his handling were such that the crockery was in no real danger. He seemed to wax furious in his excitement; and flinging the plates up into the air one after another caught them again, and kept the round in motion, crying out all the while at the top of his voice. He danced back and forth, addressing himself now to one group and now to another, and gradually diminishing the upset price of his goods until he reached his "very lowest figger." Then he paused; and after a little hesitation one or two women stepped shyly forward and bought half a dozen each. After seeing him make one or two more sales in this manner, I turned away. It was growing late. The people began to disperse. They were putting out the lights in the show booths; and I went to my inn. But something *was* going on even in Warwick, and my entertainment was better, I am sure, than it would have been at a theatre. .

Among the striking features of old English towns are the massive gates that are found standing in them across some of the principal streets. In olden time almost all these towns were walled. The walls have fallen into decay, and have been removed, but many of the gateways are left standing. Warwick has at least one such, through which I passed several times without observing anything in it to interest me particularly, except its massiveness and its age. But one afternoon, as I was walking out of the town, I saw an exceeding small boy trying to drive an exceeding big swine through this gate. The boy was one of the smallest I ever saw intrusted with any office, the beast was the hugest living pork that has yet come under my observation. He was a very long pig, but he also was a very broad one; surely greater in girth than in length. His hams were so big that as he presented his vast rear to me he seemed to obscure a goodly part of the horizon, and as to the boy, they must for him have blotted out the whole heavens; for the little man's head was not so high as the big beast's back. The group reminded me of Falstaff's exclamation to his dwarfish page, "I do here walk before thee like a sow that hath overwhelmed all her litter but one." Now the pig, for some altogether piggish reason, did not wish to go through the gate. Perhaps he thought it was too small, although armies with banners had gone out of it to battle. He turned his head to one side and the other, willing to take the pathway which passed around the gate, through which his pigmy driver, however, was determined that he should go. Whereat the latter spread out his little hands, and applying them with all his little might to the haunches of the huge creature tried to push him on. He might as well have pushed against the great tower of Warwick Castle. Then he patted the fat white hams, and coaxed and gently urged, but all in vain. Whereupon the dreadful ingenuity of boydom, early developed, came to his aid. Between the enormous haunches of the beast was an absurdly small corkscrew appendage, which for any possible use that it could be to such a monster might just as well not have been. It suggested that tails, in the course of evolution, were passing away from pigs in their progress toward some more highly developed animal of the future. But the boy put it to present and effective use. Reaching up to it as I had seen a lad reach to a door-knocker, he seized it, and with a hearty good-will gave it one more twist than it had, the consequence of which was a swinish squeal and a hurried waddle through the gateway. The contrast between the venerable dignity of this frowning old portal, with its historic suggestions and associations, and the little comedy of boy and pig enacted beneath it seemed to me one of the absurdest sights that I had ever seen.

I walked out the next morning to Guy's Cliff, the seat of Lady Spencer, which is some three miles from Warwick, the beauties of which I must pass over without particular mention. I will merely remark that in a little house, as small as house could be, in a little street on the very outmost edge of Warwick, I saw in the window a display of old blue china for sale. Who, I thought, would ever come here to buy? But this is characteristic of the Englishman of to-day. He will set up his shop in such odd out-of-the-way places that an " American " would as soon think of opening a " store " in a light-house.

On the road to Guy's Cliff, which was as trim and as well-kept as a road in Central Park, although it was only the ordinary highway, I found seats by the wayside at convenient intervals, — long, substantial benches under trees. Such provision for comfort of every kind is common all over England. And this morning I saw, although I forget exactly where, a monument erected on a wooded knoll on the spot where Sir Piers Gaveston was beheaded A. D. 1312, for the favor he enjoyed with Edward II., by the simple orders of the then Earl of Warwick. The possibility of having one's head taken off by a rich, powerful man was one of the comforts of old England which has passed entirely away. Then I turned back to Warwick, and walked rapidly to keep my appointment for the visit to Stratford-on-Avon.

CHAPTER XXII.

A VISIT TO STRATFORD-ON-AVON.

THE desire to go on pilgrimage need not be very strong in any man of English blood to take him, if he is in England, to Stratford-on-Avon. My readers may remember that the elegant woman who, while I had the pleasure of being her railway companion, earnestly advised me to read " Kenilworth " also informed me, before she suspected my nationality, that all " Americans " go to Stratford. She meant, of course, all who go to England; in which she was not quite right. To a great many of the " Americans " who do go to England (I am sorry to say to much the greater number of them) that country is a mere patch of the earth's surface over which they must pass to get to Paris. In London they do look in upon the Abbey or the Tower, and, if they are there in the season, delight our minister by sending him demands for invitations to balls and for presentation at court; but beyond this, and perhaps a visit to Brighton, their endeavor to make acquaintance with England rarely goes. But most of the " Americans " who do desire to know something more of England than may be learned by a railway journey from Liverpool to London and from London to Dover visit Stratford; the proportion of these being very much larger, I am sure, than that of the cultivated Britons who render this personal homage to him whose works are our richest common inheritance.

The reason of this is simply that the British Shake-speare lover, being always within about half a day's journey of Stratford, knows that he may go there at any time; and as for that purpose one time is as good as another, he sometimes passes his life without going there at all. To my surprise, I found many intelligent and highly educated people in London who had never seen Canterbury Cathedral, although it is only about three hours from the metropolis. One of these had been in India and in "the States," and had seen them both not without advantage to others as well as to himself. But although he was a London man, he made his first visit to the great cathedral while I was in England, stimulated to do so, I believe, partly at least, by the example of his Yankee friend. This seeming indifference to the great things near at hand is not peculiar to the natives of any country.

I decided to drive from Warwick to Stratford instead of going by rail. If I had been alone I should have walked; for the places are only nine miles apart, and of all ways of going through a country one really wishes to see there is none like that provided by nature; and this is especially true of England. The hostess of the "Warwick Arms" undertook to provide me with a fly, which in rural England is any vehicle that does the office of a cab, and which in this case proved to be a sort of modest one-horse phaeton. And, by the way, the cost of the use of this vehicle the greater part of a day was 13s. 6d., which, with two shillings to a careful, civil driver, who knew the country and all its noteworthy places well, is equal to about four dollars. Here I could not have had the same thing (if I could have had it at all) for less than seven dollars and a half, or more likely ten, with expectation of at least the same gratuity.

The scenery of Warwickshire is not striking; it is not even picturesque, except as it has been made so by the hand of man.   In the part which I saw there are no hills of sufficient height to give the landscape variety of form, either far or near.   It is simply a gently rolling agricultural country.   Tame as its natural features are, however, it is made beautiful by cultivation, by parks, by meadows of vivid green, by clumps of trees, by old churches, old country-seats, and timber-and-plaster farm-houses and cottages.   As we rolled gently along, almost every turn of the road brought us in sight of some object of this kind, which often was beautiful, or, if not beautiful, interesting.   My companion had stories to tell me of people who lived in these houses, many of whom were odd characters, or good.

Erelong we came to Barford, which consisted chiefly of a church, quite new, a beautiful little Gothic building, the architect of which was Gilbert Scott.   It was built entirely at the expense of Miss Ryland, who is the Lady Bountiful of this neighborhood, and whose country-seat we caught a glimpse of not far off.   She gave the architect *carte blanche* as to style and finish, and he produced one of the prettiest parish churches in general design and in detail to be found in all England.   It ought to atone for some of his sins of restoration, by which many of his brother architects say, in a fraternal way not uncommon among the profession, that he has spoiled not a few of the finest old churches in England.   We stopped and went in ; but as service was far advanced did not go beyond the font, which stood close by the door, as is the general custom in England.   But this font and the vestibule were so beautifully designed

and so exquisitely wrought in richly-colored marbles
that they alone were worth our visit.   Barford church
was one of several of its kind that I saw in England
which were built by individuals at their own expense
as a free gift to the parish.   It is to be remarked,
however, in regard to this munificence, that in many
cases, if not in most, the givers own the whole parish ; and often it would seem they own not only the
church, but the clergyman.

On we went again, rolling easily over the smooth,
firm road, almost as smooth and as firm as if it had
been paved with flags, and yet yielding to our horse's
tread and the turn of our wheels with a sensation to
us of ease such as comes either to pedestrian or equestrian only from a surface of hard-packed earth.   Passing between a few more broad green meadows, we
came to Charlecote church.   The fence around it
and the gate were homely and ragged to a degree
that would not be tolerated for a week by New England people, if they had a fence and a gate at all for
their church or meeting-house.   But the church is a
beautiful stone structure that combines simplicity,
irregularity, stability, and an air of rural sanctity in
a way that seems quite unattainable out of England.
There was no service in this church that day, and our
driver soon brought from a neighboring cottage the
sexton's daughter with the key, and we entered.

The chief object of our visit here was the tomb of
Sir Thomas Lucy and his wife, which is in the chancel end of the church.   Most of my readers probably
know that Sir Thomas was the squire of Charlecote
House in Shakespeare's younger days, and that the
poet is said by tradition to have been driven from
Stratford by the persecution of the knight, who un-

dertook to punish his humble neighbor severely for poaching on his manor, stealing deer from his park, and setting up lampoons upon his park gate. I doubt this. That Shakespeare poached is quite probable; that he stole deer, at least from the Lucys' park, is very improbable, because they had no deer park then.. But that there was some trouble between Sir Thomas and the young fellows of Stratford, of whom Shakespeare then was one, and nothing more, is very likely. Likely, too, that the young fellows had the worst of it, and that this particular one took his revenge, first by some verses which ridiculed the knight, and afterward, by a higher kind of ridicule in the first scene of the "Merry Wives of Windsor." For there can be no mistaking the hit at him in Justice Shallow with the luces in his coat of arms, although the punning arms of the Lucy family have three, and not a "dozen," of those fish. But Sir Thomas was no Justice Shallow. He seems to have been an intelligent, kind-hearted gentleman, a man not likely to persecute any one, much less a clever, wild boy, the son of an alderman of Stratford.

The effigies of the knight and his wife in alabaster lie in stately repose upon their tomb: he in armor, she in the full dress of a lady of the Elizabethan period. But above the tomb, on a marble recessed into the wall, is something far more interesting than these recumbent statues. It is the epitaph which Sir Thomas wrote upon his wife, who died five years before him. It tells the story of their life and of his love, and reveals the characters of both so well that I copied it. Here it is: —

Here entombed lyeth the Lady Joyce Lucy, wife of Sir Thomas Lucy, of Charlecote, in the County of Warwick, Knight, daughter and heir of

Thomas Acton, of Sutton, in the County of Worcester, Esquier, who departed out of this wretched world to her heavenly kingdome, the tenth day of February, in the year of our Lord God 1595, of her age LX and three. All the time of her life a true and faithfull servant of her good God, never detected in any crime or vice; in religion most sound; in love to her husband most faithfull and true; in friendship most constant; to what was in trust committed to her most secret; in wisdome excelling; in governing her house and bringing up of youth in the feare of God that did converse with her, most rare and singular. A great maintainer of hospitality; greatly esteemed of her betters; misliked of none unless of the envious. When all is spoken that can be said, a woman so furnished and garnished with virtue as not to be bettered, and hardly to be excelled by any. As she lived most virtuously, so she dyed most godly. Set down by him that best did know what hath been written to be true.

THOMAS LUCY.

Such a tribute to such a woman came from no pompous, shallow-pated rustic squire. Nor was the heart that prompted a man to write that last sentence one that would take delight in persecuting a lad of eighteen or twenty for trespassing, at the cost of a few hares, or birds, or even deer. There was a truly kindly nature, we may almost say a noble soul. I am with Sir Thomas in this matter; and if Shakespeare suffered any discipline at his hands, I believe that he deserved it. It does not at all follow because he wrote " Hamlet " and " King Lear " in his mature years that he might not have been a scapegrace in his youth; and we who have read " Hamlet " and " King Lear " regard their author from a very different point of view from that taken by a country gentleman who had suffered annoyance at his hands. From William Shakespeare to Sir Thomas Lucy the descent is now tremendous and precipitous; from William Shakespeare to Sir Thomas Lucy the ascent was then almost as great. This I had thought of before; but when I came to see Charlecote on the one hand, and on the other the house in which Shakespeare passed his boyhood and that from which he took his wife, it came upon me again with a very strong impression. People are apt to think of Sir Thomas hardly, as a man who oppressed a great poet in his early years. But Shakespeare was then not a great poet : and unless he had been driven from Stratford by a complication of troubles, of which, mayhap, the squire's wrath was a part, he might never have become one.

Whether the Lucys had deer in Shakespeare's time or not, they have them now by hundreds. As we skirted the park, the wooden fence of which is very rude and irregular in appearance, not unlike those that are made here of intertwisted roots and gnarled branches of trees, we saw herds of these beautiful creatures, who hardly turned their heads to look at us. Two or three stags did start up, and, tossing their antlers back upon their haunches, trot gently off, and then wheel round at gaze with distended nostrils and brightened eyes. But even this seemed rather like a little game of playing sentinel in the eyes of the she-creatures, to relieve the tedium of a dull Sunday morning ; and the does lay still and chewed the cud. The deer in the English parks have become so tame with the rest of nature there, the inhabited as well as the inhabitants, that they accept the presence of man as a matter of course, and regard him as, like themselves, a part of the great and beautiful whole.

Charlecote park gate is a lofty stone structure, which seems strangely incongruous with the ragged wooden fence that stretches away from it on either side ; but the incongruity is not uncommon in England. The house itself is noble, quite one's ideal of the stately residence of wealthy gentlemen of Elizabeth's time, and the grounds and gardens are beauti fully laid out in a somewhat formal manner. There is nothing very grand or at all baronial about the place; but to an eye accustomed only to the country houses of "America" it seems, compared with the largest and best of them, almost a palace. It has withal that thoroughly domestic, home-like look which is characteristic of the Englishman's dwelling, unless he is a duke; and even then he is apt to live very little in his Chatsworth, but to pass his really happy days in some less pretentious house, reserving his palace and its expenses for great occasions.

We did not enter Charlecote House. For I had heard that Mr. Lucy, its present owner, did not like to make a show of it; and although I was told that I might obtain a reception there, and how to do so, I preferred to respect what some people would call his whim, and others his surliness, but which seems to me merely a reasonable desire of privacy. If a man has anything beautiful or interesting in his possession, to share its enjoyment with his friends is gracious in him and wise, and, I should think, pleasant too. But many people in such a case speak and act as if strangers had a right to demand the pleasure from him, or at least as if a refusal indicated a selfish and disobliging disposition. It may do so, but in many cases it does not; and among them are those in which the object of interest is a man's own home. Nor does it appear very clear how the fact that in times long past some person about whom your forefather cared very little, and about whom, if you had been in your forefather's place, you would have cared very little yourself, was killed, or killed some one else, or was brought up for discipline in your house, should give people in general a right to expect that you would like to see

them prowling about your habitation or coming into
it. Why should Mr. Lucy be willing to have his home
invaded by staring strangers at times suited to their
convenience, merely because a wild lad, whose father
was a decent yeoman, and who afterward proved to
have the deepest insight of human nature and the
most splendid style that is known to literature, is said
by tradition to have worried and lampooned his ancestor? I cannot see why; and as I had been credibly
informed that he was not willing — although, Shakespeare or no Shakespeare, I should have been glad to
see the inside of so fine and well preserved an old
Tudor mansion — we turned away from Charlecote.

The road over which we passed must have been
often marked by Shakespeare's footsteps in his boyhood. The roadway itself, we may be sure, was not
in such admirable condition. For although there had
been no rain for some days, and a dry wind had
blown, our horse's hoofs and our carriage wheels did
not raise a particle of dust. Like this were all the
country roads that I saw and walked in England,
north, south, and midland.

Erelong we trotted gently in to Stratford. At
once a sense of disappointment fell upon me, which
weighed upon me all the time I was in the place. If
I had not been told that I was in Stratford, I should
not have suspected my whereabouts. It was the
newest-looking, rawest, most uninteresting place
that I had seen since my foot first touched British
soil. Within less than twenty-four hours after I had
landed at Liverpool I was in Chester, a town where
every street and almost every house was interesting;
and I had just come from Canterbury, from Cambridge, and from Oxford, and from rambles among

villages in Essex, in Kent, and in Sussex; and my
expectations in regard to old English towns and villages had perhaps been raised too high. But it was
disheartening to come upon Stratford, about which I
had read so much, and the topography of which I had
studied until I could have gone straight to every
place I wished to see without a guide, and to find it
more like a new "one-horse" town in "America,"
half made by a railway, than any place that I had
seen in England.

The truth is that the Stratford that I knew was
Shakespeare's Stratford; and that has passed away.
Well for Stratford folk it surely is that it has gone
never to return. For in Shakespeare's Stratford his
own father, although alderman, was fined "*quia
sterquinarium fecit*" in front of his house in Henley
Street, as others, his fellow aldermen, also did; and
sterquinaria are things not seemly to the eye, or
pleasant to the nose, nor wholesome withal. But
it was not well for me. With the march of improvement the glory had departed. I should not have
insisted upon the *sterquinaria;* I should have been
well content with old Stratford cleaned and mundi-
fied, swept and garnished. But I *had* looked forward to seeing old Stratford. I had supposed that
this small, insignificant place, out of the line of
travel in the rural heart of England, would be the
least changed of any place upon the island. But I
was to be disappointed. There could not be a clean
Stratford, it seems, without having a new one. I
had looked for a country road, and lanes dignified
with the name of streets; for old timber-and-plaster
houses with peaked gables; for cottages, and trees,
and a village green; for inn and ale house with swing-

ing sign; for humble rustics and comfortable rural
gentlefolk; for a place which, if it had no beauty
(and I expected none), had about it an air of the
antique time and of simple country life. I found
wide streets, paved, with curb-stones,— and these
curbs were a special eyesore to me,—and houses that
looked not unlike those in our older market towns.
No village green was there, no common, such as we
have in old New England villages; but there was a
town hall of startling newness and much pretense.
It was a handsome building enough; but it offended
me by being there at all. And even worse than
these absences and these presences was a smug business look, an air of money-making that would have
delighted Shakespeare, but which offended me. I
felt wronged and robbed by this thrifty, airy, clean,
hard, progressive-looking place. The truth is that
in the stead of old Stratford there is now a successful place of business. It has been found that the
Avon water makes superior beer, and a great brewery
has been set up there, which has enriched, and trans-
mogrified, and ruined the home of Shakespeare.

   We drove to the Falcon inn, and dismissed our fly;
but to our surprise we were told we could not have
rooms; the house was full. I did not care about
the rooms; but it was annoying to find at Stratford
an inn so full that two chance-coming wayfarers
could not be taken in. There was comfort, however,
in the fact that Mrs. Ford was hostess. It was Mrs.
Ford or Mrs. Page, I forget which, and it makes no
matter; she was one of the Merry Wives, and that
at least was something. After a pleasant chat with
this representative of Falstaff's deluder, who bewailed
her inability to receive us, we went to the Shake-

speare Arms. In this house the rooms are not numbered; but with an affectation, perhaps pardonable,
but to me not agreeable, they are called after the
names of Shakespeare's plays. I was lodged in "A
Midsummer Night's Dream," the name of which had
no influence upon my slumbers, and which would better have suited my feeling of disappointment if it had
been "Love's Labor's Lost" or "Much Ado about
Nothing." Here, too, I was haunted by modern progress; for my bedstead was of iron; my bed was a
spring mattress; and, worst of all, my room was lit
with gas. Had I gone through England, living in
Liverpool and Birmingham and London hotels, and
in London lodgings, visiting gentle and simple, to
sleep everywhere else in mahogany four-posters or in
carved canopied bedsteads, and upon soft yet firm
old-fashioned beds, which make going to bed a more
delightful proceeding in England than I ever found
it elsewhere; had I delighted in the darkness visible
which is revealed by one candle, except when I lit my
"dressing candles" (as two extra articles of that
kind are called), to come to Stratford-on-Avon, of all
places, to sleep upon an iron bedstead and a spring
mattress, after undressing in a room that was a blaze
of light until I turned off the gas! It was my first
misfortune of the kind, and it was my last. I turned
to find the stationary washstand and the Croton fau-
cets, with hot water and cold, but this only possible
aggravation of my hard lot, except a bath-room with
gas in it, I was spared.

We first visited the church where Shakespeare was
baptized and buried, of which two facts, almost the
only precisely ascertained and well-authenticated
events of his life, I read the contemporary record in

the old parish register, a parchment folio that looks
outside as if it were one of John a Combe's account
books. I stood over Shakespeare's grave and before
his monument; but even my moderate expectations
of interest were not fulfilled. I was no more impressed than if I were looking at the monument of
some departed Knickerbocker in the church of St.
Mark's in the Bowery. The monument is ugly; the
staring, painted, figure-head-like bust hideous; and
the famous curse engraven upon the tombstone did
not interest me nearly so much when I saw it on the
stone as when I had mused upon it in imagination.

One cause of all this disappointment was the
church itself, which is a fine building, but which
I found lacking in all those rich and sombre effects which had charmed me in other old English
churches. Its exterior is pleasing enough in form;
but it is nearly white, and it looks strangely new.
Inside it almost glares with unmellowed light. And,
to cap the climax of Stratford newness, in this really
venerable Gothic structure, galleries had been put up.
Gas and galleries in Stratford! They go well together. From the moment I saw them Stratford
seemed all gas and galleries. And seriously the introduction of these galleries has destroyed all the
venerable and ecclesiastical air which the building
might otherwise have had. Even this old church
had been made to look like some imitation Gothic
thing put up on contract yesterday by a firm of carpenters and builders.

There, in a corner, is the tomb of Shakespeare's
friend, John a Combe, who lent money on usury, but
who seems nevertheless to have been a good, respectable man. The squibbish epigram upon his death,

ending, "Ho, ho, quoth the devil, 't is my John a Combe," is an adaptation of one that had been written upon some other money-lender before him, and as applied to him is very likely a forgery. But the point of it, I find, is lost upon many persons who do not see the pun, which is made possible by rustic pronunciation. The devil is supposed to say, "'T is my John has come" — ha' come — a-Combe. Wandering among the graves in the church-yard, I found and copied these verses, graven by way of epitaph upon a Mrs. Mary Hands, who died A. D. 1699. The spelling is delightful, and must satisfy the highest aspirations of the most ardent advocate of phonetic spelling reform :—

> " Death creeps Abought on hard
> And steels Abroad on seen
> Hur darts are Suding and her arous keen
> Her stroks are dedly com they soon or late
> When being strook Repentance comes too late
> Deth is a minute ful of suden sorrow
> Then live to day as thou mightst die to morow."

At once, of course, the line in the "Elegy in a Country Churchyard" came to mind, "And teach the rustic moralist to die." There could not be a better example or illustration of the occasion of Gray's poem, which will ever seem as fresh, and as green, as the turf in an English church-yard, which in turn seems as carefully and finely finished as the elegy.

I could not associate Shakespeare at all with this new-looking, bright, staring church in this new-looking, bright, staring town ; but I hoped for the better on Monday, when I expected to see the house in Henley Street, — the birthplace, as it is called ; but there is no certainty as to the place where Shakespeare first opened his eyes upon the world that he was to understand so well and so to fill with great delight. The house is not open to visitors on Sunday; and we therefore strolled down to the banks of the river, from which we were promised some fine eels to our dinner. For the Avon, it seems, is famous for the fatness and fine flavor of its eels. And here, in truth, I found this famous stream better suited for the production of eels than for anything else. In Warwick Park it is beautiful, and as it flows along past Charlecote and by the roadside it is at least a pretty little stream; but here in Stratford it becomes sluggish and sedgy, and is little more than a big ditch. It looks like those little creeks that put up from the sea or the bay into the salt meadows on Long Island or New Jersey, and is as devoid as they are of stimulus to poetic inspiration. Any self-respecting boy-angler in fresh water for perch or pickerel would be sure to shun such a place as an eel-hole. And after all we did not even get our eels. When we returned to dinner, our hostess came wringing her hands like Launcelot Gobbo's cat, and saying that, to her sorrow, of eels she found there were to be had none. They were all taken up to supply the people that filled the other hotel. They must not only have our rooms but our eels. Thus it ever is: did not Rachel have both the love of Leah's husband and her son's mandrakes also? But we did have a delightful sea-coal fire, and a chat by it that lasted far into the night.

The next morning we went to the site of "New Place," which is hard by. What pleasure any lover of Shakespeare can receive by going there I cannot imagine. And this simply because there is nothing there for the lover of Shakespeare to see. On the corner of a hard-paved street, within a grassy inclosure looking wonderfully like " a vacant lot up town," are two or three small trenches, over which is laid wire netting. At the bottom of these trenches are a few stones, which were a part of the foundation of Shakespeare's house. That is all. I must confess that they were of no more interest to me than so many other stones. The connection between them and "King Lear," or its writer, was to me altogether imperceptible. But as I stood there and looked off upon the strong square tower of the Guild Chapel on the opposite corner, I thought all at once that Shakespeare had often stood there looking at it, just as I did, — no, not as I looked, but with his way of looking; and then from the air around the old gray tower came down upon me the only dreamy charm that I knew in Stratford of fancied nearness to him I had come to worship.

The mayor of Stratford, an intelligent gentleman of pleasant manners, was polite enough to show me some of the notable things of the town where he is John Shakespeare's successor ; and he took me to see a portrait of Garrick by Gainsborough. He told me that, unfortunately, it was out of its frame and laid by at present in a private house ; but I was too eager to see a portrait of such a man by such a painter to permit those drawbacks to restrain me. His honor took us to a very respectable-looking old brick house hard by, and we were taken by a very respectable-looking old man, in perfect keeping with his dwelling, up into a large low bed-chamber which had not yet been " readied up " [1] after the night's and early

---

[2] Properly, redd up.

morning's use ; to my gratification, for I prized these opportunities of seeing Mr. and Mrs. John Bull in *déshabille*, and of them I chanced to have many. There was the picture, a full length, upon a large canvas. It was leaning against the wall, not upright, but lengthways, in a somewhat helpless fashion ; for it was too tall to stand up in the room ; where it brought to mind the picture of the Vicar of Wakefield's family. To see it I was obliged to invert myself somewhat into the position of standing on my head. But it repaid me for the contortion. There must have been a great store of outbreaking vitality in that little man ; for every portrait of him shows it, not only in the eyes, but in the mouth, and in the whole carriage of the body ; and if anything can diminish the expression of this trait of character it is sitting for one's portrait. Gainsborough's is rather more placid and serene in expression than any other that I have seen, but the nervous energy is there ; and its slight suppression I suspect that we owe to looking through Gainsborough's eyes. For no portrait painter can present a man as he really is, but only as he sees him.

From here we went to the house in Henley Street, in which, if Shakespeare was not born, he passed his boyhood during the years of his father's prosperity. In going thither we passed through Rother Street. Its name, which it had in Shakespeare's day, shows that it was a place, or the way to a place, where cattle were sold, — the rother market, as it was long called ; *rother* meaning neat cattle. Might not the tradition that Shakespeare's father was a butcher have had its origin in the mere fact that his house was so near this market ? Or was he indeed a butcher, who made his home near the place where he bought his stock in trade? Of all that I saw connected with his memory this house was the most disappointing; and more, it was sad, depressing. The house has been recently "restored," and so destroyed. Its outside has an air of newness that is positively offensive. It looks like a small railway station which some architect, equally ambitious and ignorant, has chosen to design in the old style. All expression of rural antiquity has been scraped, and painted, and roofed, and clapboarded out of it. Were Shakespeare to see it now he might well say, —

> "This is no my ain house;
> I ken by the bigging o' it."

How much better to have left it as it stood twenty-five years ago, merely removing the more modern buildings which had been erected on either side of it!

Within, however, not much of this smoothing over has been done; nor was it possible without destroying all the original features of the house. My heart sank within me as I looked around upon the rude, mean dwelling-place of him who had filled the world with the splendor of his imaginings. It is called a house, and any building intended for a dwelling-place is a house; but the interior of this one is hardly that of a rustic cottage; it is almost that of a hovel, — poverty-stricken, squalid, kennel-like. A house so cheerless and comfortless I had not seen in rural England. The poorest, meanest farm-house that I had ever entered in New England or on Long Island was a more cheerful habitation. And amid these sordid surroundings William Shakespeare grew to early manhood! I thought of stately Charlecote, the

home of the Lucys, who were but simple country
gentlemen ; and then for the first time I knew and
felt from how low a condition of life Shakespeare
had arisen.   For his family were not reduced to this;
they had risen to it.   This was John Shakespeare's
home in the days of his brief prosperity ; and when I
compared it with my memory of Charlecote I knew
that Shakespeare himself must have felt what a sham
was the pretension of gentry set up for his father
when the coat of arms was asked and obtained by the
actor's money from the Heralds' College, — that coat
of arms which Shakespeare prized because it made
him "a gentleman" by birth.   This it was, even
more than the squalid appearance of the place, that
saddened me.   For I felt that Shakespeare himself
must have known how well founded was the protest
of the gentlemen who complained that Clarencieux
had made the man who lived in that house a gentleman of coat armor.   But what an unspeakable gain
to the world was the lowly birth which the son felt
so grievously, and which he sought so artfully to conceal !   If Shakespeare had been born at Charlecote,
he would probably have had a seat in Parliament,
not improbably a peerage ; but we should have had
no plays, — only a few formal poems and sonnets,
most likely, and possibly some essays, with all of
Bacon's wisdom set forth in a style more splendid
than Bacon's, but hardly so incisive.

The upper part of the house, to which you climb
by a little rude stairway that is hardly good enough
for a decent stable, has been turned into a museum
of doubtful relics and gimcracks, and is made as unlike as possible what it must have been when Shakespeare lived there.   There is a book-case containing

the principal editions of his works; but I was not to be placated by seeing that my own was honored by a place among them. Another smaller case is filled with bound volumes of manuscript notes by Mr. Halliwell-Phillips, which were presented by that devoted Shakespeare enthusiast. The case is locked, and it is to remain so, and the books are not to be opened during his life. There is a portrait of Shakespeare, of which much is made. I had heard a great deal of it, and knew it by photographs. On examining it closely, which I was kindly allowed to do, I came to the conclusion that it is a modern performance, painted from the bust and the Droeshout engraving on the title-page of the folio of 1623. There is very little in this museum that is worth attention; but there is one object of some interest. It is a letter written to Shakespeare by Richard Quiney, of Stratford, asking a loan of money. This scrap of paper has the distinction of being the only existing thing, except his will, that we know must have been in Shakespeare's hands. For, as to the Florio Montaigne in the British Museum, notwithstanding the opinion of Sir Frederick Madden, others whose judgment on such a point is worth mine ten times over, think, as I do, that it is a forgery.

I turned away from the house in Henley Street with a sense of disappointment that was almost sickening, and went to drink a glass of Stratford ale in the parlor of the Red-Horse inn, which is associated with the name of Washington Irving. It is a cosy little hostelry; and it was pleasant to see evidences in it of the honor paid to the memory of " Geoffry Crayon."

To Anne Hathaway's cottage at Shottery I went,

taking the path through the fields which Shakespeare took too often for his happiness. There is little to be said about this house, which is merely a thatched cottage of the same grade as the house in Henley Street; — in its original condition, a picturesque object in a landscape, but the lowliest sort of human habitation. I sat upon the settle by the great fireplace, where the wonderful boy of eighteen was ensnared by the woman of twenty-six. And while I talked of other things I thought — I could not help but think — of the toil, the wretchedness, the perplexity, and the shame that were born to him beneath that roof. I was given water to drink from the well in the garden, and flowers, to take away as mementoes. I was tempted to spue the water out upon the ground; and the flowers, if they can be found, any one may have who wants them.

Thus ended my visit to Stratford-on-Avon, where I advise no one to go who would preserve any elevated idea connected with Shakespeare's personality. There is little there to interest and much to dishearten a "passionate pilgrim" to the scenes of the early and the later life of him who is the great glory of our literature. I have heard of a gorgeously, and wonderfully arrayed Western dame who said, in the presence of some friends of mine, to the rector of Stratford church, who was showing her attention, that "she had ben a gooddle around, an' seen a good many places; but, for her part, for a place to live in, she had seen nawthin like Louyville, in Kaintucky." I did not so reward the kind attention of my hosts; and as to "Louyville," my knowledge of it is confined to that derived from this elegant and opportune eulogy. But nevertheless it was with a sense of mingled gloom, and wrong of rightful expectation, that I turned my back upon Stratford-on-Avon. As I drove out of the town, on my way to Kenilworth, the first object that caught my eye was an overloaded rickety wagon feebly drawn by a still more rickety horse, by the side of which tramped a man whom I at once recognized as the hero of the Dutch auction at the Warwick fair; the last was a large sign over a little shop: —

WILLIAM SHAKESPEARE, SHOEMAKER.

A fitting close, I thought, of my pilgrimage. It would have annoyed the "gentleman born" much more than it annoyed me; and for quite another reason. The only place in England which he who is sometimes honored with the name of Shakespeare's Scholar regrets having visited is that where Shakespeare was born and buried.

CHAPTER XXIII.

IN LONDON AGAIN.

RETURNING to London, after wandering in the shires, seemed to me like getting home again. A strange feeling this, it may be said, in one who had lived in the great town only a few weeks, and who had never been in England before. And so, indeed, it seemed to me, at first. But, notwithstanding the vastness of London, it impressed me greatly, and I do not know but chiefly, as a collection of homes. It has little beauty; much of it is dull and dingy; more is commonplace, although it may be neither dull nor dingy. There is very little of it that poses itself before you architecturally and asks for admiration. But the whole of it, outside of "the city" proper, from Belgravia to Bethnal Green, has this home-like look. The very shops in Regent Street and New Bond Street and Oxford Street are more expressive of the sense of human habitation than of that of trade and traffic. In part this is due to the comparative lack of display and of staring sign-boards, and the absence of street railways, in which respects the contrast to New York, and to "American" towns which imitate New York, is very marked. But it seemed to me that this home-like homeliness of London (the strange freaks of language make this qualification and distinction possible and apprehensible) was caused by its gradual growth, and by the perma nence of its not very substantially built houses. Few indeed of these are ancient, or even at all venerable for their age, but a very large proportion of them are old-fashioned. And, as man modifies even the face of nature, all the more has his presence among his own creations and his constant use of them left upon them the impression of his humanity. Even a man's coat and hat, if he wears them long enough, receive the impress of his individuality. Do we not recognize certain integuments, even upon hall tables and hat-trees? Thus generations of Englishmen have left their mark upon the houses of London, which bear upon their outsides the character of their inmates. The brain has given form and expression to the dome which is its workshop and dwelling-place.

There are nevertheless parts of London which are not without a likeness to some parts of New York and to some parts of Philadelphia, and a stronger likeness to certain parts of Boston. Edgeware Road and much of Oxford Street are very like the Sixth Avenue and the Third Avenue in New York. Give the houses in Edgeware Road, instead of their tawny, dingy outsides, walls of bright red brick, put a street railway in it, and a New Yorker carried to it on Aladdin's carpet might easily believe that he was in some part of Sixth Avenue with which he was not familiar. At least, so I thought; but, alas, this was before Sixth Avenue was traversed from end to end in mid-air by that monstrous contrivance for the confiscation of the property of many people for the convenience, or rather the pleasure and the profit, of some others, — the Elevated Railway. This abomination, in addition to the other injuries which it inflicts, gives to the many miles of New York streets through which

it runs, darkening and deforming them, a hideous unlikeness to the public highways in any other town in
the world.

Some parts of Oxford Street also have the same
sort of likeness to the second and third rate streets
of New York before the imposition of the elevated
railways. There is the same mingling of dwelling-
house and shop; a like inferior style of building; a
display in the shop windows somewhat like that which
is made in our shop-lined avenues, and quite unlike
the modest reserve which prevails in Regent Street,
St. James's, New Bond Street, and Piccadilly. The
resemblance which I have pointed out is greatly
helped by the fact that Edgeware Road and the upper part of Oxford Street are nearly straight, — the
straightest streets of any length that I saw in London, where the great thoroughfares, as well as the
small, wind this way and that in the easiest and most
natural manner possible. Only in Boston and in the
very oldest part of New York have we anything like
this natural irregularity.

In London, and in most other towns in England,
streets are passage-ways between houses; and the line
of the street was originally determined by the position of the houses, and still remains so in a great
measure. With us a street is regarded, or at least
seems to be regarded, merely as the directest possible
passage-way from one point to another, along which
houses have been allowed to be built. In the one
case, an idea of stability has governed; in the other,
an idea of movement.

There is, however, in this no indication of a difference of character between the people who built London and those who built New York and Philadelphia.

The unlikeness is produced simply by the fact that the newer and larger parts of the latter places were laid out, projected, and that the whole of the former slowly grew. When London was to be rebuilt, after the great fire (1666), in the plan proposed by a very eminent Englishman, Sir Christopher Wren, and approved by many other eminent Englishmen, including the king, the streets were all as straight as they could be drawn by rule; and the adoption of this plan was defeated only by the difficulty of settling the question of property in the land. The consequence was that the houses were rebuilt upon the old plots of land; the final result being the retention of the old irregularity of the streets.

Oxford Street, which I have mentioned, is a very characteristic example of another peculiarity of London streets. It is the longest, broadest, and in a certain sense the most important thoroughfare in London. The road begins just out of Cock Lane, a little street made famous by the Cock Lane Ghost. But here it is called Holborn, or at first Holborn Hill. It is, however, really the continuation of a great street, which runs very directly through London, from east to west, and which is called successively, beginning at the east, Mile End, Whitechapel Road, Aldgate High Street, Leadenhall Street, Cornhill, Cheapside, Newgate Street, Skinner Street, Holborn, Oxford Street. It is difficult to discover where these several divisions begin and end. There is no apparent cause for division. The road is continuous. It is as if Broadway had half a dozen names between the Bowling Green and Thirty-Fourth Street. The difference is caused merely by the great London thoroughfare's retention of the names which its different parts received from time to time in past centuries; while Broadway never had any name but that which it received at its starting-point.[1] It has shot three or four miles into infinite space within the memory of living men.

Although I found in London very much less of apparent antiquity than I had expected (and indeed it was so in most other towns that I saw in England), its general unlikeness to towns in the United States is striking, and is very much greater at the present day than it reasonably should be. It should seem that if Brown, Jones, and Robinson, whether British subjects or citizens of the United States, were to build themselves houses, whether in one place or another, under like influences of climate and habits of life, the result on the whole would be very much alike. And indeed it once was so. The New York of fifty years ago was very much like what a great part of London is now. An examination of old street views in New York will justify this remark. The lower part of Broadway, Beekman Street, Pearl Street, Greenwich Street, and the cross-streets below Canal Street, were then filled with houses which in form, in expression, and in everything except color were just like thousands of houses that make up now the better part of London west of Charing Cross. In London these houses have been allowed to stand. In New York they have been taken down, to give place to others more profitable. The conditions of property in houses and land in the

[1] This is not exactly true. One hundred years ago, that little part of this great dividing thoroughfare which stretched beyond the site of the City Hall was called Great George Street. But it retained this name for so short a time that the assertion above is correct, to all intents and purposes.

two countries are so different that they affect the
plans of owners and the stability of brick walls.
The only question here is, whether an increase of
rent can be obtained by "tearing down" and re-
building; the result of which is that not only has
the greater part of Wall Street been rebuilt twice
within thirty years, but that beautiful and substantial
houses in Fourteenth Street and on Union Square,
and in other new parts of New York, not twenty-five
years old, have been pulled down, within the last
three or four years, with as little remorse as if they
were so many old hen-coops. In England there is
no such indifference to dilapidation. There they
cannot afford it; and indeed real property is so tied
up there that houses cannot be shifted and scattered
about as they are here. The consequence is a feeling of hesitation about destroying a house. In this
there may be some inconvenience; but the general
result is not altogether unadmirable.

Crosby Hall is a witness (although the example
is an extreme one) of this unwillingness to destroy
substantial old houses by way of improvement. The
name of this building is known to all readers of
Shakespeare's "Richard III." Richard, while Duke
of Gloster, makes three appointments there. The
house was built between 1466 and 1470 by Sir John
Crosby, who was a grocer, an alderman, and a member of Parliament. It was therefore in the first gloss
of its newness in Richard's time, and is now about
four hundred and ten years old. I knew something
of its beauty and its history, and it was one of the
buildings in London that I was curious to see; but
the way in which I saw it was most unexpected, and
in effect quite ludicrous. I took my luncheon there,

one day, with some dozen or score other chance feed-
ers. This knightly residence is now a common eating-house, chiefly frequented by commercial people.
It is in Bishopsgate Street, not far from the Bank
and the Exchange, and, like many other places of
note in London and in England, is quite withdrawn
from general sight. It stands in a little court, and is
hidden by houses and shops. As it is said to be the
only remnant of the ancient domestic architecture of
London, it is a building of peculiar interest. And
certainly, if knightly grocers and aldermen customa-
rily had such houses for their dwelling-places, they
were magnificently lodged.

The hall, which was the principal room of the
house, and served as dining, drawing, and dancing
room, is some fifty or sixty feet in length, about
thirty feet wide, and the ceiling, or rather roof,
which is of oak, seems to be fifty feet high, but is, I
believe, somewhat less. It is lighted from the upper
part on both sides by arched windows, exceedingly
beautiful, and of marked simplicity of design; and
there is an oriel window so charming to the eye in
its proportions and its detail that it alone is worth
a visit. Two or three other rooms remain, not quite
so large, and not nearly so lofty, but in the same
noble style. This building seems to have come
into the possession of the crown about a hundred
years after its erection, for it was used in Queen
Elizabeth's time for the reception of ambassadors.
Since then it has passed through many changes. At
one time it was a dissenting chapel; then it was used
for public meetings, and for lectures and concerts.
But for none of these was it very convenient, and,
being useless, it was deserted. Nevertheless, it was not

"torn down," as if it had been, for example, John Hancock's house, but was allowed to stand, and at last was made an eating-house; and now hungry and thirsty trading Britons eat their chops and soles and drink their beer and port wine in the very hall where Plantagenet and Tudor monarchs held their state.

Ignorant of this, I was with a commercial friend at the hour of the midday meal, and he proposed luncheon, adding, "Let 's go to Crosby Hall." I did not quite apprehend his meaning. It was much as if he had proposed to me to take luncheon with him in Stonehenge or John o'Groat's house. But we went, and although I enjoyed the beauty of the place I also enjoyed my luncheon ; and the only result of my long-expected yet chance visit to this centre of Shakespearean and historical association was a brief memorandum in my pocket-book, thus : " October 20th. Luncheon with M. at Crosby Hall. Windows. Beautiful old marble fire-place, carved corners, unlike, used as a sink. Twelve she-waiters, — all skinny."

The last somewhat irreverent and ungallant remark records a fact worthy of special note. I have before remarked that among the many absurd notions which prevail about the people in the Old England and those in the New, not one is more unfounded and absurd than that which assigns full figures to the women of. the former and spare figures to those of the latter. It seemed to me, on the contrary, that, although I saw more obese old women in England than I was quite accustomed to, I found there notably more slight figures, pinched features, and pale faces among the women who were between eighteen and thirty-five years old than I had ever seen before; and this my Crosby Hall observation confirmed. It is, however, probable that there is no excess on either side : it is not reasonable that there should be. Why, then, those malicious caricatures, to which I have referred before, drawn by the nearest neighbors of our British cousins, the French, who see much more of them than we do, and who always represent the Englishwoman as "slab-sided" and bony, with limp, artificial side-curls, and projecting upper teeth?

On this same day I went to Guildhall, where Fortune favored me, as she often did in England. The building itself is a strange architectural medley. It was originally built in 1411 ; but almost all of it, except the walls and the crypt, was destroyed in the great fire of 1666, and the subsequent restorations and additions are poor in themselves and incongruous. The great hall, however, has the grandeur which, in architecture, is always given, in a certain degree, by size : it is one hundred and fifty feet long. The building has its name from the fact that it was erected by the united efforts of the various guilds of the city, — associations, or rather trading and social institutions, of which the very germ seems not to have crossed the ocean. We have nothing with which to compare them, or which will help to give any idea of them. Notwithstanding the changes that have taken place in society and in trade, they still exist as highly respectable and influential bodies ; and although their visible function seems to the outside world limited chiefly to the performance of their annual dinners, — a heavy task, — they do much to preserve the civic dignity and trade stability of the British metropolis.

Guildhall is the City Hall of London, and is a sort of state palace for the Lord Mayor; but it is also a place of meeting for the citizens, which our city halls are not. Like them, however, it is surrounded with courts of a minor grade, and within it some higher courts sometimes sit. The great hall contains a few statues. Among them, is one of William Pitt, and, if I remember rightly, one of Lord Chatham. They did not impress me as being of a high order of sculpture. Two other statues, or effigies, raised on high, adorned the place, — those known as Gog and Magog. I expected, of course, to see something grotesque in these famous figures; but I was not prepared for quite such an exhibition of colossal puerility. These absurd monsters look like painted and gilded toys, made to please the boys of Brobdignag. Words can hardly express their gigantic childishness. Why they are retained in their present position, and how they ever came there, seem to be beyond conjecture. They have not even the glamour of antiquity upon them; for they are, or the originals were, the production of the seventeenth century; and yet, with this recent origin, their history and purpose seem to be entirely lost. No one, not even the city antiquaries, can tell anything about them, except that these present figures were made in the last century to replace others that were worn out by being carried in Lord Mayors' shows. They stand there, wonderful and ridiculous witnesses to the immobility of British Philistinism.

There is an open space before the miserable front which Guildhall presents to the world, and this, as I approached it, was swarming with flocks of pigeons, which alternately swept down upon the ground and rose into the air. It was strange and pretty to see this multitude of gentle, winged creatures in the very heart of London. They are not always visible, I was told; but like Gog and Magog they were an "institution." They brought at once to mind the flocks that Hilda watches from her tower window, in Hawthorne's Roman romance. But not only the pigeons favored me. There was a little crowd before the hall, and some commotion; the reason of which proved to be that on that day the Lord Mayor visited the place officially. He was just coming out, and I saw him ascend his great, yellow, gilded coach, in which was a man wearing an enormous fur cap, which made him look like that domestic instrument whilom used for washing windows, called a pope's-head. A huge straight sword was thrust out of one of the windows of the carriage. The coach started, and a tall footman in a gorgeous light blue livery sprang after it, and, mounting it as it moved, took his place beside another being of like splendor, and his "lordship" was driven off. It seemed to me that a man of any sense would be very glad to get out of such a vehicular gimcrack as that, and to rid himself of such a preposterous companion as the man with the pope's-head. I wondered how they could sit in the coach and look at each other without laughing. Nothing could be more out of place, more incongruous, than this childish masquerading seemed to be with English common sense, and with the sobriety and true dignity befitting such an official person as the mayor of the city of London. But I was told that the people of London rather insist upon this puerile pageantry; and that the attempt of some previous Lord Mayors to mitigate the monstrosity of the "Lord Mayor's show" (although it is of very modern origin) was received with disfavor, and had sensibly diminished their popularity.

The number of statues and of monuments of which statues form a part is great in London. It could hardly be otherwise in the capital of a country with such a history as England's. Although few of these command much admiration as works of art, I found most of them interesting, not only on account of their associations, but as witnesses to the grateful memory in which the English people hold those who have served the country successfully, or only faithfully. Westward of Charing Cross one can hardly walk a quarter of a mile without seeing a monumental statue. Nor are only great statesmen and captains thus honored. It was a pleasing sight to see in St. James's Street a monument to the private soldiers who fell in the Crimean war. It has three typical figures of private soldiers in the uniforms of various arms of the service. And there is a monument to the Westminster scholars who fell in the same war, which is now generally admitted to have been a gigantic British blunder. But, right or wrong, Britannia never forgets those who faithfully do her bidding.

Two statues in South Kensington impressed me strongly. They are very unlike. One is that of a man of mature years, seated. He wears a robe, and on his head a kind of bonnet, something like the cap of a Doge of Venice. I was struck by the strength and the sagacity of the face, and perhaps even more by a certain expression, which, notwithstanding its unmistakable Oriental character, awoke in me a feeling of kindred quite unlike that with which I ever looked into any Hebrew or other Semitic face, either in life or in art, not to say any face of Mongol or other Turanian race. I did not know who it was, nor did I know that there was in London a statue of Sir Jamsetjee Jeejeebhoy; and yet as I drew near I felt that it must be he, as I soon found that it was, by the inscription. I had learned, from friends who had known the great Parsee merchant in India, to honor him for his sagacity, for his public spirit, and for a large and sweet benevolence which we, in our religious arrogance, would have Christian. But in true philanthropy few Christians have equaled, and none known to me have ever surpassed, this fire-worshiper. The pleasure with which I looked upon his face was enhanced by the intuitive recognition in its lineaments, before I knew whose they were, of an inexpressible something that told of his Aryan origin. And yet this may possibly have been given to him by the English sculptor. The imparting of such subtle traits is an unconscious process, which takes place even beyond the bounds of legitimate art. I remember seeing the colored photograph of a young New York lady which was taken in Switzerland, to which the Teutonic manipulator had managed to impart, it was impossible to say how or wherein, a German look that was quite ludicrous.

The other statue was the Eagle Slayer, which I thought worthy of a reputation which, so far as I know, it has not attained. It represents a young man who has just launched from his bow an arrow at the soaring bird. The lithe and supple figure — a fine embodiment of the forms of youthful manly beauty — seems as if it were bounding into the air with eagerness. The archer has shot not only his shaft, but his whole soul into the air. He wings his arrow with his breath; and yet there is that quietness about it, that instantaneous arrest of movement, which is one characteristic trait of the highest type of Greek sculpture. I saw no modern statue in England quite equal to this one, of which I had never heard. And yet I should speak of it with some reserve, for I saw it but once.

Of all the statues and monuments that I saw in London, the most ambitious was that which pleased me least. I mean the Albert monument in Hyde Park. Its first suggestion is the unfortunate question, Why should such a monument have been erected to such a man? Prince Albert was an honorable, prudent, kind-hearted, and accomplished gentleman. As princes go, he was certainly a very superior person; so that we can forgive his being just the least bit priggish, as his biography by Mr. Theodore Martin reveals him to us. But the biography and the monument both seem to be quite out of proportion to the merits of their subject. If the Prince had united the genius of Napoleon to the virtues of Washington, there might, with more show of reason, have been such a literary and such a sculptured monument raised to him so soon after the close of his blameless and useful life. But even then something more simple and sober would have been more fitting than this gilded, enthroned, enshrined, and canopied effigy of the demi-god of commonplace. In fact, this is the most obtrusively offensive monument in London. The Wellington statue on Hyde Park corner is ridiculous, but the Albert monument is ostentatiously vulgar.

At St. Saviour's church I was more impressed than anywhere else in London by the bringing together of

the dead past and the living present and by their incongruity. This church is a mere remnant — only
one transept, I believe — of the old priory church of
St. Mary Overy, which was built in the early part of
the thirteenth century, that golden age of ecclesiastical architecture. It stands near the Southwark end
of London Bridge. In it are some old monumental
tombs and slabs, at which I looked with interest.
Here is the tomb of John Gower, who atoned somewhat for his poetry by contributing largely to the
repairing of this beautiful church, in which his effigy,
painted after nature, lies enshrined above his grave.
Here is John Fletcher's grave, and Philip Massinger's; and here, too, is the grave of one Edmund
Shakespeare, an actor, who had a brother named William, also an actor; and he, Mr. John Spedding says,
wrought with John Fletcher on his play, "The Two
Noble Kinsmen." I had stood a minute or two before the stones that bore these names, and had moved
away, and was musing in the gloom over the effigy
of an unknown knight in chain armor and a cylin-
drical helmet, which lay with crossed legs almost upon
the very floor, when I was startled by the sharp whistle and the rumble of a railway train, which seemed
almost to be directly overhead. And indeed the
knight, whose good sword has been rust and whose
body has been dust for nearly five hundred years, is
lying very "convenient" to the station of the Southeastern Railway, on which, if he would but arise, he
might start for Palestine, and be there in fewer days
than it took him months to go, — if indeed he went.
For the notion that the crossed legs of an effigy indicate a crusader is, I believe, abandoned, as one of
those many bubble theories which self-deluding sci-

35

ence painfully blows up and admires, and then explodes only by blowing a little longer.

I went deliberately to Bolt Court for the sake of Dr. Johnson, who lived there in a house which is still standing. It is, I believe, the only memorial of him now existing. There is nothing at all uncommon about the place or the house; and it is chiefly remarkable because of its unlikeness to what any one not familiar with old London would expect to see. When we read of Johnson's house in Bolt Court, although we do not think of the doctor as living in any state, we do not imagine a little place like a flagged yard, entered through a dark, narrow alley, and in which we should expect to see clothes drying on the lines. But such is Bolt Court, on which look a few houses with fronts that seem as if they ought to be their backs. That which was Dr. Johnson's is a respectable brick building of three stories, in the plain, domestic style of the last century. Bolt Court is a representative place, — an example of those nooks and secluded recesses found in the towns all over England, and even in London, which are open to the public and frequented daily by many people, and which yet are so withdrawn from the public eye that by those who do not know of them, and where they are, their existence would never be suspected.

Wapping is a neighborhood of which many persons know the name, but nothing more. It is preserved from decay by an odor of tar and pitch in the song, " Wapping Old Stairs," of which some of my readers may be glad to see the first stanza; whereby they may remark how homely, and not only homely but tame and coarse and commonplace, are the folk-songs of Britain : —

"Your Molly has never been false, she declares,
  Since last time we parted at Wapping Old Stairs,
  When I swore that I still would continue the same,
  And gave you the 'bacco box marked with my name.
  When I passed a whole fortnight between decks with you,
  Did I e'er give a kiss, Tom, to one of your crew ?
  To be useful and kind with my Thomas I stayed ;
  For his trowsers I washed, and his grog, too, I made."

Wapping, too, may be remembered as having afforded
an important link in the chain of evidence against the
notorious impostor who claimed the Tichborne estate.
Immediately on his arrival at London he went to
Wapping (which Roger Tichborne would never have
done), and there he was recognized as a former resident of the place.   Wapping is a narrow strip of old
London, which lies below the Tower and between
London docks and the river.   It is, as might be expected, wholly occupied by mariners, or those who
supply their wants.   It is very damp and very dingy,
and everybody in it seems to smell of oakum.   The
"stairs" mentioned in the song (which, by the way,
is not very old, — only of the last century) are the
steps by which people descended to the river and took
boat in the days of wherries and London watermen,
when the river was the principal highway between
London and Westminster.   There were Whitehall
Stairs and many others, the names of which I do not
now remember.   Some of these stairs were of marble, with an arched and pillared gateway.   They have
disappeared only within the last half century, and
I believe one of them still remains.   As I walked
through Wapping, I saw on a dingy little card, in a
dingy little window, "Soup 1d. A good dinner 4d.
and 5d."   Comfortable words ; but as I did not visit
Wapping to dine I did not go in, and so saved my
fourpence.   And who knows but I might have been

tempted into the extravagance of the extra penny! As there was no longer a wherry to be had at Wapping Stairs, — which, if I could have had it, I should certainly have taken, — I took one of the small steamers at London Bridge, and came back that way. But I had some compensation. On the boat was a little band of minstrels, who were allowed to play for the few pence they could get. There was a fiddle, a flute, and a harp; and the harpist, although his instrument was very primitive in structure, did not quite succeed in making me understand (what I have never been altogether able to understand) how it was that harp-playing could charm away Saul's melancholy. But their music was not very bad, and mingled not unpleasantly with the plash of the boat, as we glided by the old wharves and the Thames Embankment. Euterpe had not watched carefully over these her poor votaries, who were sadly neglected and forlorn. Their clothes had plainly been worn out by predecessors in their occupancy, and had never fitted them; and they were shiny and drawn into rucks. Their trousers were darned at the knees with thread not so exactly of the color of the cloth as a punctilious tailor might have desired. And yet their shoes, although in one case tied with twine, were well blackened, and they wore chimney-pot hats; battered, indeed, and smoothed out and washed into a ghostly and sorrowful likeness to the real thing; but still they were chimney-pots. I remarked that well-blackened shoes and a chimney-pot hat seemed to be regarded by English people in their condition of life as the first steps toward respectability in dress, — the *sine qua nons* of elegant costume.

When the time had come for collecting contribu

tions, and the flute was going round, hat in hand, I
spoke to the violin, who did not resent my intrusion.
I asked him if they did well on the boats. "Purty
well, sir, thank 'e, — purty well, as things goes. But
music is n't 'preciated now as 't use t' be; 'r else
Hi should n't be 'ere." "No, indeed; you 're something of a musician, I should say." "Somethink!"
— a pause of admiring consciousness. "Wy, sir, *Hi*
'ave played in a band, — in horchesters. Hi've played
in gentlemen's 'ouses; heven in Russell Square, wen
they give their parties, — vile-in, flute, piannah," —
I expected him to add cornet, sackbut, psaltery, and
all kinds of music, but he disappointed me, and only
said, "hanythink;" and he accompanied the mention
of each of his many accomplishments with a gentle
and gracious wave of his bow. "Ah, yes, I see how
it is; and your friend, the flute-player there, I suppose, is a fair musician, too." "No p'ticler friend o'
mine, sir. Business, business. No great musician,
'ither, sir." Here he mused a moment. "Plays
well enough, but no feeling," — a slight deprecatory
shake of the head, — "no sentiment; an'" — with a
nod of conviction — "sentiment 's the thing in music,
sir." The flute-player had made his round; and just
at the hither end of his circle a gentleman dropped a
fourpence into his hat, which he then presented to a
lady and a lad sitting next the gentleman, when suddenly, with gracious flourish of the battered head
covering, he said, politely, "Beg pawdon, sir, — beg
pawdon. Same pahty, I see."

We in the United States lose a great deal by having none but foreigners in positions like this. Our
relations with those in the humbler walks of life are
always with Germans, Irish, Italians, or, most rarely,

French.   Our street musicians, for example, are invariably Germans or Italians.   And thus our sympathies are narrowed and limited, and our sight of life is all along one plane.   One of the charms of England is that you are cheerfully served by Englishmen and Englishwomen ; that from morning to night you look only into English faces, and hear your own language spoken without a brogue or a break.

I was not present as a guest at a wedding while I was in England.   None of my acquaintances assumed the bonds while I was there ; and although I am sure that some of my fair friends would have willingly been married to the right man, to please me, none of them were, and therefore I did not see that show. But I am inclined to think that I lost very little.   A wedding in itself has no attraction for a man ; and the difference between a wedding in England and one in "America" can be very slight among people of a like condition in life and of the same faith.   However, I saw one marriage ceremony.   It was at the church of St. Martin's-in-the-Fields.   The church was open as I passed, and suspecting, from a little crowd of limp, draggled girls about the door, what was going on, I went in.   The parties were of the lower-middle class.   It was just like a marriage in one of our churches, except that there was but one groomsman, or best man, and that there were none of those ridiculous "ushers," who have lately been added to the other painful impediments of the occasion.   White wedding favors were worn ; and except these trifling points I observed in the mere ceremony no peculiarity to distinguish the occasion from a similar one here among similar people.   But the bride and the two bridesmaids were pale, thin young women, and

the bridegroom was a little London "gent." In all
the wedding party there was not one fine, blooming
girl, nor one tall, well-made man. But there was
one very fat old woman. They got into three carriages at the door, and drove sadly off, as became
the occasion, without the throwing of a single shoe,
at which I was somewhat disappointed.

In this church there was a pew-opener, whose appearance and whose performance of his duty were remarkable. His function — unknown to us — is commonly committed in England to old women; but here
it was performed by a dwarfish man, the top of whose
big, half-bald head was hardly so high as the sides
of the pews. He would take intending worshipers
up the aisle, the shining top of his head rising and
falling gently along the line of the pews, open the
pew-door, usher them in with a bow, and then shut
the door with a flourish of his hand in the air, above
his head, that suggested the idea that he was drowning, and about to disappear for the last time. And
once I saw him bring down his hand, and, with an
extra flourish, pass it deftly across his nose in the
quality of what used to be called a muck-ender, until
we English-blooded people gave it a French name.
It was a very dexterous and somewhat astonishing
performance.

Funerals I saw, but also from the outside. And
indeed these occasions are much more private in England than they are with us. There is rarely such
a general attendance of friends and acquaintances
as crowds our houses of mourning, and even our
churches, with an elegantly dressed throng of sympathy and curiosity. There are the immediate family,
half a dozen very intimate friends, the pall-bearers,

the solicitor, perhaps the medical man (*finis coronat opus*), a few mourning coaches; and that is all. The mourning coaches are not mere ordinary coaches occupied by mourners; and, indeed, they are frequently quite empty. They are large, portly vehicles, covered with some black, dull-surfaced material like cloth, and are, in fact, coaches put into mourning. The harness and the horse-cloths are black, and coachman and footman are also in black, with weeds on their hats. At the death of any person of condition the event is announced to the world at large by the display of a hatchment on the front of the house, generally between two of the windows on the first floor, — that is, the first floor above the ground floor, the second story. These hatchments are of white cloth, are about four feet square, and have a black border. Upon them are blazoned the armorial bearings of the deceased person. One morning, on one of the squares, I saw three houses with these funereal decorations, on one of which the lozenge-shaped shield and the absence of a crest told that it was a lady, probably the mistress of the house, who had departed. I cannot say that this fashion impressed me favorably. These hatchments seemed to be signs of a show going on within the house. They looked like unilluminated transparencies; and suggested a brass band.

Among my great pleasures at the Garrick Club was the sight of the large and very interesting collection of dramatic portraits that has accumulated there in the course of many years. Thither almost everything fine of this sort has gravitated lately, as if by the operation of natural law. There were portraits of actors and actresses of the past and of the present, portraits in character and portraits out of character. There was the whole series of portraits in water-colors which were engraved for the fine edition of "Bell's British Theatre." Among the old ones were two of Peg Woffington, in which she did not appear so beautiful as I had expected to find her. But that was Charles Reade's fault. I should not have been disappointed, had I not fallen in love with his heroine ; and yet there he stood quite unrepentant. But all Peg's possibilities, and some of her actualities, were written in her face. She must have been a most alluring creature. There, too, was a portrait of Mrs. Robinson as Rosalind. She is standing, and is evidently in one of the forest scenes. Yet this is her costume: powdered hair, a voluminous high white cravat that swathes her whole neck, furs, and a blue surtout coat decorated with a bow. Nevertheless she is charming ; for her figure is fine, so much of it as can be seen, and her face has some beauty and much character. Her audiences were accustomed to her costume, and therefore to them its incorrectness was of no account; and it seemed to me as if, with that face and her art, she could make even us modern folk forget it.

One day I was attracted — I can hardly tell why, for the sight is not uncommon in London — by seeing a very handsome coroneted carriage, in which sat a little, ugly, wizened, peevish, middle-aged woman, dressed richly but not well. The horses were magnificent ; the coachman would have done honor to a bishop's wig ; and the footman was as fine a young man as one could wish to see ; and I could not but think how absurd it was, and what a shame, that four such splendid animals as those should be put to the use of carrying about such an insignificant creature as their mistress.   But indeed one does not have to cross the ocean for that absurdity ; we may see it almost every day at home.

CHAPTER XXIV.

THE recollections of my observation of England and its people which are recorded in the present chapter are very heterogeneous; and it might perhaps have been well to distribute most of them under appropriate headings. But I do not profess to treat my subject either with unvarying method or exhaustively; nor do I believe that anything would be gained by so doing. Those of my readers who can be thoughtful without being precise — and for such I write — will, I hope, not be repelled by the desultory character of these memories.

Among the minor material traits of England, none seemed to me more peculiar and characteristic than the many by-ways there and short cuts of common use through places that appeared to be closed to the public, and with us would be so. There is one of these in London, near the Albany, which goes right through a great block of houses. It is made of planks, and has a hand-rail. It brings one out into a little lane where there are shops which, one would think, might as well, so far as buying and selling was concerned, have been in the dome of St. Paul's or the Queen's drawing-room. But the people knew their business, and the shops would not have been there if they had had no customers. I used this by-way frequently; and one Thursday morning, when I was out early, in the midst of the Bulgarian horror time, I saw in the window of one of these little shops the " Punch " of the week. The cartoon was that one of Mr. John Tenniel's which shows Mr. Disraeli reclining in the wrappings of a bather, while Mr. Gladstone (who had then been making some very effective and disturbing speeches) approaches him as a sable attendant with coffee, and asks, " How did you like your Turkish bath, sir?" and the Hebrew prime minister replies, " Pretty well ; only you made it so confounded hot for me." I looked at it, and was turning away with a smile, when a young fellow in his shirt-sleeves, who was taking down the shutters of the next shop, caught my eye, and, smiling in turn, said, " Makes it rather hard for Dizzy, sir." We enjoyed the fun together for a passing moment, and then parted with " Good-morning." It was another pleasing manifestation of that freedom of intercourse and mutual good-feeling among strangers of all classes in England which I have mentioned before. In New York the man would have gone silently about his business, without volunteering the remark which opened my day and his with a bright, warm little ray of common pleasure. Indeed, a man so engaged in New York would hardly have been apt to appreciate and enjoy such a caricature, and would probably have taken no notice of me.

It needs hardly be said that in London I visited the South Kensington Museum more than once ; but I shall not undertake the superfluous task of describing this wilderness of treasures of art and of science. I remember, however, a few objects there which are of very general interest. There I saw Galileo's telescope, by means of which he discovered, in the year

1601, the moons of Jupiter and the spots on the sun. It is only about a yard long ; and the object-glass, now badly cracked, through which he saw these wonders, is but two inches in diameter — smaller than those through which many a dandy nowadays observes *his* star upon the stage. This instrument had been presented by Viviani to Leopold de Medici. There also was Newton's telescope, the first "reflector" which he invented and made with his own hand in 1671. It is only about one foot long, and is worked on a ball-and-socket joint, of wood. Two ungainly machines, looking like a cross between an old-fashioned fire-engine and a modern kitchen range, were George Stephenson's locomotive engines, "Puffing Billy" and "Rocket," which made it "vara bod for the coo," and the latter of which had its name because it could go at the rate of thirty miles an hour ! [1]

Very interesting, too, were the old standard measures of our forefathers, which are gathered together in a large case. There are the standard Winchester bushel, and the standard gallon of Henry VII.'s time, A. D. 1487 ; the gallon, quart, and pint of Queen Elizabeth's day, A. D. 1601; and the gallon, quart, and pint of William II.'s time, A. D. 1700. The measures, which are of copper, are remarkable for their size, the capacities of all of them being much greater than those of measures of the same name in these days, — certainly degenerate in this respect. It is remarkable that measures, unlike men, instead

[1] Some of my readers may not have heard how Stephenson, a north of England man, was asked by a peer, on a committee of inquiry into the feasibility of his proposed railways, if it would not be very bad if a cow got on the track before the engine. "Vara bod for the coo, my lord," was the prompt reply.

of growing larger as they grow older, diminish steadily in size with advancing years. Those of William's time were larger than ours, but much smaller than those of Elizabeth's; while hers were much smaller than those of Henry VII.'s. Largest of all was one that was dated fifty years earlier, A. D. 1437. It seemed that if we could go back far enough we should find a gallon, or certainly a bushel, as big as a bathing-tub. This diminution in size is a witness to the rapacity of traders, who gradually shrunk the measures by which they sold. And indeed has not our "bushel basket" dwindled away within the memory of living householders, until it now contains less than three pecks? Established standards seem unable to resist the compressing force of greed.

I have not been unready to speak of the manifold comforts of England, nor I believe half-hearted in doing so; but I passed one morning of characteristic discomfort there which I never shall forget. On my second visit to Birmingham I was at the Queen's Hotel for one night only, and was going to leave town by the midday train. I awoke ailing and in pain, to find that a cold fog had settled upon the place. Looking from my bedroom window at nine o'clock, I might have supposed myself on the banks of Newfoundland, but for the rays of a few street lamps faintly struggling through the watery gloom, across which, from time to time, flitted a phantom artisan or shop-girl on the way to work. It was only the 24th of October; but the cold went to my heart with a curdling chill that I had never felt before, even in a January northwester, with the mercury near zero. I dressed hastily, shuddering at the touch of cold water, and went to the coffee-room. It was as cheerless as the Mammoth Cave, — as damp, and almost as dark. There I breakfasted in the depressing vicinity of seven muffin-eating, Times-reading, commercial Britons. Their appetites were disgusting; their stolid calmness an offense. I took a chair by the hearth, where a chilly little fire was smouldering in the biggest, blackest grate I ever saw. The heat from it was imperceptible eighteen inches off. Again I doubted if fire was ever hot in England. I went down-stairs to pay my bill, and to make the brief preparations necessary just before departure. There was no parlor, no waiting-room, not even a chair; and there I sat in a small passage-way, in the midst of disorderly heaps of luggage, on a cold, hard bench, with damp draughts pouring in upon me from all quarters. I think I was never more thoroughly wretched in my life than in this great hotel, the best in Birmingham; and I then thought how differently such things were managed among us Yankees, where under such circumstances a degree of comfort is yet attainable by every one which in England is rarely to be had except by those who have their own private parlors and their own servants. Comfort came to me in the shape of a Birmingham friend, who gave me that care and attention which I found Englishmen always ready to bestow; and once on the railway the world soon brightened; for in fifteen minutes we steamed out of the fog, and left murky misery behind us. I shall ever remember the kindness, not only of that friend, in whose house I should have been but for the upturning consequent upon repairs, and as tenderly cared for as the wife wrapped in morell's skin, but the kindness also of a good apothecary to whom I went to make a small purchase, and who, learning that I was a stranger in Birmingham and ill, had me at once up into his private parlor, and waited upon me, he and his servant, as if I had been left in his charge, with twopence, by the good Samaritan ; for he refused all recompense except my thanks and the price of the trifle I had come for. This was the sort of surly Englishman that I found all over England.

I was surprised at the free-thinking and the free-speaking which I met with among English clergymen. Opinions as to the inspiration and the authority of the Bible, which not many years ago would have excited horror among all decent people, were expressed in private conversation by some of these gentlemen in orders with an astonishing absence of reserve. And the freedom of the thinking and of the speech seemed to me just in proportion to the intelligence and the scholarship of the speaker. One of these reverend gentlemen (and in England the title "reverend" is strictly applicable only to clergymen of the Established Church), who was also a college don and a scholar of repute, said to me, as we were discussing the value of the "Speaker's Commentary," "I wish that every one of those men [the eminent divines and church dignitaries engaged upon the work] was obliged to prefix to each book of the Pentateuch and the Prophets a declaration, upon his honor, of the time at which and the person by whom he believes it to have been written ; " and he emphasized "his honor," as if the honor of an English gentleman was something far more trustworthy as a guarantee of good faith than the professional declaration even of an English clergyman. The one came from the man as an individual ; the other was merely given as the member of a hierarchy, in the way of "business."

The truth seems to be that the thoughtful and scholarly divines of the English church, those whose acquirements and mental independence fit them to be critical, are sorely perplexed by their position. For the Church of England is a political institution so interwoven with the structure of English society that, should it be shaken, the whole social fabric might go to ruin. The feeling is prevalent (as I gathered, although I did not hear it uttered), and it is reasonable, that doing without bishops would be the first step to dispensing with dukes. And what would England be without dukes? An Englishman might lead a godless life ; but could he lead a dukeless one ? And the dukes themselves and the minor nobles look forward with the gravest apprehension to the time when, church and state being severed, a respect for rank and privilege will be no part of the English religion.

For it is not to be concealed that the English church is a gentlemanly institution. It not only teaches the lower classes deference to superiors, but its influence does much to breed that very admirable character, the English gentleman. Its teachings are wholly at variance with the spirit of social democracy. Its very catechism inculcates a content which is opposed to the restless and pushing tendencies of modern times. The catechumen is made to say, among other things, when asked what is his duty to his neighbor, " My duty to my neighbor is . . . . to submit myself to all my governors, teachers, spiritual pastors, and masters; to order myself lowly and reverently to all my betters ; . . . . and to learn and labor truly to get mine own living and to do my duty

in that state of life to which it shall please God to
call me." But now it seems to be the accepted duty
of every man of English blood, no matter on which
side of the great ocean he may be, to get himself, with
what speed he may, out of the state of life in which
he is, into a better. The virtue of content is gone,
and with it the grace of submission.

I remember intuitions of this even in my boyhood
as I repeated those words, and vainly strove to recon-
cile them with the struggle for advancement which I
saw going on around me, even among the most religious people. And there was the old story in verse,
which began, —

> " Honest John Tomkins, the hedger and ditcher,
> Although he was poor, did not want to be richer '

Honest John Tomkins was held up to me as the
model of all the Christian virtues ; and yet I saw
everybody around me, including my teachers and
spiritual pastors and masters, striving by day and by
night to be richer. And when we consider that discontent is the mother of improvement, whether for
the individual or the commonwealth, and that the
betters of the man who is taught to order himself
lowly and reverently to them became so because they
or their ancestors were not satisfied with that state
of life to which it had pleased God to call them, is it
not plain that the religion which teaches content is
doomed, and with it the whole system of governors
and masters, spiritual and temporal ? But it will be
a long time before this warfare is accomplished. Not
easily nor quickly can a form of society be uptorn
which is of such slow and sturdy growth as that of
England, and whose roots, like those of some vast
British oak, decayed and hollow at heart it may be

pierce the mould of centuries. There is much in England that is mere shell and seems mere sham; but the shell was shaped from within by living substance, and it hardened into form through the sunshine and the tempests of hundreds of years; and so it stands, and will yet stand long, although not forever. The very shams and surface shows of things in England are strong and stable.

Yet the process of change is plainly perceptible even to the eye of a passing stranger. I saw evidence of it in the very dress of the farmer folk and peasantry, in a morning's walk that I took with a Sussex squire on Sunday. We met many of these people on their way to and from church. The wives and daughters of the farmers wore silk gowns and bonnets with feathers, and carried parasols. I observed some incongruity between the apparel and the mien of those who wore it, and remarked upon it to my companion, an elderly man, who at once relieved himself by a mild and good-humored, but none the less earnest, denunciation of the absurdity. He remembered, he said, when farmers' wives never thought of appearing on Sundays in any other dress than a red cloak and a close black bonnet, and then they looked respectable; but now they come out dressed like fine ladies, — as they think. "And look at those young fellows," he said, "with their cut-aways and chimney-pots! They 're positively ridiculous. See there!" — pointing out an elderly man who wore a long brown linen garment and stout high-low shoes, which were somewhat incongruous with his shiny chimney-pot hat, — "that 's better. A smock frock, breeches, gaiters, and a round hat is the proper Sunday costume of a Sussex peasant." And indeed I thought, although

I did not say, that such a dress would be more becoming and even more respectable than the caricature of his landlord's — or of his landlord's butler's — costume which in most cases he actually did present to the passing observer.

But how, O Sussex squire, is it as to what the Sussex peasant himself thinks, and the Sussex peasantess, in her monstrous manifestation of millinery? If they feel in their inner hearts that they are "genteeler" and more elegant, and therefore in their own eyes more respectable, in that rampant rigging, what matter all your scoffs and gibes? And what can you expect but that they will wear it? And what will you do to check this blossoming absurdity, unless you make instant and open war upon the liberty of the subject, and throw yourself in your gentleman's dress before the wheels of progress? The eternal fitness of things! But what is the eternal fitness of things, or even the fitness of eternal things, to the fitness of fine raiment, and to the consciousness of being in the fashion, and of being dressed, at least one day in the week, "like a lady" or a "gentleman"! Verily, your notions as to correct costume and the eternal fitnesses smack of the church catechism and its state of life to which it has pleased, or may please, God to call us.

In London, as I was walking through New Bond Street, I saw upon the door-post of a house a small signboard, hardly larger than a man's hand, on which was "E—— J——, Jurisconsult." It was a sad sight. It brought up a story which is significantly illustrative of a likeness and a difference in social police between two peoples who are, or who have been until lately, the same in all the distinguishing characteristics of race, — the story of a man of such ability and such legal acquirement that he might reasonably have aspired to the highest honors attainable in his profession, — a member of Parliament ; a co-worker with Garibaldi ; a man whose reputation had crossed the broad Atlantic, and yet who, because of misconduct in regard to a trust reposed in him, was disbarred. Coming to New York, he was received with facile and uninquiring welcome, and on motion of very distinguished members of the New York bar was admitted to practice in the courts of the State. When a cry of surprise went up from those who knew his history, and an effort was made to rectify the hasty error, it was found to be too late. The judges decided that, having been duly admitted to the bar, and having been guilty of no misconduct since his admission, his standing here was good, and he could not be disbarred. But the result was that the courts of New York were as effectually closed to him as those of London. He could not obtain the practice which a lawyer of his standing requires ; he returned to England to set up his little sign as a "jurisconsult." Never was a reputation more utterly wrecked and ruined ; never were fairer prospects more completely blasted. The moral tone of both bars and both communities was the same ; but in England there would not have been the thoughtless precipitancy in his reception and admission which caused such a public scandal in the bar at New York. There would have been more caution, more reserve, more preliminary inquiry.

It is a characteristic distinction that at the Inns of Court men are "called to the bar" after a certain probation, while in the United States they are, upon

examination, " admitted to practice " in the courts.
The former mode is a voluntary act of grace by which
the benchers ask a man to become one of their fraternity ; the latter is in the nature of the recognition
of a right upon the fulfillment of certain conditions.
A barrister's function in England is nominally of
an honorary character, and his fee is an *honorarium*,
which cannot be sued for at law as an attorney's costs
may.   Practically, however, a barrister's services are
paid for, as a matter of course, like any other services, and the professional incomes of many successful
English barristers are very large.   Law is the noblest of all vocations in England.   It takes even
poor men into Parliament and makes them peers and
lord chancellors.

I did not have the good fortune of seeing any of
the great courts in session, for my visit was in the
long vacation ; but I saw a criminal cause tried in
one of the minor courts in Liverpool, and was much
interested in the proceedings.   First of all, I was
struck by the costume of the judge and of the barristers, whose wigs and gowns gave them an air of
dignity and authority well suited to their functions
and not without practical value.   The wigs, indeed,
did seem somewhat ridiculous, because of their absurd likeness and unlikeness to the natural covering
of the head.   The judge's wig was the least grotesque.
It was quite like the large bob wig worn by all gentlemen in the latter part of the last century, — much
like that, for example, represented in Dr. Johnson's
portraits.   But the barrister's wig is certainly the
queerest covering that was ever put upon a human
head.   The gown gives dignity to the figure and
grace to the action ; but I found it difficult to look

at the wigs without laughing. Behind and at the
sides there hang four little formal, isolated curls in
double rows, so unlike anything human, and yet so
plainly an imitation of curled and powdered human
hair, that they would seem like caricature, if they
did not, in their bald artificiality, pass all bounds of
caricature. I spoke of their absurdity to a friend
who was at the bar, and said that, while the gown
seemed worthy of respect and admiration, I wondered
why the ridiculous little wigs were not discarded.
"Discard wigs!" was his reply. "Why, we couldn't
get on without them. I couldn't try a cause without
my wig. I should feel as if I had no right to be in
court; as if the judge would be justified in taking no
notice of me; and as if the witnesses had me at their
mercy, instead of me having them at mine. I should
n't dare to cross-question a witness without my wig."
"In other words," I said, "your wig gives you an
authoritative position which enables you to bamboozle
a witness." "Why, yes," he answered, smiling,
"that's pretty much it, if you choose to put it so."
But to my trial.

The case was one of obtaining goods, silk and
satin, under false pretenses, and among the witnesses were women, who were connected in some way
with the fraud. I was impressed by the quiet ease
of the proceedings, by the gently exercised authority of the judge, and by the deference of the barristers to the bench and to each other. It was a minor
court, as I have said; but propriety and courtesy
seemed to reign absolutely within its walls. One
of the counsel, taking advantage of his wigged condition, began to press one of the female witnesses
rather hard in regard to her personal relations to

the principal culprit. After he had asked a question or two with this intent, under which she had winced visibly, the judge leaned forward, and said, in a tone of quiet and friendly remonstrance, " Mr. ——, I think I would n't pursue that course of inquiry any further. It makes no difference as to the nature of the act charged, and the witness has been very frank in her testimony." " Very well, your honor," was the reply, and the subject was dropped, and another line of inquiry was taken up.

It seemed that this witness had kept some of the goods for a long time by her, not made up, and when she was told that she might leave the box the judge called her to him, and as she stood before the bench entered into a conversation with her, in the tone which a father might adopt toward a daughter who had erred ; in the course of which he asked her a few questions as to the reasons for her conduct, which seemed to bring out the truth of the whole matter more completely than the questioning and the cross-questioning of counsel. His manner was at once colloquial and authoritative, and while it commanded the woman's respectful deference, dismissed her fears, relieved her of her worry, and begat a confidence in his uprightness and impartiality. How the trial ended I do not know, for I could not remain until its close ; but I left the court-room feeling sure that essential justice would be done, and much impressed by this slight exhibition of the simplicity and dignity of the proceedings in British courts of law.

Newspapers, advertisements, posters, an organized police force, and the telegraph have made the town-crier a figure of the past, long as unknown in America as an old watchman or a ticket-porter. And yet

I have been told by men who, although they have some gray in their beards, do not regard themselves as old, that they remember him standing at the corners of the streets in the smaller towns, ringing his great bell, and crying lost children or other articles more valuable, and making other announcements which are now made by machinery, social or other. I supposed that in England, however, he had disappeared generations ago, and I should as soon have expected to find Dogberry, Verges, and that " most senseless and fit man " George Seacoal going about with their lanterns and halberts. But there he was. In Oxford I saw him, — a somewhat forlorn and woful creature, sad of countenance and ruinous in raiment. He stood upon the curb-stone, and lifting up his voice he proclaimed lugubriously that certain articles would be sold by auction, and that the sale would commence — the very town-crier cannot say " begin " even in England — at six o'clock. He was a witness to the fast hold which old customs have upon English society. Probably he was the last of his tribe and had a vested interest in his office, from which he will pass away without a successor. He was allowed to display the vacuity of his mouth at street corners to get wherewith to put into it at home, and to fill his belly with something better than the east wind in the teeth of which he uttered his proclamation. No one but me paid the slightest attention to him. He might as well have done his crying in the desert of Sahara or on the top of Mount Ararat. His voice sounded to me like a faint echo of the speech of past ages ; and I thanked the poor fellow in my heart that he did his superfluous office within my hearing.

Some of these random recollections are in regard to points which should have been remarked upon in what I had to say as to manners and habits of life in England. Of these one is an absence of reserve in speech and action in regard to matters as to which a certain reticence is dictated almost by self-respect. Over the weaker and unlovelier points and the homelier functions of our physical nature self-love throws a veil, which, by silent mutual consent, is never lifted, unless at the bidding of a great need. To say that I did not find this in England would be quite untrue; but it is true that I found there enough disregard of it in a sufficient number of individuals to impress me very strongly. I shall refer only to two very mild manifestations of this unreserve. I was driving with two ladies, one of whom was of rank and herself of very ancient lineage, — a woman intelligent, accomplished, kind-hearted, and indeed, it could hardly be denied, well bred; and, moreover, she was not yet middle-aged. And yet, it being a morning drive, this lady did not hesitate to complete, then and there, her toilet as to ears and nose, in the face of the sun and in the eyes of her companions, in a manner which was not only conspicuous, but pickuous; and she did it in such a matter-of-course way, although so thoroughly, that I am inclined to think that half an hour afterwards she would not have remembered this perfecting of her personal graces in public. I never saw such a performance on the part of a New England or New York woman of even tolerable good-breeding or middling social position. My other example (and both are only samples of a sort) was an even more public manifestation of the same unreserve. In a first-class railway carriage was a lady who evidently regarded herself as a very high and mighty personage. She, her young daughter, and a nurse with a child in arms some six months old occupied one side of the carriage, which was full. At intervals of some fifteen minutes this lady, who was large and loud of voice, would make inquiries of the nurse, in very precise and well-articulated words, as to the natural history of that infant; and the particular attention which she gave to this subject went so far and was so very earnest that I began to look forward with some apprehension to what might be the consequences. Now, with an aversion to squeamishness and no respect for euphemism, I cannot but think that the feeling which would make such exhibitions as these, on the part of women of like condition, impossible in New England or New York is one which is not the mark of inferior sense, inferior civilization, or inferior manners, or even of the social tone of what is absurdly called a young country.

I had dined at the house of a wealthy merchant, where our evening's entertainment had been most agreeable, and where all the evidences of intelligence and cultivation were notably apparent. Luxury was almost boundless; and the dinner service was of plate. Soon after we joined the ladies in the drawing-room I was surprised to see my host sit himself down upon one end of a sofa, at the other end of which sat his pretty little wife, and stretching out his legs lay his feet in her lap. They were clothed indeed in gold-clocked silk stockings, and in the daintiest gold-buckled evening shoes; and the lady showed herself neither loath nor surprised. I do not presume to pass an opinion on the propriety of this demonstration of marital tenderness; but I shall never forget it, because it was so strange to me.

One little trait of manners and customs amazed me. The evidence of it was a bit of printed pasteboard which in plain terms was the business card of a hangman, of which I took this copy: —

WILLIAM MARWOOD,

EXECUTIONER,

CHURCH LANE,

HORNCASTLE, LINCOLNSHIRE.

◆

N. B. *All orders promptly executed.*

I thought this about the most astounding piece of paper that I ever looked upon. As it seems a settled thing that some men must be hanged, there must of course be others to hang them; and from the days of the saintly Trois Eschelles and the jocular Petit André there has been a succession of professional executioners in France, where the business at last became an inheritance, and the trick of it traditional in one family, like violin-making among the Amatis. But that hanging other men should become such a business as requires a business card, with the promise of dispatch in the execution of all orders, and that a man should thus openly seek such employment, would be incredible, were it not for this evidence.[1]

---

[1] It occurred to me, of course, as it has occurred to others, that this card might possibly refer to the execution of writs in civil suits. But so thought not the intelligent English gentleman who showed it to me, and who, impressed by it as I was, would not part with it. Moreover, according to all evidence of literature and lexicography, *executioner* has had in England, for at least three hundred years, but one meaning, — a public ..eadsman or hangman.

English footmen look like curates in livery. If I should say that the coachmen look like bishops on the box, it would be no compliment to the coachmen, who are, with rare exceptions, very fine men; whereas English bishops are not as a bench remarkable for fine presence. As to dignity, what bishop, what archbishop, what cardinal, what Pope, could hope to equal the dignity of a first-rate English coachman in the discharge of his professional functions!

I had no opportunity of seeing the Queen, nor did I hear much said of her; and what little I did hear did not convey to me the impression that she was personally liked, even by those who knew her as well as subjects can know a queen. One of these said to me when I mentioned my not having seen her, "Oh, you could n't expect that. She rarely shows in public; only on great occasions. And you would n't see much. She 's a shabby, dowdy woman; very close; and haughty and austere with the younger members of her family."

I heard interesting and amusing stories about the Queen and the royal family, which, although they were told by persons who should have been well informed, I shall not repeat. I shall not, however, conceal that in one that was told me about Canon Duckworth's affair, and which had all the marks of truth about it, the reverend gentleman appeared in every way to great advantage. So much, at least, I may say in regard to a matter already public. But the tone in which I heard the Queen and her family discussed caused me to puzzle myself with the question, What is loyalty in England nowadays? Not ignorant of what the feeling is (for I was loyal to

Charles I. when I read "Woodstock," and I don't envy the young reader who is not), I could find no evidence in English society of the existence of such a sentiment. Among the higher classes no one speaks with much respect of the family which has furnished the British throne with four Georges and a William, nor with personal regard or admiration of the present sovereign or of her children, although there seems to be no little ducking and deference to the Prince of Wales. I did, however, hear royalty spoken of with admiration, because of the dignity and picturesqueness which it, its functions, and its accompaniments bestow upon society. This, however, is not loyalty; nor was I able to discover any origin of that feeling which makes a theatre full of Britons thrill with a deep, sober, and genuine enthusiasm when the royal box is occupied, and "God Save the Queen" is sung, other than the self-conscious glorification of John Bull, and the contemplation of majesty made manifest in the flesh. When His Royal Highness entered his box, Mr. Jeames Yellowplush was "filled with hor."

During the excitement about the Turkish atrocities England not only supped, like Macbeth, full with horrors, but breakfasted full with horrors, — Bulgarian horrors; for the newspapers seemed to contain little else. There were meetings and meetings upon the subject, and speeches and speeches. In the railway carriages, people, as they exchanged newspapers, talked of little else; and few had even a word of excuse for the Turk. Now of this feeling I do not doubt the genuineness. According to my observation, there are no kindlier people than the English. Nor can it be fairly doubted that they are ready to strike a blow for the weak, and to use their power to enforce fair play. But I could not close my eyes to a strong under-current that was perceptible in all this, and much more apparent in private talk than in public discussion,— disgust as much at Turkish impecuniosity and bankruptcy as at Turkish cruelty. It was very plain that the feeling, taken as a whole, was one of resentment at the atrocities of those no-interest-paying pagans. It was abominable to use British wealth and power to support a miserable lot of Moslems, who made war in such a ferocious manner, when they could n't pay their debts. I could not but think that if the interest on the Turkish bonds had been ready there would have been less of white heat in the glow of British indignation. But how many of us have a pure and single motive in our conduct, individual or collective ? Has there been a war or a " movement " that ended in a great gain to human freedom which had not selfish interest among its springs and causes ? Magna Charta itself will not bear close investigation on this point, nor even our war for salvation of the Union and the extinction of slavery. Of all great political struggles, that which was begun by a few English gentlemen in resistance to the tyranny of Charles I. seems purest in its origin ; and even that became debased by selfishness and greed and tyranny before it was ended.

Even in this Turkish question, I could not but see, on the other hand, the elevating influence of the wideness and manifoldness of British interests. The scattering of British pounds, shillings, and pence all over the world makes the British people — those of them who think and who have interests beyond that of their daily bread — a people of wide sympathies and of varied and enriching anxieties. Their very solicitude for their profit and loss compels them to concern themselves in the affairs of the world at large. Their selfishness has become an element in their greatness. As Julius Cæsar's success was in no small degree due to his enormous indebtedness, so, conversely, Great Britain has risen to imperial power because she has compelled the whole world to become her debtor. In recognizing this fact it is not necessary to admit the purity either of Cæsar's motives or of Britain's.

The enrichment of the intellectual life of England by these causes is manifest in British journalism. The leading newspapers of London, and even of the provinces, place day by day before their readers discussions which involve a knowledge of the world's affairs "from China to Peru." Look through half a dozen numbers of the "Saturday Review" and of the "Spectator," and see how the affairs of India, of Afghanistan, of Egypt, in fact of all the countries of the world, are discussed as if they were but British dependencies, which every man between Cape Wrath and Michael's Mount must needs know something of and think about. The largeness and the complexity of these discussions are almost bewildering. They make all other journalism seem thin and tame and narrow. And it is this vastness and variety of interest which in the last hundred years has raised the statesmanship of shop-keeping Britain to such a height that it is the noblest as well as the most exacting of all professions, and makes all other statesmanship seem like shop-keeping.

CHAPTER XXV.

PHILISTIA.

HOWEVER closely the man of English race, but of New England birth and breeding, may acknowledge himself bound to his kinsmen of the motherland, and however much at home he may find himself among them, partly because of their common blood and speech, and of that sameness of mental tone and of social habits and political institutions (excepting the mere outside form given by monarchy and aristocracy) which come of their common "Anglo-Saxonism," and partly because of the frankness and heartiness with which they welcome him, he is sensible in the society of England, even when he is most nearly drawn to it, of a subtle, all-pervading influence which makes him constantly conscious that, although he cannot feel and is not made to feel that he is a foreigner, he is to a certain degree a stranger in the land of his fathers. This influence does not come from external things. Castles and cathedrals, peers and peasants, may be new to him, and he may look upon them with curious eyes ; but this is something which eyes cannot see. He is conscious of it mostly, if not only, in the intercourse of man with man. He feels it chiefly in the midst of his greatest social enjoyment. Seated in a room, perhaps at a table, where there is little, if anything, that is unlike what he has been more or less accustomed to from his childhood, sur-

rounded by men and women whose names are those
of his own race, perhaps of his own familiar friends
at home, — people whose costume, whose manners,
and whose topics of discourse are essentially the same
as those of the society in which he grew up, — he yet
feels that there is an invisible something between
them and him.   It is not a barrier ; for it does not
separate him from them : but it is an atmosphere
through which he makes his approaches.   It is the
atmosphere of Philistinism.

That what has been called Philistinism exists in
England is no new discovery, as Mr. Matthew Arnold's readers know ; but it has been supposed, and
indeed assumed and asserted, by him, if not by others,
that it is to be found only in the middle classes, —
that it is a distinctive quality of that immense division of English society which lies between the agricultural and artisan class, on the one side, and the
nobility and gentry and the professional class, on the
other.

This theory of the phenomenon in question is plau-
sible, and it is natural to a British observer who is
himself in the latter division.   But, according to my
experience, it is erroneous.   Philistinism pervades the
whole society of Great Britain south of the Tweed.
It is not found in equal proportions in all grades of
that society, in some of which it is very much denser
than it is in others.   Like all heavy things, invisible
although they may be, — like the heavier and more
poisonous gases, for example, — its tendency is down-
ward, and it sinks to the lower levels of society, where
it becomes almost palpable from the pressure of the
superincumbent mass.   From that plane upward it
gradually diminishes in quantity, and becomes more

delicate in quality as it passes from grade to grade, until, when it has reached the highest, it attains a tenuity which makes it almost imperceptible. But there it is, present to consciousness, although only as an influence, subtle, indefinable, almost indescribable. I have said before that it is felt as something between the stranger and his kindred ; and yet I am not sure that the latter are not dimly conscious of it also, as a separating, isolating power among themselves. As to this I cannot speak, because, being one of the strangers, I cannot know. But it seemed to me, sometimes, as if each Briton carried about him, like a social planet, his own little atmosphere of Philistinism, which was not only the breath of his nostrils, but the protective armor of his individuality, through which his nearest friends had to pierce in order to be in actual contact with the real man.

This subtle, isolating moral and mental atmosphere, which I have called an influence, — but which might be better named an exfluence, for it radiates from within outward, — is a non-conductor of ideas. It is the unreadiness of the Saxon Athelstane developed into a social and intellectual power of inertness. The gross result of this unreadiness is Philistinism. The surgical operation which has been said to be required to get a joke into the head of a Scotchman (most unjustly, it would seem, of a people who have produced Robert Burns, Walter Scott, and Thomas Carlyle) is far more needful to get a new idea, or even a fine idea, into the head of a British Philistine who is perfect of his kind. This being the case, Philistinism enshields and perpetuates itself. It is equally lasting and immovable. It stiffens the mental faculties, taking from them alertness and flexibility, and makes those who are wholly under its influence so set in their ways of thought and feeling that it is sometimes hard to say whether they are stable or stolid.

A trait like this is strange indeed as characteristic of a people in which there is such a richness and variety of intellectual power; a people who have produced and are producing, in all departments of human endeavor, work which in originality and in lasting value equals, and in many respects surpasses, that which is produced by any other people; a people to whom the world owes both Shakespeare and railways, inductive philosophy and the fanciful theory of evolution; who were once, if they are not now, the greatest discoverers, colonists, manufacturers, and traders in the world, and of whom it has been truly said that the sound of their drums follows the sun around the earth; a people whose very language, because of its supreme adaptation to all human needs, promises to abolish the confusion of Babel and to make all mankind again of one speech. Nor is the very literary activity of the British people less than phenomenal. The lists of new publications which appear weekly in the London "Spectator" are an ever-recurring surprise. I have counted more than one hundred and forty in a single list, not the most numerous that I remember; and, although these lists include new editions, this fact only modifies their significance. More original works are published in London and Edinburgh in a month than are published in all the United States in a year. But, notwithstanding this unmistakable sign of a vigorous intellectual activity, Philistinism exists in Old England, and to all intents and purposes does not exist in the New.

Now it is remarkable that Philistinism is a phenomenon of comparatively late manifestation in England. It is a growth of the last hundred and fifty years. There is no trace of it in the Elizabethan era. In all the voluminous dramas of that time there is no sign that this quality then existed in the Englishman. Shakespeare's plays, and Beaumont and Fletcher's, and Ben Jonson's, and Massinger's, and Heywood's, and Chapman's, and poor Dekker's are full of Englishmen of all conditions masquerading under Italian and French and Latin names; but there is not a Philistine among them. On the contrary, the English mind of that time seems to have been distinguished for its quick apprehensiveness, its flexible adaptability, its eagerness, its thirst for new thought, its readiness to receive, to welcome, and to assimilate. In the "Merry Wives of Windsor," written, if not at Elizabeth's command, certainly to please the court circle, Shakespeare would surely have given us a Philistine, if he had known such a creature. But Master Ford and Master Page, although middle-class men hardly within the pale of gentry, and who are not even small country squires, but townsmen of Windsor, are equally far from Philistinism and from snobbishness. Nor in Jonson's two best known plays, which were written professedly to present contemporary manners, is this humor embodied. Shallow and Silence, in "Henry IV.," make the nearest approach to it; but even they are only a pair of senile rustic squires.

English comedy of the Restoration is still void of this characteristic in any of its personages. But in the last century the Philistine element begins to appear. The dense-minded middle-class man, rich, purse-proud, vulgar, incapable of apprehending anything beyond the range of his own personal experience, comes upon the stage. He is the butt, it is true, of the courtier and of the traveled man; nevertheless, he is represented as the type of a large class, and as one who is becoming a power in the land, and who is recognized as one of the characteristic elements of its society. He is conscious at once of his importance and of his social inferiority; and he submits, although with surliness, to the snubbing of his superiors, which sometimes takes a very active and aggressive shape. In Farquhar's " Constant Couple," Wildair beats Alderman Smugler before Lady Lurewell, and finally throws snuff into his eyes; and the alderman raves and roars, but submits. English comedy of an earlier period has no such scenes as this. In the Elizabethan drama noblemen and gentlemen hold themselves loftily, and sometimes talk of "greasy citizens;" but they do not beat them nor throw snuff into their eyes in the presence of ladies. One reason of this is that the gentlemen of the earlier period are of higher quality and finer fibre than those of the later, and that in the later comedies the gentlemen themselves have become coarser under the velvet and ruder under the lace, which have wholly displaced the steel corselets and buff coats of their ancestors. The striking phenomenon is presented of the deterioration of a whole people in the finer traits of social and intellectual character, of a loss of the grace and charm of true gentility, of a vulgarizing of the general tone of society, while society as a whole is advancing intellectually, as well as growing stronger and richer in all that tends to progress and civilization. The lower class is coming into contact with the higher, and the higher has begun, in self defense, to enter into conflict with the lower; and in such a struggle the combatants are always sure to become tainted each with the other's coarser qualities.

The eighteenth century, fruitful of good in so many important respects, was a period of decadence for England in all that made life beautiful and graceful. In the arts that embellish life the Englishman of that time, compared with his ancestor of the time of the Tudors, was a being of inferior grade. In literature he had become conscious, weak, and prosaic; and in fine art he had sunk to a lower level than he had touched till then since he had been civilized. The rude art work of Anglo-Saxon times shows more vigor and freedom and fancy than appears in that of thirty-guinea periwigs and Pope's Odyssey. The Englishman of the Hanoverian reigns could not even appreciate the work of his forefathers. The elegant eighteenth century did more to despoil and degrade the architecture of England than was effected by the iconoclastic fury of the Puritans of the Commonwealth. They destroyed, but they did not debase. In the last century, cathedrals and monuments and country houses, when they were not wholly neglected, were made hideous by tasteless alterations. The eighteenth century was in this respect a period of paint and putty. Evidence of this is visible on all sides, and testimony to it is plentiful.

My first personal observation of this manifestation of Philistinism was at the villa of a friend, not far from London. He was in no way concerned in it except as its discoverer; for he is not only a man of remarkable intelligence and comprehensiveness of mind, but also one of fine taste and of uncommon social attractiveness. The house was built in Queen

Anne's time, and some parts of it earlier.   I remarked
to him one day upon the beauty of the wood of the
solid mahogany door of the principal entrance.   He,
laughing, replied, "Yes; but I had a hard time with
that door.   When I bought the house that door was
green."   "Green!"   "As green outside as that
grass, and white inside.   But it was blistered in
spots, and I had it repainted.   Still it would blister
in warm weather; and after two or three trials I
ordered all the paint scraped off down to the wood,
that we might begin afresh.   And what should we
find, after removing three or four coats, but this
noble old mahogany!   The paint was very old, and
so hard that it almost turned the workmen's tools.
The door had been painted again and again during
the last century."   I was amazed; but I found other
examples of the same vile taste, which was characteristic of the time when the term Gothic was used
to imply rudeness.   England at that time was full
of noble monuments which were defaced in this ridiculous and deplorable way.   In one of the old churches
of London, I forget which one, there is an elaborately
carved tomb of a John Spencer, erected A. D. 1609.
It is mostly in a beautiful green-veined marble, but
partly in variegated pale red and yellow marble
equally beautiful.   One of the church-wardens, who
was kind enough to do the honors of the place for
me, told me that this tomb as it stands now is the
result of restoration; that it was once all painted
and gilded.   The paint had been laid over this beautiful stone to the thickness of five eighths of an inch!
Since then I have found that British critics have remarked the same desecration.   Mr. De Longueville
Jones, in his description of a beautiful old country

house in Herefordshire, says, "There was the bachelor's room, a nice little square apartment, about twice as high as it was broad, all paneled in oak, which some Goth of a squire had painted light blue!"[1] And Mr. Jennings, in his delightful "Rambles among the Hills," just published, describing Charles Cotton's pew in the old church at Alstonfield, says, "It was elaborately carved, and of good old oak, but had received a thick coat of green paint at the hands of some barbarian many years before." The taste which covered beautiful veined marble and carved oaken panels with paint was Philistine. The people who sculptured the marble and carved the oak were not Philistine.

It is not strange that the houses and churches and other public buildings which were built in England during the time when such acts as this were regarded as improvements should be lacking in all the elements of beauty; and they are so, as I have remarked before. But they are not only ugly: there is about them an air of smug, yet heavy pretension, combined with respectability, which is peculiar to them among the productions of architecture. There were not vanting in England, even at the time of their conception and building, men who could see their hideousness, — men who had not yet been swallowed up and borne off in the flood of Philistinism which was beginning to pour over the country. Of this perception these lines are a record. I remember seeing them somewhere in the Dodsley poems.

> "Sure wretched Wren was taught by bungling Jones
> To murder mortar and disfigure stones."

This coarse, dull, pretentious taste became more

[1] *Essays and Papers* (originally published in *Blackwood*), 1870, page 60.

general and more firmly settled as years went on, until at the beginning of this century the art of England, especially the household art, had reached its lowest level since the days of Cerdic the Saxon. In design, the furniture and plate, the glass, the binding of books, the house decoration, were utterly lacking in grace, in beauty of any kind. They were expressive merely of dense insensibility to beauty, of the expenditure of money, and of a stolid respectability. We had plenty of this in "America," as those who recall the house-furnishing of our fathers' and grandfathers' houses must confess. It could not have been otherwise; for our furniture then either came from England, or was made upon English models. And yet at this time Wedgwood was beginning his wonderful revolution in household pottery. But we all know the struggles and the trials through which he had to pass before he could elevate the taste of the day to the appreciation of his work, about which now books are written.

The very "divinity" of the period (as religious literature is strangely called) was saturated with this influence. The "sound English divines" of the last century were all more or less Philistine. Reading their highly orthodox productions now is dreary work, not only because of the light which modern criticism has thrown upon their ignorance, but because of the expression of a smug satisfaction with their ignorance and of an admiration of it which pervade their pages. Doubtless they were honest, or thought that they were so; but they seem to have been all the while striving to produce sound English divinity, to be respectable, to do honor to their cloth, to build up the Church of England, and to buttress it in its weak places, where it had crumbled with age, or had been undermined by the slow filtering of insidious thought. Into endeavors like this they were indeed led by the very constitution of that church, which was not a revelational nor even a traditional church, but one made for the needs of the English people.

An acute and thoughtful writer, in the course of the discussion of another subject, has said of the Church of England: "By combined firmness and easiness of temper, by concessions and compromises, by unweariable good sense, a reformed church was brought into existence, — a manufacture, rather than a creation, — in which the average man might find average piety, average rationality, and an average amount of soothing appeal to the senses."[1] But it was not until after many long years and many severe struggles that the Church of England was at last thus adapted to the religious wants of the average Englishman, who wished to be reasonably and respectably religious in a thoroughly English, sober, sensible, unexalted way. The mutual adaptation of the church and the people was not wholly accomplished until the last century, when Philistinism took possession of England. It was the religious and political sentimentalism of the Jacobites which, quite as much as their mere dynastic loyalty, made them offensive to the average Englishman of the eighteenth century, who cared much more for the comfortable decencies of his homespun national church than he did for the house of Hanover. And so it was that the sound English divines of that period shored up the English church, just as the men to please whom they labored shored up Temple Bar, that Philistine

[1] Professor Dowden, *The Mind and Art of Shakspere*, chapter i.

structure, without beauty, and of use only as an obstacle to free movement.

Now, according to the best evidence, this average Englishman, who rose into power in the last century, and has since then exerted a gradually growing influence which has modified the social as well as the political surface and structure of England, was not an elegant nor in any way a very admirable creature. Mr. Matthew Arnold had very distinguished predecessors in his perception that England has "a middle class vulgarized." Fielding, in "Joseph Andrews" (Book III. chapter iii.), writes of "the lower class of the gentry and the higher of the mercantile world, who are in reality the worst bred part of mankind." Addison, in the "Freeholder" (No. 22), has a passage which shows that fox-hunting in his time was not the peculiar diversion, or rather employment, of a large part of the higher classes which it has since become, but was regarded as a mark of rudeness and rusticity. He describes his fox-hunting, small country gentleman by a motto from Velleius Paterculus, which he translates, "impolitely educated, expressing himself in vulgar language, boisterous, eager at a fray, and over-hasty in taking up an opinion;" and he makes him say that "he scarce ever knew a traveler in his life who had not forsook his principles and lost his hunting-seat," — by which it would seem that fox-hunting and Philistinism have advanced together to the possession of England.

To such testimony as this it would seem that there is no exception to be taken. And as this not well-bred man was somewhat slow of apprehension and was firmly fixed in his opinions, which yet he had rather found ready-made than formed for himself, and as his ideal of life was a dull and decent respectability, and his reverence for money and for rank equal and great, he and his modern descendant or representative do indeed fulfill Heine's notion of the Philistine, as he saw the creature in Germany; and the name has been well transferred to British soil. The Philistine is the man who is steeped in commonplace. He is not necessarily ignorant, nor lacking in good sense or good feeling; but his rule of action is precedent, and his ideal of life to do that which his little world will regard as proper; and he is filled with a calm, unquestioning conceit of national superiority.

A little touch of Philistinism in a lady decidedly not of the so-called Philistine class was amusing. She is of a family well and widely known for intellectual ability, and she herself maintains the reputation of her kindred. On my first visit at her house, she asked me how long I had been in England. I replied jocosely, " I have been in this blessed and beautiful island of yours just a fortnight to-day." " Oh," she exclaimed, " that shows what a big place you must have come from, — to call England an island!" Her brother, with a little blush, suggested to her that a country surrounded by the sea is an island, however respectable and powerful it may be, and that England was somewhat famous in history and poetry as an island. To which her answer was, " I know, I know! It's well enough for foreigners to say that." And indeed she was not without the support of the example of Walter Scott, who, in " Peveril of the Peak." (chapter xxix.), contrasts " the continent of Britain " with the Isle of Man.

But the most amazing manifestation of Philistin

ism that I have encountered came to me from England across the sea. A person whom I do not know and never saw, but who resides in one of the best neighborhoods of the West End of London, and whose letter indicates education and good breeding, wrote to me, inclosing a letter to be sent to a friend in New York, and in a postscript thoughtfully begged leave to inclose postage stamps, and actually sent me half a dozen British stamps to pay postage in the United States! It seemed the most natural thing in the world to this amiable Philistine that British stamps should carry a letter through any post-office to the ends of the earth.[1]

One striking trait of British Philistinism is ignorance of other countries, and chiefly ignorance of "America." To the Philistine this ignorance is his most cherished intellectual treasure. He guards it carefully, and plumes himself upon it. To enlarge and confirm it, he reads the travels of other Philistines in America, and in some cases visits "the States" himself, to return with a confusion of mind and perversion of fact upon the subject which is the occasion of solemn self-complacency, and which makes him for the remainder of his life an oracle upon "American" affairs among his untraveled friends and neigh-

[1] The London *Daily News*, commenting upon this passage when it was first published, remarked that similar errors were not uncommon in "American correspondents," who often sent United States postage stamps to their British friends to "defray some trifling expense." But these stamps were specifically sent to pay the postage, in New York, of an inclosed letter. Moreover, the word "American" is very vague, and is here more than usually insufficient. It may mean any person who writes from "America," and who, even if an "American citizen," may be an Irish or a German peasant, or a British Philistine, or the son of one of these. I should require very good and very well-sifted evidence to make me believe that any Yankee who lives outside of a lunatic asylum sent United States postage stamps to pay British postage.

bors.[1] Let me frankly confess, however, that a like
ignorance and confusion in regard to England among
natives of other countries is sometimes courteously
assumed by the Philistine. Some years before my
visit to England, a pretty and sweet-mannered, although not very high-class, Englishwoman was telling me, with the eyes and the voice of a dove, of
something that had happened in Manchester; and
then, with gentle condescension, she added inquiringly, " You 'ave 'eard of Manchester? " I said that
I had, and she was satisfied. There are little courts
and alleys in London, not unconnected with stables,
which are called mews; and I was kindly informed
by one or two friends, as we passed some of them,
that mews were places for the keeping of hawks in
olden time. It was impossible even to laugh at instruction so kindly given; nor did I tell my good
teachers that any " American " school-boy twelve
years old, of their condition in life, knew that as well
as they did. The elegant and very clever woman
who recommended me to read " Kenilworth " before
going to see the castle displayed this same sort of
Philistinism. What need of telling her, either, that
school-boys in " America " read " Kenilworth "!

There have been Philistines who were eminent in
their quality; men whose characters and habits of
mind and life made them perfect, and even admira-

---

[1] A Yorkshire gentleman, intelligent, a university graduate, a barrister
by profession, a man of the world, and one of the pleasantest companions
I ever met, told me, with some complacency and an air of enterprise, that
he meant to visit " the States " and to " go to Charleston and sail up the
Mississippi to Chicago "!   He was puzzled when I told him that this was
quite like going to Bristol and sailing up the Thames to Liverpool. And
t was not quite like; for the places and the r'ver that he mentioned were
more hundreds of miles from each other than those in my illustration were
iens.

ble, examples of their kind. In the last century two figures of superior position stand forth as Philistines of the highest attainments. They are George III. and Dr. Johnson. The king, who was the first true Briton of his family, showed his possession of this quality in his dogged inapprehensiveness of his Parliament, of his counselors, and of his American colonies. The " great moralist and lexicographer " hardly passed a day without the manifestation of it either in his speech or in his conduct. He found in Fleet Street, not figuratively, but actually, the full tide of human existence. Of his Philistinism in conduct, his behavior to his friend and benefactress on her marriage to Piozzi is a deplorable instance, he being in this case but the towering figure in a group of his kind ; and his preference of Nahum Tate's " King Lear," with its happy ending, by which virtue was rewarded and poetical justice done, is the most Philistine opinion recorded in literature. It is worthy of a critic in the gallery of Sadler's Wells. George III. and Dr. Johnson are the very Gog and Magog of Philistinism.

Nor in modern days are we without the supreme manifestation of this quality in high places. Lord Palmerston and Sir Alexander Cockburn, the late chief-justice of England, were Philistines of the first water. Lord Palmerston maintained his position so long, without exhibiting any remarkable qualities as a statesman, because in him the Philistinism of England found its representative and its highest expression. Fielding's lower class of the gentry and higher class of the mercantile world saw with delight a nobleman and accomplished man of society who in the tone of his mind reflected theirs. Lord Chief-Justice

Cockburn, a man of much superior mind, a man of ability nearly first rate, of great energy, of high culture and varied accomplishment, capable of vast effort, which he showed conspicuously on occasion of the Tichborne trial, attained his first great parliamentary success by supporting Lord Palmerston against Mr. Gladstone in the debate on the claims of Don Pacifico, the recognition of which is now seen to have been an egregious blunder. But it was a blunder committed for the glorification of Britons who never shall be slaves. His attitude and conduct on the Alabama commission showed that years and experience had merely deepened and hardened his Philistinism, until it could make him, a courteous gentleman, rude, conspicuously rude, in the face of the whole world, — him, an unright judge, elaborately unjust. These four eminent men, George III., Dr. Johnson, Lord Palmerston, and Chief-Justice Cockburn, stand in the annals of England as glorified types of the narrow, inflexible, inapprehensive, and I fear that, supported by the testimony of Fielding and Mr. Matthew Arnold, I must say vulgar sort of Englishman who was unheard of in England's annals before the reign of Queen Anne, and who I hope and believe will, by a radical change of heart, disappear from them in the reign of Queen Victoria.

The difference between the society of England and that of America down to the present time, or perhaps I should say until within the last twenty-five or thirty years, is due chiefly to what remained in the motherland, — to certain immovable material things which the English colonists could not bring away, and certain other movable immaterial things which they did not choose to bring away with them. The abandonment of these, on the one hand, and the circumstances of the country to which he came, on the other, effected the changes, really slight, which made the Englishman of this country differ from his kinsmen who remained in the old home. But Philistinism was a new development of the English national character, which took place after the great English colonization of "Virginia" was completed.[1] In it the "American" has not part nor lot. It is to-day the one great distinguishing difference between two societies of men of the same blood and speech, having the same laws and literature and religion, in two countries. It is the only difference which goes down beneath clothes and cuticle. British Englishmen as a mass are Philistine ; American Englishmen as a mass are not. In the American there is a nimble flexibility of mind, an apprehensive adaptability, which reminds us of the Englishman of the Elizabethan era. He is at once more logical and more imaginative than his British kinsman ; but at the same time less stable, less prudent, less sagacious. There are Philistines of a sort, in the United States, not a few of them ; but they wear their Philistinism with a difference.

That Philistinism is rare and mild in its manifestations among us, we Yankees may reasonably be glad ; but that the bird which broils upon our ugly coins should therefore plume himself and thank God in his heart that he is not as other brutes are, even as that poor British lion, is not quite so clear. For after all it must be confessed that the country under the

---

[1] What is now loosely called America was in Elizabeth's and James's reigns called Virginia; the name including the northern as well as the southern part of the country.

protection of that roaring beast, although it is so entirely given over to the domination of this strange
ism that it may truly be called Philistia, and although its people are often troubled at home and
baffled abroad, is yet, on the whole, the happiest, and
in many important respects the most admirable and
respectable, in the world. John Bull himself con-
fesses that he is a rude creature, who in some places
welcomes a stranger by "'eaving arf a brick at 'im,"
and who beats his wife in most places ; and yet England is the country of all Europe in which human life
is safest. Dreydorf, in his work on the Jesuits in
the German Empire, published in 1872, shows with
emphasis that while in Rome there is one murder for
750 inhabitants, in Naples one for 2750, in Spain one
for 4113, in Austria one for 57,000, in Prussia one
for 100,000, in England there is but one for 178,000.
And although John Bull may beat his wife, he wrongs
women in what is generally regarded as a more grievous way very little when we compare his sins with
those of other men in that respect. The same work
shows that while for 100 legitimate births there are
in Rome 243 illegitimate, in Vienna 118, in Munich
91, and in Paris 48, there is in London only one.
This makes the proportion of suffering and wrong of
this kind as follows : England 1, France 12, Germany
25, Austria 30, Italy 60. France is twelve times and
Italy sixty times worse than England in this respect !

And England is of all countries in Europe, and I
am inclined to think of all countries in the world, the
one in which there is, if not the most freedom, the
greatest degree of the best kind of freedom, — that
which is enjoyed by him who respects the freedom
and the rights of all other men. There is no other

country in the world in which the people are so little at the mercy of great corporations and of powerful individuals, and only one, if there be one, in which the poor man is so sure of the protection of the law against the rich, and the rich man is equally sure of justice if his adversary be poor.[1]

What position in the world is so enviable as that of an English gentleman! What character, on the whole, more admirable than that of an English gentleman who is recognized among his fellows as worthy of his class! He is not always quickly apprehensive and alert of mind; he is sometimes over-confident; he is often very illogical; he blunders abroad and blunders at home; but his want of logic does not always show a want of sense. Sagacity is sometimes better than syllogism; and he is wise in remedying real evils in an utterly illogical way. In his difficulties he generally wins through by stoutness of heart and steady nerve, and fixed purpose to do what he

---

[1] Let whoever is inclined to carp at and resent the former of these assertions read and consider Mr. Lloyd's article in *The Atlantic* for March, 1881, *The Story of a Great Monopoly*; truly, it seems to me, the fullest of great import and of shameful record that was ever made public in this country. As to the latter: — in 1876 a poor laboring man named Edwards was in arrears for rent fifteen shillings. His landlord sued him, got a distraint upon his goods, valued at £10, and caused the whole to be seized and sold at auction, including a coverlet on a baby lying in its cradle. The proceeds of the sale were £4 17s. 6d., and when the poor man's wife, bolder, perhaps because more distressed for her children's sake, than her husband, demanded that the surplus should be handed back to her, she was abused and driven away. Edwards thereupon sued the landlord, who put in a bill for auctioneer's fees, seven days' possession, toll, two bailiffs, and "liquor" supplied to these worthy leeches of the law. The county court decided that the distraint had been "oppressively and improperly conducted," and gave Edwards a judgment for £6 6s., with costs, the landlord to be imprisoned if the amount was not paid within one week. England, monarchical in its government and aristocratic in its society, has been since 1645 a commonwealth; and English law is no respecter of persons.

thinks is his duty. He has a singular capacity of suffering when he sees that he must suffer, and a grand ability to die in silence when he sees that he ought to do so. Other men are as brave as he, some perhaps more dashing and brilliant in feats of arms, — Frenchmen, Germans, even Spaniards and Portuguese ; but the calm, steady beat of the English heart in the face of danger is like the swing of a pendulum that obeys only the one great law of the universe. English armies have been beaten ; but they have rarely, if ever, been routed. They have left their lost fields with ranks as nearly unbroken and with as firm a step as the most exacting soldier could expect or hope for in his overpowered and retreating comrades. At Fontenoy and at Corunna there was no panic. And at Balaklava, when " it was not war," it was at least cool, unquestioning obedience to orders, in the retreat as well as in the charge. At what sight did the world ever look with more reverence — an admiration tempered with tears — than at the " Birkenhead," with her men obeying the call to quarters and standing at attention as she took them down in steady ranks into the depths, every man of them, like an imperial Cæsar, dying with decency !

If Englishmen are a little loftily conscious of English prowess and English stability, they have the right to be so, — a right given to them by such fields (not to mention others of minor fame) as Crecy, where Edward III.'s men were less in number than one to two of their opponents ; and Agincourt, where Henry V.'s were not one to four ; and Plassy, where Clive's one thousand Englishmen had such heart to spare to their two thousand auxiliaries that together they put more than ten times their number to flight, although the enemy had almost as many cannon as the little British force had field-officers. Andrew Borde, a Sussex physician, who had seen the world of his day as few men then saw it, published in 1542 a book called " The Boke of the Introduction of Knowledge," in which there are rude wood-cuts representing men of various nations, each of which has a motto or saying attached to it. That uttered by the Englishman is, —

> "I do feare no man, all men fearyth me;
> I overcome my adversaries by land and sea."

Boastful, indeed, and therein not uncharacteristic; but true, and therein also characteristic. Borde says, " I think if all the world were set agaynst England it might never be conquered, they being trew within themselfe." We know that this opinion of our forefathers and our kinsmen has been sustained by the event. But from that time to the present, of what other people in the world, who are not of English race, could this be truly said?

The bearing of all this upon our present subject is that the rise and the progress of Philistinism in England were strictly contemporaneous with her assumption of her position as a power of the first class in the world, in wealth, in strength, in empire, in glory. India was won for Britain by her middle classes; and Philistinism marched steadily forward from the victories of Marlborough to those of Wellington.

And, moreover, see the attitude of England now, and of Englishmen, towards the agitators and revolutionists — agitators and revolutionists, however just may be their cause or great their provocation — who are threatening and striving to dismember the empire. Englishmen as a race do not like Irishmen as a race, on either side of the ocean; and Irishmen have now been doing all that deeds and words could do to inflame English hatred against them. But England has stood, although indignant, considerate, not without sympathy, and reluctant to strike. The very leaders of what is legal treason, and who are on trial for their crime, take their seats in Parliament, with no man to molest them or make them afraid. Mr. Parnell, indicted traitor in Dublin, sits as a member of Parliament in Westminster, and has all the privileges and immunities of his representative function. He is as safe in the House of Commons, and, what is more, as safe in the streets of London, as if he were John Bright or Mr. Gladstone. He and his colleagues are heard patiently until they deliberately undertake to obstruct the action of Parliament, and there is not a word uttered in speech or in print to excite personal ill-will against them. This is a noble attitude, and it is one peculiarly English.

It would be well for us to admire what is worthy of admiration in such a people, rather than to carp at their errors and their failings, — to emulate their sterling virtues, and to find in our share of their ancient fame and grandeur an occasion of honorable and elevating pride. England has behaved to us too often rather as a mother-in-law than as a mother-in-blood, and some Englishmen have an unhappy mastery of the art of being personally offensive; but that is a poor and petty spirit which cannot see and admire greatness because it has received slight. And what wrong has England ever done us since we were an independent nation? She has scoffed and sneered and been insolent; and, as Plutarch says, men will forgive injurious deeds sooner than offensive words.

But after all, is it not better to forgive even offensive words when they were spoken less in malice than in overweening conceit and utter ignorance? England is the cradle and the home of Philistinism, and never has the Philistine temperament of her dominant, although not her ruling, class been more manifest than in her attitude, until lately, towards her younger brother in "America." It has been quite like that of Mr. Anthony Trollope's Marquis of Brotherton towards his younger brother. And this went on all the while that we were, to all intents and purposes, but another English nation. Now, when we are becoming year by year more and more a mixed people, she is changing her tone, because we have fought a big war and are paying a big debt. Alas, that it is so! But *we* at least can afford to be good-natured, and to smile, not merely in rueful scorn, as we take the hand that would have been so much more welcome and so much more honored if it had been offered when we were weaker and poorer.

Yet we may trust England in this matter. It is not that she is snobbish, and is ducking to us merely because she has found out that we are strong and rich; it is that our war and its consequences have partly opened her Philistine eyes, have taught her something, although yet a very little, about "America." Her ignorance was ridiculous, but it is not unpardonable, nor quite incomprehensible. After living a while in England, one begins to discover how it is that it is so much farther from London to New York than it is from New York to London. He who cannot see that must be very dull or very ignorant, — himself a Philistine, indeed.

England is not perfect, for it is upon the earth,

and it is peopled by human beings; but I do not envy the man who, being able to earn enough to get bread and cheese and beer, a whole coat, and a tight roof over his head, — chiefest need under England's sky, — cannot be happy there. He who is of a complexion to be surly because another man is called my Lord, while he is plain Mister, — she who frets because another woman may go to court, while she may only queen it at home, — can easily find occasion there to grumble or to pine. They whose chief aim is to rise in life do find there, not barriers indeed, but obstacles; to overcome which they must have *can* and *will* largely in their composition, as it is thought that they should have who rise. But they who are sufficient unto themselves, and who can take what life and the world offer with little concern as to what others may be thinking about them, may find in England the means and conditions of a sound and solid happiness. I never met a well-educated, well-bred Yankee, who had lived in England long enough to become familiar with her people, who found himself at all out of place there, or who was dissatisfied with any of his surroundings. As to Philistinism, the chief mark of distinction between the people of the two countries, one becomes used even to that, and finally forgets it. I confess, as I bid farewell to thee, Philistia, dear motherland, that while I was within thy borders I, a Yankee of the Yankees, felt at times as if I were a Philistine of the Philistines.

THE END